The Hollywood Novel

The Hollywood Novel

*A Critical Guide to Over
1200 Works with Film-Related
Themes or Characters, 1912 through 1994*

by ANTHONY SLIDE

McFarland & Company, Inc., Publishers
Jefferson, North Carolina, and London

British Library Cataloguing-in-Publication data are available

Library of Congress Cataloguing-in-Publication Data

Slide, Anthony.
   The Hollywood novel : a critical guide to over 1200 works with
film-related themes or characters, 1912 through 1994 / by Anthony Slide.
      p.   cm.
   Includes bibliographical references (p.   ) and index. ∞
   ISBN 0-7864-0044-7 (sewn softcover : 50# alk. paper)
   1. American fiction—20th century—Bibliography.   2. Hollywood
(Los Angeles, Calif.)—In literature—Bibliography.   3. Motion
picture producers and directors in literature—Bibliography.
4. Motion picture actors and actresses in literature—Bibliography.
5. Motion picture industry in literature—Bibliography.   I. Title.
Z1231.F4S58   1995
[PS374.H55]
016.813'509357—dc20   95-15512
                                                                 CIP

Manufactured in the United States of America

McFarland & Company, Inc., Publishers
   Box 611, Jefferson, North Carolina 28640

Acknowledgments

In the compilation of a bibliographic work, the primary need is access to a library, and in this day and age, when many libraries seem to be changing for the worse, one needs helpful and enthusiastic librarians more than ever. I found such individuals on the staff of the Literature Department of the Los Angeles Central Library. My thanks to the head of the department, Helene Mochedlover, and her colleagues, Robert Anderson, Christine Bocek, Bill Jankos, Glenda Prosser, and Roger Quimby. I would also like to acknowledge the pages who could find the most obscure novels with amazing speed. I might only wish the computerized cataloguing system at the Los Angeles Central Library displayed the same agility and efficiency.

In addition to the Los Angeles Central Library, I must thank the staffs of the Margaret Herrick Library of the Academy of Motion Picture Arts and Sciences, the Doheny Memorial Library of the University of Southern California, the Frances Howard Goldwyn/Hollywood Public Library, the Studio City Public Library, and, in the United Kingdom, the always-smiling women of the Berwick-upon-Tweed Public Library.

Among individuals, my greatest thanks go to Rudy Behlmer and Stacy Endres Behlmer. I would also thank Ring Lardner, Jr., Francis M. Nevins, Jr., and Howard Prouty.

Finally, I would like to acknowledge the current and past editors, critics, and compilers of those primary reference sources: *Book Review Digest*, *Contemporary Authors*, *Cumulative Book Index*, and *Kirkus*.

Contents

Preface

While there have been earlier efforts at compiling a bibliography of the Hollywood novel, this book is the first to provide a critical and historical guide to the genre. As the subtitle indicates, and the title notwithstanding, the volume is not limited to novels set within the Hollywood film industry but includes works with film-related characters, real or fictional, and film-related settings anywhere in the world. All types of relevant fiction may be found here, including, but not limited to, children's and juvenile reading, mystery novels, science fiction, and romance. Although limited to English-language publications, this historical guide does cover translated works. Books set in Los Angeles, or more particularly Hollywood, are included only if the location was chosen by the author in order to embrace a film industry storyline.

Entries are arranged alphabetically by author, with each entry providing bibliographic data and commentary with information on the storyline. In many cases, I have provided my own opinion as to a novel's worth or have offered a sampling of contemporary critical commentary. When an author has some connection to the film industry, that information is provided, and, wherever possible, I have supplied birth and death years for the writer.

The books are all indexed by title and subject for immediate access to relevant novels. Subject indexing should be particularly helpful in identifying romans à clef on a specific film industry personality, such as Marilyn Monroe. I would like to stress, however, that no matter how good a subject index is, it cannot possibly identify nuances in plot development or certain psychological manifestations in a storyline. The individual entries need to be read.

Furthermore, I have included the first tentative attempts at bibliographies of the radio novel and the television novel. Such bibliographies are obviously not complete, but they should serve as a beginning for any proposed future bibliographies of these genres. The general bibliography included here is relatively short, not because I have ignored many articles and books but rather because there is little that is relevant. Regrettably, virtually all the studies that deal with the Hollywood novel tend to concentrate on one or two obvious titles—by F. Scott Fitzgerald, Nathanael West, and others—and ignore the major body of work.

Important as *The Last Tycoon* or *The Day of the Locust* may be in American literary study, these novels are not representative of the Holly-

1

wood novel as a popular genre. Pat Booth, Jackie Collins, and Harold Robbins are the true authors of the Hollywood novel, continuing a tradition that began in 1915 when two anonymous writers produced *The Love Story of a Movie Star* and *My Strange Life: The Intimate Life Story of a Moving Picture Actress*. The ritual Hollywood novel quickly attracted the attention of established Hollywood screenwriters, such as Frances Marion and Adela Rogers St. Johns. Gossip columnists like Jimmy Starr began writing Hollywood novels, and America's last great gossip columnist, Joyce Haber, brought it up to date with *The Users* in 1976.

The Hollywood novel of the 1990s is rather like a typical American soap opera, thoroughly divorced from the reality with which most readers must cope. It is, as Terry Curtis-Fox wrote in 1985, "the story of the eternal outsider," and that is perhaps its chief appeal to the general public. It offers us, the readers, the potential to belong to a glamorous society. It does not matter too much that the Hollywood society about which the Hollywood novelist writes does not exist, and nor does it matter that there is often a dated quality to the storyline. The Hollywood studio system disappeared back in the 1960s, and yet most current Hollywood novelists do not recognize this, with their stories heavily reliant on studio moguls and stars with studio contracts. It is rather like the daytime soap operas, where everyone lives in a fictionalized town miles from anywhere but close enough to an international airport to guarantee a direct flight to a glamor capital such as Paris or Rome.

The Hollywood novel can also discuss such taboo subjects as homosexuality, and there are few contemporary novels that do not feature at least one gay character and do not include at least one lesbian encounter. Such subject matter is far from new. Today, the approach is explicit, with, for example, Joan Collins writing in *Prime Time* of a leading man who required "a unit cocksman in his contract to keep him happy on his lunch hour." But even as early as 1932 Haynes Lubou in *Reckless Hollywood* and Jack Preston in *Screen Star* made reference to gays in the film industry. That same year, Tamar Lane wrote in *Hey Diddle Diddle* of three leading men at a party, "romantic heartbreakers," for whom the opposite sex held no interest offscreen: "They appeared always far more interested in one another. It was probably fortunate that their female film admirers could not listen in on their conversation."

In 1941, Edmund Wilson complained that in Hollywood, a city of writers, "none has yet really mustered the gumption to lay bare the heart and bowels of the moving picture business." I can only imagine that Wilson had not read Cedric Belfrage's stunning exposé of a community and a way of life, *Promised Land: Notes for a History*, published in London in 1938. And, admittedly on a lesser, steadfastly comic level, there was *Queer People* (1930), written by the Graham brothers, a book so hard hitting, despite its humor, that it sent shudders throughout the film industry.

Because of the obvious interest in the two genres, I have included listings of science fiction and mystery novels within the subject index. Only eight works in the former category have been identified, but that seems a surprisingly large number since the film industry does not seem to lend itself to science fiction. Fantasy, yes; science fiction, no. As far as can be ascertained, the first mystery novel with a film-related theme was Arnold Frederick's *The Film of Fear*, published in 1917. The first major film-related mystery novel was *The Film Mystery*, published in 1921, and written by Arthur Benjamin Reeve, whose name as a writer was familiar to film-going audiences because of his popular Craig Kennedy mystery series. Carolyn Wells, a prolific mystery writer, wrote the first series of mystery novels featuring a film-related character — a former silent film star named Kenneth Carlisle — in the period 1929–1931. And by that time, Agatha Christie had already contributed to the genre.

As the chronological listing of Hollywood novels indicates, the first book in the genre was a children's novel, *Tom Swift and His Wizard Camera*, by Victor Appleton. A corporate pseudonym, "Victor Appleton" contributed more books to the Hollywood novel genre than any other writer — some 17 between 1912 and 1919, not counting those produced by the same corporate entity under the name of "Laura Lee Hope." In the course of preparing this reference work, I have come across a number of books for children with film-related themes, but most seem to be more the type one wishes a child would read than the kind the child will actually take down from the shelf.

As the years progressed, the subject matter of the Hollywood novel expanded to include film buffs, film fans, and the film-going experience. In the last category, Gilbert Adair's *The Holy Innocents* (1988) and David Lodge's *The Picturegoers* (1960) are most worthy of attention.

In the late teens, editor George Horace Latimer supposedly suggested to two contributors to the *Saturday Evening Post*, Charles E. Van Loan and Harry Leon Wilson, that they consider writing fiction based on the Hollywood film industry. After a visit to Los Angeles he told them, "I was struck with the possibilities of this new field for the fiction writer." Both Van Loan and Wilson took Latimer up on the idea. They were just two of the hundreds of writers who over the past 80 years have found fictional inspiration from the film industry. More than 1200 novels have been written to date, and there is obviously no end in sight.

—ANTHONY SLIDE

There seem to be two main schools of thought about Hollywood novels. One says, "It is impossible to write anything decent about Hollywood because it is such a fabulous, unreal place that it defies description." And the other: "When the writer comes along with guts enough to tell the real story of Hollywood, it will be one of the great books of all times."

—BUDD SCHULBERG,
"The Hollywood Novel," *Films*
1:2 (spring 1940), 68

Chronology of the Hollywood Novel

1912
Victor Appleton: *Tom Swift and His Wizard Camera.*

1913
Victor Appleton: *The Motion Picture Chums' First Venture; The Motion Picture Chums at Seaside Park; The Moving Picture Boys; The Moving Picture Boys in the West; The Moving Picture Boys on the Coast; The Moving Picture Boys in the Jungle; The Moving Picture Boys in Earthquake Land.*

1914
Victor Appleton: *The Motion Picture Chums on Broadway; The Motion Picture Chums' Outdoor Exhibition; The Motion Picture Chums' New Idea; The Moving Picture Boys and the Flood.* Laura Lee Hope: *The Moving Picture Girls; The Moving Picture Girls at Oak Farm; The Moving Picture Girls Snowbound; The Moving Picture Girls Under the Palms; The Moving Picture Girls at Rocky Ranch.*

1915
Anonymous: *The Love Story of a Movie Star; My Strange Life.* Victor Appleton: *The Motion Picture Chums at the Fair; The Moving Picture Boys at Panama.* Laura Lee Hope: *The Moving Picture Girls at Sea.*

1916
Victor Appleton: *The Moving Picture Boys Under the Sea; The Motion Picture Chums' War Spectacle.* B.M. Bower: *The Phantom Herd.* Francis William Sullivan: *Star of the North.*

1917
Arnold Fredericks: *The Film of Fear.*

1918
Victor Appleton: *The Moving Picture Boys on the War Front.* Margaret Turnbull: *The Close-Up.*

1919
Victor Appleton: *The Moving Picture Boys on the French Battlefields.* Charles E. Van Loan: *Buck Parvin and the Movies.*

1920
B.M. Bower: *The Quirt.* Mark Lee Luther: *Presenting Jane McRae.* Harry Charles Witwer: *Kid Scanlan; There's No Base Like Home.*

1921
Stephen Vincent Benét: *The Beginning of Wisdom.* Francis J. Finn: *Bobbie in Movieland.* Nina Wilcox Putnam: *West Broadway.* Arthur Benjamin Reeve: *The Film Mystery.* Henry Kitchell Webster: *Real Life.*

1922
Robert W. Chambers: *Eris.* William S. Hart: *Told Under a White Oak Tree.* Rupert Hughes: *Souls for Sale.* Nina Wilcox Putnam: *Laughter Limited.* Louis Joseph Vance: *Linda Lee Incorporated.* Harry Leon Wilson: *Merton of the Movies.*

1923
Edgar Rice Burroughs: *The Girl from Hollywood.* B.E. Stevenson: *A King in Babylon.*

5

1924
George Randolph Chester and Lilian Chester: *On the Lot and Off*. Hugh Wiley: *The Prowler*.

1925
Robert Ames Bennet: *The Rough Rider*. Agatha Christie: *Poirot Investigates*. Roy Octavus Cohen: *Bigger and Bigger*. Frances Marion: *Minnie Flynn*. Adela Rogers St. Johns: *The Skyrocket*.

1926
Victor Appleton: *The Movie Boys and the Flood; The Movie Boys and the Wreckers; The Movie Boys at the Big Fair; The Movie Boys at Seaside Park; The Movie Boys' First Showhouse; The Movie Boys in Earthquake Land; The Movie Boys in Peril; The Movie Boys in the Jungle; The Movie Boys in the Wild West; The Movie Boys' New Idea; The Movie Boys on Broadway; The Movie Boys on Call; The Movie Boys' Outdoor Exhibition; The Movie Boys Under Fire; The Movie Boys Under the Sea; The Movie Boys Under Uncle Sam*. Gardner Hunting: *The Vicarion*. Luigi Pirandello: *Shoot!* Vingie E. Roe: *Monsieur of the Rainbows*. Raymond L. Schrock and Edward Clark: *Broken Hearts of Hollywood*. Jimmy Starr: *365 Nights in Hollywood*. Jim Tully: *Jarnegan*. Harry Charles Witwer: *Bill Grimm's Progress*.

1927
Victor Appleton: *The Movie Boys' War Spectacle*. Beatrice Burton: *The Hollywood Girl*. J.G. Jéhu: *The Half Englishman*. Lorraine Maynard: *Twinkle, Little Movie Star*. Don Ryan: *Angel's Flight*. Virginia Tracy: *Starring Dulcie Jayne*.

1928
Victor Appleton: *Tom Swift and His Talking Pictures*. R.J. Cosgrif: *Wastelands*. Anita Loos: *But Gentlemen Marry Brunettes*. Carl Van Vechten: *Spider Boy*. Rob Wagner: *Tessie Moves Along*.

1929
Earl Derr Biggers: *The Black Camel*. Roy Octavus Cohen: *The Valley of Olympus*. Freeman Wills Croft: *The Purple Sickle Murders*. Phyllis Gordon Demarest: *Children of Hollywood*. Arlo C. Edington and Mrs. Carmen Ballen Edington: *The Studio Murder Mystery*. Anne Gardner: *Reputation*. Richard Halliday: *Fanfare*. Ernest Lopez: *His Awakening*. J.P. McEvoy: *Hollywood Girl*. Stella G.S. Perry: *Extra-Girl*. Edward Stilgebauer: *The Star of Hollywood*. Carolyn Wells: *Sleeping Dogs*. Harry Charles Witwer: *Yes Man's Land*.

1930
Herbert Crooker: *The Hollywood Mystery*. Phyllis Gordon Demarest: *Hollywood Gold*. Arlo C. Edington and Mrs. Carmen Ballen Edington: *The House of the Vanishing Goblets*. Ramon Gomez de la Serna: *Movieland*. Carroll and Garrett Graham: *Queer People*. Eugene Henry Huffman: *Now I Am Civilized*. Heinrich Eduard Jacob: *Blood and Celluloid*. Fannie Hislip Lea: *Happy Landings*. Mark Lee Luther and Lillian C. Ford: *The Saranoff Murder; Card 13*. Don Marquis: *Off the Arm*. Al Martin: *Dog Gone Hollywood*. Elmer L. Rice: *A Voyage to Purilia*. Don Ryan: *A Roman Holiday*. Carolyn Wells: *The Doorstep Murders*.

1931
Anonymous: *Hollywood Wife*. Oswell Blakeston: *Few Are Chosen*. Elizabeth Borton: *Pollyanna in Hollywood*. Roy Octavus Cohen: *Lillies of the Alley*. Charles Grayson: *Spotlight Madness*. J.P. McEvoy: *Society*. Arthur J. Rees: *Tragedy at Twelvetrees*. Carolyn Wells: *The Skeleton at the Feast*. Raoul Whitfield: *Death in a Bowl*. Harry Leon Wilson: *Two Black Sheep*.

1932
Nalbro Bartley: *Second Flight*. Roy Octavus Cohen: *Star of Earth*. Homer Croy: *Headed for Hollywood*. Tay Garnett: *Tall Tales from Hollywood*. John Gorman: *Hollywood's Bad Boy*. Maurice L. Kusell and M.S. Merritt: *Marquee Ballyhoo*. Tamar Lane: *Hey Diddle Diddle*. Haynes Lubou: *Reckless Hollywood*.

Keane McGrath: *Hollywood Siren.* James Morrison: *April Luck.* Jack Preston: *Screen Star.* Paul Rader: *Big Bug.* Madelon St. Denis: *The Death Kiss.* John Van Alstyn Weaver: *Joy-Girl.* Leon Zolotkoff: *From Vilna to Hollywood.*

1933

Anonymous: *City Without a Heart.* Maysie Greig: *Professional Lover.* Norman Klein: *She Loves Me.* J.B. Priestley: *Albert Goes Through.* Alma Sioux Scarberry: *Puppy Love.*

1934

Vicki Baum: *Falling Star.* Donald Henderson Clarke: *Alabam'.* Maysie Greig: *Romance for Sale.* Jack Hanley: *Star Lust.* Ernest Haycox: *Rough Air.* Richard Henry Lee: *Nights and Daze in Hollywood.* Olga Rosmanith: *Picture People.*

1935

Charles G. Booth: *The Cat and the Clock.* Genevieve Haugen: *Women with Wings.* Max Knepper: *Sodom and Gomorrah.* Victor MacClure: *Death on the Set.* Horace McCoy: *They Shoot Horses, Don't They?* Dora Macy: *Public Sweetheart No. 1.* Liam O'Flaherty: *Hollywood Cemetery.* Charles Ray: *Hollywood Shorts.* Berta Ruck: *Star in Love.* Phil Stong: *The Farmer in the Dell.* Shepard Traube: *Glory Road.* Ruthe S. Wheeler: *Janet Hardy in Hollywood.* George S. Whittaker: *Beggars of Destiny.* P.G. Wodehouse: *Blandings Castle and Elsewhere.*

1936

Faith Baldwin: *The Moon's Our Home.* Lynton Wright Brent: *Gittin' in the Movies.* Dane Coolidge: *Snake Bit Jones.* John Dos Passos: *The Big Money.* Cromwell Gibbons: *Murder in Hollywood.* Charles Grayson: *The Show Case.* Margaret Gibbons MacGill: *Hollywood Star Dust.* Nancy Pope: *Sentence of Youth.* Pauline Stiles: *Red Pavilion.* Margaret Widdemer: *This Isn't the End.* P.G. Wodehouse: *Laughing Gas; The*

Luck of the Bodkins. Peggy Wood: *Star Wagon.*

1937

Samuel Hopkins Adams: *Maiden Effort.* Madeline Brandeis: *Adventure in Hollywood.* James M. Cain: *Serenade.* Ruth Feiner: *Fires in May.* Rachael Field and Arthur Pederson: *To See Ourselves.* Margaret Grant: *Call Back Love.* Eric Hatch: *Good Old Jack.* E. Nils Holstius: *Hollywood Through the Back Door.* James Lee: *Hollywood Agent.* Cameron McCabe: *The Face on the Cutting-Room Floor.* Alice Duer Miller: *The Rising Star.* James D. O'Hanlon: *Murder at Malibu.* Martha Robinson: *Continuity Girl.* Charles Saxby: *Death Over Hollywood.* Lee Shippey: *The Girl Who Wanted Experience.* Dorothy Speare: *The Road to Needles.* Sylvia Stevenson: *The Flowering Aloe.*

1938

Jane Allen: *I Lost My Girlish Laughter.* Cedric Belfrage: *Promised Land.* Elizabeth Carfrae: *This Way to the Stars.* Clyde B. Clason: *The Whispering Ear.* William Gerhardie: *My Wife's the Least of It.* Richard Halas: *You Play the Black and the Red Comes Up.* Naomi Jacob: *Fade Out.* Eric Knight: *The Flying Yorkshireman.* Mary Louise Mabie: *The Root of the Lotus.* Horace McCoy: *I Should Have Stayed Home.* Lawrence W. Meynell: *The House in the Hills.* Vladimir Nabokov: *Laughter in the Dark.* James D. O'Hanlon: *Murder at 300 to 1.* James O'Hara: *Hope of Heaven.* Ellery Queen: *The Devil to Pay; The Four of Hearts.* Florence Ryerson and Colin Campbell Clements: *Shadows.* Lady Eleanor Furneaux Smith: *The Spanish House.* Henri Troyat: *One Minus Two.*

1939

Katherine Albert: *Remember Valerie March.* Ann Austin: *Murdered but Not Dead.* Jeffrey Dell: *Nobody Ordered Wolves.* Dorothy Cameron Disney: *The Golden Swan Murder.* Louise Platt Hauck: *Juliet, Inc.* Aldous Huxley: *After*

1939 *(continued)*

Many a Summer Dies the Swan. Patsy Ruth Miller: *The Flanagan Girl.* James D. O'Hanlon: *Murder at Coney Island.* Jack Preston: *Heil Hollywood!* Berta Ruck: *Handmaid to Fame.* Charles Saxby: *Death Cuts the Film.* Lee Shippey: *If We Only Had Money.* Nathanael West: *The Day of the Locust.*

1940

Ann Bell: *Lady's Lady.* Anthony Boucher: *The Case of the Baker Street Irregulars.* George Harmon Coxe: *The Glass Triangle.* Lillian Day: *The Youngest Profession.* Margaret Echard: *Stand-In for Death.* Ketti Frings: *Hold Back the Dawn.* Rose Gordon and Ione Reed: *Stunt Girl.* Paula Gould: *Publicity Girl.* Harold Helveston: *Maid in Hollywood.* Joan Morgan: *Camera!* James D. O'Hanlon: *As Good as Murdered.* R.C. Woodthorpe: *Rope for a Convict.*

1941

Paul Alexander: *The Hollywood Bug.* Karen De Wolf: *Take the Laughter.* Steve Fisher: *I Wake Up Screaming.* F. Scott Fitzgerald: *The Last Tycoon.* Courtland Fitzsimmons: *This—Is Murder!* Frederick Hollander: *Those Torn from Earth.* Rupert Hughes: *City of Angels.* Gypsy Rose Lee: *The G-String Murders.* Anna M. Lucas: *Tangled Lives.* William McFee: *Spenlove in Arcady.* James D. O'Hanlon: *Murder at Horsethief.* Stuart Palmer: *The Puzzle of the Happy Hooligan.* Helen Lawrence Partridge: *A Lady Goes to Hollywood.* Charles Saxby: *Out of It All.* Budd Schulberg: *What Makes Sammy Run.* Elswyth Thorne: *Remember Today.* Charles Hanson Towne: *Pretty Girls Get There.* Philip Wylie: *Salt Water Daffy.*

1942

W.T. Ballard: *Say Yes to Murder.* Leslie Charteris: *The Saint Goes West.* Maysie Greig: *No Retreat from Love.* Thornwell Jacobs: *Drums of Doomsday.* Gypsy Rose Lee: *Mother Finds a Body.* Richard Sale: *Lazarus #7.* Cecily Spaulding: *From This Day On.* Lee Thayer: *Murder on Location.* Dixie Willson: *Hollywood Starlet.* Florence Wobber: *Calico Orchids.*

1943

Michael Blankfort: *A Time to Live.* Gwen Bristow: *Tomorrow Is Forever.* Robert Carson: *The Bride Saw Red.* Norbert Davis: *Sally's in the Alley.* Clarence B. Kelland: *Archibald the Great.* Clifford Knight: *The Affair of the Fainting Butler.* Laurence Lariar: *He Died Laughing.* Lange Lewis: *Meat for Murder.* Finley McDermid: *Ghost Wanted.* John Waer: *Jade.* Irene Wilde: *Red Turban.*

1944

Florenz Branch: *The Fleshpots.* Ben Hecht: *I Hate Actors!* Virginia Lederer: *Married at Leisure.* Berta Ruck: *Shining Chance.* George Sanders: *Crime on My Hands.* Jimmy Starr: *The Corpse Came C.O.D.*

1945

Bettina and Audrey Boyers: *Murder by Proxy.* Maurice De Kobra: *The Madonna in Hollywood.* Dorothy B. Hughes: *Dread Journey.* Christopher Isherwood: *Prater Violet.* Lange Lewis: *The Birthday Murder.* Theodore Pratt: *Miss Dilly Says No.* Milton M. Raison: *Nobody Loves a Dead Man.* Jimmy Starr: *Three Short Biers.*

1946

Jane Allen and Mary Livingstone: *Thanks God! I'll Take It from Here.* Paul Bailey: *Song Everlasting.* Molly Castle: *New Winds Are Blowing.* Agatha Christie: *Murder After Hours.* Lois Eby and John C. Fleming: *Blood Runs Cold.* Lee Hutchings: *Hollywood and Vine.* Russell Janney: *The Miracle of the Bells.* Sophie Kerr: *Love Story Incidental.* Clifford Knight: *The Affair of the Corpse Escort.* Arthur Kober: *That Man Is Here Again.* Lew Lauria: *Let the Chips Fall.* M.S. Marble: *Everybody Makes Mistakes.* James S. Pollak: *The Golden Egg.* Theodore Pratt: *Valley Boy.* J.B. Priestley: *Bright Day.* Henry H. Robbes:

Hollywood Episode. Richard Sale: *Benefit Performance.* George Sanders: *Stranger at Home.* Ethel Sexton: *Count Me Among the Living.* Lloyd S. Thompson: *Death Stops the Show.* Margaret Buell Wilder: *Hurry Up and Wait.* Dana Wilson: *Make with the Brains, Please.*

1947
Ludwig Bemelmans: *Dirty Eddie.* Muriel Bradley: *Affair at Ritos Bay.* Moray Dalton: *The Condamine Case.* Jay Dratler: *The Pitfall.* Edwin Gilbert: *The Squirrel Cage.* Wilbur Hall: *Mr. Jory.* Andrew Hecht: *Hollywood Merry-Go-Round.* Edward Harris Heth: *We Are the Robbers.* Ernest Hoberecht: *Tokyo Romance.* Frank Kane: *About Face.* David Kent: *A Knife Is Silent.* Goddard Lieberson: *Three for Bedroom C.* Betty Webb Lucas: *Bright Moonlight.* Michael Morgan: *Nine More Lives.* Len Zinberg: *What D'Ya Know for Sure.*

1948
W.T. Ballard: *Say Yes to Murder.* David Broekman: *The Shoestring Symphony.* Roy Octavus Cohen: *My Love Was Black.* Leslie Ford: *The Devil's Stronghold.* James M. Fox: *Death Commits Bigamy.* Babette Hughes: *Magic Penny.* Aldous Huxley: *Ape and Essence.* Elizabeth D. Kaup: *Repeat with Laughter.* Jay Presson: *Spring Riot.* Tomlin Reed: *Call Me Mistress.* R.C. Sherriff: *Another Year.* Wilson Tucker: *The Dove.* Evelyn Waugh: *The Loved One.*

1949
Joey Adams: *The Curtain Never Falls.* Raymond Chandler: *The Little Sister.* Roy Huggins: *Lonely Lady, Pity Me.* Day Keene: *Framed in Guilt.* Ross Macdonald: *The Moving Target.* Harold Robbins: *The Dream Merchants.* Noel Streatfeild: *Movie Shoes.* Jan Tempest: *Short Cut to the Stars.*

1950
Edmund Crispin: *Frequent Hearses.* Charles Michael Daugherty: *Let 'Em Roll.* Katherine Everard: *A Star's Progress.* Leonora Hornblow: *Memory and*

Desire. Evelyn Piper: *The Motive.* Nora Roberts: *Captivated.* Budd Schulberg: *The Disenchanted.* Leon Z. Surmelian: *98.6°.*

1951
Sidney Alexander: *The Celluloid Asylum.* John and Emery Bonett: *Not in the Script.* Richard Brooks: *The Producer.* Frances Clippinger: *The Satellite.* Whitfield Cook: *Roman Comedy.* James Hilton: *Morning Journey.* Laura Z. Hobson: *The Celebrity.* William Bradford Huie: *The Revolt of Mamie Stover.* Anita Loos: *A Mouse Is Born.* Ross Macdonald: *The Way Some People Die.* David Niven: *Once Over Lightly.* D.B. Olsen: *Love Me in Death.* Ellery Queen: *The Origin of Evil.* Nicholas Sandys: *Starset and Sunrise.* William Saroyan: *Rock Wagram.* Georges Simenon. *The Heart of a Man.* P.G. Wodehouse: *The Old Reliable.*

1952
Jeanne Bowman: *Exclusively Yours.* Robert Carson: *The Magic Lantern.* Barry Devlin: *Song of the Whip.* Noel Langley: *Hocus Pocus.* Stephen Longstreet: *The Beach House.* Mary MacLaren: *The Twisted Heart.* O.D. Osborne: *Leave Her to God.* Elliot Paul: *The Golden Sparrow.* Harry Alan Smith: *Mister Zip.* Leon Riley Woodrum: *If You Hear a Song.*

1953
Jennifer Ames: *Wagon to a Star.* M.K. Argus: *A Rogue with Ease.* Jeanne Bowman: *Miss Prissy.* Malcolm Stuart Boylan: *Gold Pencil.* Roy Chanslor: *The Naked I.* Romain Gary: *Colors of the Day.* William Campbell Gault: *Blood on the Boards.* Jay Richard Kennedy: *Prince Bart.* Gladys Malvern: *Hollywood Star.* Paul Tabor: *Lighter Than Vanity.* Peter Viertel: *White Hunter, Black Heart.*

1954
Frances Clippinger: *Rocket in the Night.* John Dos Passos: *Most Likely to Succeed.* William Campbell Gault: *The Sweet Blonde Trap.* Charles Grayson: *Venus*

1954 *(continued)*
Rising. Richard Hinkel: *Two Deaths Must Die.* Speed Lamkin: *The Easter Egg Hunt.* Richard McKaye: *Portrait of the Damned.* Helga Moray: *Carla.* Stuart Palmer: *Cold Poison.* Monica Stirling: *Ladies with a Unicorn.*

1955
Niven Busch: *The Actor.* Kathleen Clifford: *It's April—Remember?* Harry Kurnitz: *Invasion of Privacy.* Ring Lardner, Jr.: *The Ecstasy of Owen Muir.* Norman Mailer: *The Deer Park.* Robin Maugham: *Behind the Mirror.* Alberto Moravia: *A Ghost at Noon.* William Murray: *Fugitive Romans.* Robert Ramsey: *Fiesta.* D. Stapleton: *The Crime, the Place and the Girl.* Elizabeth Tebbets-Taylor: *Now I Lay Me Down to Die.*

1956
Alex Austin: *Greatest Lover in the World.* W.T. Ballard: *The Package Deal.* Mary Carmody: *My Golden Egg.* Henri Catalan: *Soeur Angele and the Ghosts of Chambord.* David Chandler: *A Little More Time.* Manning Coles: *Far Traveler.* Maurice Druon: *Film of Memory.* Charles Hamblett: *The Crazy Kill.* Ross Macdonald: *The Barbarous Coast.* Pamela Moore: *Chocolates for Breakfast.* Abraham Polonsky: *A Season of Fear.* Sylvia Tate: *The Fuzzy Pink Nightgown.* Anne Taylor and Fern Mosk: *Press On Regardless.* Maritta Wolf: *The Big Nickelodeon.*

1957
Alvah Bessie: *The Un-Americans.* Libbie Block: *The Hills of Beverly.* Keith Botsford: *The Eighth-Best-Dressed-Man in the World.* Bessie Breuer: *The Actress.* Harry Carmichael: *Into Thin Air.* Alfred Coppel: *Night of Fire and Snow.* Frédérique Hebrard: *The Month of September.* James A. Howard: *Die on Easy Street.* Al Morgan: *Cast of Characters.* Wright Morris: *Love Among the Cannibals.* R.K. Narayan: *Printer of Malgudi.* Ercole Patti: *Roman Affair.* Patrick Quentin: *Suspicious Circumstances.*

1958
Robert Bloch: *Shooting Star.* Robert Carson: *Love Affair.* Berkeley Gray: *Conquest in California.* Alfred Hayes: *My Face for the World to See.* Owen Fox Jerome: *The Five Assassins.* George Kirgo: *Hercules: The Greek Story.* James Lord: *The Joys of Success.* Phineas Barton Myers: *Hollywood Murder.* Marguerite Nelson: *Jill's Hollywood Assignment.* Craig Rice: *The April Robin Murders.* Virginia Roberts: *Nurse on Location.* Walter Ross: *The Immortal.*

1959
Libbie Block: *No Man Tells Everything.* Carter Brown: *The Dame.* Thomas B. Dewey: *The Case of the Chased and the Unchaste.* David Duncan: *Yes, My Darling Daughters.* William Campbell Gault: *Death Out of Focus.* Al Hine: *The Birthday Boy.* Richard G. Hubler: *The Shattering of the Image.* Robert B. Kirsch: *In the Wrong Rain.* Gavin Lambert: *The Slide Area.* Jonathan Latimer: *Black Is the Fashion for Dying.* Lionel Olay: *The Heart of a Stranger.* Russell O'Neill: *Jonathan.* Irving Shulman: *The Velvet Knife.* Daniel Stern: *Miss America.* Isabella Taves: *The Quick Rich Fox.* Bob Thomas: *The Flesh Merchants.* Irving Wallace: *The Sins of Philip Fleming.*

1960
W.E. Butterworth: *Comfort Me with Love.* Robert Colby: *The Star Trap.* Norman Daniels: *Suddenly by Shotgun.* Brian Dunn: *The Censored Screen.* Henry Farrell: *What Ever Happened to Baby Jane?* James Kirkwood: *There Must Be a Pony.* David Lodge: *The Picturegoers.* Wade Miller: *Jungle Heat.* Al Morgan: *A Small Success.* Nick Quarry: *Till It Hurts.* Douglas Sanderson: *Catch a Fallen Starlet.* Irwin Shaw: *Two Weeks in Another Town.* Daniel M. Stein: *Wall of Noise.* Ramsay Williams: *Bitten Apples.*

1961
Carter Brown: *The Ever-Loving Blues.* Noel Clad: *Until the Real Thing Comes*

Along. Patrick Dennis: *Little Me.* Steve Fisher: *Image of Hell.* Robert Caine Frazer: *The Hollywood Hoax.* William Campbell Gault: *Vein of Violence.* Jim Harmon: *The Celluloid Scandal.* Jesse L. Lasky, Jr.: *Naked in a Cactus Garden.* Anita Loos: *No Mother to Guide Her.* Marcia Martin: *Donna Parker in Hollywood.* Floyd Miller: *Scandale.* Janet O'Daniel: *The Cliff Hangers.* Walker Percy: *The Moviegoer.* Stu Rivers: *The Casting Couchers.* Harold Robbins: *The Carpetbaggers.* Paul Russo: *Stag Starlet.* Aaron Shirley: *Body of a Young Woman.* Florence Stuart: *Happiness Hill.* John Turner: *Starlet!* Frederick Wakeman: *The Fall of the Apple.*

1962

John Carver: *The Sex Twist.* Roy Chanslor: *The Passion Makers.* Earl Conrad: *Crane Eden.* William R. Cox: *Death on Location.* Dan Cushman: *Brothers in Kickapoo.* Anne de Bolene: *Voyage to Eros.* Patrick Dennis: *Genius.* F. Scott Fitzgerald: *The Pat Hobby Stories.* William B. Greene: *Hollywood Virgin.* Corinne Griffith: *Hollywood Stories.* Christopher Isherwood: *Down There on a Visit.* Don James: *Hollywood Starlet.* Stephen Longstreet: *The Flesh Peddlers.* Bob Lucas: *Naked in Hollywood.* Arnold Marrow: *Sweet Smell of Lust.* Clayton Matthew: *Sex Dancer.* Elliott Nugent: *Of Cheat and Charmer.* James O'Hara: *The Big Laugh.* Ann Pinchot: *52 West.* Greg Randolf: *Sex Goddess.* Mack Reynolds: *This Time We Love.* Harold Robbins: *Where Love Has Gone.* Frank Rooney: *The Great Circle.* John Trinian: *House of Evil.*

1963

Hollis Alpert: *For Immediate Release.* Carter Brown: *The White Bikini.* Robert Carson: *An End to Comedy.* Peter Chambers: *Dames Can Be Deadly.* Gavin Lambert: *Inside Daisy Clover.* Wolf Mankowitz: *Cockatrice.* Alan Marcus: *Of Streets and Stars.* G. William Marshall: *The Deal.* Marguerite Nelson: *Hollywood Nurse.* Judson Philips: *The Dead Can't Love.* Donna Richards:

Hollywood Lesbian. Garret Rogers: *Scandal in Eden.* Richard Sale: *The Oscar.* Bernard Wolfe: *Come On Out, Daddy.* William Woolfolk: *My Name Is Morgan.*

1964

Mary Astor: *The O'Conners.* Leonardo Bercovici: *The Satyr and the Saint.* Carter Brown: *Murder Is a Package Deal; The Windup Doll.* Bill Gunn: *All the Rest Have Died.* Mel Heimer: *West Wind.* Harold Q. Masur: *Make a Killing.* Elick Moll: *Image of Tallie.* Al Morgan: *To Sit on a Horse.* Patricia Moyes: *Falling Star.* Richard S. Prather: *The Cockeyed Corpse.* Stephen Ransome: *Meet in Darkness.* Teo Savory: *A Penny for His Pocket.* David Stacton: *Old Acquaintance.*

1965

Jane Converse: *Nurse in Hollywood.* William Demby: *The Catacombs.* Judson Philips: *The Black Glass City.* David Weiss: *Justin Moyan.* Thomas Wiseman: *Czar.*

1966

Nigel Balchin: *In the Absence of Mrs. Petersen.* Alvah Bessie: *The Symbol.* Stephen Birmingham: *Fast Start, Fast Finish.* Herbert Brean: *The Traces of Merrilee.* Nora Johnson: *Love Letter in the Dead Letter Office.* Henry Klinger: *Lust for Murder.* Gene Lees: *And Sleep Until Noon.* Arnold Lobel: *Martha the Movie Mouse.* Gavin Lyall: *Shooting Script.* Larry McMurtry: *The Last Picture Show.* Robin Maugham: *The Green Shade.* Paul Rosner: *The Princess and the Goblin.* Wirt Williams: *The Trojans.* P.G. Wodehouse: *Plum Pie.*

1967

Michel Bataille: *Fire from Heaven.* George Beardmore: *Charlie Pocock and the Princess.* Vera Caspary: *The Rosecrest Cell.* David Chandler: *The Ramsden Case.* Diane Cilento: *The Manipulator.* Richard Condon: *The Ecstasy Business.* Morton Cooper: *The King.* E.V. Cunningham: *Samantha.* Harry Harrison:

1967 (continued)

The Technicolor® Time Machine. Hugh Hood: The Camera Always Lies. Ross Macdonald: Archer in Hollywood. Don McGuire: 1600 Floogle Street. Howard Rigsby: Calliope Reef. James Sherwood: Stradella. Georges Simenon: Maigret's Pickpocket. Howard Singer: The Devil and Henry Raffin. Henry Sutton: The Exhibitionist. Sloan Wilson: Janus Island. Sarah Woods: The Case Is Altered. William K. Zinsser: The Paradise Bit.

1968

S.N. Behrman: The Burning Glass. Remco Campert: The Gangster Girl. Harlan Ellison: Love Ain't Nothing but Sex Misspelled. Velda Johnson: House Above Hollywood. Herbert Kastle: The Movie Maker. James Leigh: Downstairs at Ramsey's. Paule Mason: Here Lies Georgia Linz. Barry Norman: The Matter of Mandrake. Akiyuki Nozaka: The Pornographers. Stuart Palmer: Rook Takes Knight. Françoise Sagan: The Heart-Keeper. Muriel Spark: The Public Image. Richard S. Usem: The Face Behind the Image. Gore Vidal: Myra Breckinridge. William Woolfolk: The Beautiful Couple.

1969

Evelyn Berckman: She Asked for It. Roger Dooley: Flashback. Timothy Findley: The Butterfly Plague. Elizabeth Hamilton Friermond: Pepper's Paradise. Renato Ghiotto: Check to the Queen. Patricia Highsmith: The Tremor of Forgery. Garson Kanin: Cast of Characters. Whit Masterson: The Last One Kills. Harold Robbins: The Inheritors. Ray Russell: The Colony. Donald E. Westlake: Who Stole Sassi Manoon?

1970

Desmond Bagley: The Spoilers. Joanna Barnes: The Deceivers. Paul Brodeus: The Stunt Man. John Creasey: A Part for a Policeman. Henry Denker: The Director. Thomas B. Dewey: The Taurus Trip. Joan Didion: Play It as It Lays. Robert Eaton: The Body Brokers. Steve Fisher: The Big Dream. Stanton Forbes: If

Laurel Shot Hardy the World Would End Tomorrow. Peter Haining: The Hollywood Nightmare. Joseph Hansen: Fadeout. Angela Huth: Somehow I Had to Find a Brass Band. Peter Marshall: Ancient and Modern. Brian Moore: Fergus. Robert Muller: Lovelife. Stanley Noyes: Shadowbox. Ellis Peters: Morning Raga. Evelyn Piper: The Stand-In. Maxine Schnall: The Broadbelters. Johannes Mario Simmel: To the Bitter End. Terry Southern: Blue Movie. Bart Spicer: Festival.

1971

Robert H. Adlerman: Annie Dean. George Axelrod: Where Am I Now— When I Need Me? Sandra Berkley: Coming Attractions. Mark Brower: The Late Great Creature. Diana Carter: Princess. Jackie Collins: Hollywood Zoo. Edwin Corley: Farewell, My Slightly Tarnished Hero. David Davidson: The Quest of Juror 19. Patrick Dennis: Acapulco. Anne Edwards: Shadow of a Lion. Gerald Fine: Fatty: The Celebrated Novel of Hollywood's First Super-Star Roscoe "Fatty" Arbuckle. Daniel Fuchs: West of the Rockies. Samuel Fuller: 144 Piccadilly. Burt Hirschfield: Acapulco. Tamara Hovey: Among the Survivors. Carolyn Jones: Twice Upon a Time. Evelyn Keyes: I Am a Billboard. Gavin Lambert: The Goodbye People. Alistair Maclean: Bear Island. James Mossman: Lifelines. Helen Nielsen: Shot on Location. Manuel Puig: Betrayed by Rita Hayworth. Mordecai Richler: St. Urbain's Horseman. J.M. Ryan: The Rat Factory. Bob Thomas: Weekend '33. F.P. Tullius: Out of the Death Bag in West Hollywood. P.G. Wodehouse: The Plot That Thickens. William Woolfolk: Maggie.

1972

Rona Barrett: The Lovomaniacs. Joan Blondell: Center Door Fancy. Russell Braddon: The Thirteenth Trick. Len Deighton: Close-Up. Henry Denker: The Kingmaker. Bryan Forbes: The Distant Laughter. Dick Francis: Smoke Screen. William Hanley: Mixed Feelings.

Burt Hirschfield: *Fire in the Embers.* Richard Karlan: *Pageant Faded.* Arthur Laurents: *The Way We Were.* Phyllis Raphael: *They Got What They Wanted.* Simon Raven: *Come Like Shadows.* Peter Townsend: *Zoom!*

1973
Hollis Alpert: *Smash.* Joanna Barnes: *Who Is Carla Hart?* Leland Cooley: *California.* Judy Feiner: *A Hot Property.* Jack Finney: *Marion's Wall.* Brett Halliday: *Kill All the Young Girls.* Edward Hannibal: *Dancing Man.* William Hegner: *The Idolaters.* John Hermansen: *The Waxman Production.* John Lahr: *The Autograph Hound.* Jack Matthews: *Pictures of the Journey Back.* Irwin Shaw: *Evening in Byzantium.* Laurence Snelling: *The Heresy.* Jerry Sohl: *The Resurrection of Frank Borchard.* Mario Soldati: *The Malacca Cane.* Ramona Stewart: *The Apparition.*

1974
Andrew Bergman: *The Big Kiss-Off of 1944.* Lionel Black: *The Life and Death of Peter Wade.* Geoffrey Bocca: *Nadine.* David Davidson: *We Few, We Happy Few.* Fitzroy Davis: *Through the Doors of Brass.* John Ehle: *The Changing of the Guard.* Bruce Jay Friedman: *About Harry Towns.* Herbert Gold: *Swiftie the Magician.* Elia Kazan: *The Understudy.* John Lahr: *Hot to Trot.* Mary Loos: *The Beggars Are Coming.* James McElroy: *Lookout Cartridge.* David Madden: *Bijou.* Dolores Pala: *Trumpet for a Walled City.* Jill Robinson: *Perdido.* Norman Spanrad: *Passing Through the Flame.* Gore Vidal: *Myron.* Irving Wallace: *The Fan Club.* Robert Wilde: *The Sound of Drums and Cymbals.* P.G. Wodehouse: *Bachelors Anonymous.*

1975
Mel Arrighi: *The Hatchet Man.* Fay Baker: *My Darling Darling Doctors.* Andrew Bergman: *Hollywood and LeVine.* DeWitt Bodeen: *13 Castle Walk.* Simon Brett: *Cast in Order of Disappearance.* Don Carpenter: *The True Life of Jody McKeegan.* Edwin Corley: *Shadows.*

Constance Gluyas: *Brief Is the Glory.* Bill Gunn: *Black Picture Show.* Sandra Harmon: *A Girl Like Me.* Elia Kazan: *The Understudy.* Peter Kortner: *Breakfast with a Stranger.* Ron Kurz: *Black Rococo.* Melisand March: *Mandrake Scream.* Daryl Ponicsan: *Tom Mix Died for Your Sins.* Melville Shavelson: *Lualda.* Douglas Sheldon: *The Rainbow Man.* Daniel Stern: *Final Cut.* Richard Yates: *Disturbing the Peace.*

1976
Bob Cox: *Jamaican American.* Robertson Davies: *World of Wonders.* Joyce Eliason: *Laid Out.* Gael Greene: *Blue Skies, No Candy.* Joyce Haber: *The Users.* Sandra Hochman: *Happiness Is Too Much Trouble.* Michael Maguire: *Scratchproof.* Samuel Peeples: *The Man Who Died Twice.* Dotson Rader: *The Dream's on Me.* Frederick Raphael: *California Time.* Hari Rhodes: *The Hollow and the Human.* Harold Robbins: *The Lonely Lady.* Bjorn Robinson Rye: *A Feast of Pikes.* Sidney Sheldon: *A Stranger in the Mirror.* Thomas Tryon: *Crowned Heads.* Marvin Werlin: *Shadow Play.*

1977
Walter Bloch and Robert L. Munger: *The Angel.* Jackie Collins: *Lovers and Gamblers.* Morton Cooper: *Rich People.* Tony Curtis: *Kid Andrew Cody & Julie Sparrow.* Gwen Davis: *The Aristocrats.* Maggie Davis: *The Sheik.* Henry Denker: *The Starmaker.* Weed Dickinson: *Dead Man Talks Too Much.* William Fadiman: *The Clay Oscar.* Andrew J. Fenady: *The Man with Bogart's Face.* John Fowles: *Daniel Martin.* Erica Jong: *How to Save Your Life.* Stuart M. Kaminsky: *Bullet for a Star; Murder on the Yellow Brick Road.* Garson Kanin: *One Hell of an Actor.* Marvin Kaye: *The Laurel and Hardy Murders.* H.F. Keating: *Filmi, Filmi, Inspector Ghote.* Charles Larson: *Muir's Blood.* Darcy O'Brien: *A Way of Life Like Any Other.* Walker Percy: *Lancelot.* Darwin Porter: *Marika.* Adrian Reid: *The Goddaughter.* Charles Reznikoff: *The Manner Music.*

1977 *(continued)*
Philip Rock: *Flickers*. David Rogers: *Somewhere There's Music*. Brad Solomon: *The Gone Man*. Jean Ure: *Bid Time Return*. Robert Watson: *Lily Lang*. Donald E. Westlake: *Enough!*

1978
Robert Ackworth: *The Takers*. Ann Ashton: *The Phantom Reflection*. Jacqueline Briskin: *Paloverde*. Leland Cooley: *The Dancer*. Morton Cooper: *Resnick's Odyssey*. Nona Coxhead: *The Richest Girl in the World*. Linda Crawford: *Something to Make Us Happy*. Lionel Davidson: *Murder Games*. Annabel Davis-Goff: *Night Tennis*. Leslie Deane: *The Girl with the Golden Hair*. Henry Denker: *The Actress*. Mark Dintenfass: *Montgomery Street*. Peter Evans: *Titles*. Joe Hyams: *The Pool*. William Jovanovich: *Madmen Must*. Stuart M. Kaminsky: *You Bet Your Life*. Adam Kennedy: *Just Like Humphrey Bogart*. Judith Krantz: *Scruples*. M. Jay Livingston: *The Prodigy*. Larry McMurtry: *Somebody's Darling*. Thomas Maremaa: *Studio*. Trevor Meldal-Johnson: *Always*. Paul Monette: *Taking Care of Mrs. Carroll*. Joe Morella and Edward Z. Epstein: *The Ince Affair*. Ann Pinchot: *Vanessa*. Herman Raucher: *There Should Have Been Castles*. Martha Rofheart: *The Savage Brood*. Rosemary Rogers: *The Crowd Pleasers*. Margaret Scherf: *The Beaded Banana*. Doris Schwein: *Leanna*. Ernest Tidyman: *Table Stakes*. Mel Tormé: *Wynner*. Mark Upton: *The Dream Lover*. Sheila Weller: *Hansel & Gretel in Beverly Hills*. Max Wilk: *The Moving Picture Boys*.

1979
Margot Arnold: *Exit Actors, Dying*. George Baxt: *The Neon Graveyard*. David Benjamin: *Idol*. Jane Bernstein: *Departures*. Norman Bogner: *Arena*. R. Wright Campbell: *Killer of Kings*. Don Carpenter: *A Couple of Comedians*. Parley J. Cooper: *The Restaurant*. Charles Dennis: *Bonfire*. Stanley Ellin: *Star Light, Star Bright*. Jonathan Fast: *The Inner Circle*. Harriet Frank, Jr.: *Special*

Effects. Daniel Fuchs: *The Apathetic Bookie Joint*. Thomas Gifford: *Hollywood Gothic*. William Goldman: *Tinsel*. Ron Goulart: *Cowboy Heaven*. Diana Hammond: *Sweet Lies*. David Hanly: *In Guilt and Glory*. Joseph Hansen: *Skinflick*. Timothy Harris: *Goodnight and Goodbye*. Maxine Herman: *Forced Feedings*. Donald Jack: *Me Bandy, You Cissie*. Stuart M. Kaminsky: *The Howard Hughes Affair*. Garson Kanin: *Moviola*. Herbert Kastle: *Ladies of the Valley*. William Kinsolving: *Born with the Century*. Michael Korda: *Charmed Lives*. Steve Krantz: *Laurel Canyon*. Christopher Leopold: *Casablack*. Bill Mahan: *The Moviola Man*. Michael Mershaw: *Land Without Shadow*. Paul Monette: *The Gold Diggers*. John Nichols: *A Ghost in the Music*. Eleanor Perry: *Blue Pages*. Manuel Puig: *Kiss of the Spider Woman*. David Snell: *Lights, Camera ... Murder*. Brad Solomon: *Jake & Katie*. Karen Stabiner: *Limited Engagements*. Colin Watson: *Blue Murder*. Kathleen Winsor: *Calais*. Mickey Ziffrin: *A Political Affair*.

1980
Marian Babson: *Murder, Murder, Little Star*. Alvah Bessie: *One for My Baby*. Dirk Bogarde: *A Gentle Occupation*. Bill Boggs: *At First Sight*. Beatrice Brandon: *The Court of Silver Shadows*. Niven Busch: *Continent's Edge*. Ramsey Campbell: *The Parasite*. R.V. Cassill: *Flame*. Alan Cheuse: *Candace and Other Stories*. Kenn Davis and John Stanley: *Bogart '48*. Joseph Di Mona: *The Eagle's Nest*. Richard Dorso: *Thicker Than Water*. Harlan Ellison: *Shatterday*. Andrew J. Fenady: *The Secret of Sam Marlow*. Robert Sydney Hopkins: *Riviera*. Tom E. Huff: *Marabelle*. Garson Kanin: *Smash*. Elinor Klein and Dora Landey: *Dazzle*. Judith Krantz: *Princess Daisy*. Elliott Lewis: *Bennett #2: Dirty Linen*. Elizabeth Linington: *Consequence of Crime*. Bill Mahan: *The Boy Who Looked Like Shirley Temple*. David Nemec: *Bright Lights, Dark Rooms*. Hugh Pentecost: *Beware Young Lovers*. Iris Rainer: *The Boys in the Mailroom*.

Ron Renaud: *Fade to Black.* Clarissa Rock: *Only Make Believe.* Leonard St. Clair: *Obsessions.* Jeannie Sakol: *Hot 30.* Mel Shavelson: *Conspiracy of Silence.* Murray Sinclair: *Tough in L.A.* Pamela Wallace: *Malibu Colony.* Sylvia Wallace: *Empress.*

1981

Bill Adler: *Positions.* John Baxter: *The Kid.* George J. Bellak: *Come Jericho.* Dirk Bogarde: *Voices in the Garden.* Don Carpenter: *Turnaround.* Pamela Chais: *Final Cut.* David Chandler: *The Middleman.* Liza Cody: *Dupe.* Alan Ebert and Janice Rotchstein: *Traditions.* Blossom Elfman: *The Return of the Whistler.* Jonathan Fast: *The Beast.* Evan Field: *What Nigel Knew.* Richard Friedel: *The Music Lover.* David Galloway: *Lamaar Ranson: Private Eye.* Robert Granit: *Another Runner in the Night.* Doris Grumbach: *Missing Persons.* Bill Gunn: *Rhinestone Sharecropping.* Jerome Jones: *Ambition's Woman.* Stuart M. Kaminsky: *Catch a Falling Crown; High Midnight.* David A. Kaufelt: *The Wine and the Music.* Norma Klein: *Domestic Arrangements.* Stephen Longstreet: *Wheel of Fortune.* Vincent McConnor: *The Paris Puzzle.* John D. MacDonald: *Free Fall in Crimson.* William Marshall: *Sci Fi.* Harold Q. Masur: *The Broker.* Joan Mellen: *Natural Tendencies.* Paul Monette: *The Long Shot:* David Niven: *Go Slowly, Come Back Quickly.* Linda Palmer: *Star Struck.* Robert B. Parker: *A Savage Place.* Don and Sue Preston: *Crazy Fox.* Carol Snyder: *Ike & Mama and the Once-in-a-Lifetime Movie.* Jacqueline Susann: *Valley of the Dolls.* David Thoreau: *The Satanic Condition.* Sabina Thorne: *Reruns.* Eric Van Lustbader: *Sirens.* Joseph Wambaugh: *The Glitter Dome.* Gary Wolf: *Who Censored Roger Rabbit?*

1982

Peter Ackroyd: *The Great Fire of London.* Robert Bloch: *Psycho II.* Susan Braudy: *Who Killed Sal Mineo.* Joan Juliet Buck: *Only Place to Be.* Leslie Caron: *Vengeance.* David Chandler:

Kelly. Virginia Coffman: *The Lombard Cavalcade.* E.V. Cunningham: *The Case of the Kidnapped Angel.* Gordon DeMarco: *The Canvas Prison.* Dominick Dunne: *The Winners.* Harlan Ellison: *Stalking the Nightmare.* Howard Engel: *Murder on Location.* Howard Fast: *Max.* Carl Flick: *A Disturbance in Paris.* Dulcie Gray: *The Glanville Women.* Martin Harry Greenburg and Charles Waugh: *Hollywood Unreal.* Joseph Hansen: *Backtrack.* MacDonald Harris: *Screenplay.* Dorothy B. Hughes: *Trade Secrets.* Richard Layman: *Out Are the Lights.* Ernest Lehman: *Farewell Performance.* Stephen Longstreet: *Golden Touch.* Gregory McDonald: *Fletch's Moxie.* D. Keith Mano: *Take Five.* Pamela Redford Russell: *Wild Flowers.* Clive Sinclair: *Bed Bugs.* Murray Sinclair: *Only in L.A.* Audrey Stainton: *Sweet Rome.* Jack L. Warner, Jr. *Bijou Dreams.*

1983

Ann Ashton: *Star Eyes.* Linda Barnes: *Bitter Finish.* Robert Leslie Bellem: *Dan Turner, Hollywood Detective.* Jacqueline Briskin: *Everything and More.* Jackie Collins: *Hollywood Wives.* Jane Dentinger: *Murder on Cue.* Carol Houlihan Flynn: *Washed in the Blood.* Richard Grenier: *The Marrakesh One-Two.* Joseph Hansen: *Job's Year.* Joe Hyams: *Murder at the Academy Awards.* Adrienne Jones: *A Matter of Spunk.* Stuart M. Kaminsky: *He Done Her Wrong.* Terence Kingsley-Smith: *The Murder of an Old-Time Movie Star.* Gavin Lambert: *Running Time.* Peter Lovesey: *Keystone.* Richard N. Nash: *Radiance.* Claire Rayner: *Shaftesbury Avenue.* Jodi Rhodes: *Winners and Losers.* Marc Rubel: *Flex.* June Flaum Singer: *Star Dreams.* Ian Watson: *Chekhov's Journey.*

1984

George Baxt: *The Dorothy Parker Murder Case.* Phil Berger: *Deadly Kisses.* John Bowen: *The McGuffin.* David Llewellyn Burdett: *Hix Nix Stix Pix.* Sara Davidson: *Friends of the Opposite Sex.* Dorothy Dunnett: *Dolly and the*

1984 *(continued)*

Bird of Paradise. Terence Feely: *Limelight.* George MacDonald Fraser: *The Pyrates.* Josh Greenfeld: *The Return of Mr. Hollywood.* Thomas Jeier and Jeffrey M. Wallman: *The Celluloid Kid.* Stuart M. Kaminsky: *Black Knight in Red Square.* Bill Knox: *The Hanging Tree.* Rosalind Laker: *What the Heart Keeps.* David L. Lindsay: *Heat from Another Son.* James McCourt: *Kate Wayfaring in Avenged.* Carolyn Meyer: *The Luck of Texas McCoy.* Mary Ruth Myers: *Friday's Daughter.* Bernice Rubens: *Go Tell the Lemming.* James Sherburne: *Poor Boy and a Long Way from Home.* June Flaum Singer: *The Movie Set.* Robert Upton: *Fade Out.* Robert Wurlitzer: *Slow Fade.* Bonnie Zindel: *Hollywood Dream Machine.* Paul Zindel: *When a Darkness Falls.*

1985

Martin Amis: *Money.* Carrol Baker: *A Roman Tale.* Ron Base: *Matinee Idol.* John Blumenthal: *The Tinseltown Murders.* Susan Braudy: *What the Movies Made Me Do.* Steve Erickson: *Days Between Stations.* Bryan Forbes: *The Rewrite Man.* Zoe Garrison: *Golden Triple Time.* E.X. Giroux: *A Death of a Darling.* Franklin Hall: *Ben Turpin, Private Eye.* Joseph Hansen: *Steps Going Down.* Mel Heimer: *A Family Affair.* Stuart M. Kaminsky: *Down for the Count.* Tabitha King: *The Trap.* Michael Korda: *Queenie.* Anne McAllister: *Starstruck.* L.A. Morse: *Sleaze.* Lawrence Payne: *Malice in Camera.* Danielle Steel: *Family Album.* Fred Mustard Stewart: *The Titan.* Jim Stimson: *Double Exposure.* David Thomson: *Suspects.* Miles Tripp: *Some Predators Are Male.* P.G. Wodehouse: *Hollywood Omnibus.*

1986

Ron Base: *Foreign Object.* George Baxt: *The Alfred Hitchcock Murder Case.* R. Wright Campbell: *In La-La Land We Trust.* Jackie Collins: *Hollywood Husbands.* Blanche D'Alpuget: *While in Jerusalem.* Judy Feiner: *Flame.* David Freeman: *A Hollywood Education.*

Thomas Gavin: *The Film of Emile Vicco.* Maureen Howard: *Expensive Habits.* Stuart M. Kaminsky: *Smart Moves.* John Mortimer: *Charade.* Anne Rampling: *Belinda.* Harold Robbins: *The Storyteller.* Elliott Roosevelt: *Murder at Hobcaw Barony.* Martin Russell: *Unwelcome Audience.* Simone Signoret: *Adieu Volodya.* Jim Stimson: *Low Angles.* Robert Stone: *Children of Light.* Thomas Tryon: *All That Glitters.* William Warnock: *Danziger's Cuts.*

1987

Marvin Albert: *Get Off at Babylon.* Marian Babson: *Reel Murder.* Stan Barstow: *B-Movie.* George Baxt: *The Tallulah Bankhead Murder Case.* Jay Cantor: *Krazy Kat.* Mary Blount Christian: *Sebastian (Super Sleuth) and the Stars-in-His-Eyes Mystery.* Robert Coover: *A Night at the Movies.* Carrie Fisher: *Postcards from the Edge.* Stuart M. Kaminsky: *Think Fast, Mr. Peters.* Mark Lindquist: *Sad Movies.* Layne Littlepage: *Murder by the Sea.* Dallas Murphy: *Lover Man.* Les Roberts: *An Infinite Number of Monkeys; Not Enough Horses.* Susan Saunders: *The Movie Mystery.* Neville Steed: *Die Cast.* L.J. Washburn: *Wild Night.* Michael Westlake: *Imaginary Women.* Phyllis A. Whitney: *Listen for the Whisperer.*

1988

Gilbert Adair: *The Holy Innocents.* Ellen Akins: *Home Movie.* James Robert Baker: *Boy Wonder.* Joan Collins: *Prime Time.* James Ellroy: *The Big Nowhere.* Elizabeth Gage: *A Glimpse of Stocking.* Douglas Glover: *The South Will Rise at Noon.* Mollie Gregory: *Triplets.* Robert Lee Hall: *Murder at San Simeon.* Joe R. Lansdale: *The Drive In.* Patricia Marx and Douglas G. McGrath: *Blockbuster.* Graham Masterton: *Mirror.* Gerald Petievich: *Shakedown.* John Rechy: *Marilyn's Daughter.* Salman Rushdie: *The Satanic Verses.* Diana Shaw: *Gone Hollywood.* Simon Shaw: *Murder Out of Tune.* Murray Sinclair: *Goodbye L.A.*

June Flaum Singer: *The President's Women*. Mary Tannen: *Second Sight*. Michael Tolkin: *The Player*. Leslie Walker: *Amazing Faith*. Donald Ward: *Death Takes the Stage*. Charles West: *Funnelweb*.

1989

Richard Alfieri: *Ricardo, Diary of a Matinee Idol*. Jacoba Atlas: *Palace of Light*. Marian Babson: *Encore Murder*. Pat Barker: *The Man Who Wasn't There*. Peter Benchley: *Rummies*. Eleanor Bergstein: *Ex-Lover*. Pat Booth: *Beverly Hills*. Charles Bukowski: *Hollywood*. Ramsey Campbell: *Ancient Images*. John Byrne Cooke: *South of the Border*. Noel B. Gerson: *The Golden Ghetto*. Howard and Susan Kaminsky: *Talent*. Stuart M. Kaminsky: *Buried Caesars*. Karen Karbo: *Trespassers Welcome Here*. Wayne Karlin: *The Extras*. Jane Kendall: *Miranda and the Movies*. Ed McBain: *Downtown*. Deena Metzger: *What Dinah Thought*. Joan Lowery Nixon: *Star Babies*. Stephen Rabley: *Future Attractions*. Simon Ritchie: *Work for a Dead Man*. Les Roberts: *A Carrot for the Donkey*. Danielle Steel: *Star*. Jim Stimson: *Truck Shot*.

1990

Steve Allen: *Murder in Manhattan*. George Baxt: *The Talking Picture Murder Case*. Pat Booth: *Malibu*. Mark Childress: *Tender*. Jackie Collins: *Lady Boss*. Joan Collins: *Love and Desire and Hate*. Bruce Cook: *Rough Cut*. Sandra Dallas: *Buster Midnight's Café*. Kirk Douglas: *Dance with the Devil*. Ron Goulart: *Skyrocket Steele*. Michael Herr: *Walter Winchell*. Hazel Wynn Jones: *Shot on Location*. Stuart M. Kaminsky: *Poor Butterfly*. Bernie Lee: *Murder at Musket Beach*. Elmore Leonard: *Get Shorty*. Jill McGown: *Murder Movie*. Claire McNab: *Death Down Under*. Lynda Obst and Carol Wolper: *Dirty Dreams*. Les Roberts: *Snake Oil*. Joann Ross: *Secret Sins*. Diane K. Shah: *As Time Goes By*. Diane Silber: *Confessions*. Tom Tolnay: *Celluloid Gangs*. Gore Vidal: *Hollywood*. L.J. Washburn: *Dog Heavies*.

1991

Marian Babson: *Shadows in Their Blood*. Gila Berkowitz: *The Brides*. Pat Booth: *Rags to Riches*. Celia Brayfield: *The Princess*. James Cohen: *Through a Lens Darkly*. Kate Coscarelli: *The Leading Lady*. Stan Cutler: *Best Performance by a Patsy; The Face on the Cutting-Room Floor*. Robertson Davies: *Murther & Walking Spirits*. Patti Davis: *A House of Secrets*. Amy Ephron: *Biodegradable Soap*. Elizabeth Ferrars: *Sleep of the Unjust*. David Freeman: *A Hollywood Life*. Mollie Gregory: *Birthstone*. Mary-Rose Hayes: *Amethyst*. Susan Isaacs: *Magic Hour*. Stuart M. Kaminsky: *The Melting Clock*. Michael Korda: *Curtain*. Bernie Lee: *Murder Without Reservation*. Richard Nehrbass: *A Perfect Death for Hollywood*. Darcy O'Brien: *Margaret*. Elizabeth Rossiter: *The Lemon Garden*. Theodore Roszak: *Flicker*. Jim Stimson: *TV Safe*. Bruce Wagner: *Force Majeure*. Eric Wright: *Final Cut*.

1992

George Baxt: *The Greta Garbo Murder Case*. Charlotte Bingham: *Stardust*. Dirk Bogarde: *Jericho*. Simon Brett: *Corporate Bodies*. Angela Carter: *Wise Children*. Robert Crais: *Lullaby Town*. Jane Dentinger: *Dead Pan*. Rupert Everett: *Hello Darling, Are You Working?* Gillian B. Farrell: *Alibi for an Actress*. Elizabeth Gage: *Taboo*. Kate Green: *Shooting Star*. David Handler: *The Boy Who Never Grew Up*. Kathryn Harvey: *Stars*. Wendy Hornsby: *Telling Lies*. William Jeffries: *Shallow Graves*. Michael Korda: *The Immortals*. Judith Krantz: *Scruples Two*. Bernie Lee: *Murder Takes Two*. John Mortimer: *Dunster*. Lillian O'Donnell: *Pushover*. Les Roberts: *Seeing the Elephant*. Henry Schwartz: *Albert Goes to Hollywood*. Simon Shaw: *Bloody Instructions*. Sam Toperoff: *Queen of Desire*. Lydia Weaver: *Child Star*. Stuart Woods: *Santa Fe Rules*.

1993

Ellen Akins: *Public Life*. James Robert Baker: *Tim and Pete*. George Baxt: *The Marlene Dietrich Murder Case*. Larry Beinhart: *American Hero*. John C. Boland: *The Seventh Bearer*. Pat Booth: *All for Love*. James Lee Burke: *In the Electric Mist with Confederate Dead*. Melissa Cleary: *Dog Collar Crimes*. Jackie Collins: *American Star*. Michael Covino: *The Negative*. Thomas Craig: *Playing with Cobras*. Stan Cutler: *Shot on Location*. Mary Daheim: *The Alpine Betrayal*. Patti Davis: *Bondage*. Kinky Friedman: *Elvis, Jesus & Coca-Cola*. Olivia Goldsmith: *Flavor of the Month*. Joseph Hansen: *Living Upstairs*. Oscar Hijuelos: *The Fourteen Sisters of Emilio Monterey O'Brien*. Wendy Hornsby: *Midnight Baby*. John Jakes: *Hollywood Kills*. Stuart M. Kaminsky: *The Devil Met a Lady*. Jillian Karr: *Something Borrowed, Something Blue*. Abbe Lane: *But Where Is Love?* Geoff Nicholson: *The Errol Flynn Novel*. Geoffrey O'Brien: *The Phantom Empire*. Katherine Hall Page: *The Body in the Cast*. Jeane Renick: *Always*. Robert Rosenberg: *The Cutting Room*. Susan Fromberg

Schaeffer: *First Nights*. Steve Shagan: *A Cast of Characters*. June Flaum Singer: *Brilliant Divorces*. Charlie Smith: *Chimney Rock*. Francesca Stanfill: *Wakefield Hall*. Teresa Weir: *Last Summer*. Phyllis A. Whitney: *Star Flight*. Don Winslow: *Way Down on the High Lonely*. Stuart Woods: *L.A. Times*.

1994

Lydia Adamson: *A Cat with No Regrets*. Hortense Calisher: *In the Palace of the Movie King*. Jill Churchill: *A Knife to Remember*. John Gregory Dunne: *Playland*. Aaron Elkins: *Dead Men's Hearts*. James Ellroy: *Hollywood Nocturnes*. Bonnie Faber: *And Down Will Come Baby*. Gillian B. Farrell: *Murder & a Muse*. Carrie Fisher: *Delusions of Grandma*. Wendy Hornsby: *Bad Intent*. William Jeffries: *Bloody River Blues*. Ruth Langan: *All That Glitters*. Richard A. Lupoff: *The Bessie Blue Killer*. Ameena Meer: *Bombay Talkie*. William F. Nolan: *The Black Mask Murders*. Constance O'Day-Flannery: *The Gift*. Denise Osborne: *Murder Offscreen*. Stuart Woods: *Dead Eyes*.

Main Entries, By Author

PETER ACKROYD (born 1949) is a British critic, poet, and biographer whose first novel was *The Great Fire of London* (Hamish Hamilton, 1982). It is very much a study of characters, a central one being Spenser Spender, who has decided to make a film of Charles Dickens's novel *Little Dorrit*, using a background of a contemporary prison and contemporary London. The author provides an amusing caricature of the head of the Film Finance Board in the form of Sir Frederick Lustlambert, and also focuses his narrative on a Cambridge professor and novelist, Rowan Phillips, who writes the script for the film and begins a homosexual relationship with a straight young man whose girlfriend comes to believe she is the modern personification of Little Dorrit. The film is very much secondary to the lives and relationships of the various players in the novel, but it does lead to the cataclysmic Great Fire of London of the title.

In 1988 Christine Edzard adapted and directed a six-hour version of *Little Dorrit*, filmed at a former warehouse in London's East End, and starring Derek Jacobi, Alec Guinness, and Joan Greenwood.

ROBERT ACKWORTH (born 1923). *The Takers* (Bobbs-Merrill, 1978) is a lurid Hollywood novel of the lives of three stars of Regency Pictures, celebrating its fortieth anniversary and surviving on the television sales of its film library and the popularity of a young rock 'n' roll singer it has under contract. Howard Stanton has been a contract player at the studio for 30 years; in the 1930s he was the lover of Leni Liebhaber, an actress with a penchant for girls and Nazis, and presumably an amalgam of Marlene Dietrich and Leni Riefenstahl. Stanton and rival actor Michael Baines both vie for the attentions of Tracy Gordon, who has an affair with a Howard Hughes–like billionaire named Wes Rainer.

GILBERT ADAIR is an American-born film critic who lives in Paris. *The Holy Innocents* (E.P. Dutton, 1988) opens in that city in February 1968, introducing the reader to the "rats de la Cinémathèque," the fanatical members of the audience at the screenings of the Cinémathèque Française who spend every evening there, sitting as close as possible to the screen. Three such "rats" are brother and sister Guillaume and Danielle, and a young American film student named Matthew. They know each other only from the screenings, but when the Cinémathèque is closed and its founder, Henri Langlois, fired on orders of Minister of Culture André Malraux, Matthew is invited to the home of Guillaume and Danielle, and eventually moves in when their parents go for a vacation in the country. The innocent and vaguely homosexual Matthew discovers that Guillaume and Danielle are sleeping together, and soon a ménage à trois develops, which owes its origins to Jean Cocteau's *Les Enfants Terribles*. The May 1968 student riots in Paris put an end to the relationship, as Matthew is killed defending Guillaume. The Cinémathèque Française reopens, and Guillaume and Danielle return to their seats.

While an intense sexual relationship dominates the central part of the novel, *The Holy Innocents* is still primarily concerned with the motion picture. The three young people ask each other esoteric film-related questions, with forfeits demanded if no answer is forthcoming. First Guillaume is required to masturbate in the nude while looking at a photograph of Gene Tierney, and then when Danielle and Matthew are unable to name a film in which a cross is shown to mark the spot of a murder, their forfeit is to make love in front of Guillaume. The forfeits lead to sexual abandon, which is again movie related, as Guillaume and Matthew masturbate together while singing "By a Waterfall" from *Footlight Parade* (1933).

The Holy Innocents is both perverse and perverted, demonstrating that the harmless games in which film buffs indulge can lead from innocence to humiliation and a breakdown of human values. It is disturbing and yet, like the films that fascinate its protagonists, addictive.

JOEY ADAMS (born 1911), once a popular comedian in and outside of the profession, is little known today. He also enjoyed a distinguished career as a writer, with some twenty books to his credit. *The Curtain Never Falls* (Frederick Fell, 1949) is the life story of comedian Jackie Mason (no connection to the current comedian of that name), who begins his career working the borscht belt and becomes "the country's number one comedian of stage, screen, and radio." Mason, like many comedians then and now, is always performing, an entertainer on whom the curtain never falls. There is perhaps a hint of Milton Berle here as Adams provides a clinical examination of a show business career. Writing in the *New York Times* (December 18, 1949), A.H. Weiler commented that "Mr. Adams' abundant local color is far more interesting than his story."

SAMUEL HOPKINS ADAMS (1871–1958). When the president of Purity Pictures discovers an attractive young debutante who wants to work in films for fun in *Maiden Effort* (Liveright Publishing, 1937), he decides to star her in a film titled *Virgin Effort*. The debutante discovers that Hollywood men are not particularly desirable and are difficult to keep at bay. She finds the man she really loves when he rescues her from a flood threatening the ranch where she is filming on location. As Nancy Brooker-Bowers points out, "The title of this satiric romance suggests the woman herself, her film debut, the title of the picture, and her situation in Hollywood society."

LYDIA ADAMSON. In *A Cat with No Regrets* (New American Library/E.P. Dutton, 1994), Alice Nestleton heads for France to make a film for producer Dorothy Dodd. The producer is promptly murdered, and cats belonging to both Nestleton and Dodd are an integral part of the plot.

ROBERT H. ADLEMAN (born 1919). *Annie Dean* (World, 1971) is as much a treatise on the supernatural as a readable Hollywood novel. It even includes a four-page bibliography. The title heroine was a schoolteacher, captured and possessed by a Native American warrior in the 1800s. One hundred years later, a middle-aged Hollywood director named Sam Brown decides to make a film of her life. His interest becomes an obsession as he falls in love with her and believes himself visited by Annie for nights of sexual passion.

BILL ADLER (born 1951). Three young women arrive in Hollywood in *Positions* (Leisure Books, 1981), each determined to reach the top in her chosen profession by using any man able and willing to help. Kelley becomes a screenwriter; Darlene a talent agent; and Anna the reigning bitch of a leading lady. Typical fare.

ELLEN AKINS's first novel, *Home Movie* (Simon & Schuster, 1988), is complex, the story of 14-year-old Joey Taylor, who meets loner David Giffard. The latter gives her piano lessons and also screens bits and pieces of a film that seems to have relevance to their lives. Joey leaves for Los Angeles to locate the actor in the "home movie." *Public Life* (HarperCollins, 1993) is a serious political novel whose protagonist made experimental films and directed television commercials before becoming media adviser to a governor and helping him win the presidential race. While the book is concerned with the manipulation of the public, as well as its characters, through the use of images, little more than a few paragraphs deal with film per se.

KATHERINE ALBERT was a minor Hollywood actress who was obviously well acquainted with the local scene. In *Remember Valerie March* (Simon & Schuster, 1939), director Conrad Powers recalls the title character actress whom he helped raise to stardom and then destroyed. "Miss Albert's book has its points: it is a good reflection of an unrestrained element in Hollywood life; its people, such as they are, are true to type, and it isn't the author's fault that they live abnormally and seem too often preoccupied with matters above which evolution has raised the minds of most men and women," wrote R.G. Doyle in the *New York Times* (July 9, 1939).

MARVIN ALBERT (born 1924) wrote the original novel on which the Pink Panther movie series is based. *Get Off at Babylon* (Macmillan, 1987) is the third mystery novel featuring Franco-American private eye Pete Sawyer, here trying to locate a young girl who has absconded with $3 million worth of heroin before the rightful owners of the drug shipment find her. She is the daughter of the first marriage of a former racing driver now married to an American ex–movie star whose previous husband, a failing film director, hopes to get financial backing for his latest production from the crooks owning the heroin. Part of the story takes place at the Cannes Film Festival, and Marvin Albert shows a thorough knowledge of the workings of that institution; he also knows his way around the south of France. Although a little short on mystery, *Get Off at Babylon* is fast paced and entertaining; the title refers to a Paris Metro stop.

PAUL ALEXANDER. *The Hollywood Bug* (Author, 1941) is little more than a short story in hard covers, identified as the first in a projected series of ten, known under the collective title of "Hollywood Bacillus Microbiensis." As far as can be ascertained, no other titles were printed. The story is about a young man from Europe, named Robert, who works as an extra in Hollywood. He is advised by a fellow extra, Antonio, to pay court to the wife of the studio head, and after bedding her Robert is indeed offered a studio contract. Unfortunately his girlfriend, Mary, is sexually harassesd by the studio head and Robert knocks him out. The young couple kiss and agree to leave. . . . "Thank goodness, the Hollywood bug hasn't gotten hold of us yet!"

SIDNEY ALEXANDER (born 1912). A serious young writer from New York is on vacation with his wife in Rome in *The Celluloid Asylum* (Bobbs-Merrill, 1951) when he is offered a large sum of money to work on a screenplay. The writer is slowly seduced by the film industry until a night with a sleazy actress brings him back to his senses and to his wife.

RICHARD ALFIERI. Written in the form of a personal journal, *Ricardo, Diary of a Matinee Idol* (John Daniel, 1989), is the story of a Jewish-Italian boy named Wayne Gould, who is brought to Hollywood by Paramount in 1925 and renamed Ricardo Cordova as a rival to Rudolph Valentino. The book introduces many real personalities, including Clara Bow, Gloria Swanson, Greta Garbo, Marlene Dietrich, Marion Davies, John Gilbert, William Randolph Hearst, Jesse L. Lasky, and Louis B. Mayer, and climaxes with the murder of actress Thelma Todd, who is described as Cordova's "one true love." His connection with the murder ends Cordova's career as he is smeared in the Hearst newspapers and released from a contract with Jack Warner. As Cordova watches the waves on the shore, he realizes that being an actor is not enough anymore. It is time to move on. The central character is perhaps modeled after Ricardo Cortez, although the similarity is slight. The novel itself is too close to reality to make for a comfortable fictional read.

JANE ALLEN was the pseudonym of Silvia Schulman (1913–92) and Jane Shore. Schulman was the personal secretary to David O. Selznick in the mid-1930s at the time he was negotiating for the rights to *Gone with the Wind*. Selznick made a pass at her, but she had fallen in love with one of the producer's junior writers, Ring Lardner, Jr., and despite opposition from both David and his wife, Irene Mayer Selznick, the couple were married on February 19, 1937; they divorced in 1945. Schulman left Selznick's employ, and with a friend and professional writer, Jane Shore, who was living at the time with Schulman and Lardner, she wrote *I Lost My Girlish Laughter* (Random House, 1938). It is obvious that the novel is based on Schulman's experiences with Selznick, and the romantic male lead (if such he may be called) is Ring Lardner, Jr., who also handled some publicity work for the producer. Selznick was so outraged by *I Lost My Girlish Laughter* that he tried, unsuccessfully, to prevent Orson Welles from adapting it for broadcast on January 27, 1939, on the CBS program "Campbell Playhouse." No doubt it was not accidental that the broadcast coincided with the start of production on *Gone with the Wind*. Selznick did prevent M-G-M's purchasing the screen rights. The producer was strongly of the opinion that Ring Lardner, Jr., wrote most of the novel; he described Lardner as "ungrateful" and thereafter always spoke disparagingly of him. Ring Lardner, Jr., has confirmed that he had absolutely nothing to do with the writing of the novel.

Through the use of personal correspondence, interoffice memoranda, and the occasional newspaper gossip item, Madge Lawrence, the central character in *I Lost My Girlish Laughter*, recounts her adventures in Hollywood. She stays at the Girls Community Club (the Hollywood Studio Club), and through a director named Max Sellers she obtains the position of secretary to Hollywood producer Sidney Brand (David O. Selznick). The work is hectic, as Brand is immersed in production of *Sinners in Asylum* (which bears no resemblance to any of Selznick's films), featuring his new star, a European import named Sarya Tarn. Brand wants to borrow Clark Gable from M-G-M to star opposite Tarn, but when the actor becomes unavailable, he signs a contract with a handsome New York stage performer named Bruce Anders. Suddenly Gable becomes available again, and Brand tries to negate the contract with Anders, but Madge, who has become fond of the actor, alerts him in time for his agent to best Brand. The film is made with Tarn and Anders, and the latter becomes a star. In all innocence, Anders mentions to Brand that this success would not have been possible had it not been for Madge. An outraged Brand fires his secretary for disloyalty, but she cares little, being about to marry Brand's publicist, Jim Palmer.

I Lost My Girlish Laughter is a delight. The author captures an innocent's enthusiasm at working in Hollywood, and the day-to-day activities of a studio are well documented from the point of view of a secretary who must not only deal with her producer-boss's business life but also with his personal one. No one can lift a phone here when there is a secretary to handle the chore.

In comparison, **Thanks God! I'll Take It from Here** (Faber and Faber, 1946), is disappointing. The style attempts to be lightweight but is often heavy-handed. It is difficult to believe that the book had the same author at the earlier one, although the problem must presumably lie in Allen's collaborator here, Mary Livingstone. The story is a fairly simple one. Christopher "Kit" Madden has written a best-selling novel titled *Reunion*. As she travels from New York to Hollywood and sends and receives telegrams from the producer who has purchased the screen rights, Kit meets a Marine lieutenant named Rusty who is the personification of her leading man. As she gets to know Rusty and his buddy Dink, she realizes that her character needs a rewrite. On arrival in Hollywood, she is the first author to welcome a rewriting of her novel for the screen. Discovering Kit's true identity, Rusty refuses to see her again, but just before to shipping off as the Second World War comes to a close he gets a three-day pass and heads for Hollywood.

In its closing pages, the novel captures something of the free spirit of *I Lost My Girlish Laughter* as the author again resorts to a series of letters, telegrams, and newspaper gossip items (by Louella Parsons and Sidney Skolsky) to tell her story. *Thanks God! I'll Take It from Here* was filmed in 1946 by RKO as *Without Reservations*, directed by Mervyn LeRoy, and with Claudette Colbert as Kit, John Wayne as Rusty, and Don DeFore as Dink.

STEVE ALLEN (born 1921). Among the myriad books, songs, television programs, and writings of this versatile American celebrity is **Murder in**

Manhattan (Zebra Books, 1990), which has Allen coming to New York to play a cameo role in a movie. He is attracted to the part because it gives him the opportunity to dress as Superman, and as a young man Allen was often told he bore a physical resemblance to Clark Kent. All is not well on the set, and it gets worse when an assistant director is murdered. Happily, Steve's wife, Jayne Meadows, has flown out to New York to join her husband, and working tandem the couple uncover the identity of the murderer in a novel that is occasionally funny, rather than witty, but too often is also pedestrian.

HOLLIS ALPERT (born 1916) is a novelist and critic who has had a long involvement with film. From 1950 to 1972, he was film critic of *Saturday Review*, and from 1953 to 1960 he held the same position with *Woman's Day*. Alpert was founding editor of *American Film* from 1975 to 1980, and he coedited *Film 68/69* (1969), *Playboy's Sex in Cinema, 1970* (1971), *Playboy's Sex in Cinema 3* (1973), and Charlton Heston's *The Actor's Life: Journals*. He is the author of *The Barrymores* (1964), *Lana: The Lady, the Legend, the Truth* (1982), *Burton* (1986), and *Fellini: A Life* (1986).

For Immediate Release (Doubleday, 1963) is a dispiriting novel told in retrospect by New York–based publicist Mike Roche. He is hired to work on a film shooting in London, and starring an actress with whom he had an affair that broke up in marriage. While on the film, Roche has an affair with an English publicist and is witness to the producer's forcing the leading lady and director off the feature, replacing them with a French director and a French actress whom he has under contract. The novel is adequately written and developed, but there is no vitality to the work, and no matter how badly the actress is treated the reader feels no sympathy for her, and certainly no empathy for the publicist character.

"Always forgive your enemies" is the slogan of those in the film industry, propounded in *For Immediate Release*. These are also words by which the central characters in *Smash* (Dial Press, 1973) live. The novel, a major improvement over the earlier work, concerns the production of a film dealing with the love affair of a young girl and an older man by Palestra Pictures. The producer has his girlfriend sleep with the studio head in order to assure funding for the film, with the understanding she will play the principal role. The screenwriter would like a young actress with whom he is in love to play the part. Once he has seen the other actress and realized problems his current girlfriend might create, the producer agrees. The producer sleeps with and marries the actress, while the other woman moves in with the screenwriter. Nobody really gets hurt and nobody really minds very much. I do not know whether it is a depressing or reassuring look at Hollywood.

Smash is apparently based on the making of *Love Story* (1970) by Paramount Pictures (Palestra Pictures), produced by Robert Evans (here called Barry Prinz), written by Erich Segal (Mike Breed), and starring Ali McGraw.

JENNIFER AMES was the pseudonym of Maysie Greig (1902–71) (q.v.). Child custody is the central issue in the melodramatic *Wagon to a Star* (Bouregy & Curl, 1953). British actor Gregg Watson and his wife are divorced and their son lives with his father. When the boy goes off to appear in a pirate picture being filmed in Jamaica and Hollywood, his mother wins him back. In Jamaica, the boy returns to his father and the mother is killed in a hurricane.

MARTIN AMIS (born 1949) is the distinguished novelist son of a distinguished British novelist, Kingsley Amis. *Money: A Suicide Note* (Viking, 1985) is something about which antihero John Self cares little as he wanders in an alcoholic daze through New York and London, a highly acclaimed director of television commercials about to make his first feature film, *Good Money* (or is it *Bad Money?*). The money for the film is apparently being provided by a wealthy young New Yorker who is to serve as producer, but ultimately it transpires that the money all along has been Self's—and it is now gone, along with most of the hero's life and all of his self-esteem. A major secondary character in the novel is a writer named Martin Amis, who agrees to help Self restructure the film's script. As with all of Amis's novels, *Money: A Suicide Note* is witty, outrageous, and totally fulfilling as a work of literature. With a keen eye for the ludicrous and offensive in contemporary society, Amis teases and taunts his readers, and here, playing himself, he allows us to know a little but not enough about his own personal existence.

ANONYMOUS. An innocent young girl is held spellbound by Hollywood in *City Without a Heart* (Houghton Mifflin, 1933). Each time she tries to make a break, acknowledging the artificiality of the community, she always returns to sign another contract.

ANONYMOUS. *Hollywood Wife* (G. Howard Watt, 1931) documents how the wife of a famous film star copes with her situation, in particular her husband's alcoholism, promiscuity, and the humiliation his behavior brings to her. Carolyn See has suggested that this novel was written by Frederick Hollander (q.v.), but that seems unlikely for Hollander may not have been in the United States at the time the book was conceived.

ANONYMOUS. *The Love Story of a Movie Star; Or, The Heart Story of a Woman in Love* (Edward J. Clode, 1915) is sometimes credited as having been written, as it may well have been, by Edward J. Clode. The title character is a film player named Nella who has an affair with and is then rejected by a fellow actor. To hide her grief, she works hard at building her career, often participating in dangerous stunts, and ponders what type of love life future actresses will enjoy. *The Love Story of a Movie Star* is a moral tome, presumably intended as positive reading for young girls who might be yearning for a screen career.

ANONYMOUS. *My Strange Life: The Intimate Life Story of a Moving Picture Actress; Illustrated with Photographs of America's Most Famous Motion Picture Actresses* (Edward J. Clode, 1915). This novel is in a vein similar to that of the previous book, and may possibly have been written by its publisher.

VICTOR APPLETON is a pseudonym created by Edward Stratemeyer (1862–1930), a prolific children's novelist who employed various ghostwriters to work on books based on his plot outlines. The most popular series written by Stratemeyer, under the name of Arthur M. Winfield, was the "Rover Boys" series (1899–1926). As Appleton, Stratemeyer created the "Tom Swift" series (1910–41), the "Motion Picture Chums" series (1913–16), and the "Moving Picture Boys" series (1913–27).

Tom Swift and His Wizard Camera; Or, Thrilling Adventures While Taking Moving Pictures (Grosset & Dunlap, 1912) is the earliest identified film-related novel. An adventure book for boys, it concerns Tom Swift's invention of a magic camera that automatically films moving pictures; Swift is hired by a producer to film news and actuality stories around the world, which he does, while at the same time thwarting the villainous and jealous Wilson Turbot.

The following is a complete listing in chronological order of Appleton's film-related children's novels; specific subject matter is indicated after each entry:

The Motion Picture Chums' First Venture; Or, Opening a Photo Playhouse in Fairlands (Grosset & Dunlap, 1913), reprinted as *The Movie Boys' First Showhouse; Or, Fighting for a Foothold in Fairlands* (Garden City Publishing, 1926). (Frank Durham, Randy Powell, and Pepperill "Pep" Smith open the Wonderland movie theater in Fairlands.)

The Motion Picture Chums at Seaside Park; Or, The Rival Photo Theatres of the Boardwalk (Grosset & Dunlap, 1913), reprinted as *The Movie Boys at Seaside Park; Or, The Rival Photo Houses of the Boardwalk* (Garden City Publishing, 1926). (The Chums open a movie theater in Seaside Park.)

The Moving Picture Boys; Or, The Perils of a Great City Depicted (Grosset & Dunlap, 1913), reprinted as *The Movie Boys on Call; Or, Filming the Perils of a Great City* (Garden City Publishing, 1926). ("The Moving Picture Boys," Joe Duncan and Blake Stewart, become newsreel cameramen and later create their own company.)

The Moving Picture Boys in the West; Or, Taking Scenes Among the Cowboys and Indians (Grosset & Dunlap, 1913), reprinted as *The Movie Boys in the Wild West; Or, Stirring Days Among the Cowboys and Indians* (Garden City Publishing, 1926). (The boys shoot Western footage in Arizona.)

The Moving Picture Boys on the Coast; Or, Showing Up the Perils of the Deep (Grosset & Dunlap, 1913), reprinted as *The Movie Boys and the Wreckers; Or, Facing the Perils of the Deep* (Garden City Publishing, 1926). (The boys shoot footage off the coast of California.)

The Moving Picture Boys in the Jungle; Or, Stirring Times Among the Wild Animals (Grosset & Dunlap, 1913), reprinted as *The Movie Boys in the Jungle; Or, Lively Times Among the Wild Beasts* (Garden City Publishing, 1926). (This story concerns filming wild animals in Africa; it was probably based on films of President Roosevelt's exploits on the same continent.)

The Moving Picture Boys in Earthquake Land; Or, Working Amid Many Perils (Grosset & Dunlap, 1913), reprinted as *The Movie*

Boys in Earthquake Land; Or, Filming Pictures Amid Strange Perils (Garden City Publishing, 1926). (The boys film a volcanic eruption on a West Indian island.)

    The Motion Picture Chums on Broadway; Or, The Mystery of the Missing Cash Box (Grosset & Dunlap, 1914), reprinted as ***The Movie Boys on Broadway; Or, The Mystery of the Missing Cash Box*** (Garden City Publishing, 1926). (The Chums open a movie theater on Broadway.)

    The Motion Picture Chums' Outdoor Exhibition; Or, The Film That Solved a Mystery (Grosset & Dunlap, 1914), reprinted as ***The Movie Boys' Outdoor Exhibition; Or, The Film That Solved a Mystery*** (Garden City Publishing, 1926). (The Chums open the "Airdome," or open-air cinema, in Riverside Grove.)

    The Motion Picture Chums' New Idea; Or, The First Educational Photo Playhouse (Grosset & Dunlap, 1914), reprinted as ***The Movie Boys' New Idea; Or, Getting the Best of Their Enemies*** (Garden City Publishing, 1926). (The Chums get involved in educational film production, opening a movie theater to screen such endeavors on the Boston Common.)

    The Moving Picture Boys and the Flood; Or, Perilous Days on the Mississippi (Grosset & Dunlap, 1914), reprinted as ***The Movie Boys and the Flood; Or, Perilous Days on the Mississippi*** (Garden City Publishing, 1926). (Joe Duncan and Blake Stewart are in Hannibal, Missouri, searching for members of a film company believed lost in a flood.)

    The Motion Picture Chums at the Fair; Or, The Greatest Film Ever Exhibited (Grosset & Dunlap, 1915), reprinted as ***The Movie Boys at the Big Fair; Or, The Greatest Film Ever Exhibited*** (Garden City Publishing, 1926). (The Chums shoot footage at the Panama-Pacific International Exposition in San Francisco.)

    The Moving Picture Boys at Panama; Or, Stirring Adventures Along the Great Canal (Grosset & Dunlap, 1915), reprinted as ***The Movie Boys in Peril; Or, Strenuous Days Along the Panama Canal*** (Garden City Publishing, 1926). (Filming the final stages of the making of the Panama Canal.)

    The Moving Picture Boys Under the Sea; Or, The Treasure of the Lost Ship (Grosset & Dunlap, 1916), reprinted as ***The Movie Boys Under the Sea; Or, The Treasure of the Lost Ship*** (Garden City Publishing, 1926). (Underwater filming; this was obviously based on the work of the Williamson Brothers, who the year this novel was published produced *20,000 Leagues Under the Sea*.)

    The Motion Picture Chums' War Spectacle; Or, The Film That Won the Prize (Grosset & Dunlap, 1916), reprinted as ***The Movie Boys' War Spectacle; Or, The Film That Won the Prize*** (Garden City Publishing, 1927). (The Chums are now operating seven movie theaters, and here make a film on the life of George Washington.)

    The Moving Picture Boys on the War Front; Or, The Hunt for the Stolen Army Films (Grosset & Dunlap, 1918), reprinted as ***The Movie Boys Under Fire; Or, The Search for the Stolen Film*** (Garden

City Publishing, 1926). (Making U.S. propaganda films in the European battlefields.)

The Moving Picture Boys on the French Battlefields; Or, Taking Pictures for the U.S. Army (Grosset & Dunlap, 1919), reprinted as *The Movie Boys Under Uncle Sam; Or, Taking Pictures for the Army* (Garden City Publishing, 1926). (Further adventures filming in front of and behind enemy lines.)

Tom Swift and His Talking Pictures; Or, The Greatest Invention on Record (Grosset & Dunlap, 1928). (Tom Swift's "magic camera" is now able to make talkies thanks to its owner's invention of a "radio machine.")

M.K. ARGUS was the pseudonym of Mikhail Konstantinovich Jeleznov. *A Rogue with Ease* (Harper, 1953) casts a bemused eye on Russian aristocracy in the United States in the 1920s. One of the heroes here is neither Russian nor aristocratic, while the other is merely Russian, but they pass themselves off as a Russian prince and count, first in New York and eventually in Hollywood, "a devout and pious city where the spirit reigns supreme and flesh is disdained." Of course in Hollywood at the time, Russians of royal birth were always well received, and the industry happily finds employment for the pair.

MARGOT ARNOLD is the pseudonym of Petronella Marguerite Mary Cook (born 1925), who has written a series of mystery novels featuring archaeologist Tobias Merlin Glendower and anthropologist Penelope Athene Spring. The merry and entertaining pair appears in *Exit Actors, Dying* (Playboy Press, 1979), which is set in Turkey and involves the murders of various members of a film company. The motive is drug smuggling, and the murderer proves to be a director who had been driven out of the United States by the House Un-American Activities Committee. Heroine Spring is sympathetic toward the murderer and thinks that his life of crime stems from the committee's witch-hunt.

MEL ARRIGHI (1933–86). *The Hatchet Man* (Harcourt Brace Jovanovich, 1975) is a suspense novel wherein an investigative reporter researches a profile on the movie star daughter of a senator and discovers fraud in her husband's background. "One cannot deny the author's talent for creating suspense, or the seriousness of the ethical question he raises," wrote K.J. Henderson in the *Christian Science Monitor* (August 27, 1975).

ANN ASHTON is one of the pseudonyms of John M. Kimbro (born 1929), who also writes for film and television. Set in the 1930s, *The Phantom Reflection* (Doubleday, 1978) has a Hollywood star, Stella Raye, becoming increasingly confused by memory lapses and haunted by a phantom reflection. While on location at a rustic Spanish estate near San Luis Obispo, it seems as if she has murdered the film's script girl and her leading man. The reality is that Stella has an evil twin named Rachael. *Star Eyes* (Doubleday, 1983) is a romance wherein former child actress Maggie Tyler is cast as the understudy in a Broadway play. She must deal with the egotistical tantrums of the star and a burgeoning love affair with the director.

MARY ASTOR (1906–87), a superior actress in both American silent and sound films, gained considerable notoriety in 1936 when the diaries, in which she wrote of the men to whom she had made love, were published. Aside from those diaries, Astor wrote two autobiographies, *My Story* (Doubleday, 1959) and *A Life on Film* (Delacorte, 1967), and several novels.

The O'Conners (Doubleday, 1964) are Pauline Bassett and Gareth O'Connor (named for silent screen star Gareth Hughes), two actors who meet in the unemployment line. They marry and move to a home owned by Bassett in the San Fernando Valley. O'Connor stars in a play on Broadway, while Bassett is active in television in Los Angeles. Their separate careers and egos lead to quarrels and divorce, but in the final pages, the pair is reunited. Not too much of consequence happens in the 374 pages of this novel. There is a lot of talk and quite a lot of time spent in line for unemployment benefits, which does not make much sense in view of the couple's prominence in the industry, a prominence that also raises questions as to why the O'Connors have so little money. It is probably true that when actors get together all they talk about is acting and what they have to say is often boring to an outsider. Much of what is said here lacks interest and the dialogue often sounds superficial. At the same time, the author obviously knows of what she writes and does provide what is probably a realistic picture of work primarily in television. This is the only novel that describes what an actress is like after a hard day's filming:

> In the bathroom Pauline stripped and surveyed herself in the long mirror on the door. Her make-up was caked around her nose and mouth; her hair was sticky and dull with repeated swooshings of lacquer; under her breasts were soiled lines of perspiration, and her ankles and feet were black with the dust of the studio floor. "Wow! Glamorous," she said wryly. "Just like Greer Garson." And then she smiled with satisfaction and added, "Just *exactly* like Miss G. after a day's work at the studio!" Being a big star was no exemption from the sweat and the dirt.

JACOBA ATLAS. Beginning in New York in 1912 and moving on to Los Angeles, *Palace of Light* (E.P. Dutton, 1989) links the early years of the motion picture industry, and the fight of the independent filmmakers against the Motion Picture Patents Company, to the rise of the labor movement in the United States. The principal players are Mirah Mishkin, whose father becomes a prominent filmmaker as a result of his move to California, and whose brother, Danny, is a revolutionary labor leader; and Jameson Horgan, a wealthy young man who is a friend of Danny and has fallen in love with Mirah. The author has well researched the history of the labor movement in the United States and has a general understanding of early filmmaking (at the time the novel was published she was producer of the "Today" show). The characters she has created are lively and complex. The terrorist acts committed by Danny Mishkin and his followers are more exciting, more worthy of the description "pioneering" than are the activities of the early filmmakers, but then, as Danny says, in comparing his work to that of his screenwriting sister, "Just like my sister, I'm creating distractions for their petty lives. Only my stories are real."

ALEX AUSTIN. *Greatest Lover in the World* (Rinehart, 1956) has an interesting concept, but the "humor" of the plot fails to entertain. The title character is a dead silent screen star, Ramon Ramano (born Willie Schus-bruber), who was once the idol of millions of women. He is sent back to Earth by the devil to find the greatest contemporary lover in the world. The outcome of his global search is a Jackson Heights, Long Island, dentist named John Don-ner. When the latter spends a night with former silent screen siren Gerda Galdi, "the most beautiful woman in the world," he does become the world's greatest lover. The two silent stars, in name only, are based on Ramon Novarro and Nita Naldi.

"You may, just possibly, find an amusing tale here," wrote J.C. Neff in the *New York Times* (November 11, 1956). Leland Windreich, in *Library Journal* (December 1, 1956), was even less enthusiastic: "Although this harmless trifle sets no high goals for itself, it does offend by attempting to be exceedingly funny and not getting to first base."

ANN AUSTIN. *Murdered but Not Dead* (Macmillan, 1939) is a mystery novel about a screen star whose murder is solved by a gossip columnist.

GEORGE AXELROD (born 1922) was once a fashionable novelist, playwright, and screenwriter, whose films include *The Seven Year Itch* (1955, based on his 1952 play), *Bus Stop* (1956), *Breakfast at Tiffany's* (1961), *The Manchurian Candidate* (1962), and *Lord Love a Duck* (1966). *Where Am I Now— When I Need Me?* (Viking Press, 1971) is a farcical Hollywood tale, one of whose principal characters is an egotistical movie star who thwarts an airplane hijacking while drunk and, as a result, loses his popular appeal. "Though more than a literary spoof, with Mr. Axelrod busily sticking pins into any balloon he passes, his story does not wholly satisfy as a comic fiction," wrote Haskel Frankel in *Saturday Review* (August 14, 1971).

MARIAN BABSON is an American-born mystery novelist who has lived in the United Kingdom for many years but still manages to write about its inhabitants as if they are quaint and maladjusted. Her books are filled with characters whose behavior and conversation are often silly, and her four film-oriented novels are no exception.

Murder, Murder, Little Star (Walker, 1980) begins with widowed Frances Armitage's obtaining a job as chaperone to a ten-year-old American child star named "Twinkle," who has come to London to star in her latest feature. She is an obnoxious child, to whom her newspaper-reading costar comments, "So many obituaries, and always for the wrong people." Of course, someone is apparently trying to murder Twinkle (with good reason); first, a continuity girl is drugged from drinking the child star's milk, and then the screenwriter dies after demonstrating a faulty harness the actress was to have worn. The murderer turns out to be the producer, who is after the insurance money.

Reel Murder (St. Martin's Press, 1987) begins with Evangeline Sinclair, a Hollywood star of the 1930s and 1940s, and her sidekick on screen, Trixie Dolan, heading for London, where there is to be a retrospective of Sinclair's work. The festival is organized by Sinclair's former leading man, Beauregard Sylvester, who not only operates a film theater in London but has his own private film archives and vaults, with a staff restoring and preserving films. This allows author Babson to give a considerable amount of misinformation on methods of film preservation and the history of nitrate film. For reasons that are quite preposterous, Sinclair and Dolan became involved in a couple of murders, and the novel ends with their rescuing two women, one of them Sylvester's former actress wife, from the railroad tracks, to which they have been tied by the villainess. The latter was the woman in charge of film preservation and restoration, who chose this modus operandi because, as Sinclair explains, "A woman who spends her days restoring old films has her head filled with the early cinematic visions more surely than the old actresses who played the original roles. After all, we have moved on in time, done other things, and are looking to the future. We can hardly remember most of the roles we played. But they were all fresh in her mind."

Evangeline and Trixie stay on in England for **Encore Murder** (St. Martin's Press, 1989), in which Trixie's daughter (who is really Evangeline's daughter) is planning to marry a successful British theatrical entrepreneur. Just as the latter's ex-wife is about to star Evangeline in a feminist version of *King Lear*, she is murdered at Evangeline and Trixie's London home. Characters rush in and out in great confusion for both the plot and the reader, which is perhaps why it is difficult to spot the killers. Who could remember the two character actors who worked with the ex-wife in a television costume drama series and were now being denied potential residuals because the woman refused to permit the series to be re-aired?

At the end of *Encore Murder*, Trixie and Evangeline are about to be signed to appear in a new screen adaptation of Dracula. **Shadows in Their Blood** (St. Martin's Press, 1991) opens with the film on location in Whitby, where the vampire first landed in England. There is a maniacal director, a film buff with a large collection of movie memorabilia, and a murder—of the egotistical leading man. Babson displays a total lack of knowledge of location shooting and assumes her readers are already familiar with the main and supplemental characters—or perhaps the publisher cut a chapter or two, as there are references to events that simply are not here in the book.

DESMOND BAGLEY (1923–83). *The Spoilers* (Doubleday, 1970) concerns the activities of an English doctor in activating a film script set in Iran. "A fairly standard razzle-dazzle, with three spectacular shoot-em-outs and two eye-popping coincidences to prove that the good doctor is on the side of the angels," reported A.J. Hubin in the *New York Times* (March 15, 1970).

PAUL BAILEY (1906–87). In *Song Everlasting* (Westernlore Press, 1946), newlyweds Emil and Gail Warren come to Hollywood and Emil begins work on a novel that a studio plans to film. He starts drinking and the couple split, with the religious-minded Gail singing in concert at the Hollywood Bowl. The couple reunites, but Emil is accidentally killed. Gail tries to commit suicide and pays a temporary visit to heaven, where she talks to Emil and decides to continue living. Ferenc Molnár's *Liliom* revisited!

CARROL BAKER (born 1931) was on screen as an actress from 1953, but she came to fame in 1956 with her performance as the child-wife in *Baby Doll*.

With her career in decline, Baker relocated to Italy in the late 1960s, a move that provided material for her only novel, *A Roman Tale* (Donald I. Fine, 1985). The plotline concerns American actress Madeline Mandell, who "for twelve years ... had been a slave to the studio and its system, to the studio bosses and most (worst) of all to her sex-symbol image," thanks to her first film *Venus Awakening*. She comes to Italy to compete with three European stars for a leading role in *Boccaccio Volgare*, a production consisting of four separate Boccaccio tales directed by four leading Italian filmmakers, and with each episode starring the country's biggest male star, Umberto Cassino. Eventually Madeline gets the role, and marries Umberto in the final chapter.

Baker describes the vagaries of Italian production and film finance, but the bulk of the novel is concerned with explicit sex, with a heavy sampling of racy dialogue. A variety of bedroom scenes favored by the various actresses in the novel are discussed in entertaining detail, with the heaviest sex involving a French boy named Jean Claude, who is passed around among the women. Happily, there is some humor to the sexual situations, as when Umberto gets his penis caught in his zipper and the studio doctor has to be called. Of its type, *A Roman Tale* is not without merit, and, obviously, Baker might have enjoyed a career as a novelist. She has written two autobiographical works: *Baby Doll: An Autobiography* (1983) and *To Africa with Love: A True Romantic Adventure* (1985).

FAY BAKER. *My Darling Darling Doctors* (George Braziller, 1975) is written in the form of letters to a quack doctor and her agent and entries in her diary by Hollywood actress Valerie Daphne Taylor, whose husband is a screenwriter who had helped create her legend. The content of the letters and entries relates to Taylor's back problems and the various treatments available to her. The author defies the reader not to laugh. I found it relatively easy.

JAMES ROBERT BAKER. *Boy Wonder* (New American Library, 1988) tells, through the comments of various friends and acquaintances, the life story of filmmaker Shark Trager, born during a 1950 drive-in screening of *Gun Crazy*. His first film, *Sex Kill a Go-Go*, is an immediate success because of the similarity of the plot to the Sharon Tate murder and the suggestion that Charles Manson might have seen the film. He did not. Shark's first artistic success is *White Desert*, screened at the Cannes Film Festival. At the Academy Awards presentation, Shark's *Blue Light* is the big winner, despite the efforts of members desperately trying to recant their votes following word of the producer's outrageous behavior during a visit to Ronald and Nancy Reagan at the White House. The ceremony is hosted by Hector Preck, a wicked parody of Charlton Heston. The following night, Shark takes a murderous drive through a drive-in theater and is shot down by police.

Boy Wonder is only a moderately successful parody on a Hollywood theme, but Baker's *Tim and Pete* (Simon & Schuster, 1993) is one of the best of the contemporary gay novels; it recounts a harrowing but at the same time often amusing 24 hours in the lives of Tim and his ex-lover Pete as they travel from Laguna Beach to Los Angeles. Tim works at the California Film Archives in Los Angeles, and that appears to be a cross between the UCLA Film and Television

Archive and the Margaret Herrick Library of the Academy of Motion Picture Arts and Sciences. One of the characters whom Tim and Pete encounter on their journey is Kevin, an independent filmmaker from San Francisco. He is into the occult and relatively sane among this novel's extraordinary and fascinating cast of characters.

NIGEL BALCHIN (1908–70). While screenwriter Jim Petersen is on assignment in Hollywood in *In the Absence of Mrs. Petersen* (Simon & Schuster, 1966), his wife, Sarah, is killed in a plane crash. When Petersen gets to Paris, on his return to Europe, he meets his wife's mirror image, a woman named Katherine Field, who asks him to take her to Yugoslavia on Sarah's passport. From then on, the story is typical Nigel Balchin intrigue and suspense.

FAITH BALDWIN (1893–19??). *The Moon's Our Home* (Farrar & Rinehart, 1936) is best known as a 1936 Walter Wanger production for Paramount release, directed by William A. Seiter, and starring Margaret Sullavan and Henry Fonda, rather than as a best-selling romantic novel. In the film, the central character, Cherry Chester, is a debutante–film star, but in the book she is merely a tempestuous Hollywood star. The storyline concerns her love for explorer Anthony Amberton and the personal conflicts in their relationship.

W. (Willis) T. (Todhunter) BALLARD (1903–80). When temperamental actor Leon Heyworth disappears in *Say Yes to Murder* (G.P. Putnam's Sons, 1942), Bill Lennox is sent by General Studios to find him. The actor is discovered dead in the apartment of starlet Jean Jeffries, whose grandmother Mary Morris was a popular Hollywood leading lady. Out of respect for Morris, Lennox determines to clear Jeffries's name of any part in Heyworth's murder. (There was a British screen actress named Mary Morris, but she was not known in the United States at this time.)

Bill Lennox returns in *Dealing Out Death* (David McKay, 1948). Actress Renee Wilson leaves the studio in the middle of a picture to go to Las Vegas, where her brother has inherited a hotel. When he is murdered and Wilson becomes implicated in his death, only Lennox can solve the crime.

Jerry Moore is a failed scriptwriter who enters television as a writer and decides to pursue a ruthless course in order to become a producer in *The Package Deal* (Appleton-Century-Crofts, 1956). Unlike the central character, the book "doesn't get out of the small time," commented *Kirkus* (March 2, 1956).

PAT BARKER (born 1943). *The Man Who Wasn't There* (Virago Press, 1989) covers a few days in a decaying English seaside resort, as 12-year-old Colin tries to discover the identity of his father, killed during the Second World War. Colin lives partially in a fantasy world, a war drama of his own making, based on the films he has seen at the local Odeon cinema. The novel is quite brilliant in capturing the dialogue and thinking of a 12-year-old, as fantasy created by British films becomes blurred with reality; it is short, poignant, and intense.

JOANNA BARNES (born 1933) is an actress who has also enjoyed success as a popular novelist. *The Deceivers* (Arbor House, 1970) is the story of

Laura Curtis, a child actress who loses a beauty contest at the age of 13 and ten years later is a star. When her husband is killed, reality rears its ugly head in Laura's tinsel world. *Who Is Carla Hart?* (Arbor House, 1973). The answer is, a beautiful and talented star of stage and screen, who finds security in her acting but who must also discover her innermost self.

LINDA BARNES (born 1949) has written four mystery novels featuring handsome and wealthy Michael Spraggue. In the second, *Bitter Finish* (St. Martin's Press, 1983), Spraggue leaves a Hollywood set, where he is embarking on a new career as an actor, to help his ex-girlfriend and business partner in a vineyard operation, who is being held for murder. The lessons he learns from a stuntman in the novel's opening chapter help him at the book's conclusion.

RONA BARRETT (born 1936) was once one of the best known Hollywood commentators. She began her career as a columnist in 1957 with "Rona Barrett's Young Hollywood." "Rona Barrett's Hollywood" was first aired on ABC in 1969. She was an interviewer on "Good Morning America" from 1975 to 1980, when she moved over to the "Today" and "Tomorrow" shows. Barrett published her autobiography, *Miss Rona*, in 1974.

   The Lovomaniacs (Nash Publishing, 1972) is Barrett's first novel. In view of the author's background, one would be tempted to dismiss the book as a typical trashy Hollywood novel. One would be very, very wrong. *The Lovomaniacs* is an extraordinarily complex novel, overlaid with astrological lore, and narrated alternately by each of the major characters. Its plot is as tangled and twisted as the lives of the main antagonists as the novel opens on what must be a typical industry Christmas. The movie moguls are flying home, and the young son of one makes a date with the stewardess on their chartered plane. The leading man of the group's latest film is drinking himself into a stupor in New York and eventually wanders into Central Park, where he services half a dozen men. A navy ship is commandeered to serve in the filming of a Hollywood production, and, as a result, it is not protecting a naval vessel on a secret assignment off Cuba. The boat and its crew are captured by Fidel Castro. The actor, permanently affected by a dose of LSD, hijacks a civilian jetliner and has it fly to Cuba to deliver ransom money for the crew, but the copilot attacks the actor and the plane is blown up. This brief plot summary does not give an adequate overview of this novel's contents. It has to be read! The title refers to those who can only take but never give love.

STAN BARSTOW (born 1928) published his first novel, *A Kind of Loving*, in 1960; it was filmed by John Schlesinger in 1962. Despite its title, *B-Movie* (Michael Joseph, 1987) does not contain a film theme but rather is a bleak tale of two young men, cousins, who come for a week's holiday at Blackpool. One has committed a crime and the other is forced to betray him. The novel's style is intended as a tribute to the B movies of the 1940s and 1950s, and is vaguely reminiscent of the 1947 British feature *It Always Rains on Sunday*.

NALBRO BARTLEY. *Second Flight* (Farrar & Rinehart, 1932) is the story of a young woman's divorce from a film star and her second marriage—on the same day as the divorce—to a small-town businessman. The chief aim of Bartley is character development, and here she is fairly successful, but ultimately the story is relatively uninteresting, in large part because the central character, Posy, does not appear to know her own mind.

RON BASE is the film critic for the *Toronto Sun*. *Matinee Idol* (Doubleday, 1985) is a superior mystery novel with a strong film-related theme. Celebrity interviewer Tom Coward believes that his ex-girlfriend is dating a man, Ash Conley, who has murdered two women once associated with him on a student film project. Conley is a handsome man who "wanted to be bigger than life . . . wanted to be special," like Cary Grant, Clark Gable, and Gary Cooper, whose photographs he collected as a child. Much of the action takes place in Toronto, as Coward tries to persuade his ex of the truth of his accusation, but it is only a partly accurate assessment of the situation, for one of the murders is committed by Conley's mother, who had murdered his father in front of the young boy.

Tom Coward returns in *Foreign Object* (Doubleday, 1986), wherein he is at the Cannes Film Festival, interviewing Lacy Bergen, an actress who bears a strong resemblance to Brooke Shields. Coward gets involved with the producer of a schlock epic titled *Saudi* after flirting with the man's wife and getting attacked and knocked out for his effort. It transpires that the producer has stolen millions of dollars from an Egyptian gangster. "There's lots of Cannes and movie color, but perhaps too much childish-hip dialogue," commented *Publisher's Weekly* (December 5, 1986).

MICHEL BATAILLE. The bulk of *Fire from Heaven* (Crown, 1967), translated from the French by Arthur Train, Jr., is devoted to the story of fifteenth-century French historical character Gilles de Rais, who fought alongside Joan of Arc and was also a pederast who raped, tortured, and murdered young boys. French director Antoine Alboni plans a film of de Rais's life, and as he works on the script, he becomes involved with a young woman whom he loses through mutual misunderstanding. The reader learns a great deal about Gilles de Rais and French history from 1415 through 1440 but very little about French production. *Fire from Heaven*, the title of Alboni's proposed film, was originally published in France in 1964 under the title *Le feu du ciel*.

VICKI BAUM (1888–1960) was a novelist, playwright, and screenwriter of German extraction, best known for her 1930 play *Grand Hotel*. *Falling Star* (Doubleday, Doran, 1934) begins at the premiere of *Cardogan*, the latest film of Ria Mara and English-born Oliver Dent. Ria Mara's career is in decline and will fall still further because of the actress whom Dent is escorting to the premiere. This is former silent star Donka Morescu, who has taken speech lessons and rid herself of a heavy Central European accent. At the premiere, Dent meets his former stand-in Richard Aldens and a would-be actress named Frances Warrens. Their story is a secondary one here, as are those of others at the studio. Dent is in need of a vacation and despite an infatuation with Morescu leaves Los Angeles. As he travels with a devoted dog, Dent gradually sickens until, when he reaches New York, he has become seriously ill. The news of his illness is kept from Morescu by the studio so that she will complete a film. When she learns the truth, she rushes to New York, only to discover Ria Mara basking in the reflected glory of supposedly being Dent's lover, while Dent himself has just died.

Falling Star is a beautifully conceived and written novel. The final chapters of Dent's travels are heartrending, and I do not believe any other writer has more clearly understood the psyche of a dog than did Vicki Baum. If anything, it is a little Sealyham terrier named Tobias who dominates the novel's second half. Baum's characterizations are matched by her descriptions, such as the following of the night sky of Hollywood during a premiere: "But over the town itself there were no stars. The town was too bright and would tolerate neither the night nor the sky over her head. She flung her own lights upward against the canopy of moist vapor suspended in midair. The streets were glittering nets, laced by the blazing ribbons of the boulevards."

Here is one of the great, forgotten Hollywood novels, well worthy of resurrection.

GEORGE BAXT (born 1923) published his first mystery novel—the first of four featuring New York detective Pharaoh Love—*a Queer Kind of Death* in 1966. He has authored a number of screenplays in the horror genre: *Circus of Horrors* (1960), *The City of the Dead/Horror Hotel* (1960), *The Shadow of the Cat* (1961), *Payroll* (1961), *Night of the Eagle/Burn Witch Burn* (1962), *Strangler's Web* (1965), *Thunder in Dixie* (1965), *Vampire Circus* (1971), and *Beyond the Fog* (1981). In recent years he has gained some fame for a series of mystery novels with film-related themes, all noted for their witty and often bitchy dialogue: *The Dorothy Parker Murder Case* (St. Martin's Press, 1984), *The Alfred Hitchcock Murder Case* (St. Martin's Press, 1986), *The Tallulah Bankhead Murder Case* (St. Martin's Press, 1987), *The Talking Picture Murder Case* (St. Martin's Press, 1990), *The Greta Garbo Murder Case* (St. Martin's Press, 1992), and *The Marlene Dietrich Murder Case* (St. Martin's Press, 1993).

The Neon Graveyard (St. Martin's Press, 1979) has a secret service agent coming to Los Angeles to investigate a blackmail ring headed by a former movie ice-skating star, who lives in a castle built by her husband, next to the home of a legendary Hollywood sex symbol who bears a striking resemblance to Mae West. There is murder and mayhem before the story is over, but the novel does not contain the ususal homosexual camp humor of Baxt's other works, although he does come up with the occasional witty phrase, describing the lights of Hollywood, for example, as "a whore wearing sequins."

JOHN BAXTER (born 1939) is an Australian-born writer who came to prominence in the 1970s with a considerable number of film-related volumes: *Hollywood in the Thirties* (1968), *The Gangster Films* (1970), *Science Fiction in the Cinema* (1970), *The Cinema of John Ford* (1971), *The Cinema of Josef von Sternberg* (1971), *Hollywood in the Sixties* (1972), *Sixty Years of Hollywood* (1973), *An Appalling Talent: Ken Russell* (1973), *Stunt: The Story of the Great Movie Stunt Men* (1974), *The Hollywood Exiles* (1976), and *King Vidor* (1976).

There is little secret as to whom *The Kid* (Viking Press, 1981) is based on. A caricature of Chaplin's face graces the dust jacket and the book is dedicated to "Charlie." Chaplin is here called Thomas "Tommy" Timpson and is introduced in the first chapter as he receives his knighthood in the wheelchair that has been his home for the past ten years. The book traces his roots in the poverty of Victorian London, his beginnings in the British Music Hall working for Sid Santo (based on Fred Karno), his first trip to the United States and his signing by comedy producer Frank McManus (based on Mack Sennett), and his rise to stardom. Chaplin's penchant for young girls is discussed but never fully explained; he enjoys a long relationship with actress Enid Stuyvesant (based on Edna Purviance) and a happy, if brief, marriage to Geraldine Kingsley (based on Paulette Goddard), with whom he stars in *Our Times* (based on *Modern Times*).

Other characters featured in the book include Bill Whitewood and Frances Merrian (Douglas Fairbanks, Sr., and Mary Pickford) and Arthur Ryan (George K. Arthur). Two women in Chaplin's life, Lita Grey Chaplin and Joan Barry, are merged in the character of Dorothy Carmody. The author provides an extremely good and well-rounded portrait of Chaplin's brother Sydney, here called Jack, the one thoroughly decent and reliable figure in the book. As in all Chaplin biographies, Chaplin's private persona proves impossible to pin down on paper. Thomas Timpson is as self-engrossed as the real-life Chaplin, worried about his image and shocked to learn that his father was Jewish.

The Kid concentrates on Chaplin's life and career up through *Modern Times*, but glosses over the 1940s and later, covering his virtual "deportation" from the United States in one line. It departs dramatically from the reality of Chaplin's life in the final chapter, as its central character pays a visit to Berlin. He meets a representative of his own film distribution company who has been forced to hide his Jewish background and, inadvertently, from little more than pure selfishness, he leads the man to his death at the hands of the Nazis. It is this incident that persuades Chaplin to make *The Great Dictator*.

If nothing else, *The Kid* is a good deal more entertaining and readable than Chaplin's own autobiography, and it is infinitely superior to the 1992 film *Chaplin*. The latter failed to come to terms with Syd Chaplin's place in his younger brother's life. *The Kid* understands the Syd Chaplin character and builds him up almost as the hero of the novel.

GEORGE BEARDMORE (1908–79). *Charlie Pocock and the Princess* (Viking Press, 1967) is a curious novel—sentimental, humorous, and wistful—whose author, like its title character, was a rent collector in London's East End. Pocock meets a 15-year-old Hindu orphan named Devi, marries her, and sends her off to school in Kent. Three years later, Devi is a lesbian who has little connection to Charlie's world. She becomes an Italian movie star and only returns to Charlie's life when she has a need for something. The novel was first published in the United Kingdom under the title *Charlie Pocock's Indian Bride*.

S. (Samuel) N. (Nathaniel) BEHRMAN (1893–1973) was a noted American novelist, playwright, and screenwriter. Among his plays are *Biography* (1932), *Love Story* (1933) and *End of Summer* (1936). His films include *Liliom* (1930), *Cavalcade* (1933), *A Tale of Two Cities* (1935), *Waterloo Bridge* (1940), *Two-Faced Woman* (1941), and *Fanny* (1961).

The Burning Glass (Little, Brown, 1968) uses some plot elements from the play *End of Summer*. The novel is a multicharacter study, a central character being American playwright and screenwriter Stanley Grant, who has changed his name to escape from his Jewish heritage. Much of the work is taken up with attitudes toward and attitudes of Jews, with the question of homosexuality coming in a distant and far less sympathetic second. Grant is first met by the reader in Salzburg in 1938 and reintroduced in Hollywood and New York. In the Hollywood section, he is working on the script for *Liliom*, actually produced eight years earlier and kept waiting by Irving Thalberg, who died two years earlier. Behrman makes mention of *The Last Tycoon* as based on Thalberg, noting, "Fitzgerald does not remotely approach him nor the business he represented." Aside from Grant, the other major character is Grant's mentor, Alexander Lowe, who dies at the novel's conclusion.

LARRY BEINHART invents the interesting theory that President George Bush hired a movie director to stage the Gulf War in *American Hero* (Pantheon Books, 1993). Members of the old Washington, D.C., gang are all here in a brilliant parody of the Woodward and Bernstein investigative style.

CEDRIC BELFRAGE (1904–90) was the Hollywood correspondent for a number of British newspapers as well as the *New York Herald Tribune* and the *New York Sun* from 1927 to 1930. In 1930 he returned to London, where he was born, to serve as public relations representative for Samuel Goldwyn, and he later worked as film and theater critic for the *Daily Express* and the *Sunday Express*. In 1936 Belfrage came back to the United States, founding and editing the leftist publication *National Guardian*. He wrote a number of books, beginning with *Away from It All* (Simon & Schuster, 1937). On May 5, 1953, Belfrage appeared before the House Un-American Activities Committee and monotonously invoked the Fifth Amendment to a score of questions, ranging from "What is the *National Guardian*?" to "Are you a member of the Communist Party?" He was arrested for deportation on May 15, 1953, and after spending time as a reporter for various left-wing publications around the world, he settled in Mexico in 1963.

In my opinion, the best and certainly the most underrated of all Hollywood novels is *Promised Land: Notes for a History* (Victor Gollancz, 1938). Dealing with the lives of ordinary people, it traces the development of Hollywood from 1857 to 1936, offering hope at its close that Hollywood is "getting to be a place a man can almost be proud to live." The novel is at its most angry when discussing the hypocrisy of Hollywood personalities after the United States' entry into the First World War, in documenting the Lasky Home Guard, membership in which "saved" many Hollywood types from service abroad, and the wealthy in the industry who bought bonds and were tireless in exposing the less patriotic (and poorer). As another example of Hollywood hypocrisy, Belfrage mentions actor Conrad Nagel's movement to build a wall around Hollywood: "'It may never be built,' he says, 'but figuratively it is always there, keeping out much of this fusion some call progress, and keeping in the peace and happiness and beauty we all love and cherish.'"

Novelist H.E. Bates wrote, "Almost the highest honor . . . that I can pay Mr. Belfrage is to say that no nice newspaper would print twenty consecutive unbowdlerized pages of his book. But I will go further and say that his book is great stuff—the most salutary travel book in years." In *Films* (Spring 1940), Budd Schulberg described *Promised Land* as "the most interesting and comprehensive novel yet to be written about Hollywood, loose and sprawling, but an important milestone as the first work which attempts to be definitive."

In 1978 *Promised Land* was reprinted by Garland in its Classics of Film Literature series.

ANN BELL. *Lady's Lady* (House of Field, 1940) is a semipornographic novel detailing the life of Bunny Flower, who is sexually ill-treated by the world. She comes to Hollywood in an attempt to become a companion, or lady's lady, to a wealthy woman. In the film capital, Bunny's sexual ill-treatment continues, as she is assaulted by sundry producers, becomes involved in lesbian relationships, and undergoes an abortion. Later, in New York, she has plastic surgery and then with her brother moves to Hawaii, where she marries a wealthy doctor. Finally, Bunny returns to Hollywood to help those who had been kind to her there. This is a novel of which Jackie Collins would be proud!

GEORGE J. BELLAK. *Come Jericho* (William Morrow, 1981) is a thriller dealing with a ruthless Hollywood director who is shooting a drama about the Vietnam War in a remote area of Mexico. When repeated acts of sabotage are directed against this film, the director becomes friendly with the local guerrilla leader, only to turn him in to the police later. The novel is narrated by the film's editor, who does not share the director's indecent, overriding concern that the film be made whatever the moral and ethical cost. The novel was obviously influenced by Francis Ford Coppola's production of *Apocalypse Now*.

ROBERT LESLIE BELLEM (1902–68) was a pulp fiction writer who created the Hollywood private eye Dan Turner, who became so popular that in 1942 he was given his own magazine, *Dan Turner, Hollywood Detective* (later *Hollywood Detective*). In the 1950s, Bellem wrote for such popular television series as *The Lone Ranger* and *Perry Mason*. Dan Turner was never featured in any of Bellem's novels, but this hero, whom S.J. Perelman described in *The New Yorker* as "the apotheosis of all private detectives . . . out of Ma Barker by Dashiell Hammett's Sam Spade," is anthologized in *Dan Turner, Hollywood Detective* (Bowling Green University Popular Press, 1983). Seven short stories are collected together here from the pages of *Hollywood Detective*, *Spicy Detective*, *Speed Detective*, and *Private Detective*.

LUDWIG BEMELMANS (1898–1962) was a prolific novelist and essayist and also a restauranteur; he is best remembered as a children's writer, with the "Madeline" books published between 1939 and 1961. The title character in *Dirty Eddie* (Viking Press, 1947) is a small black pig, but he does not appear until late in the novel, chapters of which can stand in their own right as short stories. The novel opens in New York, where Hollywood producer Vanya Vashvily signs elevator operator Marie O'Neill (renamed Belinda) to a contract. The story then moves to Los Angeles, where leftist New York writer Ludlow Mumm has arrived with a contract as a screenwriter on Vashvily's new film. He is paired with another writer, Maurice Cassard. The latter demonstrates to

Mumm how little work is required of screenwriters and how it is possible to string along both producers and studio heads for inordinate lengths of time. Cassard also falls in love with Belinda, and Eddie enters the picture when Belinda accidentally hits him with her car. So lovable and photogenic is Eddie that he is signed to a studio contract and becomes the star of the Vashvily film. Unfortunately, because films are not shot in chronological order and no one at the studio takes into account that Eddie is a growing pig, when the rushes are examined it is found that he gets smaller rather than larger during the production. A triumph is pulled from disaster when the film is turned into a comedy, Cassard marries Belinda, and Mumm is signed to a new contract.

The names of the characters might sound outrageous, but as the author writes, in reference to Mumm's meeting various individuals at the studio: "In a town that contains firms like Utter McKinley, the undertakers; a real estate firm of Read and Wright; two Prinzmetals; LeRoy Prinz; a Jack Skirball; a Jerry Rothschild; a law firm by the name of Dull and Twist; and musicians called Amphitheatrof and Bakaleinakoff, he had become accustomed to unusual and distinctive names."

Dirty Eddie provides an entertaining parody of the lives of Hollywood screenwriters. Writing in the *New York Herald Tribune* (August 17, 1947), Richard Mealand commented, "It is the funniest, most ridiculous, truest, craziest, sharpest satire on the motion-picture world to be presented to the other half since George S. Kaufman and Moss Hart wrote *Once in a Lifetime.*" *Dirty Eddie* is in no way as amusing as the latter play, but it is better than the negative contemporary reviews in the *Atlantic, The Nation,* and *Saturday Review of Literature* might suggest.

PETER BENCHLEY (born 1940) came to fame in 1974 with the publication of his novel *Jaws.* His sixth novel, **Rummies** (Random House, 1989), is set in a drug and alcohol rehabilitation center, operated by a legendary male screen star. When an actress dies shortly after leaving the center, the actor's own drug and alcohol dependence is revealed. Despite its serious overtones, *Rummies* is a comic-tragedy that follows New York book editor Scott Preston as he is forced to visit the center to try to overcome his alcoholism. The former occupation of the actor seems relatively unimportant, as does that of the murder victim. The antics of Preston and his fellow inmates is what holds the attention of the reader, although the ending may seem somewhat disappointing.

STEPHEN VINCENT BENÉT (1898–1943) was noted for his retelling of popular American history and for winning the Pulitzer Prize for Poetry for *John Brown's Body* (1928). **The Beginning of Wisdom** (Henry Holt, 1921) is a biographical novel about a poet, from his birth in California through his acquisition of a farm and marriage to his childhood sweetheart. Just before joining the army during the First World War, he becomes a movie star. "Some two-thirds of the book are interesting and vital. The rest is tedious," commented the *New York Times* (October 28, 1921), while Gilbert Seldes in *Dial* (November 1920) wrote, "Of creative power this book does not show the faintest indication."

DAVID BENJAMIN is the pseudonym of David Ryman Slavitt (born 1935), and *Idol* (G.P. Putnam's Sons, 1979) is a roman à clef about the life and career of Elizabeth Taylor from the Second World War to the present. Obvious and certainly predictable.

ROBERT AMES BENNET (1870–1954). *The Rough Rider* (A.L. Burt, 1925) is the story of a cowboy who enters the film industry as a stuntman and eventually marries the leading lady.

EVELYN BERCKMAN (born 1900). There is a hint of *What Ever Happened to Baby Jane?* in *She Asked for It* (Doubleday, 1969). Fiftyish, faded Hollywood star Nell Harriot lives with her crippled secretary, Monica Cowdray, who has spent the last 18 years of her life in service to Nell. When the latter marries a younger man, hidden passions are aroused...

LEONARDO BERCOVICI. In *The Satyr and the Saint* (Charles Scribner's Sons, 1964), Italian actor-director Urbani becomes the mentor of screenwriter Eduardo. The thrice-married older man is amused that his protégé will have no part of *la dolce vita*, is determined to remain chaste and to marry a virgin. "In this, his first novel, Bercovici has exploited [a] basic comic situation with taste and humor, aiming his satire with good effect," commented the reviewer in *Library Journal* (September 1, 1964).

PHIL BERGER (born 1942). Set in the 1930s, *Deadly Kisses* (Charter Books, 1984) has newspaper reporter Harry Krim investigating the death of silent film star and former lover Eve Payton. A series of additional murders follows, as Krim discovers that Payton and other screen actresses were forced to appear in pornographic movies with studio head H.B. Meyer. (Not only is the name similar to that of M-G-M studio boss Louis B. Mayer, but also the description of the two men matches in most details.) The book concludes with silent screen star Gilbert May (who is loosely modeled on John Gilbert) attacking Meyer's mansion with a tank, killing himself, the studio head, and the latter's cohorts. Despite an original, if totally unbelievable, plotline, the novel is formulaic, particularly in the various sex scenes presented for the reader's pleasure. The anecdotes relating to Hollywood history are well known. Like Horace McCoy in *I Should Have Stayed Home*, the author has a scene take place in front of "Aspiration," a statue dedicated to the memory of Rudolph Valentino in Hollywood's DeLongpre Park.

ANDREW BERGMAN is a Hollywood screenwriter who began his career with two nonfiction works on film—*We're in the Money: Depression America and Its Films* (1971) and *James Cagney* (1973)—and two mystery novels. New York private detective Jack LeVine is introduced in *The Big Kiss-Off of 1944* (Holt, Rinehart and Winston, 1974), in which the detective tries to recover a pornographic film starring the daughter of a wealthy Philadelphia banker. The film is being used as blackmail by forces within the Democratic party to prevent the banker from financing Thomas Dewey's presidential election campaign against Roosevelt's third term. The plot is highly original, unusual in that the

Republicans are the good guys, and the novel is great fun. In ***Hollywood and LeVine*** (Holt, Rinehart and Winston, 1975) it is 1947 and LeVine is called to Hollywood by a writer buddy who wants the detective to investigate why the Hollywood studios will no longer hire him. When LeVine arrives in Los Angeles, he finds his client dead on the Warner Bros. lot, and his investigation leads to another one with highly political undertones, the House Un-American Activities Committee. Richard Nixon plays a prominent part, as he leads a witch-hunt in the film industry, seeking out "Reds." Bergman's knowledge of film history is apparent, as is his delight in creating a hard-boiled 1940s-era detective.

ELEANOR BERGSTEIN (born 1938) gave her first novel an intriguing title, *Advancing Paul Newman* (Viking Press, 1973), but it lacked a Hollywood theme. More than a decade later, she published a second novel, ***Ex-Lover*** (Random House, 1989), which is narrated by a playwright named Jessie Gerard, who has been hired to write an in-depth piece on the filming of a New York–based production. She is insecure, often confused, and here writes not only about the film but also about her personal life as she begins an affair with the director of photography. Even before the leading lady is brutally murdered, Jessie senses an undercurrent of violence on the set but fails to understand that it emanates from the actress's stand-in and stuntwoman. The scenes of location shooting in New York are well drawn, but in this work the personal thoughts and activities of the narrator are more important than the background filming.

SANDRA BERKLEY. ***Coming Attractions*** (E.P. Dutton, 1971), set in the 1930s, is the story of a young girl named Cassie, who comes to Hollywood with her mother to live with the latter's second husband, an assistant director. Cassie preserves her virginity until her marriage on a radio program. Martin Levin in the *New York Times* (February 14, 1971) commented that this "novel of Hollywood in the 1930s operates on the principle of Murphy's Law: if something can go wrong, it will. Four-year-old Cassie Keen comes West to meet her new step-daddy—and he turns out to be a child molester. . . . There is fine opportunity here to depict the soft underbelly of the old Hollywood, but Ms. Berkley is too strident for satire. Written in an archaic, present-tense, screen treatment style, filled with directions to 'pan' and 'cut' and 'dissolve,' the novel rolls heavily from one campy deadfall to another."

GILA BERKOWITZ. ***The Brides*** (St. Martin's Press, 1991) is a heavy romantic drama of three women of the 1970s who are linked through a Fifth Avenue, New York, bridal salon named Goldsmith's. One of the protagonists is the beautiful Melissa John, who begins her acting career by modeling bridal gowns at Goldsmith's, where the owner becomes her mentor. At the age of 26, Melissa marries 67-year-old superagent Chuck Lloyd and seems destined for a major career in Hollywood, but she becomes as well known for her marriages and immorality as for her acting career.

JANE BERNSTEIN (born 1949). The departures that central character Lydia is haunted by in ***Departures*** (Holt, Rinehart & Winston, 1979) are the deaths of her father and grandfather, and then the abrupt parting with her lover, a film technician. The novel recounts Lydia's search for love.

ALVAH BESSIE (1904–85) was one of the screenwriters investigated by the House Un-American Activities Committee in 1947 and jailed for contempt of Congress as one of the "Hollywood Ten." *The Un-Americans* (Cameron Associates, 1957) would appear to be a roman à clef, with Bessie disguised as good Communist Ben Blau. The novel is more a document than a work of fiction, written in black-and-white terms with no room for differences of opinion with its author. The *Times Literary Supplement* (February 14, 1958) felt that it could only be considered as "a piece of propaganda."

The Symbol (Random House, 1966) is very much a roman à clef about the life of Marilyn Monroe, here called Emmaline Kelly/Wanda Oliver. The book was not a critical success, but it sold very well and was the basis for ABC's 1973 television movie *The Sex Symbol*.

One for My Baby (Holt, Rinehart & Winston, 1980) is a monologue by a Lenny Bruce–like nightclub comedian named Sidney Sauerstein, known as Dr. Sour. In the course of his commentary, Sour discusses his unhappy life and his connection with all aspects of show business, including the legitimate stage and motion pictures.

EARL DERR BIGGERS (1884–1933) is best remembered for the six-volume Charlie Chan series, featuring the Honolulu-based detective, which formed the basis for more than forty films produced between 1926 and 1981. *The Black Camel* (Bobbs-Merrill, 1929) is the fourth novel in the series, and was filmed in 1931 with Warner Oland as Chan. Beautiful Hollywood leading lady Shelah Fane arrives in Honolulu, where she visits a fortune-teller named Tarneverro the Great and reveals to him the name of the murderer of a Hollywood actor named Denny Mayo, killed some years earlier. That same night, Miss Fane is murdered, and Chan's investigation identifies Fane as the murderer of Mayo, Tarneverro as Mayo's brother, and Fane's maid as Mayo's wife and her mistress's killer. The Charlie Chan mysteries are light reading but always great fun. The title is taken from one of Chan's many sayings: "Death is the black camel that kneels unbid at every door."

CHARLOTTE BINGHAM (born 1942) is a best-selling British novelist who has also written many television productions. Covering the 1950s through the 1970s, *Stardust* (Doubleday, 1992) examines the lives of two contract players, the beautiful Elizabeth Lawrence and the handsome Jerome Didier, as they become international stars of stage and screen. The ruthless Elizabeth destroys Jerome's marriage through poison pen letters and later the seduction of her leading man. Didier's wife flees to France, where she gives birth to his daughter, of whom he is unaware. Later, the daughter plots revenge against her father but realizes the breakup of her parents' marriage was primarily the fault of Elizabeth, who turns to alcohol, drugs, and starvation in a desperate attempt to retain her youth and beauty. Much of Elizabeth's later life is spent on the brink of madness, while Didier remarries and becomes reconciled with his first wife.

Dmitri Boska, the owner of the film studio where Elizabeth and Didier first meet, bears a slight resemblance to Alexander Korda, while the two players are obviously based on Laurence Olivier and Vivien Leigh. The novel's style is elegant and graceful, and although it contains some explicit dialogue and sexual sequences, overall the book reads like a dramatization for "Masterpiece Theatre"; perhaps not unsurprisingly author Bingham and her husband, Terence Brady, co-wrote "Upstairs Downstairs."

STEPHEN BIRMINGHAM (born 1932). *Fast Start, Fast Finish* (New American Library, 1966) is a study of a suburban group in Connecticut, one of whose number is commissioned to paint a portrait of a nymphomaniac movie star. "It's Harold Robbins in O'Hara territory," opined *Kirkus* (May 11, 1966).

LIONEL BLACK was the pseudonym of Dudley Barker (1910–80). In the mystery novel *The Life and Death of Peter Wade* (Stein and Day, 1974), journalist Johnny Trott is hired to write the biography of a dead actor.

OSWELL BLAKESTON (1907–85) was a British writer, artist, and critic involved with the early avant-garde film magazine *Close Up*. With American photographer Francis Bruguière, he produced an early abstract film, *Light Rhythms*, and with photographs by Bruguière, Blakeston also authored *Few Are Chosen: Studies in the Theatrical Lighting of Life's Theatre* (privately subscribed by Eric Patridge Ltd. at the Scholartis Press, 1931). The book is a collection of esoteric short stories, the first of which, "Arc Lights," concerns Connie, who moons down London's Wardour Street (the center of British film distribution) and obtains a pass to a film studio. It is not the glamorous world she imagined. Other stories contain filmic allusions; for example, a mother is compared to a character from a Russian film by Eisenstein.

MICHAEL BLANKFORT (1907–82) was a novelist, playwright, and screenwriter; his films include *Blind Alley* (1939), *The Caine Mutiny* (1954), and *The Plainsman* (1965). *A Time to Live* (Harcourt, Brace, 1943) reveals Blankfort's leftist viewpoint as it documents the life of New York playwright and professor Ernest Cripton. At one point Cripton comes to Hollywood as a screenwriter but feels isolated there.

ROBERT BLOCH (1917–94) wrote the original 1959 novel on which Alfred Hitchcock's 1960 film *Psycho* was based. The successor novel, *Psycho II* (Warner Books, 1982), has Norman Bates escaping from a mental institution and heading for Hollywood where a "mad slasher" film is being made of his life. Great fun! Bloch also casts a jaundiced eye on Hollywood in an earlier novel, *Shooting Star* (Ace Books, 1958), a mystery replete with liberal doses of Hollywood history and a Hollywood funeral.

WALTER BLOCH and ROBERT L. MUNGER. *The Angel* (Ward Ritchie Press, 1977) is a religious fantasy concerning an alcoholic, unemployed film producer under obligation to the Mafia whose soul is saved by his guardian angel in the body of a 17-year-old guitar-playing boy. Miracles can happen—particularly to born-again Christians.

LIBBIE BLOCK (1910–72). *The Hills of Beverly* (Doubleday, 1957) is a gentle parody of life in Beverly Hills, written in the style of a seventeenth-century French diarist. The principal characters are studio owner David Staver, his beautiful wife, Sophie, and film executive James Darcy. Reviews were mixed. "It is the work of a brilliant storyteller, and most pleasing of all there isn't a queer in the cast," wrote Richard Blakesley in the *Chicago Tribune* (August 4, 1957). "As novels about the pent-up people in the movie colony go," commented Bosley Crowther in the *New York Times* (September 1, 1957), "this one runs smoothly and freely and comparatively true to form." *The New Yorker* (August 24, 1957) thought, "The parody is rather skillful, but since Miss Block does not provide much evidence for the point of view behind it, the book dwindles into an interminable, manner-of-the-world parlor game."

No Man Tells Everything (Doubleday, 1959), edited by Pat Duggan, is a collection of 20 previously published short stories. One concerns a movie star who is plagued by an overzealous fan.

JOAN BLONDELL (1909–79) enjoyed a long career in vaudeville, a shorter one on the New York stage, and an extremely lengthy one in Hollywood films, from 1930 through 1979. She is best remembered for her featured roles in Warner Bros. productions of the 1930s, including, from 1933, *Gold Diggers of 1933* and *Footlight Parade* (in which she sang "Remember My Forgotten Man").

Center Door Fancy (Delacorte Press, 1972) is narrated by Nora Marten, who is introduced to vaudeville at the age of five by her father. At 16, she is appearing on Broadway, and then comes to Hollywood, where Marten plays the leads or "girl Fridays" in comedies and musicals and is married three times. The novel is obviously based on Blondell's own life, but although its writing may have been cathartic for the actress it is oddly unexciting to the reader, not badly written but with little sense of drama and understanding of climactic plot development.

JOHN BLUMENTHAL (born 1949). *The Tinseltown Murders* (Simon & Schuster, 1985) must be one of the most childishly humorous mystery novels ever written. It is full of outrageously awful puns—a Chinese houseboy is named Lo Fat, a police detective is Lieutenant Lou Tennant—and concerns New York private eye Mac Slade who comes to Hollywood at the request of a buddy, finds him dead, and begins questioning suspects, including a glamorous movie star and her agent. Don't bother reading this. The murderer, if anyone cares, is a gay hairdresser who is really a female stripper in disguise.

GEOFFREY BOCCA (1923–83). The title character in *Nadine* (G.P. Putnam's Sons, 1974) is an international star who lives in France with her sexually perverted husband, Raoul. The body of Raoul's bodyguard is found in the trunk of Nadine's car at the Cannes Film Festival, a homosexual pimp friend of Raoul disappears, and Nadine and Raoul must prove they have had nothing to do with what has happened. At the novel's close, the two divorce. If not for the lurid and explicit sex and the homosexual angle, the melodramatics of this novel might suggest that it was written in 1914.

DeWITT BODEEN (1908–88) wrote the screenplays for a number of well-known Hollywood films of the 1940s and 1950s, including *Cat People* (1942), *The Enchanted Cottage* (1945), and *I Remember Mama* (1948), and was also a film buff who contributed many career articles to *Films in Review* and other periodicals.

13 Castle Walk (Pyramid Books, 1975) is a fictionalized account of the 1922 unsolved murder of the Hollywood director William Desmond Taylor. Set in the present, the gothic mystery novel features a young woman released on parole from prison, where she had been serving time for the mercy killing of her husband. She goes to work for former silent screen star Mary Miles Minter (here called Jennie Jill Jerrard), and becomes fascinated with the murder of Minter's director, William Desmond Taylor (here called Andrew Riley Rutherford). It is revealed that Rutherford was bisexual, that he directed a porno film starring Mary Pickford's brother Jack (here called Johnny Carfax), and that Carfax murdered Rutherford after he had been infected by him with syphilis. Film buffs will be titillated by the story, which mixes fictional Hollywood personalities with famous names from the silent era. The book also provides something of a nostalgic glimpse at Hollywood in the 1970s, and even the story of the porno film is based on an extant silent pornographic comedy preserved at the Library of Congress.

DIRK BOGARDE (born 1920) was a popular and handsome British leading man of the 1940s and 1950s who revitalized his career by appearances in such film as *The Servant* (1963) and *Death in Venice* (1971). He achieved literary success with a series of autobiographical volumes, beginning in 1977 with *A Postillion Struck by Lightning* (Henry Holt), and three semiautobiographical novels.

A Gentle Occupation (Alfred A. Knopf, 1980) is based on its author's experiences on the island of Java at the end of the Second World War. The novel is set on a fictitious island near Java and Borneo during the same time period, with the British policing the native population following a Dutch colonial regime and a Japanese military occupation. "Bogarde has a terrific ear for dialogue, creating characters through speech the way actors do on stage and film," commented Jean Strouse in *Newsweek* (June 2, 1980).

Voices in the Garden (Alfred A. Knopf, 1981) is concerned with the relationship between youth and old age, as a 68-year-old woman, living on the French Riviera, falls in love with a 19-year-old boy. An Italian film producer seeks a homosexual relationship with the latter, offering the boy a role in his latest film, and the boy is seduced by the Italian's leading lady. "Mr. Bogarde has seen a lot of movies and still has an almost innocent enthusiasm for plot," wrote Anatole Broyard in the *New York Times* (September 12, 1981). "There's more than he needs—not all of it brand new—in *Voices in the Garden*. He's not pretentious, though, for the book has a happy ending." The novel is dedicated to actress Charlotte Rampling (with whom Bogarde costarred in the 1974 film *The Night Porter*) and her composer husband, Jean-Michel Jarre.

The central character in *Jericho* (Viking, 1992) discovers the perfect home for himself in French Provence (just as did Bogarde in the late 1960s). There is also a considerable amount of homosexual sadomasochism, which somehow one cannot imagine is linked to the private life of the author, who has always denied he is gay. "Autobiography-hunters will have a field day," noted *The Observer* (January 5, 1992).

BILL BOGGS (born 1942). The central character in *At First Sight* (Grosset & Dunlap, 1980) is forced to choose between a Parisian sculpture student and the daughter of a Hollywood movie mogul. The latter seduces him with cocaine and a part in a Sean Connery feature film, but our hero eventually comes to his senses and heads for Paris and the student.

NORMAN BOGNER (born 1935). *Arena* (Delacorte Press, 1979) is the story of two Jewish and two Italian families who both escape Nazi Germany at the same time and settle in the United States. The Stones (previously Steins) open a boxing arena in Brooklyn, while the Wests (formerly Weissbecks) start a hotel in the Catskills. Vittorio (Victor) Conte becomes a Hollywood agent and has an obligatory encounter with Howard Hughes. The arena of the title is a sports arena that Jonathan Stone builds to rival Madison Square Garden. *The California Dreamers* (Wyndham Books, 1981) are three young people from the East Coast: Bobby wants to be a leading architect, Claire wants to open a store on Rodeo Drive, and Madeleine just wants to be a movie star.

JOHN C. BOLAND. *The Seventh Bearer* (Pocket Books, 1993) features stockbroker Donald McCarry, who talks a major client out of investing in a movie deal and then plans rest and relaxation on the French Riviera. Adversaries in the international financial community have other ideas.

JOHN and EMERY BONETT. While a Hollywood film company is shooting on location in a small American town in *Not in the Script* (Doubleday, 1951), the set designer is accused of murder. One of the women of the community, who has fallen in love with him, helps track down the killer.

CHARLES G. (Gordon) BOOTH (1896–1949). *The Cat and the Clock* (Doubleday, Doran, 1935) is "an ingenious, fast-moving story of life and death in a community where bizarre personalities abound and the unexpected is the order of the day," wrote Isaac Anderson in the *New York Times* (January 5, 1936). The narrator is a press agent and the murder victim his client, a female dancer. The Hollywood police detective investigating the crime is hampered by the fact that the most likely suspect is the reform candidate for mayor.

PAT BOOTH (born 1942) is an author who proves the validity of the warning to readers of Hollywood novels: Beware of books named for glamorous places; they are nothing more than television soap operas transferred to print.

Beverly Hills (Crown, 1989) has as its central character Hollywood superstar Robert Hartford, whose dream is to own the Sunset Hotel (presumably based on the Beverly Hills Hotel). He falls in love with penniless Paula Hope, who, though her interior decorator mentor, comes to own the Chateau Madrid (presumably based on the Chateau Marmont). Through many trials and tribulations and with much melodramatics in the final pages, the two lovers and their respected hotels are united. The writing is heavy-handed, with exuberant purple prose reserved for Hartford's sex scenes; the best line: "the fruits and the nuts and the flakes of the muesli that was Southern California."

Malibu (Crown, 1990) pits an industrialist intent on building a movie studio in the Malibu hills against an aging biker-photographer. The latter wins. The industrialist owns a celebrity magazine managed by an evil, female British editor who plots revenge against up-and-coming actor Tony Valentino and his girlfriend, a photographer who is to direct his first film. When it is revealed that Valentino is the industrialist's son, the editor loses in her blackmail attempt against the industrialist and commits suicide. Valentino takes an average of four pages for each sexual climax. The novel reaches its climax midway through, and what is left of the plot is reduced to silly melodrama. Best line: "Hollywood had been sold lock, stock, cock, and its barrel to the grey corporations."

Rags to Riches (Crown, 1991) is a sequel to *The Lady and the Champ*, in which East End boxer Tommy Booth gave up his career after winning the world heavyweight championship while his mistress, the wife of the British prime minister, bled to death at the ringside. Now Booth is in Los Angeles and living with a well-known actress, Charlotte Christie. His former manager, Lewis Klein, embarks on a new career as a film producer and decides to star Booth and his lover in a screen adaptation of the boxer's life. After much sex and a little violence (including a castration), the film of Booth's life wins four Oscars, but Klein cannot enjoy the triumph—that same night his wife murders him in response to his sexual dalliances and his criminal activities.

As always, author Booth demonstrates her knowledge of the lives of Hollywood's beautiful people, all of whom seem more self-centered and arrogant than nice. She even manages to invent an interview by former gossip columnist Roderick Mann with Charlotte Christie, which does little but raise questions about the reason for writers such as Mann in today's world. The best that can be said is that Pat Booth is an equal opportunity writer when it comes to sex scenes—they are equally titillating to both female and male readers.

All for Love (Crown, 1993) is the story of Tarleton "Tari" Jones, a medical student and "adopted daughter of God," and it has little to do with Hollywood except for the character of Rickey Cage, an actor and biker whose girlfriend has compromising photographs of Tari.

ELIZABETH BORTON is the pseudonym of Elizabeth Borton de Trevino (born 1904). The first of five Pollyanna novels written by Borton is **Pollyanna in Hollywood** (Kirby Page, 1931), in which the child heroine of earlier days is now a wife and mother. With her family, she travels to Hollywood to view the various attractions and feels contentment that she is just a simple soul and not a Hollywood star with all the baggage that goes along with the title.

KEITH BOTSFORD (born 1928). *The Eighth-Best-Dressed Man in the World* (Harcourt, Brace, 1957) tells the tale of the younger son of an Italian nobleman, Count Cosmo Annibale Casasola, who emigrates to the United States prior to the First World War, becomes a successful male model and later a Hollywood actor, and returns to Italy and an arranged marriage in 1937. In the *New York Herald Tribune* (September 1, 1957), Anne Ross wrote,

"Mr. Botsford's slight novel gives only the sketchiest account of Cosmo's bitter career. He tells it in flashes, through the eyes of an American-born relative. But somehow in this apparently hit-or-miss fashion, he does convey an almost touching portrait of Cosmo, the shell of a man, who, born in a simpler society, might have been happy."

ANTHONY BOUCHER was the pseudonym of William Anthony Parker (1911–68). *The Case of the Baker Street Irregulars* (Simon & Schuster, 1940) has the Sherlock Holmes fan club of the title, led by the trusty Dr. Rufus Bottomley, heading for Hollywood, where Metropolis Pictures is filming the Arthur Conan Doyle story "The Speckled Band." The group's initial concern is that there be no tampering with the writings of the master, but Bottomley and company must also solve a murder when the film's highly unpopular screenwriter, Stephen Worth, is murdered. "The Speckled Band" has been filmed four times, in 1912, 1923, 1931, and 1949; it has also been adapted for the stage and television.

JOHN BOWEN (born 1924). Stylishly written and a well-crafted thriller, *The McGuffin* (Atlantic Monthly Press, 1984) contains many of the elements of an Alfred Hitchcock drama. It begins with Paul Hatcher, a London film critic, observing something strange in the rear window of an apartment opposite. The old lady who lives there has been joined by a woman, who is obviously a man, and a large dog. As in Hitchcock's film *Rear Window*, Hatcher becomes obsessed with the puzzle. He confronts the two "women" while offering to walk the dog, and discovers that the younger "woman" is indeed a man in hiding. When both are murdered, Hatcher takes in the dog and becomes intensely involved in an international situation. Hidden in the dog's collar are negatives showing four men sexually abusing a young man and later killing him. Hatcher is unable to determine whom to trust, as his ex-wife is murdered and he is invited to attend what turns out to be a pornographic film festival in the capital city of Liechtenstein. Filled with film references, *The McGuffin* reads at times like a comic-tragedy, but for its protagonist the story ultimately proves to be a deadly serious game.

B.M. BOWER was the pseudonym for Bertha Muzzy Cowan Sinclair (1874–1940). Her two Hollywood novels both relate to the difference between the West as depicted on film and that of reality. In *The Phantom Herd* (Little, Brown, 1916), Luck Lindsay tries to persuade the film company for which he is general manager to make a Western showing nineteenth-century life as it really was on the prairie. When his bosses reject the idea, claiming the public wants only stock, melodramatic Westerns, Lindsay produces his own film with the help of the owners of the Flying U Ranch. The heroine of *The Quirt* (Little, Brown, 1920) visits a ranch in Idaho, hoping to enjoy a true Western atmosphere, but upon discovering a cattle feud and sundry uncivilized behavior, she decides that the Hollywood concept of the Western is far safer and more reassuring.

JEANNE BOWMAN was the pseudonym of Peggy O'More (1895–19??), a prolific writer of romantic novels. In *Exclusively Yours* (Arcadia House,

1952), a wife does not understand how her movie star husband can sacrifice their privacy for the adoration of millions of fans. *Miss Prissy* (Arcadia House, 1953) is the story of two young people in Hollywood: Priscilla works in an office and hopes for a screen test, while Art has become a major star.

BETTINA and AUDREY BOYERS. When Australian Poldi Buck comes to Hollywood in *Murder by Proxy* (Doubleday, Doran, 1945) to be with her husband, who is writing a screenplay based on his best-selling novel, she has a premonition that something awful will happen to her. Her worries take on reality when she is pushed in front of a truck. "Good slant on the telling, with Hollywood life plausible instead of exaggerated, and with fresh interest in spite of drawbacks," commented *Kirkus* (June 1, 1945).

MALCOLM STUART BOYLAN. *Gold Pencil* (Little, Brown, 1953) is the story of Joshua Doty, who has made colonel during the First World War, prior to his twentieth birthday. In 1919, Doty comes to Hollywood and becomes a press agent. "Boylan doesn't overlook a bet. His sly comments on the foibles of movie making, his artistically casual asides on lovemaking, and his intrusion of the serious, plus a good story to tell, should fasten the reader's hands to the book until the end," wrote Seymour Korman in the *Chicago Sunday Tribune* (April 26, 1953).

RUSSELL BRADDON (born 1921). In *The Thirteenth Trick* (W.W. Norton, 1972), a young female British hitchhiker is murdered and her body found in the rear seats of an English cinema. "Not a bad tale," according to Jacques Barzun in *A Catalogue of Crime* (Harper & Row, 1989).

MURIEL BRADLEY. *Affair at Ritos Bay* (Doubleday, 1947) is a mystery novel wherein screenwriter Dan Garrett and his secretary take a working vacation at Ritos Bay. While there, Garrett finds himself a suspect in three murders. "Her [Bradley's] exploration is rather deft and about as deep as a coat of veneer," commented James Sandoe in the *Chicago Sun Book Week* (July 6, 1947).

FLORENZ BRANCH was a pseudonym. *The Fleshpots* (Phoenix Press, 1944) is a fairly explicit (for its day) romance, involving a beauty contest winner, Shirley Pierce, who comes to Hollywood looking for success but does not get beyond extra work. She meets attractive war correspondent Bill Hilliard, who offers to help her meet some Hollywood big shots in return for helping him have some fun. The first night at a Hollywood nightspot, Shirley is the subject of a much publicized fight between Hilliard and movie star Ralph Wharton. Shirley and Hilliard go to a beach house and have sex, but in the morning Shirley deserts Hilliard for Wharton and a party in Palm Springs. At Hilliard's urging, Wharton's wife tries to dissuade Shirley from associating with her husband. Shirley ignores the advice, but eventually she and Hilliard are reunited, marry, and Shirley gives up on Hollywood.

MADELINE BRANDEIS (1897–1937). *Adventure in Hollywood: A Story of the Movies for Girls* (Coward-McCann, 1937) is a novel for teenage girls. When the heroine, who works with a local theater group in Hollywood, meets the son of a wealthy movie mogul, she is promised work in films, but the work is that of an extra. Disillusioned, she returns to the theater group, but is seen there by a casting director and a return to motion pictures seems imminent.

BEATRICE BRANDON was the pseudonym of Robert W. Krepps (1919–80), whose *The Court of Silver Shadows* (Doubleday, 1980), a self-described "novel of romantic suspense," is one of the more ludicrous offerings in any fictionl genre. Laurel Warrick takes up a position as a live-in librarian at the mysterious Sablecroft Hall in St. Petersburg, Florida. She is immediately frightened by the atmosphere at the Hall, and little wonder, for its megalo-maniacal residents spend their days quoting lines from old movies and preparing audiotapes of speeches for playing at inappropriate moments. After a screening of *Little Caesar* in the Hall's private theater, one of the family members explains to Laurel:

> That's the real world up there. That's your family and your closest friends, your kids, your bosses, even the gods that run the universe. Compare *that* with what's out there! Did you ever have a friend like Cooper, who'd go through fire for you? Did you ever woo a woman as fascinating as Colbert or Vivien Leigh or either of the Hepburns? Take your troubles to anyone as kind and wise as Travers or Kellaway or Davenport—look up to anyone as you could to Tracy, Gable, Hawkins, Mason, four-score others? You're damn right you didn't! The people in the movies never failed you, never let you down. As *nobody* does in what's called "real" life, they acted faithfully, nobly, skillfully, entertainingly...

Laurel has been hired to catalogue the collection of film books, movie memorabilia, tapes, and films collected by the doyenne of Sablecroft Hall, Sibella Callingwood. In such an atmosphere, it is no surprise that romance and murder flourish, and eventually Laurel is forced to speak harshly to the family:

> I've been thinking that all the stupid, evil things that happened here were the direct result of living in the movies. Some of you, at least one for sure, has no conception of the realities of life because he was born in the middle of ten thousand films—some masterpieces, some very jolly, some intellec-tually stimulating, but many, many of them presenting a world that's false, based on false values, idealized notions of human nature, sentimental slush, and immoral gratifications of the bravery, nobility, and all-around superiority of the criminal mind.

After wading through this novel, readers can only agree with Laurel's estimation of the characters she encounters—they "talk like the opening of a bad horror movie out of the early forties."

SUSAN BRAUDY (born 1941). *Who Killed Sal Mineo?* (Wyndham Books, 1982) is a fictional account of newspaper reporter Sara Martin's investi-gation into the stabbing death of the actor, which took place at 8567 Holloway Drive, West Hollywood, on February 12, 1976. Much is made of Mineo's homo-sexuality or possible bisexuality, and helping the reporter is Mineo's fictional close friend, a gay singer named Mark Loren. Curiously, all the characters with whom the reporter comes in contact are fictional, with one exception, and that is director Nicholas Ray. Few readers will have the energy to read this book through to its conclusion, and so, perhaps, it is not unfair to reveal that, according to the author, Sal Mineo's killing was a senseless one engineered by the wife of a Paramount producer, with whose drug dealings the actor was interfering.

What the Movies Made Me Do (Alfred A. Knopf, 1985) is plenty as far as New York film executive Carol Young is concerned. At the age of 40, she has cause to reflect on her decision to choose a career over marriage and a family. Her long-planned film *Jesus the Prophet* is shooting on location in Israel, and the female director has walked off the set after a confrontation with Jack Hanscombe, the leading man. There is no alternative but for Carol to head for Israel, where she must also deal with her personal feelings for Jack, with whom she has had a long, on and off relationship. The novel was well received, being "impossible to put down," according to *Publisher's Weekly*, and "pure pleasure," according to *Library Journal*.

CELIA BRAYFIELD (born 1945). *The Princess* (Bantam Books, 1991) is typical romantic fare. Prince Richard, Duke of Sussex, must decide whom he wants to marry: a Hollywood star, a supermodel, or a British aristocrat with a past.

HERBERT BREAN (1907–73). There are murders and the disappearance of the title character in *The Traces of Merrilee* (William Morrow, 1966), wherein sex symbol Merrilee Moore sails for Europe to star in a $15 million feature production.

LYNTON WRIGHT BRENT. *Gittin' in the Movies: Adventures of a Country Boy in Hollywood; Pictures by the Author* (Moderncraft Publishers, 1936) consists of a series of semi-illiterate letters home, written by Lem G. Whillikins, who has come to Hollywood, where he makes a film starring a cow.

SIMON BRETT (born 1945) is the author of a series of mystery novels that are both witty and highly evocative of the British theatrical scene. They feature actor Charles Paris, who is generally unemployed, separated from his wife, and overly fond of Bell's whiskey. The background is generally the stage, although there are occasional forays into the worlds of film, radio, and television.

Charles Paris is introduced, at the age of 47, in *Cast, In Order of Disappearance* (Charles Scribner's Sons, 1975), wherein he confronts a blackmailer and impersonates a Scotland Yard detective, both in the interests of a young lady to whom he is attracted. Paris also gets shot in the arm while appearing in a horror film titled *The Zombie Walks*, directed by "a little Cockney who gloried in the name of Jean-Luc Roussel."

Corporate Bodies (Charles Scribner's Sons, 1992) is not one of the better novels in the series. Now well into his fifties, Paris has taken a job performing in a corporate video for a food and drinks conglomerate. As usual, when Paris accepts an assignment, murder closely follows.

BESSIE BREUER (1893–1975). *The Actress* (Harper, 1957) is the romantic story of a small-town girl named Joanna Trask, who becomes a Hollywood star. On her second visit to Rome—on both occasions she is working—Trask finds romance. The novel was first conceived as a short story, "The Phantom Script," published in the June 1955 issue of *Mademoiselle*. "It is the human being's constant capacity for renewal which the author confirms in this rewarding book, and her own womanly compassion gives depth and significance to a story so simple that one wonders why it has not been told before," commented Kay Boyle in the *New York Times* (October 6, 1957).

JACQUELINE BRISKIN (born 1927). Against a background of the oil boom and the silent film industry, the love of two brothers for the same woman in the period between the 1880s and the 1920s is told in *Paloverde* (G.P. Putnam's Sons, 1978). *Everything and More* (G.P. Putnam's Sons, 1983) uses a film background as it documents the intertwined lives of three Beverly Hills women who first became friends in high school.

GWEN BRISTOW (1903–80). The heroine of *Tomorrow Is Forever* (Grosset & Dunlap, 1943), Elizabeth Herlong, loses her first husband in 1918, when he is killed at Chateau Thierry. She moves to Hollywood and meets and marries studio publicist Spratt Herlong, who later becomes a major producer at Vertex Studio. Her second marriage is a happy one until she comes face to face with her dead husband. Here is a dramatic and suspenseful novel that still holds the reader's attention despite what today might seem a somewhat trite plotline. The novel was filmed in 1946 by RKO, under the direction of Irving Pichel.

PAUL BRODEUR (born 1931). While AWOL, a young army recruit meets up with a director on the verge of blindness in a resort town in *The Stunt Man* (Atheneum, 1970). The soldier needs to hide from the army and the director needs a stuntman. All goes well until the soldier realizes that the director is revising the script to reflect the soldier's own life, and that the last stunt in the film may well end with his death. The novel was enthusiastically received, hailed by *Library Journal* (March 15, 1970) as "absolutely first-rate" and by *Book World* (March 29, 1970) as "both intellectually powerful and artistically strong." *The Stunt Man* was filmed in 1978 by producer Melvin Simon, under the direction of Richard Rush, and starring Peter O'Toole, Steve Railsback, and Barbara Hershey.

DAVID BROEKMAN. *The Shoestring Symphony* (Simon & Schuster, 1948) is a semiautobiographical work based on its author's two years of unemployment during the Depression, while he was a Hollywood conductor and composer. "On the whole an amusing book, with the humor often cut in with a keen-edge blade, it is also a tactful book," wrote Nancy Ladd in the *New York Times* (May 2, 1948). "For the characters who are recognizable, Mr. Broekman has nothing but good to say; for the characters who are not persons but types, he has nothing good to say. Sound practice for an artist with two fortes—he never can tell when he'll meet up with a musician who can read."

RICHARD BROOKS (1912–92) had a career as a screenwriter, beginning in 1942, before becoming a director in 1950. In the latter capacity, his best works are *The Blackboard Jungle* (1955), *Cat on a Hot Tin Roof* (1958), *Elmer Gantry* (1960), *Sweet Bird of Youth* (1962), and *In Cold Blood* (1967). *The Producer* (Simon & Schuster, 1951) makes good use of Brooks's experiences in Hollywood as it documents producer Matt Gibbons's attempt to make an independent production, while dealing with everything from marital problems to congressional investigations. According to Carolyn See, Gibbons and his wife are based on Mark Hellinger and Gladys George.

BROCK BROWER (born 1931). *The Late Great Creature* (Atheneum, 1971) of the title is Simon Morro, a horror star of the 1930s, who has some of the attributes of Bela Lugosi, Boris Karloff, and Peter Lorre. In his late sixties, Morro plans a comeback in a horror film not unlike Poe's "The Raven" and produced by a company that bears a remarkable resemblance to American-International. Unfortunately, Morro takes himself too seriously—or is it the author?—and has a coffin built in which he will ship himself back to Transylvania or Vienna. Instead, Morro suffocates inside it. "For some, certainly eclectic," wrote *Kirkus* (October 13, 1971), "with all that cineaste-ing around, but also clever and bitter and disruptive since Brower is a wordsmith of decisive sophistication."

CARTER BROWN, a prolific mystery novelist, was the pseudonym of Alan Geoffrey Yates (1923–85). One of his regular heroes, Lieutenant Al Wheeler, is called in to investigate threats against the life of film star Judy Manne in *The Dame* (Horwitz, 1959). In *The Ever-Loving Blues* (New American Library, 1961), private detective Danny Boyd escorts a glamorous movie star from Florida to Hollywood and encounters a murder en route. And in *The Windup Doll* (New American Library, 1964), Denny solves a murder and helps an aging child star come to grips with his maturity. Another Carter Brown regular, Rick Holman, is hired to help a movie actress with a blackmail problem in *Murder Is a Package Deal* (Horwitz, 1964). Additionally, Carolyn See identifies *The White Bikini* (New American Library, 1963) as a Hollywood novel.

JOAN JULIET BUCK (born 1948). *Only Place to Be* (Random House, 1982) is the story of Iris Bromley, who begins life as a precocious child in Paris, becomes a debutante in Monte Carlo, a society reporter in New York, and a show business journalist in Rome.

CHARLES BUKOWSKI (1920–93) has a considerable cult reputation as an author of both poetry and prose. *Hollywood* (Black Sparrow Press, 1989) is a curious novel in which Bukowski's alter ego Henry Chinaski tells about writing the screenplay of *The Dance of Jim Beam*, its production, and critical reception. *Hollywood* is an autobiographical novel about the making of an autobiographical film: while using fictitious names and situations, it documents the making of the 1987 feature *Barfly*, which Bukowski wrote and based on his life as the "patron saint of hard-drinking poets." The book is dedicated to Barbet

Schroeder, who directed *Barfly* as his first U.S. film, and who is identified here as Jon Pinchot; similarly Mickey Rourke, who gave a "quirky, unpredictable, most engaging performance as the boozy hero" (*Daily Variety*, May 13, 1987), and Faye Dunaway are identified in the novel as Jack Bledsoe and Francine Bowers. Throughout, Bukowski plays name games, with references to Jon-Luc Modard (Jean-Luc Godard), Werner Zergog (Werner Herzog), Francis Ford Lopalla (Francis Ford Coppola, who served as executive producer on *Barfly*), and others. One of the few critics who actively disliked *Barfly* was Pauline Kael, who wrote in *The New Yorker* (November 2, 1987), "You wouldn't guess at Bukowski's talent from this movie. His script is a pastiche of his earlier writing." She is singled out for more explicit identification in *Hollywood*. Also, Bukowski offers this comment, "What was the difference between a movie critic and the average moviegoer? Answer: the critic didn't have to pay."

DAVID LLEWELLYN BURDETT. *Hix Nix Stix Pix: A Kaleidoscope of Talk and Events* (E.P. Dutton, 1984) is a parody of history from the First to the Second World War, set against a Hollywood background. It is a unique novel, a satirical montage, which reads rather like a Robertson Davies work—but with a sense of humor. The central character is Phillip Inshroin, introduced at studios of Drewstone Films in Hollywood, just before he goes off to film First World War battlefront footage in Europe. As Inshroin's career as an actor progresses, the novel recounts Charlie Chaplin's visit to a hospital for wounded soldiers, the trips of the Prince of Wales and Winston Churchill to the United States, the rise of Hitler in Germany, Upton Sinclair's campaign for the governorship of California, the religious services of Aimee Semple McPherson, the activities of the Federal Theatre Project, and the rise of anti–Semitism. The title is a well-known headline from *Variety* (meaning the Middle West is opposed to rural dramas on screen). The author is Welsh, and this was his first book.

JAMES LEE BURKE (born 1936). *In the Electric Mist with Confederate Dead* (Hyperion, 1993) is the sixth mystery novel to feature Cajun police detective Dave Robicheaux, who has a hard time dealing with the modern world. A film is being made in southern Louisiana, financed by local mobster Baby Feet Balboni. When the film's star Elrod Sykes is arrested for drunk driving, he tells Robicheaux of a skeleton wrapped in chains unearthed during filming in a bayou, which reminds Robicheaux of the 35-year-old murder of a black man by two whites to which the policeman was a witness. When Sykes's costar is shot to death, mistaken for Robicheaux, the detective becomes determined to bring about the downfall of Balboni, despite objections from locals who are happy with the money the filmmakers are bringing to the community. What is unusual about *In the Electric Mist with Confederate Dead* is that it is more than just a mystery, with the supernatural playing a significant role as Robicheaux experiences dreamlike encounters with a troop of Confederate soldiers led by General John Bell Hood. Critics have found elements of both William Faulkner and F. Scott Fitzgerald here, unusual comparisons for a mystery novel.

EDGAR RICE BURROUGHS (1875–1950). The creator of *Tarzan of the Apes* (1914) wrote one novel with a Hollywood theme. A classic melodrama,

The Girl from Hollywood (Frank A. Munsey, 1922) warns about the danger of drug use, which Burroughs argues will be a far more serious problem in the future than alcohol abuse. The story begins in an idyllic California ranch setting, with youthful Custer Pennington in love with a neighbor, Grace Evans. Before settling down to marriage, she is anxious to experience life by becoming an actress in Hollywood. Meanwhile, her brother Gus is helping a bootlegger hide alcohol on the property but is not aware that the bootlegger, Slick Allen, is also involved in drug trafficking. In Hollywood, director/actor Wilson Crumb has seduced a young actress named Gaza de Lure, introduced her to cocaine, and is now using her to peddle the drug, obtained from Allen. Gaza de Lure's real name is Shannon Burke, and her mother is a neighbor of the Penningtons. When the mother becomes ill and subsequently dies, Shannon returns home, fights the drug habit, and slowly falls in love with Custer Pennington. Back in Hollywood, Crumb has managed to have Allen arrested and has now set up Grace Evans to replace Gaza de Lure in his life. Federal marshals investigating bootlegging implicate the innocent Custer Pennington, and he is sent to jail. After his release, Wilson Crumb comes to the ranch to film on location and is murdered. Custer Pennington is arrested again, tried, and sentenced to death for the crime. Only through the efforts of Shannon Burke does the real murderer, Gus Evans, confess—he had taken his revenge for what happened to his sister. At the novel's close, Shannon Burke also confesses—that Allen is her father.

The Girl from Hollywood was presumably influenced by the film industry scandals of the period, including the drug-induced illness and subsequent death of leading man Wallace Reid. Still highly entertaining, even for non–Burroughs fans, the novel's anti–Hollywood theme makes curious reading in view of the financial success its author enjoyed by permitting his Tarzan stories to be filmed.

BEATRICE BURTON. *The Hollywood Girl* (Grosset & Dunlap, 1927) is an atypical juvenile novel, warning about the dangerous lure of Hollywood. The heroine discovers that she can be a success in the film industry, but that she is better off in her hometown and married to her childhood sweetheart.

NIVEN BUSCH (1903–91) was a prominent Hollywood screenwriter— *The Postman Always Rings Twice* (1946), *Pursued* (1947), and others—who became a major novelist, working first in the field of the psychological Western with *Duel in the Sun*. *The Actor* (Simon & Schuster, 1955) is the classic Hollywood novel about an actor on the way down, his aggressive wife, and his director son who hates his father. "He knows the Hollywood half-world—the fading, shabby, shoddy level of those who haven't quite made it, and of those who had made it and somehow lost it," commented J.H. Jackson in the *San Francisco Chronicle* (June 13, 1955). The Hollywood community plays a secondary role in *Continent's Edge* (Simon and Schuster, 1980), which is primarily concerned with an oil-rich family.

W.E. BUTTERWORTH. The central character in *Comfort Me with Love* (New American Library, 1960) is an uptight Southern screen personality who has an affair with a black starlet in Hollywood. He is repulsed when he discovers she has made a porno film, which his friends and colleagues have seen.

Returning to the South, the man is seduced by the wife of his best friend, and he then decides to come back to Hollywood and rekindle his relationship with the willing starlet. *The Love-Go-Round* (Berkley Books, 1962) is one of a series of novels with a Hollywood background, described by Carolyn See as "semi-pornographic." Additionally, *Hot Seat* (New American Library, 1961) is identified by Carolyn See as a Hollywood novel.

JAMES M. (Mallahan) CAIN (1892–1977) was one of the leading exponents of the hard-boiled school of mystery fiction. His best-known novels, *The Postman Always Rings Twice* (1934), *Mildred Pierce* (1941), and *Double Indemnity* (1943), all became classic Hollywood films.

It is difficult to know who would be most offended by *Serenade* (Alfred A. Knopf, 1937), the people of Mexico or America's gay community. It is an extraordinary novel that leaves the reader with a feeling of total disbelief—and in many cases outrage. We first meet the central character, John Howard Sharp, down and out in Mexico. He was, apparently, once an opera singer, but he is now penniless. He meets a prostitute named Juana Montes, and with the help of a kindly, opera-loving American sea captain, he comes with her to the United States. After taking over a role at the last minute at the Hollywood Bowl, Sharp is able to obtain a film contract. From Hollywood, he and Juana move to New York, where Juana and the reader are first introduced to wealthy conductor Winston Hawes. The latter is in love with Sharp, and, apparently, his obsession with the singer led to Sharp's losing his voice and fleeing to Mexico. It is not clear whether the two men had a sexual relationship, or to what extent Sharp returned Hawes's affection, but the singer does refer to himself at one point as a "fag." Hawes turns Juana in to the immigration authorities, and she kills him. Again with the aid of the same sea captain, Sharp and Juana flee the country, traveling first to Guatemala and then to Mexico, where Juana is killed but Sharp recovers his voice.

Serenade was filmed in 1956 as a vehicle for Mario Lanza; the gay angle was dropped, and the story concerned a love triangle between the singer and two women.

HORTENSE CALISHER (born 1911). The main protagonist in *In the Palace of the Movie King* (Random House, 1994) is director Paul Gonchev, born in Russia, raised in Japan, and a leading figure in Balkan cinema, who is brought to the United States. According to Brad Hooper in *Booklist* (September 15, 1993), "This novel is far too cerebral for its own good. It lives entirely in the author's head, like the pupa of a moth that, had it completed its full cycle, could have been a magnificent creature, but because of some malfunction of nature never breaks from its chrysalis."

R. WRIGHT CAMPBELL (born 1927) now writes mystery novels under the name of Robert Campbell; he was nominated for an Academy Award for his screenplay for *Man with a Thousand Faces* (1957). *Killer of Kings* (Bobbs-Merrill, 1979) concerns an embittered 20th Century–Fox security guard named Harry Smiley, who finds himself in a self-created feud with Hollywood star Michael Nordland. Smiley's rage and frustration with the rich and powerful lead him and a group of misfit friends to plan the destruction of the Oscar

ceremony. As Nordland goes up to receive his award for best actor, bombs planted in the chandeliers of the Dorothy Chandler Pavilion in Los Angeles explode, leading to the deaths of 31 in the film community. Nordland and his leading lady, winner of the best actress Oscar, are taken hostage, but the former is able to overcome the nightmares resulting from his service in Korea and save the actress. The novel is great fun, if highly implausible because of the relative ease with which Smiley and colleagues are able to infiltrate the awards ceremony. The book's dust jacket features the Oscar statuette with a bloody bullet wound through the heart. Bob Hope and Elliott Gould appear briefly as themselves at the Oscar show; presumably neither was among the 31 dead.

Pornographic films at their most virulent—child pornography and snuff films—are the subject of *In La-La Land We Trust* (Mysterious Press, 1986), which takes place in Los Angeles and New Orleans. The hero is a private eye named Whistler and the chief villain, a Los Angeles mogul with a penchant for young boys. The story is sordid but fascinating—perhaps in part for the wrong reasons.

RAMSEY CAMPBELL (born 1946) is noted for his horror novels and short stories. *The Parasite* (Macmillan, 1980) is typical of the works for which he has become well known. Its central character is a 30-year-old film critic, Rose Tierney, who went through a traumatic experience as a child. A mugging in New York reawakens childhood fears, which in turn lead to out-of-body experiences. Three critics helped the author in the creation of his main protagonist: Philip Strick, David Thomson, and Robin Wood.

In *Ancient Images* (Charles Scribner's Sons, 1989), a "lost" 1938 British film starring Bela Lugosi and Boris Karloff, titled *Tower of Fear*, is a clue to something mysterious and evil in the town of Redfield. A young London film editor, Sandy Allen, goes on its trail when her friend Graham claims to have found a copy of the film and then leaps to his death from the roof of his ten-story apartment building. Intriguing and suspenseful—a perfect novel for horror film buffs—the lost film is perhaps based on the Boris Karloff 1933 vehicle *The Ghoul*, a British film that was thought for many years no longer to exist in any form.

REMCO CAMPERT. In *The Gangster Girl* (Rupert Hart-Davis, 1968), a British screenwriter is given the assignment of writing a script with a gangster theme for fashion models. While gathering ideas for the film, he builds a vivid picture of his life and family.

JAY CANTOR. *Krazy Kat* (Alfred A. Knopf, 1987) is an attempt to bring to life, or at least to the novel form, the George Herriman comic strip character "Krazy Kat." It begins in 1945 as Krazy Kat and the reader's world is shattered by the atomic bomb. Krazy Kat refuses to work again, and Ignatz Mouse must do everything he can to change her outlook on life, including bringing in a Hollywood producer with the offer of screen stardom. That section of the book allows the author to retell a few somewhat stale jokes about the film industry, including the story of the Polish starlet who slept with the writer.

ELIZABETH CARFRAE. *This Way to the Stars* (Mills & Boon, 1938) is a romance about a parson's daughter who comes to London in hopes of becoming a film star. "This novel is for people who like to read detailed accounts of literary tea parties where no tea is served and brilliant conversation is reported with no samples," commented the reviewer in the *New York Times* (January 16, 1938).

HARRY CARMICHAEL was the pseudonym of Leopold Horace Ognall (1908–79). In *Into Thin Air* (Crime Club/Doubleday, 1957), a British screen actress disappears from her hotel just before an appointment with Carmichael's regular hero, insurance investigator John Piper.

MARY CARMODY. *My Golden Egg* (Vantage Press, 1956) is identified by Carolyn See as a Hollywood novel.

LESLIE CARON (born 1931) is a legendary Hollywood actress and dancer, born in France, who made her screen debut in 1951 with *An American in Paris*. Her best-known films include *Lili* (1953), *Daddy Long Legs* (1955), *Gigi* (1958), *The L-Shaped Room* (1962), and *Father Goose* (1964). She first began writing in 1967, following the death of her mother. "Nothing in these stories is entirely truthful, yet there is an element of truth in each," Caron writes in her foreword to *Vengeance* (Doubleday, 1982), a collection of 12 short stories. Two have film-related themes. "King of the Mountains" has producer A.C. Weston moving his house across town to Beverly Hills while learning, as it moves slowly at night, that his career is over. "Stardom at Last" concerns Eve Gordon, who puts her film career above the life of her prematurely born baby; when told of its death, she responds, "I mustn't think about it now . . . I must get on with my work." Good as these stories undoubtedly are, there is a cold, almost clinical approach to writing, much as Caron embraces her work as an actress. The stories were published in Caron's native France by Balland in 1983.

DON CARPENTER (born 1931). *The True Life of Jody McKeegan* (E.P. Dutton, 1975) is a truncated one. We first meet her, as a teenager, in Portland, Oregon, living with her mother and present as her sister dies following an illegally performed abortion. That part of Jody's story is interesting in and of itself. In part two of the novel, Jody is 35 years old and living in Hollywood, where she has yet to find employment as an actress. She meets and moves in with a producer who thinks she is right for a small part in his latest film but is unwilling to cast her without the approval of the director. When the director agrees with his producer's opinion, Jody flies to Georgia for location shooting, argues with her producer-lover about how her character should die, and goes out in search of drugs. The novel ends abruptly, apparently with her turning down heroin and returning to shoot the final scene.

The novel is at its best in describing the behind-the-scenes happenings that go into getting a production under way, and in its depiction of relatively unsympathetic location shooting. Ultimately, it is not Jody but her producer-lover for whom the reader feels sympathy and understanding.

A Couple of Comedians (Simon & Schuster, 1979) could be Dean Martin and Jerry Lewis. Here, they are named comedian David Ogilvie, who narrates the novel, and straightman and singer Jim Larson. Friends since high school and highly successful for a number of years, the pair make one movie a year together, with an annual pilgrimage to Las Vegas. But their lives are empty, except for drugs, alcohol, and sex; they are, in Larson's words, "dumbfounded and bored and sick of the whole shithouse mess." Despite or perhaps because of it all, the reader actually feels sympathy for these two.

Turnaround (Simon & Schuster, 1981) is a cautionary tale about how luck and timing can be so important in career breaks in Hollywood. A would-be screenwriter, Jerry Rexford, arrives in town. A first-time producer-director, Rick Heidelberg, is looking for a new property that studio head Alexander Hellstrom, talented and dignified, is willing to back. Heidelberg's choice is Rexford's script for Raymond Chandler's *The Lady in the Lake*. This is the weakest of Carpenter's three Hollywood novels.

ROBERT CARSON (1909–83) was a prominent Hollywood screenwriter whose credits include *A Star Is Born* (1937), *Beau Geste* (1939), *Western Union* (1941), *Bedside Manner* (1945), and *Bundle of Joy* (1956). He also wrote many novels, several set in California. His second, **The Bride Saw Red** (G.P. Putnam's Sons, 1943), is the story of the spoiled son of a rich mother, who marries a Hollywood extra in Las Vegas. The mother stops her son's allowance, but the wife sees red and stands by her husband.

The Magic Lantern (Henry Holt, 1952) is the story of the rise to power in the silent era of movie mogul Frank P. Silversmith. When his wife dies in childbirth, he deserts his son, Ellis. "Pretty dull," opined Robert Lowry in the *New York Times* (November 30, 1952). "But the book's documentation of an industry's birth is better than its story or its style." *The New Yorker* (December 13, 1952) agreed: "Mr. Carson's characters are hollow, but he keeps them talking and moving around, and his account of the early days of Hollywood is diverting reading."

When Christopher McClaren meets Deane Gregory in **Love Affair** (Henry Holt, 1958), he is an extra. The couple marry, and she helps build his career. But he fails to recognize his reliance on her; they divorce, and McClaren's career fails until he remarries Gregory. "The authentic Hollywood idiom is captured in this excellent novel as in few others," wrote Seymour Korman in the *Chicago (Sunday) Tribune* (September 21, 1958).

In **An End to Comedy** (Bobbs-Merrill, 1963), a starlet comes of age as an actress while on location in Spain, thanks to her director and to a respected British actress.

ANGELA CARTER (born 1940). **Wise Children** (Farrar Straus Giroux, 1992) contains a chapter on Hollywood. The book was first published in England in 1991 by Chatto & Windus.

DIANA CARTER. *Princess* (G.P. Putnam's Sons, 1971) is pretty much standard fare, a roman à clef about a Hollywood movie star (Grace Kelly) who marries the ruler of a tiny European nation (Prince Rainier of Monaco).

JOHN CARVER. *The Sex Twist* (Beacon Books, 1962) is one of a series of novels with a Hollywood background, identified by Carolyn See as "semipornographic." No other information is available.

VERA CASPARY (1899–1987). *The Rosecrest Cell* (G.P. Putnam's Sons, 1967) is the story of a small Communist cell in a small Connecticut town in the 1930s and early 1940s. A Hollywood screenwriter moves there and joins the "literary" gatherings of the cell, but the Second World War helps him become disaffected with politics. The plotline is obviously influenced by the activities of the House Un-American Activities Committee and the Hollywood Ten.

R. (Ronald) V. (Verlin) CASSILL (born 1919). *Flame* (Arbor House, 1980) is obviously based on the life of Susan Hayward, and in case there should be any doubt the full-color head-and-shoulders drawing on the book's dust jacket bears a remarkable resemblance to the actress. The novel's fictional heroine is Kelly Rayburn, who is brought to Hollywood to test for the role of Scarlett O'Hara in *Gone with the Wind* (as was Hayward). Pregnant, she is ordered by her studio to marry a minor but good-looking "B" picture actor, and has twins. (Hayward married "B" picture actor Jess Barker and gave birth to twins.) When the marriage fails, Rayburn marries a Nashville businessman. When he dies, her career slumps; she appears in a Las Vegas nightclub act, has a brief lesbian fling, and dies of a brain tumor. As did Susan Hayward in *With a Song in My Heart*, the fictional Rayburn appears in a film as a singer confined to a wheelchair, and just as Susan Hayward's greatest film is generally considered to be *I Want to Live*, Rayburn's biggest success is *Let Me Live*. The novel is overwritten, and readers will feel little empathy with the leading character, who comes across as neither a great actress nor a particularly remarkable woman.

MOLLY CASTLE. English Peg and her American-born husband, Steve, must face adjustments in their lives and careers in *New Winds Are Blowing* (Thomas Y. Crowell, 1946). The couple meet as film actors in England but face problems with the Second World War and new careers in Hollywood. Lisle Bell in *Weekly Book Review* (August 18, 1946) commented, "In tracing Peg's spectacular rise to the peaks of romance and equally spectacular skid into the bleak valley of lost allure, *New Winds Are Blowing* boxes the compass in sex relations, and says some very wise things vigorously and entertainingly."

HENRI CATALAN was the pseudonym of Henri Dupuy-Mazuel (1885–19??). In *Soeur Angele and the Ghosts of Chambord* (Sheed & Ward, 1956), the title heroine takes a group of children from broken homes for a walk in the woods near Chambord and finds a member of a film unit dying of poison. "The telling is very brisk and free, as are the sexual relations of the movie crowd," writes Jacques Barzun in *A Catalogue of Crime* (Harper & Row, 1989).

PAMELA CHAIS (born 1930) is the daughter of Hollywood screenwriter F. Hugh Herbert. She has written an entertaining and fast-moving mystery novel in *Final Cut* (Simon and Schuster, 1981), which concerns the murder of Beverly Hills agent D.P. Koenig. Investigating the case is Beverly Hills detective Bud Bacola, who was once a child star, under contract to Koenig, whom he blames (unfairly, as it transpires) for the death of his father. A variety of diverting characters are introduced by the author, including Koenig's personable gay male secretary, a faded Hollywood screenwriter. As he investigates the case, Bacola comes to terms with the end of his acting career and the death of his father; he begins a new personal relationship, and even manages to come to grips with his fear of putting on weight.

PETER CHAMBERS is the pseudonym of Dennis John Phillips. Hollywood private eye Mark Preston investigates the information and funding source for a newspaper that publishes "dirt" on the Hollywood community during the McCarthy era in *Dames Can Be Deadly* (Abelard-Schuman, 1963). It transpires that a respected Hollywood gossip columnist is behind the newspaper and is using blackmail money from Hollywood celebrities to aid ex–Nazis living in South America.

ROBERT W. CHAMBERS (1865–1933) was a prolific and popular novelist in his day (which is long past). Many silent films were based on his books: *The Common Law* (1916), *The Fighting Chance* (1916), *The Girl Phillipa* (1916), *The Fettered Woman* (1917), *The Hidden Children* (1917), *Who Goes There!* (1917), *The Business of Life* (1918), *The Danger Mark* (1918), *The Woman Between Friends* (1918), *The Cambric Mask* (1919), *The Dark Star* (1919), *The Firing Line* (1919), *Even As Eve* (1920), *The Fighting Chance* (1920), *The Restless Sex* (1920), *The Turning Point* (1920), *Unseen Forces* (1920), *Cardigan* (1922), *The Common Law* (1923), and *Between Friends* (1924).

Eris (George H. Doran, 1922) is Eris Odell, the unwanted child of a farmer—he was only interested in having a son—who is named by the delivering doctor after the Greek goddess of discord. At the age of 20, as the First World War comes to a close, she meets an executive of the Crystal Films Corporation who is fishing on her father's land, and obtains a contract with the organization. When the company goes under, Eris is forced to sleep in the open in Central Park, conserving her meager savings of $20. A journalist writes up her story and helps her obtain work as an actress. Eris then goes to Hollywood and becomes a star. She overcomes various problems, including a producer who tries to seduce her and the return of a husband who deserted her on their wedding day. At the novel's close, she marries the journalist and retires from the screen.

While there is little to recommend the novel to modern readers, Chambers does present an interesting line in social commentary. For example, he writes, "There is little to learn in American schools. No notion is more illiterate. And in the sort of school she went to the ignorant are taught by the half educated." The novel is surprisingly free of anti–Semitic comment, and at one point, the journalist notes, "Gentile or Jew—who cares in these days how an educated gentleman worships God? But a Christian blackguard or a Jewish blackguard, there's the pair that are ruining pictures.... Whether they finance a picture, direct it, or exhibit it, these two vermin are likely to do it to death."

DAVID CHANDLER (born 1934). Screenwriter Paul Mather becomes disillusioned with Hollywood in *A Little More Time* (John Day, 1956), tries to kill his movie star wife, and ends up on skid row. He is revitalized as a result of a trip to India and studies under an Anglo-Indian doctor-cum-mystic.

Lengthy courtroom scenes dominate *The Ramsden Case* (Simon & Schuster, 1967), in which a former playwright and Hollywood screenwriter is tried for the murder of a Southern sheriff. The screenwriter had returned to his hometown to make a citizen's arrest of the sheriff whom he thought guilty of the murder of four civil rights workers, and had accidentally shot him as the two struggled for a gun.

The Middleman (Arbor House, 1981) is a lawyer named Burton Z. Hammond, who is a crucial figure in the workings of many studio boardrooms, but whose primary concern is revenge against the man who destroyed his father. "Superficial, simplistic characters and a facile style" was the opinion of Rex E. Klett in *Library Journal* (January 1, 1981).

Kelly (Arbor House, 1982) is Kelly Armstrong, who works her way up from "bit" player to studio production head, using and discarding lovers en route. The story is told from the viewpoints of those men.

RAYMOND CHANDLER (1888–1959). *The Little Sister* (Houghton Mifflin, 1949) is Orfamay Quest of Manhattan, Kansas, who hires private detective Philip Marlowe to find her brother, Orrin. Only after a search through Hollywood does Marlowe discover that Orfamay wants him to locate her brother so she can share in the blackmail money he has obtained from the pair's older sister, who is now a Hollywood leading lady.

ROY CHANSLOR (1899–1964) is best known as the author of *Johnny Guitar*. In *The Naked I* (Crown, 1953), Eve wants her newspaper reporter husband Sam to leave Hollywood and write the Great American Novel. Perversely, when Sam and Eve divorce (and it's a messy one), as a result of Sam's falling in love with Hollywood star Maggy, he does produce the book that Eve wanted. *The Passion Makers* (Universal Distributor, 1962) is identified by Carolyn See as a Hollywood novel.

LESLIE CHARTERIS (1907–93). *The Saint Goes West: Some Further Exploits of Simon Templar* (Doubleday, Doran, 1942) is the twenty-sixth volume in a series that began in 1928 with *Meet the Tiger*. This particular book is a collection of three novellas. In the final story, Templar is signed to play himself on screen, the producer is murdered, and the Saint begins a romance with a film comedienne.

GEORGE RANDOLPH CHESTER (1869–1924) **and LILLIAN CHESTER** (1888–19??) were a husband-and-wife writing team active in films, primarily with the Vitagraph Company, from 1915 to 1923. *On the Lot and Off* (Harper, 1924) is a series of interrelated short stories featuring Izzy Iskowitch, who, at the age of 17, is determined to become a motion picture magnate. The final chapter, "Just Beginning," is concerned with a William Desmond Taylor–like murder, the victim here called Henry Lord Candysh. The authors note, "When the blistering breath of scandal creeps quivering on the air of Hollywood, then all good motion-picture folk and all the bad ones, if there be any such, which is not averred, scurry into the darkest corners, and, falling on their hunker bones, begin crossing themselves madly, gibbering the while; for, lo! we are come on virtuous days when the censorship spirit has written a morality clause into every contract."

ALAN CHEUSE (born 1940). *Candace and Other Stories* (Applewood Press, 1980) consists of a novella and four short stories. The title novella concerns a young girl who comes to Hollywood in the 1930s and goes through vaudeville, marriage to a producer, various samples of sleazy sex, and then dies as the mistress of a Nazi in occupied France.

MARK CHILDRESS (born 1957). The title and the illustration on the dust jacket leave no doubt that *Tender* (Harmony Books, 1990) is a thinly veiled fictionalized life of Elvis Presley, here called Leroy Kirby, from Tupelo, Mississippi. He comes to Memphis and within a year is America's most famous rock 'n' roll singer. A possessive manager watches over young Leroy as he becomes inexorably hooked on drugs and alcohol. The novel closes with his induction into the army following completion of the film *Prisonhouse Blues*.

MARY BLOUNT CHRISTIAN (born 1933). The children's novel *Sebastian (Super Sleuth) and the Stars-in-His-Eyes Mystery* (Macmillan, 1987) has Sebastian stunting for Chummy the Wonder Dog, who is in Hollywood working on a production plagued by "accidents." In case you were in doubt, Sebastian is also a dog.

AGATHA CHRISTIE (1890–1976), the Queen of Crime, kept relatively clear of film-related stories, concentrating on crime in the more restrained atmosphere of the English countryside. At the time of her death, she had written 95 books, which had sold more than 400 million copies, but only two are relevant here. Christie's fourth book, and her third featuring Belgian detective Hercule Poirot, *Poirot Investigates* (Dodd, Mead, 1925), consists of a series of short stories. One is "The Adventures of 'The Western Star,'" in which a famous screen actress, Miss Mary Marvell, asks Poirot's help after receiving three threatening letters. Poirot is also the central character in the other book, *Murder After Hours* (Dodd, Mead, 1946), in which the detective arrives in time for what appears to be a staged murder, involving glamorous film star Veronica Cry.

JILL CHURCHILL. Location shooting and the resultant inconveniences to local residents form the background to the mystery novel *A Knife to Remember* (Avon Books, 1994). The problems are exacerbated by a cast of performers whose careers are at a low ebb. *A Knife to Remember* is the fifth in the series featuring Jane Jeffry.

DIANE CILENTO (born 1933) is an actress who made her screen debut in 1952 and was nominated for an Academy Award for her performance in *Tom Jones* (1963). The first of her two novels is *The Manipulator* (Charles Scribner's Sons, 1967). The title character is film producer Nicholas Jebb, who heads the British delegation to a film festival in Acapulco. He insinuates himself into the lives of a promoter, a screenwriter, a leading lady, and two starlets. "Sexy and scenic" was the general critical opinion at the time of the book's publication.

NOEL CLAD. *Love and Money* (Random House, 1959) is the story of stockbroker Max Armand, from his arrival in the United States as an enemy alien in 1917 through the Second World War. Armand sells stock in various film companies in the 1920s and 1930s, and after the death of his first wife marries a Hollywood star.

The heroine of *Until the Real Thing Comes Along* (Random House, 1961) is able to overcome spinal meningitis and become a Hollywood star in the 1930s, but her chilly personality prevents her from finding true friendship and love. In view of the film industry's longstanding inability to deal with physical handicaps in actors and actresses, this novel is no example of art imitating life.

EDWARD CLARK *see* **RAYMOND L. SCHROCK and EDWARD CLARK**

DONALD HENDERSON CLARKE. *Alabam'* (Vanguard Press, 1934) recounts the adventures of a Southern beauty who hitchhikes to Hollywood and becomes a star. "We recall other novels by Mr. Clarke which contained a livelier interest, racier action and rowdier characters than those of his latest, but were no more faithful in their depiction of a special phase of life than *Alabam'*," wrote a reviewer in the *New York Times* (January 7, 1934). "The story seemed to us artless and commonplace, devoid of distinction, though the character of Ida, that of a winsome dumb-bell, is completely convincing, as are those of various types of Hollywood people by whom she is surrounded."

CLYDE B. CLASON. Against a Hollywood background, Professor Theocitus Lucius Westborough solves a murder involving a bad twin who impersonates his famous brother, in *The Whispering Ear* (Doubleday, Doran, 1938).

MELISSA CLEARY. When two basset hounds are the only witnesses to the murder of their master, Jackie Walsh, a film instructor at fictitious Rodgers University, investigates, in *Dog Collar Crimes* (Diamond, 1993). When the dogs angrily confront the murderer, Walsh is with them, pointing out that they are just as smart as any human. A poorly written novel, strictly for dog lovers.

COLIN CAMPBELL CLEMENTS *see* **FLORENCE RYERSON and COLIN CAMPBELL CLEMENTS**

KATHLEEN CLIFFORD (1876–1963) was a male impersonator on the vaudeville stage in the teens and twenties who starred in a number of films from 1917 through 1928. *It's April—Remember? A Novel of Hollywood* (Exposition Press, 1955) is a roman à clef based on Clifford's years in Hollywood and her marriage to a Yugoslavian.

FRANCES CLIPPINGER. In *The Satellite* (Random House, 1951), Jimmy Keefer is a "pimp and a slob and a sucker." He marries his high school sweetheart, Elinda Bates; she obtains a part in a Broadway show, followed by a film contract. Jimmy follows her to Hollywood and then leaves her.

Darwin Hayes, actor, director, and producer, is the *Rocket in the Night* (Random House, 1954), whose ambition takes him from summer stock to fame in Hollywood, but who ultimately discovers he has sacrificed his integrity in vain. "The sensitivity, knowledge and imagination of a keen observer are obvious in this delineation of an *enfant terrible*," wrote A.H. Weiler in the *New York Times* (April 4, 1954). "Miss Clippinger offers an interested reader a chance to reconstruct prototypes for her hero, Darwin Hayes, and his coterie."

LIZA CODY introduced her likable London private investigator Anna Lee in *Dupe* (Charles Scribner's Sons, 1981). While investigating the past of a fatal accident victim, she talks to many of the victim's friends and employers, most of whom are involved in the film industry. Anna Lee is, of course, the name of a British-born film and soap opera leading lady.

VIRGINIA COFFMAN (born 1914). *The Lombard Cavalcade* (Arbor House, 1982) is the second novel in the saga of the Lombard family of San Francisco; it is long-winded, tedious, and so full of characters that it is virtually impossible for the reader to remember the relationship of one to another. In an unlikely scenario, Tony Lombard is shot down over France while directing a documentary at the close of the Second World War. He takes refuge in Paris with brother and sister Carl and Jany Friedrich, whose parents were both leading players in German silent films. Lombard falls in love with Jany, but she rejects his advances, knowing that he has an actress wife and a daughter back in the United States. Lombard is liberated at just about the same time that Paris is liberated, and the novel's first half comes to close. In part two, Carl and Jany come to San Francisco. Both are anxious to meet producer Leo Prysing, whom their father helped escape from occupied Austria and who supposedly glorified their father's anti–Nazi activities in a film titled *Journey*. Despite the difference in their ages, Jany and Prysing are married. Carl obtains studio work and constantly seeks to view a print of *Journey*. When, eventually, he does so, he discovers that his father was a Nazi collaborator, portrayed in the film by Conrad Veidt. The House Un-American Activities Committee is examining Hollywood's Communist connections, and, in revenge for *Journey*, Carl persuades his former Communist mistress from Paris to come to San Francisco and implicate Prysing. Instead, she meets with Hedda Hopper and implicates Tony Lombard. Carl sacrifices himself to the authorities to save Lombard and returns to Paris. Leo Prysing has a convenient and fatal heart attack after discovering Jany in Lombard's arms, and Lombard's wife conveniently agrees to free him from the marriage.

JAMES COHEN (born 1956). *Through a Lens Darkly* (Donald I. Fine, 1991) is a powerful thriller whose images of violence are in every way as disturbing as those to be seen on screen. Two young filmmakers have made a video documentary on death, using actual footage of car crashes, suicides, murders, and the like. The subject has become an obsession to them; so much so that the novel opens with one of the filmmakers shooting himself on camera. The other is in Iowa filming a public service documentary when he begins to suspect that a local farming family is, in reality, involved in murder. As the filmmaker audio- and videotapes the family, he is drawn into the vortex. It is no longer a matter of recording the life of a serial killer, but rather of becoming his target. The search for and fixation with footage of death leads only to the grave.

ROY OCTAVUS COHEN (1892–1959) was noted for his stories of African American life which, in retrospect, often appear racist in the extreme. *Bigger and Blacker* (Little, Brown, 1925) introduces the Midnight Pictures Corporation, an African American owned and operated concern, and considers the trials and tribulations of its employees. Eight stories are included, the titles demonstrating the puns of which Cohen was so fond: "Every Little Movie," "Double Double," "The Bathing Body," "A Little Child Shall Feed Them," "Inside Inflammation," "Miss Directed," "The Lion and the Uniform," and "Write and Wrong." "His stories, cleverly enough constructed, are never more than farce dyed by an obvious sort of humor; his characters are never more than flashy burlesques of city types," commented the *New York Times* (May 17, 1925).

A further collection of short stories, *Lillies of the Alley* (D. Appleton, 1931), is concerned with the efforts of the Midnight Pictures Corporation to make talkies. "It is not necessary to appraise these stories as any part of true literature about the negro," wrote *Saturday Review of Literature*. "They are highly entertaining sketches of their kind, and Mr. Cohen doubtless claims no more for them."

Cohen also wrote three nonblack novels with film-related storylines. Lawyer Larry Wycoff marries Swedish actress Tyra Karlson in *The Valley of Olympus* (D. Appleton, 1929) so that she can remain in the United States and continue her film career. From a business relationship, the marriage develops into one of love. A detective named Jim Hanvey solves the murder of a mountaineer turned film star in *Star of Earth* (D. Appleton, 1932). *My Love Wears Black* (Macmillan, 1948) is a complex murder mystery in which a movie star and her fiancé discover the body of the former's first husband. Fearful of being implicated in the crime, they pretend ignorance of it but must then deal with the problem of another body's showing up in place of the ex-husband's.

ROBERT COLBY. *The Star Trap* (Fawcett, 1960) is identified by Carolyn See as a Hollywood novel.

MANNING COLES was the pseudonym of British novelists Adelaide Frances Olive Manning and Cyril Henry Coles (1899–1965). With perhaps a slight nod to the film *The Ghost Goes West*, *Far Traveler* (Doubleday, 1956) concerns the efforts of an English film company to shoot the life of Count Graf von Grauhugel at his castle on the Rhine. The ghosts of the Graf and his servant appear to help straighten out some misconceptions about their lives. Seymour Korman in the *Chicago (Sunday) Tribune* (August 12, 1956) thought the players in the novel to be "stock characters with no more depth than extras on a movie screen," but H.H. Holmes in the *New York Herald Tribune* (August 5, 1956) opined that "*Far Traveler* provides the most entertaining glimpse of ghostly activities since Noel Coward's *Blithe Spirit*."

JACKIE COLLINS is the preeminent writer of the contemporary Hollywood novel, of the "sex-drenched, best-selling sleaze" (Joy Fielding in the *Toronto Globe & Mail*) variety. Her novels are flashy television soap operas transferred to the printed page, and, not surprisingly, three of her books—*Chances*, *Hollywood Wifes*, and *Lucky*—have been adapted as television miniseries. Collins published her first novel, *Married Men*, in 1968; her first Hollywood novel was **Hollywood Zoo** (Pinnacle Books, 1971).

Lovers and Gamblers (Fred Jordan Books/Grosset & Dunlap, 1977) features Dallas, who has slept her way to stardom, and Al King, a rock superstar; both are egotists and both are washed-up sexually.

Jackie Collins is one of those contemporary writers who knows how to tease her readers. She teases the mind by introducing a score of characters to keep track of, and by giving only a part of the story of one before moving on to the next. And she teases the genitals by allowing those characters to perform the most outrageous sexual couplings. **Hollywood Wives** (Simon and Schuster, 1983) is pure, unadulterated (but adulterous) Collins. A major Hollywood actor and his wife break up after throwing a glitzy party; he is known for the size of his penis and an affection for women with large breasts. A young stud arrives in town, newly married, and is signed to stardom by a female agent who discovered the first actor. The latter hopes to star in a new film, whose director gets stuck while having intercourse with the actress he would like to have star in that film. The director dies of a heart attack, and his wife, who wrote the film, takes over the direction, only to have the producer cancel it in return for a large insurance payoff. There is much, much more, including a crazed killer who is out to kill half of Hollywood but ends up murdering only the gay assistant to the agent. Gays are treated sympathetically here, but they have to expect to die.

The sequel to *Hollywood Wives* is **Hollywood Husbands** (Simon & Schuster, 1986)—"Trash transcendent," wrote *Kirkus*—which features a 47-year-old soap opera star named Silver Anderson, married to a minor actor/hustler. (Presumably it is only coincidence that Jackie Collins's sister Joan Collins was the star of the soap opera *Dynasty*.) Supporting players in this novel include Silver's brother, a talk show host, whose lover is an Academy Award-winning actress; a studio head with a drug problem; and a musclebound leading man. "The book's clichéd characters and repetitive plot soon grow tiresome," opined *Publishers Weekly* (September 5, 1986).

Lady Boss (Simon & Schuster, 1990) is yet another Hollywood novel. Unbeknownst to her husband, a film comedian, Lucky Santangelo buys Panther Studios, which specializes in sexploitation films. But for six weeks prior to the deal's finalization, Lucky works in the studio as a secretary, finding out what is really going on behind the scenes. Lucky was also featured in *Chances* (1980) and *Lucky* (1985).

American Star (Simon & Schuster, 1993) is the story of three kids from the Midwest, Nick Angelo, his half-sister, Cyndra, and his girlfriend, Lauren Roberts. After various melodramatic trials and tribulations, Nick and Cyndra leave their hometown, and shortly thereafter a tornado conveniently hits, killing off a lot of surplus characters and also destroying a note from Nick to Lauren explaining why he was leaving. Eventually, Nick becomes a big movie star with a wife and daughter. Cyndra dumps her first husband and bigamously marries a second, who helps her become a recording star. Lauren marries an older man and becomes a top model. Conveniently, Nick's wife (who knows a dark secret about his and Cyndra's past) and his daughter are killed in a head-on car crash, Cyndra's first husband bleeds to death, and Lauren's husband decides to leave her for a woman of his own age. At last Nick and Lauren can find happiness together. Now, if only for the reader's sake it could have happened 600 pages earlier.

JOAN COLLINS (born 1933) is a British-born actress who made her screen debut in 1952 and achieved widespread fame in 1981 when she began appearing on the ABC nighttime soap opera *Dynasty*. That soap opera is obviously the basis for *Saga*, which plays a leading part in *Prime Time* (Linden Press/Simon & Schuster, 1988). Five actresses, all with film careers, are tested for the leading role in the soap opera which eventually goes to the English Chloe Carriere. An obsessive fan of one of the actresses murders one of the rivals and is determined to kill Carriere. There is much random sex, the husband of one of the actresses is gay and eventually kills himself when he discovers he has AIDS, and Carriere and her ex–rock star husband are separated but reunited at the novel's close. There is a ragged quality to the plot development, an awkwardness to the story, and characters and situations that seem irrelevant and unnecessary to the storyline. There are minor elements suggestive of a roman à clef—including some incidents obviously based on the author's past—but this is primarily a work of fiction.

Love and Desire and Hate (Linden Press/Simon & Schuster, 1990) provides the perfect combination of intrigue and Hollywood misdoings. Prostitute Ines Dessault falls in love with an English actor, Julian Brooks, and goes with him to Hollywood. Brooks is cast in a feature whose producer Ines had known in wartime Paris as a Fascist Italian officer and thought she had killed. Then the film's Greek director realizes the producer had killed his mother during the war, the film's French ingenue decides to seduce Brooks—and all comes to a head on location in Acapulco. Best line in the novel: "That spring of 1943 the Gestapo seemed to be everywhere in Paris."

RICHARD CONDON (born 1915). *The Ecstasy Business* (Dial Press, 1967) is a Hollywood satire featuring egotistical Hollywood star Tynan Bryson ("an unzipped fly in amber") and his actress wife, Caterina Largo, whom he has married and divorced three times. The couple is making a film in Germany, and a former SS major is threatening Bryson's life. One of the funniest lines concerns plans for a modern screen version of *Uncle Tom's Cabin* in which the film's would-be producer hints that Laurence Olivier would like to play Tom. "A quickly forgotten book" was the opinion of Patricia Stiles in *Library Journal* (October 1, 1967).

EARL CONRAD (1912–86) ghostwrote Errol Flynn's autobiography, *My Wicked, Wicked Ways* (G.P. Putnam's Sons, 1960), and it is very obvious that the title character in *Crane Eden* (Bernard Geis Associates, 1962) is based on Flynn. Eden is an aging Hollywood star on location with his mistress in the Caribbean, and he is desperately trying through drugs, alcohol, stunts, and fistfights to prove that he is still young. His behavior leads to his dying of a heart attack. The book was not well received, with *Library Journal*'s reviewer describing it as "a third-rate imitation of *The Carpetbaggers*."

JANE CONVERSE. A typical romance that manages to embrace both the nursing and Hollywood genres, *Nurse in Hollywood* (New American

Library, 1965) has a Hollywood producer trying to lure a student nurse away from her chosen profession for a career on screen. Of course she rejects the offer.

BRUCE COOK (born 1932). *Rough Cut* (St. Martin's Press, 1990) is the second mystery novel to feature ex–Los Angeles cop and now private investigator Antonio "Chico" Cervantes. Here, he is hired to protect the daughter of a German filmmaker from a gang that plans to kidnap and use her to halt production of her father's film. The background of the novel is the Los Angeles drug trade.

WHITFIELD COOK (born 1909) wrote many television programs and film scripts, notably *Stage Fright* (1950) and *Strangers on a Train* (1951). *Roman Comedy: An Impolite Extravaganza* (Coward-McCann, 1951) is a biting and cruel satire on Hollywood, and concerns a middle-aged movie star who goes to Rome to star in a film, *A Night with Mr. Primrose*, directed by Anna Stagnaro. "It is somewhat prosaically descended from *Once in a Lifetime* and Evelyn Waugh's *The Loved One*," wrote A.H. Weiler in the *New York Times* (July 29, 1951). "The author, in short, seems to be having a high time thumbing his nose while wielding a scalpel."

JOHN BYRNE COOKE (born 1940). *South of the Border* (Bantam Books, 1989) is supposedly authored by Charlie Siringo, a former Texas cowboy and ex–Pinkerton detective who had long pursued Butch Cassidy. In 1919, he is living in Hollywood at a boardinghouse, where he meets a young lady who is featured in Western serials. With her, Siringo goes to Mexico to film *The Trail of Pancho Villa*, meeting both the film's title character and Butch Cassidy. Cooke has researched early Hollywood history, but his primary interest is in what happened to Butch Cassidy, and whether he really did die in Bolivia. Carl Laemmle is the Hollywood producer most mentioned in the novel, whose supposed author, as the real author points out, is not a fictional character but a Pinkerton detective who moved to Hollywood in 1922 and died there in October 1928.

LELAND COOLEY (born 1909). *California* (Stein and Day, 1973) is the saga of a California family which begins in 1839 with the arrival of a 19-year-old sailor from Connecticut. His descendants get involved in railroads, banking, land speculation, and, of course, movies. *The Dancer* (Stein and Day, 1978) is Leya Marks, who dreams of becoming a classical ballerina but is forced to face the grim reality of commercial success as a dancer on the Broadway stage and in Hollywood.

DANE COOLIDGE. A Hollywood millionaire brings in some Hollywood beauties to seduce prospector Snake Bit Jones and find the location of his gold mine in *Snake Bit Jones* (E.P. Dutton, 1936). Some think that the novel was suggested by the legend of Death Valley Scotty, but that seems unlikely.

MORTON COOPER. *The King* (Bernard Geis Associates, 1967) is the story of Italian American pop singer Harry Orlando and his rise to fame. He divorces his wife to marry a movie star and is friendly with a young president and an actor who would like to be president. The novel would appear to be loosely based on the life of Frank Sinatra. *Time* (June 23, 1967) commented that the book's "author and his publisher have aimed confidently at the bestseller list, although Cooper's literary defects and unerring tastelessness would fill an office wastebasket."

Rich People (Evans/J.B. Lippincott, 1977) is a roman à clef based on William Randolph Hearst (here called Adam Scofield) and his dynasty. Marion Davies (Venus Montgomery) is present, and the story brings the saga up to date with Carole Scofield (obviously Patty Hearst) and her kidnapping by the Resistance Army. "Fetid junk," wrote the reviewer in *Library Journal* (May 1, 1977).

Resnick's Odyssey (William Morrow, 1978) is the story of 50-year-old executive Charlie Resnick, who leaves his wife and family to head for California and the decadent Hollywood scene, where he meets up with a porno star.

PARLEY J. (Joseph) COOPER (born 1937). The restaurant in *The Restaurant* (Macmillan, 1979) is where a Mafia assassin has planted a bomb to blow up California governor-elect Raymond Fielding (Jerry Brown). In an adjacent room, two aged movie star sisters, Jeanette and Martine Devore are, as usual, fighting. No prize for identifying their real life counterparts as Olivia de Havilland and Joan Fontaine.

ROBERT COOVER (born 1932) uses the short story form in innovative fashion with *A Night at the Movies* (Linden Press/Simon & Schuster, 1987). The stories are more musings than standard items of fiction, reliant on word-plays, remembered moments from semiforgotten feature films, and a blend of fantasy and reality. The first story, "The Phantom of the Movie Palace," presents the surrealistic vision of a projectionist. In "Cartoon," a cartoon man drives his cartoon car into the cartoon town and runs over a real man. *Brief Encounter* is the basis for "Milford Junction, 1939," and *Casablanca* for "You Must Remember This." Charlie Chaplin is the central character in "Charlie in the House of Rue." Other stories are titled "After Lazarus," "Shootout at Gentry's Junction," "Gilda's Dream," "Inside the Frame," "Lap Dissolves," "Intermission," and "Top Hat."

ALFRED COPPEL (born 1921). Screenwriter Miguel Rinehart fights his conscience in *Night of Fire and Snow* (Simon & Schuster, 1957). The former wife of a childhood friend and now a movie star had persuaded Rinehart to enter the film industry, but now he has doubts as to whether he has made the right decision. Reviews were overwhelmingly negative. *Kirkus* (February 1, 1957) called the novel "uninteresting and routine." S.P. Mansten in the *Saturday Review* (April 6, 1957) wrote, "As a clinical study of a social behavior this novel has its points; as literature it leaves much to be desired."

EDWIN CORLEY (1931–81). *Farewell, My Slightly Tarnished Hero* (Dodd, Mead, 1971) is a roman à clef based on the life of James Dean.

Shadows (Stein and Day, 1975) opens in February 1940 on the night of the Academy Awards presentation. Screenwriter Mitch Gardner joins the celebrities on the train to William Randolph Hearst's party at San Simeon, where he pitches his idea for a film on the Donner party, to star Marion Davies. Hearst agrees to fund the production on the understanding that Gardner's father, a prominent stage actor, will play opposite Davies. After many trials and tribulations, Gardner persuades his father to appear in the film and the production gets under way, but with Gardner's shooting a more realistic film than that approved by his backers. The novel closes with the death of Gardner's father and Hearst's ordering the destruction of the film because it failed to show Marion Davies in a "fairytale" characterization.

A host of film personalities appear as themselves in the novel, including Tallulah Bankhead, John Barrymore, F. Scott Fitzgerald, Errol Flynn, Clark Gable, Judy Garland, Hedda Hopper, Louella Parsons, David O. Selznick, and Spencer Tracy. The dialogue the writer forces them to speak is extremely artificial: whenever a celebrity opens his or her mouth it is to make a comment relating to film history. Gable explains how he won the Oscar for his performance in *It Happened One Night* to Carole Lombard. In the M-G-M commissary, Garland asks the contents of a Charles Laughton sandwich. Gardner, who has been in the film industry for more than a decade, has to ask what MOS (without sound) means. *Shadows* has little to recommend it, for it is exploitive and contrived.

Mitch Gardner returns in **Long Shots** (Doubleday, 1981). He is called to appear before the House Un-American Activities Committee, and, in retrospect, describes the filming of *The Battle of Russia* during the Second World War, and his attempt to make a documentary exposing the Japanese American internment camps in California. A commendable if not totally successful effort.

KATE COSCARELLI. *The Leading Lady* (St. Martin's Press, 1991) of the novel's title is Bunny Thomas, who begins her career in Hollywood as a child star in the 1930s and develops into a popular leading lady, thanks to the efforts of her mother, who is so determined that her daughter succeed that she even permits the child to be sexually abused as an eight-year-old by the studio head. Aside from Bunny and her mother, the third major female character in the novel is Bunny's daughter, Chelsea, the only sensible member of the family, who eventually understands that the only way she can achieve happiness is by turning away from her grandmother and mother; the former eventually dies of cancer, and Bunny kills herself shortly thereafter. A subplot involving Bunny's agent, Hilda Marx, and a diary in which she records various Hollywood secrets is irrelevant to the basic storyline. *Leading Lady* is entertaining and engrossing for two-thirds of its length, but then deteriorates into a saccharine romance, becoming increasingly unbelievable as human kindness toward Chelsea Thomas overflows and overwhelms.

R.J. COSGRIF. *Wastelands* (Wetzel Publishing, 1928) is an early plea for reforestation, sincere but poorly written by an unknown author. The principal character, Rad Shea, had appeared in movies prior to becoming an advocate for reforestation in Oregon.

MICHAEL COVINO has, with his first novel, *The Negative* (Viking, 1993), produced a witty and original black comedy, which displays a cynicism and a healthy disrespect for the film industry of the 1990s. Recently released from prison, a white-collar criminal is approached by a bumbling film professor with a unique proposal. The two of them will steal the original negative of director Doug Lowell's new film just before it is sent to the laboratory for release prints to be made. The film professor is certain that Lowell will pay for the negative's return rather than approach the police. Unfortunately for the pair, Lowell has serious doubts about the artistic value of his new work, into which he has sunk most of his personal fortune, and the "kidnapping" of the negative is most opportune. He will allow the pair to destroy the negative and claim his investment back from the insurers. In a desperate effort to prove to Lowell that his film is worthwhile, the pair then kidnaps a couple of film critics named Alfred Egert and Morgan Meany, who have become household names through television. The film critics like the film greatly, but professional conduct prohibits their reviewing a film prior to its release. The plot becomes more confused as the reader learns of an earlier relationship between Lowell and the film professor, and between Lowell and the film professor's girlfriend. Unfortunately, Covino cannot sustain the fun through to the end, and the book's final chapters are a little disappointing.

The story is narrated, in turn, by the white-collar criminal and by Lowell. The latter is a megalomaniacal bearded filmmaker who hangs out on an isolated estate just outside San Francisco. Perhaps coincidentally, the author once worked as a reader for Francis Ford Coppola. A short piece of dialogue between Lowell and the white-collar criminal will help the reader appreciate Covino's fine understanding of the manner in which Hollywood works:

"I'll still be able to work. . . . They gave Spielberg work after *1941*. They gave Cimino work after *Heaven's Gate*. They gave Coppola work after *One from the Heart*—"

"They gave Polanski work after he screwed that child."

"Never an issue. What counts is they gave Polanski work after *Pirates*."

The Negative may well be destined to become a classic Hollywood novel. Doug Lowell is no Sammy Glick, but he is the stereotypical indolent and arrogant Hollywood filmmaker of the 1990s.

BOB COX. *Jamaican American* (Quail Street, 1976) concerns six graduates from the University of Southern California of mixed ethnic and racial heritage. The female of the group, who wants to prove that a woman can be "more than a baby machine," forms a talent agency and signs up the others as a novelist, screenwriter, actor, cinematographer, and so forth, to make a film with a football theme. "There ought to be a law to prevent books this bad from being published," opined Frances Seamster in *Library Journal* (October 1, 1976). "The language is stilted and full of clichés. Unreadable."

WILLIAM R. COX (1901–88). Private detective Tom Kincaid investigates a drug-related murder that takes place in Nevada, where a Hollywood film crew is on location, in *Death on Location* (New American Library, 1962).

GEORGE HARMON COXE (born 1901) wrote a series of mystery novels featuring a Boston newspaper photographer and part-time detective,

Kent Murdock. In *The Glass Triangle* (Alfred A. Knopf, 1940), Murdock's photographs of a film director who is later murdered help to identify the killer among various members of the Hollywood community in Boston for the preview of the director's latest (and last) film.

NONA COXHEAD. *The Richest Girl in the World* (Doubleday, 1978) is Lily Boeker, and one of her many husbands is a film star named George. The story runs from 1927 to the present and may have been suggested by the life of Barbara Hutton.

THOMAS CRAIG. In *Playing with Cobras* (HarperCollins, 1993), a British secret service agent in India is held for the murder of his mistress, a famous Indian movie star and the wife of the prime minister. Now he must prove his innocence.

ROBERT CRAIS. *Lullaby Town* (Bantam Books, 1992) is the third mystery novel to feature Los Angeles private investigator Elvis Cole, a likable guy, the story of whose exploits is always well written and entertaining. Here he is hired by a brilliantly obnoxious director named Peter Alan Nelsen to find his divorced wive and 12-year-old son, whom he has not seen in as many years. Cole finds the couple, but the wife has gotten herself involved with the Mafia, and as the detective tries to sort everything out Nelsen arrives on the scene, incapable of understanding that powerful as he may be in Hollywood he is no match for the Mafia. In the climax, Nelsen is forced physically to defend his ex-wife and son, and for the first time becomes a real man as opposed to a Hollywood creation. Perhaps the scenes at Paramount studios with Nelsen, his yes-men, and a cringing executive are somewhat overdrawn, but who knows...

LINDA CRAWFORD (born 1938). *Something to Make Us Happy* (Simon & Schuster, 1978), Crawford's second novel, is the story of a couple from Scotland who settle in Detroit. The wife is obsessed with the movies and heads for Hollywood in 1932, daily visiting Pickfair, meeting with Tallulah Bankhead, collecting movie memorabilia, and even wearing black to her son's wedding because she is still in mourning for Rudolph Valentino.

JOHN CREASEY (1908–73) wrote a vast quantity of mystery novels, including the Toff series (1938–39), the Inspector Roger "Handsome" West series (1942–78), the Sexton Blake series (1937–43), and the Dr. Palfrey series (1942–79). Under one of his many pseudonyms, J.J. Marric, he wrote the Gideon series (1953–76), and as Anthony Morton, the Baron series (1937–79). A number of films have been based on Creasey novels, notably John Ford's *Gideon's Day/ Gideon of Scotland Yard* (1958).

A Part for a Policeman (Charles Scribner's Sons, 1970) is typical Creasey fare. While watching a film with his wife, Janet, Inspector West is called to investigate the murder of the movie's star, Danny O'Hara. A second film star, Raymond Greatorex, is attacked, and there are two additional murders, including that of a policeman, before West discovers the murderer and the crime—related to the smuggling of foreign currency and the fencing of stolen goods. Along the way, West visits the Borelee Studios (presumably named after Borehamwood Studios on the outskirts of London) and is privy to the workings of a security force on the lot. The motive behind the various attacks and murders is more than a little difficult to follow, and even at the novel's conclusion it is not always clear what has been taking place.

See also **ROBERT CAINE FRAZER.**

EDMUND CRISPIN was the pseudonym of Bruce Montgomery (1921–78), and the author of the classic 1946 British mystery novel *The Moving Toyshop*. While **Frequent Hearses** (Dodd, Mead, 1950) is neither as witty nor as inventive as the former, it does feature the same hero in the shape of Oxford don Gervase Fen and contains many amusing literary allusions and comments. For example, the author describes *The Ambassadors* as "narcotic," and continues, "I always feel that Henry James ought to be dealt with in the Dangerous Drugs Act, and perhaps used in childbirth as an alternative to trilene."

Here, Gervase Fen is at the Long Fulton studio, just outside London, serving as an adviser on a film based on the life of Alexander Pope. Since Bruce Montgomery's primary occupation was that of a film composer, the author is able to provide some caustic commentary on the workings of the film industry. He details the activities of a music department and the technicalities of film scoring, and has the principal female character in the story active in the music department. The plotline concerns the suicide of a young actress and the revenge killings of a leading lady, a cameraman, and a director, all siblings, each of whom had contributed to the girl's taking her own life. Neither Gervase Fen nor the author offers much sympathy toward the murder victims, but whether this is because they were relatively heartless or typical of the film community is not entirely clear. What is apparent is that Fen is as much at home in the unreal world of filmmaking as in his ivory tower at Oxford.

FREEMAN WILLS CROFT (1879–1957) wrote a series of mystery novels featuring Inspector Joseph French of Scotland Yard. Known in the United Kingdom as *The Box Office Murders*, **The Purple Sickle Murders** (Harper, 1929) concerns the murder of three women employed as cashiers in English cinemas, with the killings related to counterfeiting.

HERBERT CROOKER. In *The Hollywood Murder Mystery* (Macaulay, 1930), when lovely star Berylyn Bovary is murdered following a Hollywood party, blithe criminologist Clay Brooke unmasks the killer. "Movie fans should enjoy the story, but judged by the standards of first rate mystery fiction the book is a sad affair," commented the *New York World* (May 18, 1930).

HOMER CROY (1883–1963) was a novelist whose works were frequently made into films in the 1920s and 1930s; he wrote his autobiography, *Country Cured*, in 1943, and also authored two filmed-related nonfiction books: *How Motion Pictures Are Made* (1918) and *Star Maker: The Story of D. W. Griffith* (1959).

Headed for Hollywood (Harper & Brothers, 1932) concerns Pearl Piper of Iowa, who wins the Tri-State Motion Picture Beauty contest and comes to Hollywood with her Aunt Minnie and her father, Andy (who operates a medicine show). She makes a test for Auditone, is given a small part in its production of *Chapped Knees*, but at the film's premiere, she discovers her role has been cut. With his anti–Semitism and blundering, Andy does little to help his daughter, but Pearl makes the rounds of the studios and registers with central casting. The family takes in a lodger, a minor actress named Ginger O'Day, who eventually kills herself—"That's Hollywood," says Andy bitterly. Pearl begins dating Joe, the son of Auditone's head, Nat Gumpertz, and he gives her a small part in his epic *War Bonnets*. Joe's father is opposed to the couple's marriage plans, as is Andy, who persuades Pearl's Iowa sweetheart, Gene, to come to Hollywood. As the family becomes disillusioned with the Hollywood scene, Nat Gumpertz helps Andy make a film about his patent medicine and modernize the medicine show with the introduction of a motion picture presentation. The family is ready to return to Iowa.

Headed for Hollywood is wonderfully evocative of the period as the Piper family explores Hollywood and its environs, and Homer Croy's descriptive passages are excellent. Of Hollywood Boulevard, he writes, "All life seemed to flow into it and in some miraculous manner to be renewed, like blood in the lungs." Nat and Joe Gumpertz are presumably based on Carl Laemmle, the head of Universal, and his son, Junior.

E.V. CUNNINGHAM is the pseudonym of Howard Fast (born 1914), who introduced his highly original mystery novel hero, Detective Sargeant Masao Masuto of the Beverly Hills Police Department, in **Samantha** (William Morrow, 1967). The lady of the title was a Hollywood hopeful of a decade or more ago, and the men with whom she slept in the hope of obtaining a screen role are being murdered one by one. To add to the mystery that Masuto must unravel, each of the men is married to a woman who might be Samantha.

Angel, the wife of film star Mike Barton, is kidnapped in **The Case of the Kidnapped Angel** (Delacorte Press, 1982). When Barton goes to deliver the ransom money, he is shot, and then Angel and her chauffeur are murdered. In a complicated plot solution, Masuto discovers that Angel (a former man who had undergone a sex change operation) killed Mike; the latter's business partner killed the chauffeur; and Barton's lover/secretary murdered Angel in revenge for her killing of Mike.

TONY CURTIS (born 1925) was a popular Hollywood leading man whose career has diminished in recent years. Among his better films are *Houdini* (1953), *The Sweet Smell of Success* (1957), *The Defiant Ones* (1958), and *Some Like It Hot* (1959). His first novel, **Kid Andrew Cody & Julie Sparrow** (Doubleday, 1977) is the story of two young men who, unbeknownst to each other, have the same father. Cody (who is perhaps very loosely based on the author) grows up to become a stuntman and later a Hollywood star. He has a long-running and vicious feud with a female gossip columnist whom he punches in the face. Sparrow opens a casino in Las Vegas and dies in a gun battle with the New York gangster for whom he had once worked. At times the dialogue and sexual situations are unnecessarily crude. There are too many incidents irrelevant to the basic storyline, and an inadequate development of characters. At the end, the reader is left wondering what it was all about. All in all, this is a confused and confusing novel that needed either heavy editing or a collaborative hand.

DAN CUSHMAN (born 1909). ***Brothers in Kickapoo*** (McGraw-Hill, 1962) is a satire on small-town American life. A middle-aged insurance agent in a Midwestern town persuades an overbudgeted Hollywood production company to make a film there. Martin Levin in the *New York Times* (April 29, 1962) described the novel as "a fresh rendering of life in a small American town."

STAN CUTLER (born 1925) has written three mystery novels featuring gay ghostwriter Mark Bradley and straight Hollywood private detective Rayford Goodman. The chapters in these books are alternatively narrated by each of these two, and both novels are notable for complex if ultimately tedious plots. ***Best Performance by a Patsy*** (Dutton, 1991) has Bradley hired to write Goodman's autobiography, which is concerned mainly with his solving a celebrated murder case of the 1960s. As the two men work together on the book, it becomes obvious that he wrong man was convicted. In ***The Face on the Cutting Room Floor*** (Dutton, 1991), Goodman is asked by a Mafia figure, introduced in the previous novel, to protect an aging Hollywood director, and Bradley begins work on the same director's autobiography. The director is the second person killed in a long series of murders that pepper the book.

In ***Shot on Location*** (Dutton, 1993), the son of an Oscar-winning actor confesses to the murder of his sister's lover. Goodman and Bradley reunite to write the true story, but there are complications when the son recants his confession, and Goodman finds himself on the jury trying the man for murder. "Cutler's real talent for light banter and heavy plotting gets lost in the shuffle," commented *Kirkus* (December 1, 1992). "The guy needs a good coauthor."

MARY DAHEIM (born 1937) has written a series of mystery novels featuring editor Emma Lord and all set in Alpine, Washington. In ***The Alpine Betrayal*** (Ballantine, 1993), Hollywood star Dani Marsh returns home to Alpine to shoot a film, and an ex-husband turns homicidal.

SANDRA DALLAS (born 1939). ***Buster Midnight's Café*** (Random House, 1990) is the simple story of a girl from Butte, Montana, who is seen in a Movietone News item and given a screen test, and then she becomes a Hollywood star in the 1930s. Her childhood boyfriend becomes a boxer, follows her to Hollywood, and kills an actor who beats her up. After a short prison term, the friend returns to Butte, where the star finances his diner, Buster Midnight's Café. The star dies at the height of her fame. What makes *Buster Midnight's Café* stand out among similar Hollywood novels is that it is written in narrative form by a female childhood friend now in late middle age. The author has a marvelous ear for how a typical small town woman from Montana might speak and write — "Hollywood was not the fine place you might think" — and fills her story with fascinating details of life in Montana in the 1920s, 1930s, and 1940s.

BLANCHE D'ALPUGET (born 1944), like the central character in ***Winter in Jerusalem*** (Simon & Schuster, 1986), is an Australian. Her heroine,

Danielle, is also a screenwriter who returns to her birthplace, Israel, after a 30-year absence to write a film based on the mass suicide at Masada. She reunites with her father and gets romantically involved with Bernie, the film's ruthless director. The story is played out against a background of Israeli politics. "In sum," wrote *Kirkus*, "a startling, searching and sinewy novel, alive with a tortuous-to-fantastic 'laminate of clans,' old stones resting on the past's 'lake of human blood,' all under the miraculous skies of Jerusalem."

MORAY DALTON. In the mystery novel *The Condamine Case* (Low, Marston, 1947), English Detective Inspector Collier investigates two murders that take place during the filming of a story of sixteenth-century witch-hunting in the West of England.

NORMAN DANIELS. *Suddenly by Shotgun* (Fawcett, 1960) is identified by Carolyn See as a Hollywood novel.

CHARLES MICHAEL DAUGHERTY (born 1914). *Let 'Em Roll* (Junior Literary Guild/Viking Press, 1950) is a novel for a teenage readership, in which young Josh Beacon spends a summer in Hollywood with his famous director-uncle Tex, and pursues his ambition to become a film director. Josh's experiences in Hollywood help awaken his interest in American history.

DAVID DAVIDSON (1908–85). *The Quest of Juror 19* (Doubleday, 1971) chronicles the growing bitterness of a television and film director who serves on a New York grand jury and begins to contemplate a special crime that he might commit. A portion of the book is concerned with the central character's direction of a telethon.

During the filming of a documentary on the scrapping of a World War II aircraft carrier, relations among the film crew, veterans, and war protesters become tense in *We Few, We Happy Few* (Crown, 1974).

LIONEL DAVIDSON (born 1922). *Murder Games* (Coward, McCann & Geoghegan, 1978) is a tense thriller involving a series of murders in Chelsea, with the victims' initials matching those of literary figures who lived in the London borough. While the murders are taking place, three young men of doubtful sexual persuasion are trying to produce a modern "silent" film in the area. The police, and the reader, determine that one of the three is a killer, which is true—but not the likeliest suspect. This novel was originally published in the United Kingdom in 1978 by Jonathan Cape under the title *The Chelsea Murders*, and was reprinted in the United States under that same title by Penguin Books in 1980.

SARA DAVIDSON (born 1943). *Friends of the Opposite Sex* (Doubleday, 1984) is described by its publisher as a novel for the 1980s. It is a study of relationships as two filmmakers, Lucy Rosser and Joe Sachs, meet, become lovers, and try to fashion a permanent relationship as they work together as coproducers for Rosser-Sachs Films.

ROBERTSON DAVIES (born 1913) is a distinguished Canadian novelist, playwright, and critic. He is also obviously a film buff, with several of his books using the motion picture as a springboard for the development of the story.

World of Wonders (Viking Press, 1976) is the name of a traveling carnival in which the central character, magician Magnus Eisengrim, worked as a teenager. He is starring in a BBC film, *Un Hommage à Robert Houdin*, playing the central character of the pioneering French illusionist, and as the film is being made in Switzerland and London, he tells his two closest friends the story of his life. He is encouraged by the film's director, who views Eisengrim's life as a subtext for his film, just as it proves to be a subtext for the novel's central theme of who killed the man who as a child threw a snowball at Eisengrim's mother, thus resulting in a premature birth. The emphasis here is on carnival, vaudeville, and the legitimate stage rather than the motion picture.

Murther & Walking Spirits (Viking Press, 1991) demonstrates Davies's belief in the words of Samuel Butler that "Where Murthers and Walking Spirits meet, there is no other Narrative can come near." When "Gil" Gilmartin, the entertainment editor of a Toronto newspaper is murdered by his wife's lover, his spirit attends the screenings of a retrospective at the city's international film festival. The films he views are real—*The Spirit of '76* (1917), *Shadows of [Our] Forgotten Ancestors* (1964), *The Master Builder* (1939), and *Scenes from a Marriage* (1973)—but their contents are changed by the author to provide a panoramic history of the Gage family, which flees revolutionary New York to start a new life in Canada, and marries into the Gilmartin family.

FITZROY DAVIS (1912–80). *Through the Doors of Brass* (Dodd, Mead, 1974) refers to the doors of a Hollywood studio, which in this novel would appear to be M-G-M. The two principal characters are introduced attending a performance of Chekhov's *The Sea Gull* at the Biltmore Theatre in downtown Los Angeles. Paul Ellison is a top Hollywood director, who wants to make a film of Chekhov's *The Cherry Orchard*, starring a retired Hollywood star. When she rejects the part, he realizes that he should continue to make the sort of commercial productions for which he is best known and which his studio expects him to direct. Violet Lang is a once-great Hollywood star who has been blacklisted for a couple of years as a result of her behavior, not clearly defined but part of which involved morality. She is now married to a successful businessman and realizes that to keep her marriage secure she must accept a part in a B picture to be produced by a poverty row studio. The story takes place in Hollywood in the late 1940s, when the suggestion of a film based on a Russian play immediately generates concerns about Communism. The Hollywood studios pay too much attention to the gossip columnists and to the inhabitants of Los Angeles, about whom Ellison comments, "Why should you judge all America by those people? They aren't average Americans, believe me; they are the off-scourings of the whole country."

Through the Doors of Brass is not particularly well written. It is a little reactionary, a little in need of a stronger storyline, and, unfortunately, a little dull.

GWEN DAVIS (born 1936). *The Aristocrats* (Playboy Press/Simon & Schuster, 1977) is a confused novel—with plenty of incest, drug use, and lesbianism—involving serial killings and the production of a major motion picture. It illustrates Davis's reputation, as described by *Kirkus*, as "a kind of poor woman's Jacqueline Susann writing novels with a scene, a lot of characters and sluttish sex." Additionally, *Naked in Babylon* (New American Library, 1960) is identified by Carolyn See as a Hollywood novel.

KENN DAVIS and JOHN STANLEY (born 1940). Humphrey Bogart and friends are involved in stopping a plot to blow up the 1948 Academy Awards presentation in *Bogart '48* (Dell, 1980).

MAGGIE DAVIS. Sheik Abdullah al Asmari is sent to Hollywood on a bank-buying mission by his father, the Emir of Rahsmani, in *The Sheik* (William Morrow, 1977). There he has a good time thanks in large part to his friend, an Egyptian movie star named Ali Hassan, but he is quickly recalled when a revolution breaks out in Rahsmani.

NORBERT DAVIS. Hollywood plays only a secondary role in *Sally's in the Alley* (William Morrow, 1943) as the Justice Department hires a private eye to locate a miner in the Mojave Desert who knows the location of an ore deposit. Helping the private eye is movie star Susan Sally. "A rich morsel for readers who like them tough and raucous," opined *Time* (October 11, 1943). "Rarely have homicide and detection been made more entertaining" was the opinion of Isaac Anderson in the *New York Times* (September 26, 1943).

PATTI DAVIS (born 1952) attracted considerable controversy when she published *A House of Secrets* (Birch Lane Press, 1991), the intense story of a young girl's growing up in southern California with a domineering mother and a passive father. A study of emotional and psychological abuse within an affluent family, the novel has no Hollywood theme, aside from its Los Angeles setting, but is worthy of note since the author is the youngest daughter of actor-turned-president Ronald Reagan and has perhaps some reality in the background of Patti Davis's childhood.

There has been no published reaction from Ronald and Nancy to their daughter's novel *Bondage* (Simon & Schuster, 1993), whose costume designer heroine has a sadomasochistic relationship with a rebel film director. After the director has bound and humiliated her in his dungeon in front of a producer and assorted friends, the costume designer decides it is time to curb her sexual appetite. According to *Kirkus* (November 15, 1993), "Former First Daughter Davis has churned out a gloriously self-serious saga of sexual power and dependency that's neither as explicit nor as psychologically penetrating as *9½ Weeks*—much less the *Story of O*—but represents instead a triumph of marketing over insight and style."

ANNABEL DAVIS-GOFF (born 1942). *Night Tennis* (Coward, McCann & Geoghegan, 1978) opens the day before Julia's forty-third birthday. Like all the characters in the novel, Julia has no last name. She is directing a film at Pinewood Studios in England, having problems with an aging romantic actor and an arrogant, unintelligent French actress, and coping in part thanks to the loyalty of her friend, Catherine, the film's costume designer, who is having an affair with a major Hollywood star named James. Back in Beverly Hills is Julia's teenage son by her first marriage, Mark, and her husband, Christopher, with whom she no longer has a sexual relationship and of whose extramarital activities she is fully aware. Into Julia's life comes 20-year-old Nick, the stepson of the French actress, and the pair begin an affair despite the difference in their ages. After a brief sojourn with her husband at the Cannes Film Festival, Julia realizes she is still in love with Nick. He follows her to Los Angeles, and later to Bakersfield where she is filming a television movie with James. After an angry confrontation, Nick and Julia break up. Christopher confronts Julia with the affair, but she reminds him of his infidelities. The novel concludes as Julia is about to receive a meaningless award for the film she shot in England, the editing of which was taken away from her by the producer.

Few novels are able to examine and analyze a relationship between an older woman and a younger man as does *Night Tennis*. The two major female characters, Julia and Catherine, are beautifully delineated; the author also examines the basic selfishness of each of the male characters. Further, the novel provides the best fictional portrait yet of film production in an English studio, the vagaries of the crew, the obstacles of the unions. *Night Tennis* deserves recognition as one of the classic film novels of recent decades.

LILLIAN DAY (1893–19??). *The Youngest Profession* (Doubleday, Doran, 1940) is the diary of a 16-year-old movie fan named Jane, who vigorously stalks film stars in an effort to collect their autographs. In 1943 the novel was adapted as a stageplay, *A Woman of Fifteen*, and also filmed by M-G-M under the original title, directed by Edward Buzzell, and starring Jean Porter (as Jane) and Virginia Weidler (as her friend Barbara).

LESLIE DEANE. *The Girl with the Golden Hair* (Jove, 1978) is Darla Dawson, who rises from a model to a television spokeswoman for a mouthwash to the star of a television adventure series to the dream of millions of red-blooded American males. Could this possibly be the veiled life story of one of the stars of "Charlie's Angels"? "The 'inside info' on the entertainment industry is shoddy. A real turkey" was the considered opinion of Joyce Smothers in *Library Journal* (November 15, 1978).

ANNE de BOLENE. *Voyage to Eros* (Berkeley Publishing, 1962) is one of a series of novels with a Hollywood background, identified by Carolyn See as "semi-pornographic." No other information is available.

LEN DEIGHTON (born 1929). *Close-Up* (Atheneum, 1972) is a change of pace for an author best known for his spy thrillers. The novel recounts the life of a British screen star named Marshall Stone as it is seen by biographer Peter Anson, who just happens to be married to Stone's ex-wife. The book indicates a strong dislike by Deighton for the film industry, which he perceives as hypocritical, squalid, and devoid of intelligence. As Arthur Cooper wrote in *Newsweek* (January 26, 1972), Deighton "believes the film industry is run by cretins who pander to youth and who would be content to turn out nothing but trash as long as it turned out a profit. ... We can share Deighton's concern without accepting his art."

MAURICE DEKOBRA was the pseudonym of Maurice Tessier (1885–1973). *The Madonna in Hollywood* (T. Werner Laurie, 1945) was first published in New York in 1943 as *La Madone à Hollywood* and is a sequel to *La Madone des Sleepings: Roman Cosmopolite* (1925)/*The Madonna of the Sleeping Cars* (1927). English noblewoman Lady Diana Wyndham leaves her French convent, helps an RAF pilot escape from the Nazis, and comes to Hollywood to make a propaganda film. While there, she coproduces *A Carnival of Ghosts*, a comedy based on *Hamlet*, and then returns to her convent.

JEFFREY DELL (1899–1985) was a writer and contributor to *Punch*; he became a film director in his native United Kingdom in 1943. Dell's first novel, *Nobody Ordered Wolves* (Heinemann, 1939), is described by *Contemporary Authors* as "a well-regarded comedy about filmmaking." The novel was reviewed in the April 27, 1940, edition of *Motion Picture Herald*, and the central character was, apparently, based on producer/director Alexander Korda.

GORDON DeMARCO. *The Canvas Prison* (Germinal Press, 1982) is set in 1949 and has private eye Riley Kovachs investigating rumors that Frances Farmer, held in a mental institution, is to be lobotomized. Screenwriter Dalton Trumbo is in some way involved, and the whole plot is linked to the Hollywood Ten.

PHYLLIS GORDON DEMAREST. There is little film-related material in *Children of Hollywood* (Macaulay, 1929). The story involves Boy Kent and Toni Martin of Hollywood, who are in love with each other but marry elsewhere. Eventually, after several years of unhappiness, they are reunited through the sacrifice of Kent's wife. "*Children of Hollywood* has, at best, only a spurious and imperfect kind of life," opined the reviewer in the *New York Times* (January 20, 1929).

Hollywood Gold (Macauley, 1930) is a typical Hollywood romance, perhaps a little more daring than many of the period. Eden is a Hollywood extra who becomes a script girl, thanks in part to the support of a tough director named Julian Falcon. She is attracted to an extra named Terry O'Day, brings him to the attention of Falcon, and the two become lovers. When O'Day is featured opposite Gay Maynard, the latter decides to seduce him, interested in the fact that at the age of 35 he will inherit a fortune from his father's estate. O'Day leaves Eden and marries Maynard, unaware that Eden is pregnant. Falcon takes an interest in Eden and is able to promote her as a screenwriter at his studio. Accidentally, Maynard kills Falcon, but it is O'Day who is tried for the crime. He is acquitted, but both he and Maynard are blacklisted by the studios. After discovering that his wife is having an affair with an English film promoter, O'Day decides to divorce her, but she agrees to the divorce only after Eden threatens to expose her as the murderer of Falcon. Demarest obviously knows of what she writes, explaining carefully to the reader what is required of an extra and a script girl. At one point she brings the story to a halt for a two-page discussion of the Vitaphone sound-on-disc system.

WILLIAM DEMBY (born 1922) is the narrator of *The Catacombs* (Pantheon, 1965). The principal character is Doris, whom Demby meets in Rome while she is playing one of Elizabeth Taylor's handmaidens in *Cleopatra*. Both Davis and Demby are African Americans, and he writes a diary of Doris's life. She is introduced to an Italian count, becomes his mistress, and is made pregnant by him. Unfortunately, the diary Demby keeps is as much a critical commentary on America and its politics from 1962 to 1964 as it is a diary of Doris's work in *Cleopatra*.

HENRY DENKER (born 1912). *The Director* (Richard W. Baron, 1970) is a roman à clef based on the making of *The Misfits* (here called *Mustang!*), starring Clark Gable (Preston Carr) and Marilyn Monroe (Daisy O'Donnell), on location in Nevada. The main difference between *The Misfits* and *Mustang!* is that the former was directed by John Huston, who bears no resemblance to the novel's new wave director, Jock Finley. *The Kingmaker* (David McKay, 1972) is a roman à clef that raises issues most in Hollywood would prefer not to know about. The central character is Dr. Isadore Cohen (obviously Dr. Jules Stein), who builds a major talent agency, Talent Corporation of America, or TCA (Music Corporation of America, or MCA). As the agency enters television and film production, it needs an industry figure to help fight charges of monopoly, and finds such an individual in Jeff Jefferson, a "has-been" actor (obviously Ronald Reagan). Dr. Cohen builds Jefferson into a major political figure—and we all know what happens next. *The Starmaker* (Simon and Schuster, 1977) is the story of Hollywood mogul H.P. Koenig of Magna Pictures, and his protégé, David Cole. Koenig is obviously based on Louis B. Mayer. Cole is not Irving Thalberg—there is no character resemblance, and a Thalberg-like figure has just died prior to Cole's joining Magna in 1947. *The Actress* (Simon and Schuster, 1978) is Kit Lawrence of the theater, rather than motion pictures, who stars in a play based on her life and personal problems in an effort to come to terms with her inner conflicts.

CHARLES DENNIS (born 1946). *Bonfire* (Dell, 1979) is the story of actor Alan Farrel, beginning in the slums of New York in 1937 and ending in 1951 with him as a major star whose wife has the capacity to destroy him.

PATRICK DENNIS was the pseudonym of Edward Everett Tanner III (1921–76), who also wrote as Virginia Rowans. He is best known as the author of *Auntie Mame* (1955), which was adapted as a 1956 Broadway show and filmed in 1958. A musical version opened on Broadway in 1966 and was filmed in 1974. Under his own name, Tanner was drama critic of *The New Republic* from 1957 to 1971.

The title of *Little Me: The Intimate Memoirs of That Great Star of Stage, Screen and Television Belle Poitrine* (E.P. Dutton, 1961) says it all, as does the dedication to those actresses who have written their memoirs "and those whose life stories will follow." The book is the ultimate parody of show business autobiographies, with a witty text and equally amusing posed photographs. There is a gay undertone to the novel which some readers may find slightly infantile. A musical adaptation of *Little Me*, with book by Neil Simon, music by Cy Coleman, and lyrics by Carolyn Leigh, opened on Broadway at the Lunt-Fontanne Theatre on November 17, 1962, with the multitalented Sid Caesar playing a variety of roles.

Acapulco is the setting for *Paradise* (Harcourt Brace Jovanovich, 1971), which is similar in style and construction to *Auntie Mame,* and which features Liz Parkhurst Martinez, who has a penchant for marrying the wrong man. Also included in the cast of characters is an aging actor, Rex Roman, noted as the Tarzan of the screen.

Genius (Harcourt Brace Jovanovich, 1962) has director Leander Starr checking into a Mexico City hotel operated by one of his ex-stars, and, despite the intrusion of an Internal Revenue Service agent, making an art film on a shoestring budget in a single week. In the *New York Herald Tribune* (October 21, 1962), R.D. Spector wrote, "He [Dennis] has little concern for credibility and less for the niceties of character delineation. But with great gusto and a genuine gift for creating the wild and boisterous scene, farcical situations, and bizarre settings, he can't miss."

JANE DENTINGER (born 1951) introduced actress–private detective Jocelyn O'Roarke in *Murder on Cue* (Crime Club/Doubleday, 1983). In the fourth novel in the series, *Dead Pan* (Viking, 1992), O'Roarke is invited to Hollywood by friend Austin Frost to appear in a television movie. No sooner does she arrive on the set than the director of photography is murdered. O'Roarke is assisted in her efforts to find the killer by a male studio hairdresser, who, cast against stereotype, is not gay. O'Roarke returned to the theatrical world for her next mystery, *The Queen Is Dead* (Viking, 1994).

BARRY DEVLIN. *Song of the Whip* (Beacon Books, 1952) is one of a series of novels with a Hollywood background, identified by Carolyn See as "semi-pornographic." No other information is available.

THOMAS B. (Blanchard) DEWEY (born 1915). *The Case of the Chased and the Unchaste* (Random House, 1959) has a Chicago detective known as "Mac" investigating the kidnapping of the child of a Hollywood producer. In *The Taurus Trip* (Simon & Schuster, 1970), Mac is asked by a former silent film star to find out what the problem is facing a fellow actor who shares her home. An old Hollywood murder forms the background to the plot.

KAREN De WOLF. *Take the Laughter* (Bobbs-Merrill, 1941) is the story of a young girl from the Midwest who is determined to become a Hollywood star. She achieves success as a writer, and then must decide among the three men in her life. "Most of the complicated story is revealed in dialogue, fortunately of the kind commonly described as brittle. Much of it is both naughty and amusing," wrote Charlotte Dean in the *New York Times* (March 9, 1941).

WEED DICKINSON. A studio public relations man goes to Mexico to retrieve a drunken film actress but finds only her double in *Dead Man Talks Too Much* (J.B. Lippincott, 1937). When the son of the director turns up murdered, apparently by the star, the public relations man has more to deal with than he bargained for. Will Cuppy in the *New York Herald Tribune* (November 14, 1937) called this "a good-natured carefree picture of screen people on the loose."

JOAN DIDION (born 1934). *Play It as It Lays* (Farrar, Straus & Giroux, 1970) is the study of a former fashion model's moral and social flight from Hollywood (where she makes a few films) to New York and to Las Vegas. "A punchy, fast, scathing novel, distilling venom in tiny drops, revealing devastation in a sneer and fear in a handful of atomic dust," wrote J.R. Frakes in *Book World* (August 9, 1970). The novel was filmed in 1972 by Universal, under the direction of Frank Perry, with Tuesday Weld and Anthony Perkins.

JOSEPH Di MONA. In *The Eagle's Nest* (William Morrow, 1980), an American director, leading man, and starlet are kidnapped by the Baader-Meinhof gang while filming *The Secret Life of Hitler* on location in Germany. The starlet's lover rescues the group.

MARK DINTENFASS (born 1941). The narrator of *Montgomery Street* (Harper & Row, 1978) is filmmaker Stephen Mandreg, whose latest production is well received at the Cannes Film Festival. His new film, with the novel's title, is about his childhood neighborhood in Brooklyn and the relationship between a 14-year-old boy and a shopkeeper/neighbor. David Sterritt in the *Christian Science Monitor* (May 12, 1978) wrote, "While *Montgomery Street* is a winning book, its muted tone and familiar aphorisms get wearying. A few flashes of color and a little bold music on the soundtrack might have worked wonders."

DOROTHY CAMERON DISNEY. Amateur detective and spinster Susan Page is called to Hollywood by her film star niece in *The Golden Swan Murder* (Harper, 1939). The niece's ex-husband has been found dead in bed in her guestroom, and it is up to Page to clear her niece's name. "Despite all its thrills and able writing, story wilts under poisonous miasmas of cinema colony and crew of unpleasant characters. Entertaining—at that," reported the reviewer in the *Saturday Review of Literature* (October 14, 1939).

ROGER DOOLEY (born 1920) is obviously something of a film buff. In *Flashback* (Crime Club/Doubleday, 1969) he mentions such varied items as *Films in Review*, Cinema 16, the Theodore Huff Memorial Film Society, and countless silent screen personalities. He is not enough of a film buff, however, to know that the Academy Award for Best Supporting Actress does not date back to 1933, as he claims, but was first presented in 1936. The novel begins when film magazine writer Joel Goodman receives a telephone call from former silent screen star Juan Madero. Shortly thereafter, Madero is dead, and the police cajole Goodman into investigating. Goodman discovers that Madero's one-time leading lady, who later became a popular Nazi screen star, had a child who is now starring in a film directed by her mother's discoverer and first director. It is difficult to ascertain who apart from film buffs would enjoy this contrived mystery novel, in which the dialogue is as believable as the plotline.

RICHARD DORSO. The story of the making of a contemporary motion picture is told by a female casting director in *Thicker Than Water* (Harcourt

Brace Jovanovich, 1980), but this is no typical Hollywood film. The director, Casey, has walked off his last film and is in a tenuous financial position. Rocky, an actor who has worked frequently with the director in the past, offers to put up the money for Casey's next film, in which he will star. Additional funding comes from a yogurt manufacturer after he has been seduced by the leading lady. Shooting commences on the Universal lot—with Lew Wasserman putting in a guest appearance—with a married cinematographer who is having a tempestuous sexual relationship with a minor actor, a threatened directors' strike, and an oversexed leading man named Tommy Allsworth. The casting director gives the cinematographer's boyfriend a small role in the picture in order to keep the two happy. After Tommy fails to pay a high-class prostitute, he is raped by a group of prostitutes who force him to endure multiple orgasms. His sex life in ruins, Tommy forms a ménage à trois with two of the women. The biggest shock comes when a blackmailer forces Rocky to confess to Casey that he is a transsexual. The book opens and closes with Rocky's funeral, the casting director surmising that the actor has staged his own death in a plane crash in order to embark on a new life. Oh Hollywood, where is thy shame?

JOHN DOS PASSOS (1896–1970) was described by Jean-Paul Sartre as "the best novelist of our time"—and that time was the 1920s and 1930s. Dos Passos was hired by Paramount in the summer of 1934, on a five-week contract, to work with Joseph von Sternberg on Pierre Louys's *La Femme et le Pantin*, released as *The Devil Is a Woman* (1935); Dos Passos did not receive screen credit. For more information on John Dos Passos, see *The Fourteenth Chronicle: The Letters and Diaries of John Dos Passos*, edited by Townsend Ludington (Gambit, 1973), and *John Dos Passos: A 20th Century Odyssey*, by Townsend Ludington (E.P. Dutton, 1980).

   The Big Money (Harcourt, Brace, 1936) is the last volume in the "U.S.A." trilogy that began with *The 42nd Parallel* (1930) and *1919* (1932); the trilogy was reprinted in one volume as *U.S.A.* by Houghton Mifflin in 1938. *The Big Money* includes a biographical sketch of Rudolph Valentino, and one of its characters is Margo Dowling, who comes from nowhere to become a Hollywood star.

   Whereas *The Big Money* was widely praised, **Most Likely to Succeed** (Prentice-Hall, 1954) was not. *The Nation* (October 9, 1954) commented, "The book might be said to resemble a scratchily written Lillian Ross type of 'profile' which would be rejected by the *New Yorker*. Though its central figure is a phony, a mental incompetent, and a moral castrate, *Most Likely to Succeed* cannot even be called venomous. It is merely libelous." That character is Jed Morris, an idealistic New York playwright who becomes a major Hollywood screenwriter. He is depicted as torn between love for the money that Hollywood can provide and his attraction to an idealistic world as envisioned by the Communist Party.

KIRK DOUGLAS (born 1916) is a major Hollywood actor, who made his screen debut in 1946 with *The Strange Love of Martha Ivers* and became a star in 1949 with *Champion*. He published his first novel, **Dance with the Devil** (Random House), in 1990. San Sabba Camp in Trieste, Italy, is the initial point of connection between director Danny Dennison and would-be actress (and apparently part-time prostitute) Luba. When Dennison was at San Sabba as a child, it was a concentration camp; when Luba came there from Poland as a teenager, it was a camp for refugees. The two first meet on the set of a 1987 film, and the book moves backward and then forward in time, recounting their lives as they become lovers. Dennison is determined to deny his Jewish identity (of little relevance here, however, in the setting of the Hollywood film industry), and his most important and first serious film, *Everyman*, proves to be a disastrous flop. The book concludes with Dennison back at the camp on a visit and accepting his spiritual past. The novel is well written and entertaining, with plenty of the type of explicit sex one has come to expect from contemporary Hollywood novels. It is unusual to find one sex sequence in which Luba persuades Dennison to perform fellatio. Few male writers, let alone a major Hollywood star, would be willing to embrace such a possibility.

JAY DRATLER (born 1911). *The Pitfall* (Thomas Y. Crowell, 1947) was the basis for the important noir film *Pitfall*, made in 1948 by Regal Films for United Artists release, directed by Andre de Toth, and starring Dick Powell, Lizabeth Scott, Jane Wyatt, and Raymond Burr. There are major differences between the film and the novel, from the change in the title, to that of principal character John Forbes's occupation, from screenwriter to insurance sales- man. Forbes is a happily married man who commits adultery and gets involved with a blackmailing private detective, whom Forbes's lover kills. The *San Francisco Chronicle* (March 9, 1947) wrote, "The beginning of the plot is a little hard to accept; the ending is only neatly twisted melodrama. But the body of the book is a hard, tense, almost nerve-wracking study of the miseries of adulthood, the torments of the man who wants both wife and mistress. The picture business background is unglamorously true, and the fast, easy tempo has a disquieting impact."

MAURICE DRUON (born 1918). *Film of Memory* (Charles Scribner's, 1956), translated by Moura Budberg, straddles the dividing line between fantasy and reality as a once-famous courtesan, La Sanziani, slowly dies in a cheap Rome hotel and tells her past to one of the maids. "What fortune shall I hold in my hands. What fabulous city shall I inhabit," the maid asks herself each night as she enters La Sanziani's room. Because of her friendship with the elderly woman, the maid falls in love with a screenwriter and is discovered by a well-known Italian film director. Both the *Saturday Review of Literature* (April 7, 1956) and the *New York Times* (April 22, 1956) agreed that the novel sinks into conventionality when the author examines the maid's burgeoning film career.

DAVID DUNCAN (born 1913). The central character in *Yes, My Darling Daughters* (Doubleday, 1959) is Ben Archer, who writes science fiction scripts for Intercontinental Studios, but is more interested in writing a novel about colonist James Nestor, a free love advocate. When the studio decides no longer to produce science fiction films, Archer wonders how he will take care of his many daughters, but one of them has accidentally mixed up his manuscripts. The studio receives the Nestor novel and decides to film it.

BRIAN DUNN. *The Censored Screen* (Newsstand Library, 1960) is one of a series of novels with a Hollywood background, identified by Carolyn See as "semi-pornographic." No other information is available.

DOMINICK DUNNE (born 1925) is a television and film producer as well as a novelist. *The Winners* (Simon & Schuster, 1982) is billed as "Part II of Joyce Haber's *The Users*," but it features an entirely different set of characters. The main figure here is overweight and vulgar secretary Mona Berg, who takes advantage of her agent boss's heart attack to take over the business. She creates a career for a young stud she picks up, and destroys that of an actress who walks out on her, and so on and so forth. Lots of dirty sex but not up to the "style" (if such it can be called) of the earlier volume.

JOHN GREGORY DUNNE (born 1932). "I did not want to write a roman à clef about contemporary Hollywood. I think contemporary Hollywood is terribly boring," Dunne told *The New Yorker* (August 1, 1994), but *Playland* (Random House, 1994) is the story of a juvenile screen star named Blue Tyler, who bears more than a passing resemblance to Natalie Wood. Another character in the novel is a homosexual director named Chuckie O'Hara ("He's my favorite character in the entire book," said Dunne), who, one must assume, is based on George Cukor.

DOROTHY DUNNETT (born 1923). *Dolly and the Bird of Paradise* (Alfred A. Knopf, 1984) is the sixth mystery novel to feature portrait painter and British secret agent Johnson Johnson. Here, Johnson, with the help of his yacht *Dolly*, assists Scottish makeup artist Rita Geddes in solving a murder in a Hollywood film crew on location on the island of Madeira.

ROBERT EATON. *The Body Brokers* (Nash Publishing, 1970) would have been a far better book had its author brought each subplot to a logical conclusion. As it is, the novel introduces a variety of characters, several of whom have no relevance to the plotline and who are suddenly dropped just as they become interesting. The theme, presumably, is that politics and motion pictures are similar in that both use the bodies of their participants to an immoral end. The characters here include a best-selling author who is broken by the film industry but then fights back to become as vicious and conniving as those who first took him over; a nymphomaniac movie star and her equally sexually obsessed daughter; a wealthy duke whose power extends into the American political scene; a would-be president who will use any means at his disposal to achieve his goal; and a director with extreme sexual interests who escapes the clutches of politics and films, declaring he "will never get within smelling distance of this pig sty again." The book's final scenes take place at the Cannes Film Festival. Ultimately, *The Body Brokers* is the waste of a good idea and a good book.

ALAN EBERT (born 1935) **and JANICE ROTCHSTEIN** (born 1944). *Traditions* (Crown, 1981) is the saga of the Tiernan family over four decades. The focus is on two sisters, Carolyn and Margaret, whose fame leads them from the stages of Hollywood to the stages of Broadway and London's West End. Very long!

LOIS EBY (born 1908) **and JOHN C. (Chester) FLEMING** (1906–64) were first cousins. In *Blood Runs Cold* (E.P. Dutton, 1946), Tommy

Marvel investigates the murder of a film columnist who was actively involved in blackmailing members of the Hollywood community. "Well dressed Hollywood" opined *Kirkus* (July 1, 1946).

MARGARET ECHARD. When a stand-in is shot after being mistaken for the star in *Stand-In for Death* (Doubleday, Doran, 1940), the star, a radio gossip columnist, and the husband of a second radio gossip columnist who has a psychotic hatred for the actor decide to investigate.

ARLO C. EDINGTON and MRS. CARMEN BALLEN EDINGTON. *The Studio Murder Mystery* (Reilley & Lee, 1929) is an early mystery novel with a film background. Chief Detective Smith investigates when screen heavy Dwight Hardell is stabbed to death on stage six at the studios of Superior Films the night before the completion of his "masterpiece." Smith's problem is that not only had several individuals threatened to kill Hardell, but also three have confessed to the crime. "A good close-up of moving-picture people at work, as well as an original work-out," commented the reviewer in *Bookman* (July 1, 1929).

The House of the Vanishing Goblets (Century, 1930) is an old dark house murder mystery with a Hollywood twist. A film company arrives at an abandoned mansion to shoot interior scenes—and the director and a leading actor are promptly murdered.

ANNE EDWARDS (born 1927) is best known for a series of popular biographies, including *Judy Garland* (1975), *Vivien Leigh* (1976), *A Remarkable Woman: A Biography of Katharine Hepburn* (1985), *Early Reagan: The Rise of Power* (1987), *The De Milles: An American Family* (1988), and *Shirley Temple: American Princess* (1988). *Shadow of a Lion* (Coward, McCann & Geoghegan, 1971) is the story of a 1940s producer, Maxwell Seaman, who by his personal behavior destroys the lives of his family members and then, by informing before the House Un-American Activities Committee, destroys the careers of his colleagues. "The portions regarding the House Un-American Activities Committee hearings on 'communist influences' in the film industry are chilling and authentic. However, the novel is basically an absorbing chronicle of the life of a troubled modern-day family," wrote Richard H. Rossichan in *Library Journal* (May 15, 1971).

JOHN EHLE (born 1925). *The Changing of the Guard* (Random House, 1974) examines the conflicts between the new and old schools of filmmaking. Fifty-something film star Richie comes to the Studio De Boulogne on the outskirts of Paris to star as Louis XVI in a new film on the French Revolution. His wife, Kate is to costar as Louis's mistress, and a close friend, Annie Logan, is to play Marie Antoinette. All three look forward to the production until the arrival of a brash, young, new wave director, Doug Sigler. As the latter strives for total realism on the set, the Revolution of the story becomes inexorably blended into the reality of day-to-day filmmaking. The novel is dedicated to screenwriter Bella Spewack.

BLOSSOM ELFMAN (born 1924). The central character in *The Return of the Whistler* (Houghton Mifflin, 1981) is Arnie Schlatter, who compensates for low academic standards by developing a shrill whistle, with which he irritates his teacher. In reward for his behavior, a fellow student, Barry Fletcher, invites Arnie to a party at his famous producer-father's Malibu beach house. The virginal Arnie has a date with Francie, the daughter of a well-known actress, and when he is introduced to the world of teenage drugs and alcohol, he must struggle to decide his own values in life.

JOYCE ELIASON (born 1934). *Laid Out* (Harper & Row, 1976) is the story of a young film director named Wally, whose life and career is recounted by five of the many women attending his funeral.

AARON ELKINS (born 1935). In *Dead Men's Hearts* (Mysterious Press, 1994), Elkins's long-time hero Gideon Elkins comes to Egypt's Valley of the Nile to appear in a documentary film, and a skeleton turns up in the trash at the Egyptological Institute.

STANLEY ELLIN (1916–86). In *Star Light, Star Bright* (Random House, 1979), billionaire Andrew Quist invites seven strangers, all of them involved in the making of a film, to his Palm Beach estate. When one of the guests receives death threats, private investigator John Milano is called in, but he is loath to take the case, having previously known, in the biblical sense, Quist's superstar wife.

HARLAN ELLISON (born 1934) has a cult reputation as a short story writer, a writer for film and television, and a New Age guru. Hollywood and its lost stars are the subjects of one of the stories in *Love Ain't Nothing but Sex Misspelled* (Trident Press, 1968). Also worthy of investigation are stories in *Shatterday* (Houghton Mifflin, 1980) and *Stalking the Nightmare* (Phantasia Press, 1982).

JAMES ELLROY (born 1948). *The Big Nowhere* (Mysterious Press, 1988) is a very long and complex mystery, and somewhat confusing to readers. Like the author's previous novel, *The Black Dahlia*, it mixes fact with fiction. The year is 1950 and the setting Los Angeles, as a young homicide detective with the sheriff's department, a deeply closeted gay man, investigates a series of brutal mutilation murders of homosexuals. At the same time, Howard Hughes is signing up starlets at RKO in order to set them up for sexual exploitation. Gangsters Mickey Cohen and Johnny Stompanato (both of whom play prominent parts in the story) are supporting the Teamsters Union in a jurisdictional dispute with the United Alliance of Extras and Stagehands. The latter organization is on strike, and the Teamsters and the studio bosses are determined to destroy the union, aided in their efforts by the Los Angeles Police Department, which sees the United Alliance as a Communist front organization. As the detective investigating the gay murders is named to the task force investigating the union, the two stories come together—sort of. The murders are shown to relate to the earlier Sleepy Lagoon killing, and the detective kills himself because of his homosexuality. At the book's close, there are no heroes, only dead bodies, a cop on the run, and a still-powerful group of Teamsters and gangsters.

Hollywood Nocturnes (Penzler/Macmillan, 1994) consists of a novella and five short stories. In "Out of the Past," a film actress whose career is stalled arranges to have himself and a starlet kidnapped, but matters get out of control. "Since I Don't Have You" is about a carhop who is a close personal friend of both Mickey Cohen and Howard Hughes.

HOWARD ENGEL (born 1931) has written a series of mystery novels featuring Grantham, Ontario, private investigator Benny Cooperman. In *Murder on Location* (St. Martin's Press, 1982), Cooperman searches for the missing wife/actress of a local realtor and becomes embroiled with a Hollywood film company shooting on location at Niagara Falls. Cooperman is considered by many, including the *New York Times*, as the most realistic of Canada's fictional private eyes.

AMY EPHRON (born 1955) has written a comedy of social anthropology with *Biodegradable Soap* (Houghton Mifflin, 1991), in which a Hollywood housewife and her agent husband split up. She becomes increasingly concerned with the environment, and he has an affair with an Italian actress. Many other incidents occur among the couple's friends in a brilliantly satirical and somewhat abbreviated novel, which, of course, ends happily with the husband's return.

STEVE ERICKSON's first novel, *Days Between Stations* (Poseidon, 1985), is set in the Los Angeles and Paris of the near future. While the world tries to recover from devastation caused by catastrophic weather changes, amnesiac Michael Sarasan seeks a lost film masterpiece (*Napoleon*) made by his grandfather (Abel Gance), and also, coincidentally, to rediscover his own past. This original science fiction novel is surrealistic in form and makes use of various cinematic techniques translated to the printed page. Reviews were negative; *Publishers Weekly* called it "impenetrable," and *Kirkus* "unbelievably jejune."

PETER EVANS. *Titles* (Ballantine Books, 1978) is a roman à clef based on the marriage of Prince Rainier of Monaco to Grace Kelly (here called Prince Philippe and Georgina Game). "It would be more exciting to watch the kinescopes of the 1956 Rainier/Kelly nuptials," commented Mary A. Pradt in *Library Journal* (September 15, 1978).

KATHERINE EVERARD. *A Star's Progress* (E.P. Dutton, 1950) is a cautionary tale for any woman who might be tempted to become a Hollywood star. Graziella Serrano is introduced as a ten-year-old Mexican with a passion for dancing. The family moves to New Orleans, where the girl gets a job as a striptease dancer in a nightclub. An older man falls in love with her; they marry, but Hollywood beckons and Graziella insists on a divorce. In Hollywood, Graziella becomes a star and also discovers that she is a lesbian. After a fling with a Balkan prince, scandal destroys the woman's career and Graziella Serrano, now Grace Carter, is last seen in a cheap hotel room in New Orleans, an alcoholic taking an overdose of sleeping pills. "A first novel that holds little promise of a future," opined *Kirkus* (February 15, 1950).

RUPERT EVERETT (born 1961) is a lean, tall, and good-looking British actor of stage and screen who first came to prominence with his performance in *Another Country* (1984). Just how much of Everett is in the central player in his first novel, *Hello Darling, Are You Working?* (Sinclair-Stevenson, 1992), only the author knows. The character Rhys Waverall is an extraordinary camp creation, introduced at the age of eight, when he discovers he will never be a great actress: "There it was, sticking out in front of him like a sore thumb: his penis—and his first showbiz disappointment—shattering all his dreams." Rhys enjoys a brief moment of fame as the star of an American soap opera, but when that is canceled, he becomes a high-class prostitute, catering to a rich, ugly, and aging American woman. It is not a new experience for Rhys, who in his teen years had readily sold his body to any man with the requisite fee. While there is an occasional and sobering reference to AIDS, Rupert Everett has primarily written a novel of great humor, very camp and very gay, despite its hero being more bisexual than homosexual. The entire book is virtually an exercise in camp humor, and far easier to read than any Susan Sontag essay on the subject. If Everett has used his book as a coming-out exercise, we should encourage more actors of his generation similarly to put pen to paper.

BONNIE FABER. In *And Down Will Come Baby* (Windsor, 1994), a star returns home to write her memoirs and is stalked by a mad killer.

WILLIAM FADIMAN. Since *The Clay Oscar* (Major Books, 1977) has nothing to do with either an Oscar or the Academy of Motion Picture Arts and Sciences, the title is somewhat misleading. The book is the story of a screenwriter whose observations and comments (such as "Hollywood, where nothing counts but the now—not the past, not the future, just the now") are all too obvious. The narrator Jed Wilkins is a washed-up writer whose wife has divorced him and who is verging on alcoholism. He is hired to rewrite and rework a script, and steals from an earlier, unproduced, but sold script of his own. Found out by the studio, Wilkins is fired, and the producer's wife whom he has been servicing sexually also tells him that he is no longer needed. On a drunken binge in Mexico, Wilkins learns that the same producer's wife has been murdered by his brother, who has also been providing stud services. Wilkins ends up writing porno films. The final letter to his psychiatrist, missives to whom end each chapter, begins, "I'm getting kind of tired of this book-thing you asked me to do." Readers will heartily concur.

GILLIAN B. FARRELL. Actress Annie McGrogan is introduced in *Alibi for an Actress* (Pocket Books, 1992), in which she leaves her career in Hollywood and moves to New York, where she decides to become a part-time private detective. Her first assignment is protecting a daytime soap opera star. In *Murder and a Muse* (Pocket Books, 1994), Annie is hired for a role in a "nouveau film noir," and while scouting locations in an old mountain resort she comes upon a dead body.

HENRY FARRELL. The plot of *What Ever Happened to Baby Jane?* (Rinehart, 1960), about two aging sisters who were once famous in show business and about the hatred that is tearing them apart, is well known thanks to the 1962 Warner Bros. release, directed by Robert Aldrich, and starring Bette Davis (in the title role) and Joan Crawford. Baby Jane had been a child star, while her sister, Blanche, was a legendary Hollywood star whose career was cut short by a car accident engineered by Jane. "True Grand Guignol, exquisitely calibrated," exclaimed James Sandoe in the *New York Herald Tribune* (March 13, 1960), but Anthony Boucher in the *New York Times* (March 13, 1960) found it "lacking the insight and skill to raise its shocks above the level of the screams in a horror movie."

HOWARD FAST (born 1914). The central character in *Max* (Houghton Mifflin, 1982) is Max Bitsky, a composition of various movie moguls, whose life and career is documented from New York in the 1890s through Los Angeles in the teens and twenties and back to New York in the 1930s. "In all," commented *Kirkus*, "a homey, easy-listening mini-saga—with an endearing tycoon-hero, attractive museum displays of familiar (though ever-lively) cinema history, but *without* the ornate implausibilities of the recent Fast epics."
    See also **E.V. CUNNINGHAM.**

JONATHAN FAST (born 1948) has authored one of the funniest and most original books of recent years with *The Inner Circle* (Delacorte Press, 1979). Screenwriter Louis Pinkle stumbles upon a mysterious cult dating back to the teens called "The Inner Circle." It worships a Mexican panther god and each ten years must provide fresh human meat to appease the deity. The human meat is selected from among prominent members of the film industry, and in the past the victims have included Jean Harrold (Jean Harlow), Rosalee Romain (Marilyn Monroe) and Dean Jamison (James Dean). The current victim is Pinkle's friend Tony Valenti (Freddie Prinz).
    The Beast (Random House, 1981) is a modern southern California version of *Beauty and the Beast.* When agent Leslie Horowitz's car breaks down in the Mojave Desert, he seeks refuge in the home of millionaire Henry Wallace Breeze III, whose face was destroyed in the Vietnam War. Breeze has a large film library and is familiar with Horowitz's client, the beautiful actress Rebecca Weiss. He will allow Horowitz to leave only if she takes his place. Love and sex follow; no fairy tale this.

TERENCE FEELY has written novels, plays, and television series. Liverpudlian Tara Stewart embarks on a career in documentary filmmaking with a burglary in *Limelight* (William Morrow, 1984). Her contacts with the criminal fraternity of Liverpool help Stewart build a reputation as a documentary producer/presenter with Alhambra Television, while at the same time she uses the films in a fight to clear her father of a robbery conviction. Tara Stewart is a fun heroine even if the plotline is decidedly contrived, and it is doubtful the documentary field could ever embrace such a character or allow her such freedom of choice and expression in her projects. Only in the final chapters does Stewart's to free her father become a little tedious. Author Feely does come up with the occasional amusing comment, as in his description of Aylesbury duckling, "its skin as crisp and brown as a seventy-year-old film producer's at the Cannes Film Festival."

JUDY FEINER. After writing a novel based on her screen career, B-movie star Faye Cassidy Oppenheim publishes a second book on her love affairs in *A Hot Property* (Random House, 1973). Her book is only moderately successful, and she is chagrined when her 15-year-old daughter writes a similar book on the same subject, featuring the same lovers, and it becomes a best-seller. *A Hot Property* is unusual in that it is a Hollywood novel about Hollywood novels.

In 1930s Hollywood, Buck Herman is a would-be screenwriter and studio musician in *Flame* (Delacorte Press, 1986). His son, Nick, becomes a Hollywood psychiatrist, one of whose clients is movie star George Warren. The problems of the cast of this novel would take an army of psychiatrists from Hollywood or elsewhere to sort out.

RUTH FEINER. *Fires in May* (G.P. Harrap, 1937), translated from the German by Norman Alexander, is the story of a young German refugee, Vera Hansen, who comes to England, finds work as a screenwriter, and later becomes a playwright. "The book is frankly a popular light romance," wrote Fanny Butcher in the *Chicago Daily Tribune* (March 14, 1936), "but it is something more than ordinary romance. It is filled with keen observations of the British temperament, made by a young German refugee. Miss Feiner, like her heroine born and brought up in Germany, has lived in London since the Nazi regime in her fatherland."

ANDREW J. FENADY (born 1928) is a Hollywood film and television producer who came up with an original idea for a series of mysteries. His hero undergoes plastic surgery and acquires Humphrey Bogart's face; he changes his name to Sam Marlow, sets up as a private detective, and drives a 1933 Plymouth. The character was introduced in *The Man with Bogart's Face* (Henry Regnery, 1977), in which he goes in search of a pair of perfectly matched sapphires, the Eyes of Alexander. He encounters types who resemble Gene Tierney and Zachary Scott, and has a gunfight at the Hollywood Bowl. A second novel, *The Secret of Sam Marlow* (Contemporary Books, 1980), chronicles "The Further Adventures of the Man with Bogart's Face."

ELIZABETH FERRARS is the pseudonym of Morna Doris Brown (born 1907), who also writes as E.X. Ferrars. Under either name, her novels are frightfully English middle-class. The style is often terse and the central characters, Virginia Freer and her estranged husband, Felix, in the series from which comes *Sleep of the Unjust* (Crime Club/Doubleday, 1991), are somewhat tiresome. Here, a Hollywood movie actor is murdered when he returns to England for the wedding of his cousin and former fiancée. The character behaves like no known film actor, and Ferrars appears to have little idea as to how a Hollywood star might think or feel.

CARL FICK. *A Disturbance in Paris* (Little, Brown, 1982) is an original thriller—*Library Journal* described it as "well written"—in which Alex Marin, a failed American screenwriter in Paris, gets involved with the Baader-Meinhof gang. A member of the group helps Marin dispose of the body of his actress/mistress when she commits suicide, and in return, the screenwriter agrees to run an errand for the gang, not knowing that his contact is a local Israeli agent. Marin is to produce a film tribute to Ulrike Meinhof, but he eventually escapes with a new lover, one of the terrorists.

EVAN FIELD is the pseudonym of "two well-known writers on film." When America's most powerful and most disliked gossip columnist, Nigel Whitly, is found strangled by his own typewriter ribbon in a screening room at the New York Film Festival in *What Nigel Knew* (Clarkson N. Potter, 1981), the suspects include an actor-turned-director whose latest film was about to receive a scathing review from Nigel; a pill-popping starlet; an Italian director whose career was destroyed by Nigel; an Italian actress determined to break into Hollywood films; and a slick Hollywood producer. The novel is witty but perhaps a little too clever for its own good.

RACHAEL FIELD (1894–1942) **and ARTHUR PEDERSON**. *To See Ourselves* (Macmillan, 1937) is the bittersweet story of the Hamilton Bosworths, Jr., of Morgan, Idaho, who are bitter by the Hollywood bug when Mr. Bosworth receives a letter from an old college friend who is earning $500 a week as a writer for Victory, Ltd. The Bosworths leave their dry goods and furniture store and head for Hollywood, determined to become screenwriters. "*To See Ourselves* is by no means the evaluating analysis of Hollywood's street scene which may some day be written," commented the reviewer in the *New York Herald Tribune* (November 21, 1937). "But for a rendering of rise and fall of emotion in marriage it is a lovely accomplishment, gentle and honest in portraying both the world-known locale and its unknown intimacies."

TIMOTHY FINDLEY. *The Butterfly Plague* (Viking Press, 1969) is a highly original and complex novel, written at times in what would appear to be experimental form. It is set in the period 1936–38, primarily on the Topanga Beach just outside Los Angeles, but with a section in Germany, where one of the principal characters, Ruth Damarosch, has gone to compete as a swimmer in the 1936 Olympic Games. The novel open with her return to Los Angeles, where she is met by her brother, Adolphus, a director known by the nickname "Dolly" (in partial reference to his homosexuality) and by Dolly's current screen star, Myra Jacobs. Ruth's parents were both in the film industry, the father a director and the mother a leading lady. Her father deserted his wife after discovering the hemophilia in her family, of which Dolly is a victim, and had an affair with a silent screen star, Letitia Virden, known as the Little Virgin, who makes a comeback film in the course of the novel. By the novel's close, Dolly and Ruth's parents are dead, and Ruth has gone through a false pregnancy. *The Butterfly Plague* is not a novel that can be easily summarized, because so much that takes place may only, like Ruth's pregnancy, be fantasy. The chief reality of the novel is that the monarch butterflies of the title do migrate for the winter to California, but overstay their visit until areas of the state are plagued by them. This is quite an extraordinary book, extremely engrossing, well worthy of revived interest for its multiform themes.

GERALD FINE. A self-published book, *Fatty: The Celebrated Novel of Hollywood's First Super-Star Roscoe "Fatty" Arbuckle* (Fine, 1971) is nothing more than a biography of the silent film comedian which might just as well have been published as such, except that the names of a number of the supporting characters in Arbuckle's life have been changed.

FRANCIS J. (James) FINN (1859–1928). The central character in *Bobbie in Movieland* (Benziger Brothers, 1921) is a young boy separated from his mother and "adopted" by a fat comedian named John Compton (presumably an amalgam of John Bunny and "Fatty" Arbuckle). With Compton's help, Bobbie becomes a child star, but he yearns not only to return to his mother but also to renew his allegiance to the Catholic Church. When the dissipated Compton and his crew attend Bobbie's First Communion, they repent of their past lives, and eventually Bobbie and his mother are reunited.

JACK FINNEY is the pseudonym of Walter Braden Finney (born 1921). *Marion's Wall* (Simon & Schuster, 1973) employed an amusing idea and caused quite a stir among film buffs when it was first published. A young married couple moves into a San Francisco apartment formerly owned by the late silent screen star Marion Marsh. Her ghost still inhabits the place and takes over the wife's body, goes to Hollywood, and tries to re-enter films. The couple meets a film buff, living in Vilma Banky's old home, and he has prints of all the lost films, including the complete *Greed*, but the nitrate films are destroyed in a projector fire that also disposes of Marion's ghost.

CARRIE FISHER (born 1956) is the actress daughter of Debbie Reynolds and Eddie Fisher. Her first novel, *Postcards from the Edge* (Simon and Schuster, 1987), follows Hollywood actress Suzanne Vale from the harrowing experience of a drug rehabilitation center through her comeback film, in which she must cope with three producers who do not believe she is delivering enough, to a presumed happy relationship with a novelist. The book is very much of its time, witty and outrageous, but often too clever for its own good. About halfway through, the author does provide an excellent overview of what it is like for an actress to arrive on a location set early in the morning and go through the various rituals before shooting begins. She has attempted to offer the reader a sympathetic portrait of the central character, but ultimately only those who have been through the same difficulties will feel much empathy with the actress. *Postcards from the Edge* was filmed in 1990, with Meryl Streep as Suzanne Vale, and Shirley MacLaine as her mother, a role more obviously based on Debbie Reynolds on screen and relatively unimportant in the novel.

Delusions of Grandma (Simon & Schuster, 1994) is a seriocomic novel, narrated by screenwriter Cora Sharpe as she awaits the arrival of her baby. She breaks up with her Hollywood lawyer boyfriend and deals with her flamboyant and eccentric mother, a retired costume designer.

STEVE FISHER (1912–80) was a novelist and screenwriter, whose best-known work is the novel *I Wake Up Screaming*, filmed in 1941 and remade in 1953 under the title *Vicki*. *I Wake Up Screaming* (Dodd, Mead, 1941) is a lurid and passionate melodrama about a down-on-his-luck screenwriter accused of murdering a young Hollywood starlet named Vicki Lynn. "While we are being afforded glimpses of life in Hollywood and of an unconventional love affair, there is always the menace of arrest hanging over the head of the leading character. Both the background and the mystery element are skillfully handled," commented Isaac Anderson in the *New York Times* (March 16, 1941).

It is not well known that when *I Wake Up Screaming* was reprinted in paperback, Steve Fisher rewrote portions in an effort to "modernize" the setting, changing the names of places and personalities mentioned. For example, in the 1941 edition, the book begins with the central character in white flannels visiting the Hollywood Roosevelt's Cine-Grill and ordering a Baccardi. In the later edition, he is wearing a Sy Devore suit, visits Mike Romanoff's, and orders a Canadian Club old fashioned. It is the later edition, not the 1941 original, that was reprinted by Black Lizard Books in 1988.

Image of Hell (E.P. Dutton, 1961) is a tale of revenge as a psychiatrist, rejected by a Hollywood star after he tries to make love to her, first tries to ruin her life and then decides to murder her.

Hollywood studio head Jack Stuart faces a variety of crises and problems in *The Big Dream* (Doubleday, 1970). The studio is suffering a major financial crisis thanks to a recent flop, and Stuart's position is in jeopardy. Murder threats have been made against one of the female stars, and her male counterpart's participation in a homosexual relationship is about to be exposed. As if that were not enough, Stuart's wife is considering a move to Italy where she will star in films with nude scenes. In intriguing fashion, Fisher brings every problem to a satisfying solution, leading Jack Stuart to conclude, "Once in a great while you win the whole shooting match."

F. (Francis) SCOTT FITZGERALD (1896–1941) is generally credited with having written the best-regarded Hollywood novel, in large part because of his reputation as one of America's finest novelists of the 1920s, and also because of his personal knowledge of life in Hollywood, since he had tried his luck there as a screenwriter in 1927, 1931, and 1937. The romantic image of him as an alcoholic, spurned by the film industry, did not hurt his posthumous reputation. The reality is that the novel, *The Last Tycoon*, was nothing more than an unfinished 50,000-word draft when Fitzgerald died, and it was edited and completed by Edmund Wilson. Fitzgerald's best books, indeed virtually all of them, date from the 1920s — *This Side of Paradise* (1920), *The Beautiful and the Damned* (1922), *Tales of the Jazz Age* (1922), *The Great Gatsby* (1925), and *All the Sad Young Men* (1926) — and are representative of that era in American history. Like *Tender Is the Night* from 1934, they are studied more as monuments to a dead age than as the works of a timeless literary hero.

Described by one critic as "perhaps the most highly regarded fragment in American literature," the novel was originally published under the title *The Last Tycoon: An Unfinished Novel; Together with the Great Gatsy and Selected Stories* (Charles Scribner's Sons, 1941), and, as already indicated, edited by Edmund Wilson. It consisted of half of the novel, all that Fitzgerald had completed, a summary of the remainder of the story, a letter to Fitzgerald's publisher, a reprint in its entirety of *The Great Gatsby* (whose central character is somewhat similar to the hero here), and five of Fitzgerald's short stories.

The Last Tycoon is narrated by Cecilia, the daughter of producer Pat Brady, who bears a striking resemblance to Louis B. Mayer. The central character is Monroe Stahr (based on M-G-M production head Irving Thalberg), who had become an important figure in film production after the First World War and who is involved in a power struggle with Brady. A widower, Stahr falls in love with an Englishwoman named Kathleen Moore, whose husband is a film technician involved in union activities. Much of the story is taken up with Communist organizing of the writers at the studio, a wage cut ordered by Brady, and the studio stockholders' distrust of Stahr.

As early as 1936, Fitzgerald planned a novel based on Irving Thalberg, but he did not start in earnest on the task until 1939. In 1937 he met British gossip columnist Sheilah Graham, took her as his mistress, and based the character of Kathleen Moore on her.

In the *New York Times* (November 9, 1941) J.D. Adams wrote,

> *The Last Tycoon* is an ambitious book, but, uncompleted though it is, one would be blind indeed not to see that it would have been Fitzgerald's best novel and a very fine one. Even in this truncated form it not only makes absorbing reading; it is the best piece of creative writing that we have about one phase of American life—Hollywood and the movies. Both in the unfinished draft and the sheaf of Fitzgerald's notes which Mr. Wilson has appended to the story it is plainly to be seen how firm was his grasp of his material, how much he had deepened and grown as an observer of life. His sudden death, we see now, was as tragic as that of Thomas Wolfe.

Clifton Fadiman in *The New Yorker* (November 15, 1941) commented,

> *The Last Tycoon*, even as it stands, is the only grownup novel about Hollywood that I have knowledge of.... His story therefore has a solidity and depth lacking in such merely readable narratives as *What Makes Sammy Run?* It might have turned out to be his masterpiece, and even in its present state it is an advance over *The Great Gatsby*, which, by the way, is unexpectedly rereadable.

To the critic at *Time* (November 3, 1941),

> F. Scott Fitzgerald was the last U.S. romantic. To the end his writing was preoccupied with flowers, perfume, rain, the rustle of women's clothes, warm darkness and music in the night. He sometimes deliberately blurred his narrative line, resulting now in effective suspense, now in mere teasing. Yet this fragment contains scenes of beauty and power. Completed, it might or might not have been a *Citizen Kane* about the movie industry.

More recently, Fitzgerald scholar Matthew J. Bruccoli presented a revisionist edition of the novel, *The Love of the Last Tycoon: A Western* (Cambridge University Press, 1994). Bruccoli argues that the title under which the novel was published was Wilson's choice and not that of Fitzgerald.

Aside from *The Last Tycoon*, Fitzgerald published a series of Hollywood-related short stories, one in each issue of *Esquire* from January 1940 through May 1941, featuring Pat Hobby, a hack Hollywood writer, "who was hot stuff when the movies were dumb." These short stories were published in book form as *The Pat Hobby Stories* (Charles Scribner's Sons, 1962), edited by Arnold Gingrich.

In 1976, Sam Spiegel produced a film version of *The Last Tycoon* for Paramount release, directed by Elia Kazan, and starring Robert DeNiro, Tony Curtis, Robert Mitchum, Jeanne Moreau, and Jack Nicholson. Harold Pinter adapted Fitzgerald's novel. For more information on Fitzgerald's Hollywood career, see *Crazy Sundays: F. Scott Fitzgerald in Hollywood*, by Aaron Latham (Viking Press, 1971).

COURTLAND FITZSIMMONS (1893–1949) wrote a couple of mystery novels with film-related backgrounds. *This—Is Murder!* (Frederick A. Stokes, 1941), coauthored with Gerald Adams, was described by *Kirkus* (September 10, 1941) as "manufactured, but well done." A murder is committed on board a yacht, whose complement includes a gossip columnist and a number of stars and studio executives. Could this plotline have been influenced by the 1924 death of producer Thomas H. Ince, who was taken ill aboard William Randolph Hearst's yacht? In *The Evil Men Do* (Frederick A. Stokes, 1941), Stella Wayne calls her 80-year-old great-aunt Ethel Thomas to Hollywood, where the old lady solves two murders.

CAROL HOULIHAN FLYNN (born 1945). *Washed in the Blood* (Seaview/Putnam, 1983) takes as its background Los Angeles in 1939, at the moment when police and political corruption is halted, but while "Okies" are still considered little more than "Red" agitators. Someone is committing a series of murders and sending the police department "screen tests" of the victims, shot immediately prior to the killings. Detectives Able Garret and Roy Jasper are assigned to the case, and the former receives considerable publicity as the city's only "clean cop," tracking down a perpetrator dubbed the "Red Slayer." One of the victims is found dressed as Scarlett O'Hara on the Atlanta set of *Gone with the Wind*, just as it is about to be burned for the movie. Another is found in Santa's sleigh in the annual Hollywood Christmas Parade. The killer hires one of the Munchkins from *The Wizard of Oz*, dresses him as Shirley Temple, and has him perform a dance on film, waving the Stars and Stripes in one hand and the hammer and sickle in the other.

The plot is complicated by Garret's home life and his wife's mourning the death of their only son; a neighbor who is a former child actress; and an evangelist who is the killer's last victim. The author has obviously well researched the period in Los Angeles history, but at times historical data overwhelms the mystery's entertainment value. Truth and reality are blended in such a way that at times the reader is uncertain which is which. When it seemed that Shirley Temple herself had been kidnapped, did indeed President Roosevelt order a troop of Marines to protect her, did Stalin award her honorary Soviet citizenship, did Mrs. Temple decline the offer on behalf of her daughter? No!

BRYAN FORBES (born 1926) was a bland actor in British films—*The Small Back Room* (1949), *The Wooden Horse* (1950), *An Inspector Calls* (1954),

Guns of Navarone (1961), and others—who became an equally insipid director, with such films as *The L-Shaped Room* (1962), *The Madwoman of Chaillot* (1969), and *The Slipper and the Rose* (1976). He published his autobiography, *Notes for a Life*, in 1974.

Forbes began writing **The Distant Laughter** (Harper & Row, 1972) 20 years prior to its publication. In his autobiography he comments, "Each succeeding version became more sterile with perfection. There was no fire in my works, only the embers of a burnt-out imagination." While not exactly original, the storyline is not uninteresting. The book is intelligently written, and Forbes often comes up with a nice turn of phrase. But ultimately *The Distant Laughter* is as bland as most of its creator's projects. It is narrated by director Richard Warren as he returns to England to work on his new film. Changes in the management of the U.S.-based production company affect its start. Warren's marriage to a celebrated actress is affected by a revived relationship with a former lover. The film is eventually completed but shelved by yet another new management. The relationship ends, but the novel concludes with Warren's wife filing for divorce. Bryan Forbes is, of course, married to actress Nanette Newman, but at the front of the novel he writes, "It is no secret that I am a film director married, and happily so, to an actress, but I am not the Warren of this story nor is my wife the Susan."

The Rewrite Man (Simon and Schuster, 1985) is a powerful novel, showing Forbes to be a superb storyteller when he wants to be. Again the background is the making of a film, with this time the narrator a screenwriter named Harvey Burgess. He comes to the Victorine Studios in Nice to doctor a script of a film with a British director and an American producer. The director has fallen in love with a young actress, to whom Burgess is strongly attracted and with whom he has an affair. When the film is completed, Burgess loses touch with her but later discovers that she died in childbirth—and the child was his. As in the previous novel, Forbes has a lot to say about the behavior of publicists. The one here is named Marvin, and he deliberately sabotages a speech by the producer before committing suicide. Aside from its emotional impact, *The Rewrite Man* provides a splendid and obviously factually accurate account of the making of an English-language film on location in a French studio.

STANTON FORBES (born 1923). *If Laurel Shot Hardy the World Would End Tomorrow* (Crime Club/Doubleday, 1970) is a great title for a mystery novel that is a little disappointing. When students in the Classical Cinema Department of an eastern college decide to dress up as Laurel and Hardy, two actors take advantage of the situation and murder the president of a nearby electronics corporation. Public Relations Director Larry Evans is implicated in the crime and thus forced to investigate. Depending on one's point of view, the writing is either witty and clever or irritating and mindless.

LESLIE FORD was the pseudonym of Zenith Brown (1898–1983). In **The Devil's Stronghold** (Charles Scribner's Sons, 1948), widow and amateur sleuth Grace Latham goes to Hollywood where her son is helping promote the career of a movie actress with links to two murders. Beatrice Sherman in the *New York Times* (July 25, 1948) commented, "Here is a fresh, amiable mystery set in

Hollywood. In spite of two murders and a number of sinister circumstances, it manages to maintain a cheerful, amusing atmosphere."

LILLIAN C. (Cape) FORD *see* MARK LEE LUTHER

JOHN FOWLES (born 1926) has seen three of his novels turned into successful and literate films: *The Collector* (1963), *The Magus* (1966, with a screenplay by Fowles) and *The French Lieutenant's Woman* (1969). The central character in **Daniel Martin** (Little, Brown, 1977) is a successful Hollywood screenwriter who returns to his native England at the request of his estranged former brother-in-law, who is dying. There he must come to terms with a collapsed marriage, his mistress, his adult daughter, and the realization that he should have married his wife's sister. "Few novels in recent years have been more thoroughly textured with contemporary history or more rigorously reluctant to offer pat solutions," commented Paul Gray in *Time* (September 12, 1977).

JAMES M. FOX was the pseudonym of James M.W. Knipscheer (born 1908). His Hollywood private eye, John Marshall, who narrates the novel, appears to have caused the death of a man called Chester McFarland in **Death Commits Bigamy** (Coward-McCann, 1948). McFarland was about to reveal his bigamous marriage to a film star who was currently married to a film actor. "The plot is ingenious enough, although it seems slightly irrational in spots," wrote Isaac Anderson in the *New York Times* (January 11, 1948).

DICK FRANCIS (born 1920) is the best known exponent of the horse racing mystery novel. His eleventh book, **Smoke Screen** (Harper & Row, 1972), takes place in South Africa, where Edward Link, a noted womanizer and screen star, is called by a dying friend. The adventures he is about to undertake are far scarier than any he has been involved with on film.

HARRIET FRANK, JR., is a prestigious Hollywood screenwriter who has written scripts for a number of films with her husband, Irving Ravetch, including *The Long, Hot Summer* (1958), *Hud* (1963), *Conrack* (1974), and *Norma Rae* (1979). **Special Effects** (Houghton Mifflin, 1979) is a heartwarming and very modern novel about screenwriter Emma Howard, whose husband has left her for a younger woman and whose two sons are coping with their newfound sexuality, with the one boy involved with a much older, motherly Hollywood agent. Throughout the drama of life, Emma Howard keeps her spirits high, and she is a character whom readers will admire and support no matter the circumstances she is facing. Emma's tolerance and love for all around make her an appealing and admirable heroine.

GEORGE MacDONALD FRASER (born 1925) is best known for his series of novels featuring the character Flashman, and **The Pyrates** (Alfred A. Knopf, 1984) is very much in the same outrageous style, mixing historical fact and fiction. A novel set in the seventeenth century (sort of) might seem an odd work to include in a study of film-related fiction, but it is the "sort of" that is the basis for commentary here. While the novel concerns the efforts of dashing hero Captain Avery to convey the Madagascar crown from London to the island in the Indian ocean, the story is told as a parody of Hollywood adventure films featuring Douglas Fairbanks, Sr., Errol Flynn, and Tyrone Power. As the publisher notes, here is a novel in Technicolor, with stereophonic sound and music by Erich Wolfgang Korngold. Throughout, the characters are described in comparison to their Hollywood counterparts and situations have more to do with scenes in Hollywood movies than with seventeenth-century reality.

Though not based on the novel, the 1986 Roman Polanski feature film *Pirates* attempts, unsuccessfully, to find the same spirit of tongue-in-cheek adventure.

ROBERT CAINE FRAZER was the pseudonym of John Creasey (1908–73). In *The Hollywood Hoax* (Pocket Books, 1961), Mark Kirby of the Regal Investment Security Corporation helps the son of a Hollywood producer investigate a series of murders related to an attempt to acquire the producer's father's company.

ARNOLD FREDERICKS. *The Film of Fear* (W.J. Watt, 1917) is the oldest known mystery novel with a filmmaking theme. It is set within the film industry of New York and environs. No other information is available.

DAVID FREEMAN is a screenwriter—*Street Smart* (1987) and *The Border* (1982)—and a journalist. He combined both talents for the 1984 book *The Last Days of Alfred Hitchcock*, in which he documented his collaboration with the ailing director on the screenplay for the unproduced thriller *The Short Night*. Freeman has used his Hollywood background for two fictional volumes.

A Hollywood Education: Tale of Movie Dreams and Easy Money (G.P. Putnam's Sons, 1986) consists of a series of self-contained short stories narrated by an unnamed Hollywood screenwriter who quits his job as a reporter for the *New York Post* after discovering it is easier to concoct news stories than relate the facts. All of the stories are entertaining, with the wittiest being "Deus ex Machina," in which an insecure Hollywood director arrives at his class reunion by helicopter, accompanied by a starlet and a sycophantic aide. The longest (34 pages), "The Senator and the Movie Star," involves a married politician who needs a studio head to cover his infidelity; the price he pays is that he must introduce in Congress whatever legislation the movie executive would like passed. "Deus ex Machina" begins at Schwab's drugstore, and the last story in the collection reports the closing of the venerable pharmacy and coffee shop. It is just one of the many real Los Angeles landmarks depicted in this book, which is a pleasant blend of fantasy and reality, with the former never too far removed from the truth.

A Hollywood Life (Simon & Schuster, 1991) is the story of former child actress turned Hollywood legend Carla Tate, told by Gene Burton, a screenwriter and Tate's one-time lover. In the final stages of making a film, Carla Tate has died in a drowning accident while on her boat. The similarity to the November 29, 1981, death of Natalie Wood is obvious, and just as Wood's last film, *Brainstorm*, had to be cobbled together from extant footage, so is Carla Tate's last film the subject of a frantic retrieval effort. Narrator Burton even mentions the same rumors that circulated in Hollywood following Wood's unexplained death. However, aside from their both having been child actresses, there is little resemblance between the lives and careers of the two. Tate has a longtime, secret relationship with a powerful Hollywood lawyer, Jack Markel, and has two children by a screenwriter, whereas Natalie Wood's romantic life was closely tied to actor Robert Wagner (to whom she was twice married).

David Freeman, as expected, displays a solid knowledge of Hollywood history, but in passing on information to the reader his writing is often reduced to the level of an academic text, with the characters having to provide expository conversation. For a work of fiction, *A Hollywood Life* does offer considerable detail on the reality of contemporary film production.

RICHARD FRIEDEL. Compared by *Library Journal* (June 1, 1981) to *Auntie Mame*—"Not since . . . has the saga of a poor little rich kid's growing up been so delightfully told"—*The Movie Lover* (Coward, McCann & Geoghegan, 1981) is the fictional autobiography of twenty-something Burton Raider, an unabashed homosexual who wants to be a screenwriter. He obtains a job on a morning television program, and after seeing a former glamorous movie star shoplifting (obviously Hedy Lamarr), he persuades her to star in a film that he will both write and produce. Here is a novel to appeal to both the film buff and the gay reader, and since the two are often one, it is surprising that *The Movie Lover* has not generated more of a cult appeal.

BRUCE JAY FRIEDMAN (born 1930). The central character in *About Harry Towns* (Alfred A. Knopf, 1974) is a New York screenwriter who tries unsuccessfully to come to terms with a bad marriage and the deaths of his parents. Endless affairs and a steady diet of cocaine are not the answer. As J.R. Fraker explained in the *New York Times* (June 23, 1974), "Harry writes scripts for Hollywood and scripts for the lives of himself and everyone else. The professional scripts sell and are evidently successful; the others are absorbed by flaky circumstances."

KINKY FRIEDMAN has enjoyed a career as a country music and rock 'n' roll singer/composer, with his group, the Texas Jew Boys, and as a recording artist with a number of fairly outrageous songs, including "They Ain't Making Jews Like Jesus Anymore" and "Waitress, Please Waitress, Come Sit on My Face." He became a mystery novelist in 1986 with *Greenwich Killing Time*, in which the principal character was himself. Friedman is again the star in *Elvis, Jesus and Coca-Cola* (Simon & Schuster, 1993), in which his best friend is working on a revealing film about Elvis impersonators. When the friend dies, the film disappears, and Kinky sets out to find it. The novel is replete with quirky comments by Kinky as well as descriptions of his love life.

ELIZABETH HAMILTON FRIERMOND (born 1903). In order to save her father's theater business in 1927–28, Kitty must persuade her parents to embrace the talkies in *Pepper's Paradise* (Doubleday, 1969). A novel for juveniles.

KETTI FRINGS's (1915–81) first novel, *Hold Back the Dawn* (Duell, Sloan & Pearce, 1940), is a touching tale of a group of would-be immigrants waiting in Tijuana for admission to the United States. Among the group is a young man whose wife works in Hollywood, writing stories for movie magazines, and who drives down to see him each week. The novel was filmed in 1941 by Paramount, directed by Mitchell Leisen, and starring Olivia de Havilland, Paulette Goddard, and Charles Boyer.

DANIEL FUCHS (1909–93) was a novelist turned Hollywood screenwriter who won the Academy Award for Best Writing—Motion Picture Story for *Love Me or Leave Me* (1955). *West of the Rockies* (Alfred A. Knopf, 1971) is a deceptively simple novel of a grifter named Burt Claris who works for a talent agency through the influence of his wife's relations. When screen star Adele Hogue walks off her current production and holes up in a Palm Springs hotel, Claris is sent to sort out the problem because he is known to have had an affair with the actress. Hogue is oblivious to the harm her departure from the set has caused, to the financial problems it creates for the producer, and to the emotional problems it creates for Claris. At the novel's close, Claris has lost both his wife and his job, and Hogue is holding a press conference announcing their engagement. *West of the Rockies* has more to do with characters than situations, and reads more like an intellectual novel of the 1920s or 1930s than a work from the midfifties.

The Apathetic Bookie Joint (Methuen, 1979) consists of a series of short stories and the novella "Triplicate," which is about a New York producer who crashes a Hollywood party.

SAMUEL FULLER (born 1912) is a well-regarded Hollywood "cult" director whose films include *The Steel Helmet* (1951), *China Gate* (1957), *Shock Corridor* (1963), and *The Naked Kiss* (1964). He is also a screenwriter (1937–82) and novelist (1935–90). *144 Piccadilly* (Richard W. Baron Publishing, 1971) is probably based on an actual incident that took place on Piccadilly when a group of squatters took over a building almost next door to the offices of a major American film company. Here, the emphasis is on sex, drugs, and violence as an American film director living in London helps some hippies take over an abandoned mansion on Piccadilly.

ELIZABETH GAGE is a pseudonym of (according to her publisher) "one of storytelling's brightest stars." *Kirkus* (February 15, 1988) described *A Glimpse of Stocking* (Simon & Schuster, 1988), as "a tale of greed, sex, violence, and Hollywood in the grand Krantz/Collins tradition." Sex certainly predominates in Gage's first novel as a young New York model, Annie Havilland, comes to Hollywood in 1967. After testing for her first screen role, she is raped by the head of the studio, and when she tries to press charges against him, she is blacklisted. Annie perseveres and stars in a film that gets her typecast as a "sex angel." There is much, much more in a similar vein, with Annie's past and unbelievable coincidences playing important parts.

Taboo (Pocket Books, 1992) is typical of current, popular Hollywood novels in the way it begins by introducing three disparate characters and a decade later has their lives closely intertwined. The writing is turgid, and the sex and violence fail to titillate; in fact, the central players lead rather boring sex lives.

The story begins in 1930 with the reader meeting sexually abused Kate Hamilton, handsome and determined Joseph Knight, and child star Eve Sinclair. After wandering around the United States, Hamilton ends up in Hollywood, where she is discovered by Knight, who has become a successful writer/producer, and where Sinclair's career is in decline. After time out for the Second World War, Hamilton and Knight settle down to married life, only to have an unsavory episode from Hamilton's past come back to haunt her. Hamilton commits murder in order to put that part of the past behind; she is neither accused nor asked to pay a price for her crime except that her husband is killed by Sinclair in a car crash that also takes her own life. This is not good, but as *Kirkus* (January 1, 1993) commented, "The psychology is primitive, but Gage knows her market."

DAVID GALLOWAY (born 1937) wrote his first mystery novel with his third book, *Lamaar Ransom: Private Eye* (Riverrun Press, 1981). With the backdrop of World War II, the book's heroine, Hollywood-based, lesbian private investigator Lamaar Ransom looks into the disappearance of a student from a finishing school for young women wishing to enter the film industry. The school's backer is a Howard Hughes–type character who uses the institution to provide himself with partners willing to participate in his curious sexual practices. The style is flippant and occasionally witty, but much of the novel's dialogue reads like the script for a shoddy Hollywood *film noir* feature. In view of the film background, it is unfortunate that the author did not research his topic a little more thoroughly and that he made no effort to spell correctly the names of the various Hollywood personalities mentioned throughout.

ANNE GARDNER was the pseudonym of Gladys Denny Shultz (1895–19??). The subtitle of *Reputation* (A.L. Burt, 1929), "A Story of April Low, Known as 'The Wickedest Woman in Hollywood,'" is intended as irony. The woman in question is a farmgirl from Arkansas who enters vaudeville, is discovered, and is brought to Broadway as a sex siren. She becomes notorious after being named in a divorce action and is signed to a Hollywood contract. April is introduced to her first Hollywood party, at which opium is smoked, and stars in *Jezebel of the Ages*. When the man who tries to seduce her is killed, it appears that April's adopted brother is the murderer, but another actress confesses, and April and the brother decide to marry.

TAY GARNETT (1894–1977) began his Hollywood career as a screenwriter in 1920; he began directing in 1928, and his films include *Her Man* (1930), *China Seas* (1935), *Trade Winds* (1939), *Seven Sinners* (1940), *The Postman Always Rings Twice* (1946), and *Soldiers Three* (1951). He published his autobiography, *Light Up Your Torches and Pull Up Your Tights*, in 1973. *Tall Tales from Hollywood* (Horace Liveright, 1932) is a short, 96-page parody of the history of Hollywood, beginning with Ginsburg's discovery of a moving-picture machine, his realization of its commercial potential, and the formation of a corporation, Ginsburg, Ginsburg, Feinstein, Murphy, Schmaltz, Schmaltz and Ginsburg. The infant grows... No names are mentioned, only the character roles, and the style is flashy but badly dated and resolutely unfunny by 1990s standards.

ZOE GARRISON is, according to her publisher, "the pseudonym of two women, one an editor at a New York book publishing house, the other a vice president of a major film company." *Golden Triple Time* (New American Library, 1985) takes its title from the film term *golden time*, referring to when a film crew is working triple overtime. That is a prospect facing the latest production of Kit Ransome, the head of a production company, funded by her cousin Archer Ransome. Kit Ransome is a former actress who has fought her way into production by sleeping with a production executive; she is also the daughter of an eccentric but well-known artist who makes her home in a small North African country. As a magazine writer named Liberty Adams works on the story of Kit Ransome's rise to fame, the reader learns that Archer Ransome is not only her cousin but also her father, that Liberty Adams is her sister, and that the daughter of Archer Ransome's business partner, who is seeking to destroy him financially, is also Kit's sister! Sex in many varieties, but seldom the missionary position, plays an important part in *Golden Triple Time*. The novel might prove that female executives have a hard time getting to the top in Hollywood, but they certainly enjoy themselves along the way. Similarly, magazine writers such as Liberty Adams enjoy the good life, eating at the Plaza and sleeping with congressmen. Edith M. Hull, author of the 1919 romantic melodrama *The Sheik*, would be proud of Zoe Garrison's ability to mingle twentieth-century Western culture with traditional Arab philosophies.

ROMAIN GARY (1914–80). An eccentric Hollywood producer, his wife, and his father-in-law gather at Nice on the French Riviera in *Colors of the Day* (Simon & Schuster, 1953), translated from the French by Stephen Becker. "Mr. Gary tells his story with artistry that makes one accept the inevitability of the meeting of the two lovers and its bizarre and tragic aftermath. But better than the story itself is the sharp and biting characterization of the persons involved, each one rising up as an individual out of the complicated past that has produced him," wrote Rose Field in the *New York Herald Tribune* (September 27, 1953).

WILLIAM CAMPBELL GAULT (born 1910). Director Steve Leander faces a moral dilemma in *Death Out of Focus* (Random House, 1959) as he considers the death of his leading man, whose life was heavily insured by the producer of his latest film. The actor's death was accidental, but a second killing leads Steve to his producer's wife. At one point, Steve wonders whether the film industry can survive against the onslaught of television, only to be told, "I hope you don't think a commercial-studded wrestling match will ever replace Laurence Olivier." In the *New York Times* (March 22, 1959) Anthony Boucher described this novel as "a sharp, cynical, credible story, with nicely ironic tone and realistically ambivalent." The writing style is reminiscent of Patricia Highsmith, but the characters seem too remote for the reader to feel empathy with them.

Gault wrote three other novels with Hollywood themes: *Blood on the Boards* (E.P. Dutton, 1953), *The Sweet Blonde Trap* (Zenith Books, 1954), and *Vein of Violence* (Simon & Schuster, 1961). The first features a Los Angeles policeman whose inheritance permits him to retire; he moves to an expensive neighborhood, joins an amateur dramatic company, and sets out to prove that one of its members, a Hollywood starlet, is guilty of a series of murders. In *Vein of Violence*, a Hollywood detective's aunt and uncle purchase the mansion of a former star; when she is murdered, the detective investigates and suspects a number of her former colleagues to be guilty of the crime.

THOMAS GAVIN (born 1941). *The Last Film of Emile Vico* (Viking, 1986) takes the reader back to Hollywood in 1938 and the disappearance of actor/director Emile Vico, who has simply walked off the set of his current film. The novel is narrated by cameraman G.R. Farley and by his split personality, Spyhawk. As Spyhawk, Farley has been sending Vico disturbing "fan" letters and disseminating stories of unpleasantness on the set to a gossip columnist. It is Skyhawk who traces Vico to Death Valley, with which Vico has been obsessed since seeing *Greed*, and where he is holed up with a stuntman who was disfigured as a result of doubling for Vico on one of his films. If anything, *The Last Film of Emile Vico* is stream-of-consciousness storytelling, offering long-winded passages on filmmaking, and moving backward in time through both Vico's career and the childhood of Farley. The author tries to recount the story through a cameraman's eyes, aware that what we see or read is determined by the manner in which it is presented, how the cameraman chooses to frame the image. Coincidentally, the final scenes are viewed by Farley not through the lens of his camera but through the telescopic sight of a rifle. The only nonfictional characters in the work are Lon Chaney (a photograph of the both of them is prized by Vico), and the actors and director from *Greed*. Vico is said to have the allure of Valentino, the ingenuity of Orson Welles, and the chameleon versatility of Lon Chaney. Most readers will feel he most closely resembles Orson Welles.

WILLIAM GERHARDIE (1895–1977). At the age of 61, Charles Baldridge, the central character in *My Wife's the Least of It* (Faber and Faber, 1938), feels he has reached "a philosophical condition of life." Unfortunately his calm is shattered when a young man named Harold Burke recognizes the cinematic possibilities of Baldridge's pre–World War I novel *Dixie*. One of the characters in the book is a film magnate named Lord Comet, who also appears (or, to be more precise, is always absent) in Gerhardie's *Pending Heaven* (Harper, 1930). *My Wife's the Least of It* was reprinted in 1973 as part of the revised, definitive works of William Gerhardie, with an introduction by Michael Holroyd.

NOEL B. (Bertram) GERSON (1914–88). The principal character in *The Golden Ghetto* (M. Evans, 1989) is a New York tycoon named Max Berman, who backs underground filmmaker Lance Balutis. Introduced to a world of drugs and pop culture, Berman comes to his senses only after Balutis is murdered.

RENATO GHIOTTO. On publication, *Check to the Queen* (G.P. Putnam's Sons, 1969), translated by Isabel Quigley, was compared to *The Story of O*. The book simply documents the relationship between masochist Silvia, whose marriage has just broken up, and sadistic screen actress Margaret. Silvia's relationship with the steadily mentally deteriorating Margaret leads to her dehumanization and denigration.

CROMWELL GIBBONS (1893–19??) was apparently a screenwriter, although no films appear to have been credited to his name. The *Murder in Hollywood* (David Kemp, 1936) is of director William Whalen. Scientific detective Rex Huxford investigates the crime, checking on a film mogul, a drug-addicted actress, and a studio secretary. The critic for the *Saturday Review of Literature* (April 4, 1936) thought this "run of mill," while C.W. Morton, Jr., in the *Boston Transcript* (March 28, 1936) complained, "Our interest began to wane when we were informed that a Los Angeles newspaper headlined the case as follows: 'William Whalen Found Dead—Police Hint at Murder.' If our judgement is worth a sou, we should assert it as a fundamental truth that when anyone is ill in Hollywood he is always dying, and when he dies he is invariably murdered."

THOMAS GIFFORD (born 1937). *Hollywood Gothic* (G.P. Putnam's Sons, 1979) begins very badly with outlandish plot development but then rights itself with reasonable speed to become an engrossing suspense yarn. Screenwriter Toby Challis is on his way to prison for the murder of his wife when the helicopter in which he is traveling comes down in a snowstorm. The crew and prison officer are killed, but Challis survives and is helped back to Hollywood by the owner of a mystery bookshop whose father had been a well-known director. Challis's wife, Goldie, had been unfaithful and got her head bashed in with the Oscar statuette that her husband had won. When the police found Challis, holding the Oscar, at the side of his wife's body at their Malibu beach home, there was no reason to doubt the identity of the killer. Challis confronts Goldie's father, a movie mogul, and her grandfather, the founder of the studio that his son now controls, and they are willing to help him escape, having little love for Goldie. As Challis digs deeper, he finds unpleasant happenings in the past of his in-laws and also has a run-in with the Mafia, which is trying to take over the studio. At the novel's close, it appears that Goldie's grandfather had killed her, but as Challis sets off for a new life, he realizes the truth: he killed his wife after finding her in a compromising situation with a beachboy and then blotted out the event from his memory.

EDWIN GILBERT (1907–76) was a novelist and screenwriter of *All Through the Night* (1942) and *Larceny Incorporated* (1942). His observations of Hollywood were used to good effect in *The Squirrel Cage* (Doubleday, 1947), in which Tony Willard, a New York playwright, comes to the Millikin Studios in Hollywood. He finds his play rewritten, credit given to another, and is then fired after being branded a Communist for owning copies of the works of Chekov and Dostoevsky. "As a compendium of information on Hollywood jargon and mores, the book has a certain clinical interest," wrote the reviewer in *The New Yorker* (October 4, 1947), "but the author's major purpose—to give the film people a sound literary thrashing—has been carried out with greater sting and dexterity in many other novels."

E.X. GIROUX is a pseudonym used by Doris Shannon (born 1924) in writing a series of prim, determinedly middle-class mystery novels featuring British barrister Robert Forsythe and his aging secretary, Miss Sanderson. In

A Death of a Darling (St. Martin's Press, 1985), Miss Sanderson invites For-sythe to the country home of an elderly friend, which is about to be used for the shooting of a modern version of *Wuthering Heights*. Staying there are members of the film company, including actress Erika Von Farr, a beloved screen idol of Forsythe, and the good-looking and arrogant leading man, Mickey Darling. When the latter is subject to a murder attempt, which leaves a former girlfriend actress of Darling dead, Forsythe investigates, with the complete blessing of the police department—and comes up with the wrong solution. When Forsythe eventually figures out what happened, Darling has been shot by the film's cine-matographer, whose daughter was drugged and seduced by Darling, and Miss Sanderson declares that justice has been served. As for Erike Von Farr, Forsythe admits she is a great actress, "and that is all Erika Von Farr will ever be."

DOUGLAS GLOVER (born 1948). After a month in jail, drunken and feckless Tully Stamper returns to Gomez Gap, Florida, in *The South Will Rise at Noon* (Viking, 1988). He finds his ex-wife in bed with the director of a Civil War drama being filmed in the town, a film that gets out of control as the racist inhabitants of Gomez Gap decide it is time for the South to rise again—and to rise against Tully Stamper. The latter is a vaguely likable antihero, and the novel is disarmingly crazy.

CONSTANCE GLUYAS (born 1920). *Brief Is the Glory* (David McKay, 1975) documents the life of the son of a well-known Mexican bullfighter who becomes a major Hollywood star.

HERBERT GOLD (born 1924) unleashes a flood of consciousness in *Swiftie the Magician* (McGraw-Hill, 1974) as 40-year-old narrator Frank Curtis reviews his life in the 1960s, moving from television writer/director in New York to film writer/director in Hollywood. As Curtis discusses his two lovers, Kathy and Karen, the book provides a popular culture view of American society in a decade that began in a time "when love and money solved every-thing. Ike still smiled almost daily. The country was dressed for the senior prom." The title character is a female designer friend of Kathy, with whom Cur-tis has one sexual encounter and from whom he contracts a venereal disease. She is also the subject of the best line in the novel: "She played herself on a projector not adapted for cinemascope; she came out long and narrow, abruptly an anachronism."

WILLIAM GOLDMAN (born 1931) is a highly regarded novelist and screenwriter. He won Academy Awards for his scripts for *Butch Cassidy and the Sundance Kid* (1970) and *All the President's Men* (1976); his other screenplays in-clude *Marathon Man* (1976) and *Heat* (1987), both from his own novels.

Tinsel (Delacorte Press, 1979) is the story of Hollywood mogul Julian Garvey, whose son would like to follow in his father's footsteps. Garvey tries to help the young man by giving him the opportunity to produce a script based on the final hours of Marilyn Monroe's life. "*Tinsel* is not so much a story as a bright idea surrounded by halfhearted attempts to create character," wrote Michael Wood in *American Film* (September 1979).

It is something like a do-it-yourself Hollywood novel, in which Goldman reminds us of the proper clichés, and we do the rest. The writing could hardly be slacker. People give affirmative answers instead of saying yes, and murmer things like "Would that it were that easy." ... When Goldman wants to do a New York sequence, he simply names schools and streets and says an apartment is "antique laden." Any old realistic hack would blush at the prospect of leaving things so completely to the set designer. Still, there is something here, even if the fantasy is entirely unreconstructed.

OLIVIA GOLDSMITH. *Flavor of the Month* (Poseidon Press, 1993) is the story of three women who are brought together to costar in a television series. Mary Jane Moran is a plump New York actress. When her lover and director, Sam Shields, leaves her for a Hollywood career, she undergoes extensive plastic surgery, reducing her weight, beautifying her face, knocking years off her age, and renaming herself Jahne Moore. Sharleen Smith, a poor woman from Texas, is apparently having an incestuous relationship with her brother Dean. Lila Kyle is the daughter of legendary Hollywood star Theresa O'Donnell, who would perform a ventriloquist act with two dummies, more precious to her than her daughter. Lila Kyle is mentally unstable, and as the popularity of her costars grows, she seeks to destroy them by revealing their past to gossip columnists and tabloid newspapers. Jahne Moore's plastic surgery is exposed after she gets back together with Sam Shields. (He had directed her first feature film, which, after shooting, and with the use of body doubles, was turned into an explicit sexual feature.) After Sharleen Smith's relationship with her brother is reported, it is learned that Dean is not her blood brother. Stars flock to Jahne Moore's defense, endorsing her plastic surgery. All three stars are nominated for the Emmy for Best Actress, but at the ceremony an out-of-work stand-up comedian, whom Jahne Moore had known and liked in New York, goes berserk and shoots Lila Kaye out of anger over nepotism in the entertainment industry. At the hospital, Lila Kaye is found to be, in reality, a transvestite. Jahne Moore marries her plastic surgeon, and Sharleen Smith and Dean discover a new life on a Wyoming ranch.

This is a novel of epic proportions—some 700 pages in length—which requires fortitude and a suspension of disbelief by the reader. On the plus side, the author does manage to work in numerous negative comments on the Hollywood scene, for which she obviously has little respect. The book is supposedly written by a gossip columnist, who occasionally ingratiates herself into the pages, but the concept does not work well since these interruptions are so few and far between that the reader tends to forget who the narrator is. Aside from the basic plotline, there are a number of subplots and a host of secondary characters. The attitude of the author and her characters toward homosexuality is patronizing, and the notion that a woman would undergo extensive plastic surgery in order to win back her lover is one that surely must diplease a feminist audience.

RAMON GOMEZ de la SERNA (1886–1963). *Movieland* (Macaulay Company, 1930), translated from the Spanish by Angel Flores, presents a highly fictionalized look at Hollywood, its stars, and its great films, "events too beautiful to be true." Originally published under the title *Cinelandia*, the author was a Spaniard who never set foot in Los Angeles.

ROSE GORDON and IONE REED. *Stunt Girl* (George Palmer Putnam, 1940) features stunt girl Carol Raymond, the novel's narrator, who falls in love with "suicide director" Bill Woollcott. After a stunt goes wrong and she hurtles down a cliff at 60 miles an hour, the director's attitude toward her changes and the two are married. They recommence their careers, part, and are reunited. Coauthor Ione Reed was a Hollywood stunt girl.

JOHN GORMAN was not a writer of distinction, although *Hollywood's Bad Boy* (Eugene V. Brewster, 1932) does adopt a moral tone in the suggestion that there is nothing wrong with the women of Hollywood or its directors; only producers and production supervisors expect extras to sleep with them. The novel opens with director Robert Marlin's divorce from his second wife. In celebration, he throws a drunken party attended by his assistant director, Joe, Joe's girlfriend, Daisy, and an actress named Tolly Lane. Daisy dies of alcoholism, and Joe and Tolly sort out the mess. Marlin decides that Tolly must escape from the degeneracy that is Hollywood and sets her up in a Beverly Hills house with a pet dog, a new car, and a monthly check. He expects nothing from her in return. The director is delighted when he is invited to make a new film starring Betsy Earl. He meets her and her mother, and discovers that the actress neither drinks nor smokes. The two fall in love while on location and plan to marry on return to Hollywood, but once there Betsy's mother dies and Betsy inadvertently signs a contract with a morals clause that forbids her to marry for three years. The couple have no alternative but to hide their relationship. Betsy takes to drinking and must undergo an appendicitis operation (a Hollywood euphemism for abortion). Only when the three years are up does Marlin discover that Betsy has become a drug addict. He is later shot, presumably by the drug dealer, and Tolly nurses him back to health. Betsy goes off to Europe for treatment, but unable to recover fully, she decides to marry a fellow drug addict, who is Chinese. Marlin discovers that all along he was in love with Tolly: "A year later, not in Hollywood, but far away where they would find peace and happiness, Bob and Tolly were quietly married." Interestingly, the publisher, Eugene V. Brewster, once headed a fan magazine publishing empire that included *Motion Picture Magazine* and *Motion Picture Classic*.

RON GOULART (born 1933) is a prolific author of science fiction novels and short stories. He has been referred to as the Woody Allen of science fiction. His comedy bent is very apparent in *Cowboy Heaven* (Doubleday, 1979). Here, Andy Stokes takes time out from pursuing the gossip columnist for *Screenfreak* magazine to help out a former stuntman, Bronc Swanley, from the Cowboy Heaven Museum in Texas. Aging cowboy star Jake Troop is too ill to work on an upcoming multimillion-dollar movie, and so Stokes creates an android of the actor. But the robot is too good a replica and takes on all the personality traits of Troop, including his heavy drinking.

Set in 1940 or 1941, *Skyrocket Steele* (Pocket Books, 1990) has pulp fiction writer Pete Tinsley obtain a job as screenwriter on the serial *Skyrocket*

Steele for Star-Spangled Studios. He falls in love with an assistant to the head of the studio and discovers that she has remarkable powers: she can elevate and throw her victims great distances without touching them. After that initial shock, Tinsley is less surprised to discover that she and various senior executives at the studio are, in reality, aliens from another planet. They are using the subterfuge of moviemaking to build spaceships and weapons that can be used to conquer Earth. A rival group of aliens from another planet arrives on the scene, and a battle ensues, leaving both sides decimated but Tinsley's girlfriend intact and able to face the future at his side.

PAULA GOULD. In *Publicity Girl* (House of Field, 1940), eighteen-year-old New Yorker Constance Carey obtains a job as a stenographer in the publicity department of Supreme Pictures. Within a year, she is one of the publicity team and quickly makes a name for herself. In the meantime, she meets and sleeps with handsome newspaperman Tony Wayne. He goes on assignment to Russia, fails to keep in touch with her, and when he returns is accompanied by a new wife. Constance is unable to break with Tony, and the two begin an affair; Tony's wife refuses a divorce and turns the table on publicist Constance by publicizing her relationship with Tony. As a result of the publicity, the Hays Office orders Supreme Pictures to fire Constance as her behavior reflects badly on the film industry. Tony and his bride leave for Argentina, and at the novel's close, Constance rejects suicide but still faces the future in a tragic mood. *Publicity Girl* was originally promoted as a romance, but, for its time, it is a remarkably powerful and original work, deserving of wider attention.

CARROLL and **GARRET GRAHAM** were two brothers who wrote *Queer People* (Vanguard Press, 1930), in its day the most scandalous novel ever written about Hollywood, one that everyone in the film community read but which no one dared to be seen reading. The screen rights were acquired by Howard Hughes, who throughout the 1930s threatened to film the novel but never did. It is a work of comedy though of such biting intensity that its authors obviously despise the film industry and most of its senior members.

Queer People is the story of newspaperman Theodore Anthony "Whitey" White, who arrives penniless in Los Angeles from Chicago. Most of his time in Los Angeles is spent partying, but in between and often as a result of those parties he takes on various jobs. First, by mistaken identity, he is hired as a member of the scenario department at Colossal Pictures, whose president is the benevolent Jacob Schmalz, known as "Papa Jake," who has many relatives on the payroll and a son serving as a senior executive. There is little question that Schmalz and son are based on Carl and Junior Laemmle. When Whitey is found out to be a fraud, he is not removed from the lot but instead becomes a press agent, organizing a banquet to honor Junior Schmalz. "John Barrymore, as was his custom, wired regrets." When Jacob Schmalz uses the event as an excuse to fire his general manager and replace him with his son, Whitey denounces the mogul and walks off the lot. Next, he becomes publicist for an Elinor Glyn type. He seeks revenge, through blackmail, on an executive who has sexually abused a woman whom he secretly loves. He sells a film script. He obtains a position in a popular Hollywood brothel. He sings off-camera for a former silent star who has no voice for the talkies. Finally, he takes responsibility for a killing by the same woman to whom he is devoted. He is acquitted and leaves Los Angeles for New York, but not before placing his footprints surreptitiously in the cement at Grauman's Chinese Theatre.

There is much great descriptive material and capturing of the essence of Hollywood personalities in *Queer People*. The Grahams write that the junction of Wilcox and Cahuenga avenues forms the apex of a triangle ("unconsciously phallic") of which Hollywood Boulevard is the base. They continue:

> Between those streets one can find actors, authors, artists, acrobats and astrologers, coon-shouters, chorus girls, confidence men, comedians, camera-crankers, Christian Scientists, and call-houses, directors, gangmen, song writers, sadists, psalm singers, soothsayers, and sycophants, press agents, pugilists, policemen, perverts, pickpockets, panhandlers, pimps, playwrights, prostitutes, and parsons and playgirls (both unfrocked), bootleggers, bandits, bookmakers and Babbits, remittance men, radio announcers and realtors, Jews, Gentiles, Mohammedans and Rosicrucians, all living like Mormons, manicurists, misanthropes, misogynists and masochists, women of all sexes and men of none.

It is one of the most brilliantly evocative passages in the entire history of the Hollywood novel.

Budd Schulberg criticized the Grahams, writing in *Films* (Spring 1940),

> Actually, its characters form an unbelievable procession of unmitigated frauds. Hollywood may have its share of such men, but it seems careless and even dangerous to assume that they are any more indigenous to Hollywood and motion pictures than to any other American community or industry. Nor, even granting that they do exist, have the Grahams revealed what produces them, how they think and feel. In other words, the Grahams have failed to supply that without which no book can be good or real—compassion.

Queer People was republished in 1976 by Southern Illinois University Press as part of its "Lost American Fiction" series. Schulberg contributed an afterword, which was somewhat more complimentary about the book.

The novel was immensely popular, going through 11 printings, when it was first published. It gave birth to two sequel volumes, neither of which was concerned with the film industry: *Whitey; the Playboy of "Queer People" Runs Riot in Manhattan* (Vanguard Press, 1931), and *Kings Back to Back: Whitey, the Irrepressible, Infests Europe* (Vanguard Press, 1932).

ROBERT GRANIT is a pseudonym used by an author who is also the central character and narrator of ***Another Runner in the Night*** (A&W Publishers, 1981). Granit has produced two grade-B movies and one low-rated Movie of the Week for ABC. That was when he was dating Kate Kantor, the daughter of Simon Kantor, chief of production at ZKI Pictures. Now Granit is openly gay, and with his lover, J.B., he flies to Hollywood with plans to produce a script he has written for a singer, well loved by gay audiences, who has previously turned down all film offers but who likes Granit. The film is to be made by Kantor's studio. Granit's life and what is left of his career fall apart in Los Angeles as his gay lifestyle overwhelms him. He kicks and beats a gossip columnist with whom he has had a longstanding feud, and J.B. drops him for a promiscuous lifestyle and the leading role in a television series. With nothing left, Granit returns to New York.

The publisher describes *Another Runner in the Night* as a roman à clef, but it is difficult to identify any of the players, including Granit. Presumably the aging gay director here called Wesley Strich is George Cukor. A guest at the director's parties, Ray Dankoff, is obviously Paul Lynde. J.B.'s former Hollywood lover, here called Alex Bostwick, is probably Sal Mineo. The novel presents a depressing view of the film community. As a cocaine dealer describes it:

> There are money lenders at every studio, every TV. . . . Do you know how many major stars have gambling habits? And drug habits! Jesus, they import more cocaine in this town than they make movies. This is the city of illusions, my man, and everybody puts on a big show here, but underneath it they're all broke. They have to scrape it together to pay their Mexican maids. They live on advances from their agents, if the agent is lucky enough to be solvent.

The primary appeal of *Another Runner in the Night* is as a document of gay culture in the late 1970s and early 1980s, the gay man's fixation with sex, and the gay mafia. More than drugs and alcohol, it is the gay lifestyle that destroys the central figure here. He wants to be liberated but is unwilling to accept the limits placed on his lifestyle by the Hollywood establishment.

MARGARET GRANT was the joint pseudonym of the husband-and-wife writing team of Rose D. (Dorothy) Franken (1895–1988) and William Brown Meloney (1905–71). ***Call Back Love*** (Farrar & Rinehart, 1937) compares the lives of a five-year-old girl who becomes a star and remains unspoiled and that of her mother, who would like to be a star. "It is unfair to dwell on the fundamental silliness of a book like this, because it makes no pretensions to be anything but what the jacket calls 'a gay and tender story.' If it seems neither especially gay nor tender, it is at least about Hollywood, and a wide public regards Hollywood as sure fire stuff no matter what. Here we have no matter what," wrote the critic for the *Saturday Review of Literature* (October 2, 1937).

BERKELEY GRAY was the pseudonym of Edwy Searles Brooks. ***Conquest in California*** (William Collins & Sons, 1958) is identified by Carolyn See as a Hollywood novel.

DULCIE GRAY (born 1919) was a popular British stage and screen actress—*Mine Own Executioner* (1947), *The Glass Mountain* (1948), and others—who often worked with her husband, Michael Denison. She is also the author of a number of novels, including ***The Glanville Women*** (Michael Joseph, 1982). Described by Rebecca West as "Thackerayan," this is the saga of three women, Kate, Bess, and Laura Glanville, three generations of a famous British theatrical family. It begins in 1910 with the marriage of Kate, whose parents, Madge and Harry Glanville, are two of the country's best-known theatrical personalities, and concludes in the 1970s with her granddaughter Laura's writing a novel based on the family history. Much of Kate's story takes place in Malaya (where Dulcie Gray was born and grew up); there is considerable theatrical history and folklore recorded, with brief appearances by many nonfictional theatrical figures of the day. Bess becomes a film star with Gainsborough Pictures in the 1940s, and the novel contains a brief description of the company, presumably based on first-hand knowledge. The book is well written in a somewhat staid fashion and highly engrossing; its only fault is the author's obsession with trivia, much of it unrelated to the plot or the characters.

CHARLES GRAYSON (born 1905). *Spotlight Madness* (Liveright, 1931) follows the rise to fame of screen actor Ethan Doyle, whose self-love conquers all his emotions but loses the girl for him. "Apart from its shrewd character study, *Spotlight Madness* indicates that the author knows thoroughly his Hollywood background from the inside out," wrote the reviewer in *Bookman* (April 1931). Less enthusiastic was the critic for the *New York Times* (March 8, 1931): "The paraphernalia of the book clogs its development; technical talk and a persistent vein of Hollywood gossip stand in the way of mature dissection. Yet in its pages there are flashes of quick observation, an occasional trenchancy of phrase, sparks of a satiric irony which are all too often stalemated by the author's tendency to remind himself that he must get on with the story, that he has a climax to meet some pages hence."

The Show Case (Green Circle Books, 1936) studies the various individuals involved in film production, with particular emphasis on publicity writers. The novel concludes with the suicide of a former Hollywood star. "Readers who are perennially interested in the parties, wire-pulling and scandals of film city will find *The Show Case* revelations satisfactory," noted the reviewer in the *New York Times* (June 28, 1936). "It is the same old lurid Hollywood heartbreak, dished up in thin, spicy slices."

In *Venus Rising* (Henry Holt, 1954), a New York obstetrician hopes to marry one actress but is attracted to another when she comes to him for hormone injections. In an ironic twist, the novel ends as the doctor is helping the second actress retain a role in a Hollywood film in order that her rival, the first actress, will return to him.

KATE GREEN. *Shooting Star* (HarperCollins, 1992) is a suspense novel involving actress Nyia Wyatt, who is stalked by an obsessive fan while shooting on location in New Mexico. When she discovers she is being secretly videotaped, the actress has no choice but to turn to the local police for help.

MARTIN HARRY GREENBERG (born 1945) **and CHARLES WAUGH** (born 1943), editors. *Hollywood Unreal* (Taplinger, 1982) anthologizes 13 science fiction and fantasy stories inspired by Hollywood:

"Werewind," by J. Michael Reaves (1981)
"Payment Anticipated," by C.S. Forester (1951)
"The Gahan Wilson Horror Movie Pocket Computer" by Gahan Wilson (1980)
"E for Effort," by T.L. Sherred (1947)
"The Missing Idol," by Ben Hecht (1939)
"The Never-Ending Western Movie," by Robert Sheckley (1976)

"The Movie People," by Robert Bloch (1969)
"The Meadow," by Ray Bradbury (1948)
"Double Take," by Jack Finney (1965)
"Really Unlimited," by Robert Silverberg (1957)
"The Movie House," by Harold Fast (1980)
"The Jocelin Shrager Story," by Thomas M. Disch (1975)
"The Movie-Makers," by Henry Slesar (1956)

GAEL GREENE's first novel, *Blue Skies, No Candy* (William Morrow, 1976), is the story of a happily married and successful screenwriter, Kate Alexander, who, at the age of 40, has a steamy love affair. The author was the restaurant critic for *New York* magazine, and reviewers at the time noted her penchant for describing exotic meals herein.

WILLIAM B. GREENE. *Hollywood Virgin* (Carousel Books, 1962) is one of a series of novels with a Hollywood background identified by Carolyn See as "semi-pornographic." No other information is available.

JOSH GREENFELD (born 1928) co-wrote the 1974 novel and screenplay *Harry and Tonto*, and the central character in *The Return of Mr. Hollywood* (Doubleday, 1984) would appear to be based on Greenfeld's collaborator, Paul Mazursky. "Mr. Hollywood" is Larry Lazar, a crude, vulgar, and presumably authentic Hollywood director/screenwriter who considers himself something of an auteur but has, in fact, relied for success on ideas stolen from collaborators. He is, in the words of writer Max Isaacs (Josh Greenfeld?), "an evil phony, a congenital liar, and a dilettante prick." The bulk of the novel concerns Lazar's return to New York for his mother's funeral. Greenfeld obviously disliked his Hollywood fling, and this is a venal attack on the community and its inhabitants.

MOLLIE GREGORY. *Triplets* (Franklin Watts, 1988) begins in the 1930s with the births of Sara Bay, Stephanie Skylar, and Edward Vail Wyman to a wealthy San Francisco family. Sara and Sky are determined to be actresses, while Vail (against the wishes of his mother) wants to be a writer. He experiences the sexual freedom and the drug appeal of the 1960s and 1970s, Sky journeys through the degradation of Hollywood, and Sara becomes a film director in Rome. A novel of five decades, *Triplets* is long but entertaining to those who revel in family sagas.

With the opening of *Birthstone* (Jove, 1991), only Sara, still a director, and Vail, a film critic, are alive. Much of what the pair face is left over from the previous novel. The deranged fan who murdered Sky is out of prison and proving troublesome to both Sara and her mother. Sara's daughter Lindy is also out of prison, having served time there and in a mental institution for the murder of her lover, Archie. Her son by Archie is now being brought up by Vail and his wife, Patsy. Lindy embarks on a career as an assistant to a temperamental film director. And so it goes on . . .

MAYSIE GREIG (1902–71) wrote more than 200 romantic novels. *Professional Lover* (Doubleday, Doran, 1933) is a typical romance in the

Hollywood genre. Attractive reporter Starr Thayle interviews Hollywood star Rex Brandon, takes an instant dislike to him, writes a negative article, and is fired. Brandon hires the reporter and tries to change her attitude toward him. The novel ends with her a star, playing love scenes opposite him both on screen and in real life. *Professional Lover* was reprinted in 1943 by Doubleday, Doran and Triangle Books.

The central character in *Romance for Sale* (Doubleday, Doran, 1934) is actress Odette Cosway; she and Lance Furner are known as "Britain's Most Perfect Screen Lovers." She is devoted to the film industry until she becomes innocently involved in scandal. The story is set in London, Morocco, and Hollywood. "Film fans who dote on everything about the movies, particularly the perils to a young star's virtue, will probably find it well up to the standards of the motion picture magazines," commented a reviewer in the *New York Times* (August 12, 1934).

No Retreat from Love (Doubleday, Doran, 1942) begins in England with Penny's objecting to her foster brother Alex's marriage to film star Felicity Summers. Penny goes to Hollywood to take care of their child. She and Felicity become romantically involved with the same British screen star, but a gossip columnist helps Penny win out in the end. *Kirkus* (August 21, 1942) compared this to "a penny dreadful," condemning it as "tripe."

See also **Jennifer Ames**.

RICHARD GRENIER. *The Marrakesh One-Two* (Houghton Mifflin, 1983) is more concerned with the Arab than with the film world as screenwriter Burt Nelson struggles to complete a film version of the life of Mohammed. In the process, he must deal with the mysteries of Arab culture, an attempted coup against the king of Morocco, a terrorist kidnapping, a meeting with Colonel Kaddafi of Libya, and the activities of the CIA. Senator Daniel Patrick Moynihan is apparently a fan of the author and describes the novel as "immensely entertaining."

CORINNE GRIFFITH (1894–1979) was a major star of the late teens and twenties who claimed a decade later not to be the actress but her stand-in, who took over when the real Corinne Griffith died; friends and colleagues could perceive no difference between the "old" and the "new" Corinne Griffith.

Of *Hollywood Stories* (Frederick Fell, 1962), the publisher explains, "Based somewhat on fact, and artfully enlivened by the author's imagination, each tale is not only dedicated to one of Hollywood's 'greats,' but challenges the reader to imagine his favorite player in its central role." "Heaven by the Tale" is for Marilyn Monroe; "Hollywood Story" for Frank Sinatra; "Somewhat Seventeen" for David Niven; "Tan Diddy! Tan Diddy! Tan Diddy! Ahuntin' We Will Go!" for Corinne Griffith; "Unfinished Story" for Gary Cooper; "D Street, Southeast" for Eddie "Rochester" Anderson; "Sports Is for Sports" for Bob Hope; and "It's My Life" for a performer selected by the reader. Definitely not a book that should be considered for reprinting.

DORIS GRUMBACH (born 1918). In the early days of the talkies and in *Missing Persons* (G.P. Putnam's Sons, 1981), blonde star Franny Fuller is so overwhelmed by her success that she turns to drugs and alcohol and attempts to sleep her life away.

BILL GUNN (1934–89) was an African American novelist, playwright, and screenwriter (eight films between 1968 and 1976). His first novel, *All the Rest Have Died* (Delacorte Press, 1964), is semiautobiographical, the story of Barney Gifford, who comes to New York from Philadelphia in order to embark on an acting career. *Black Picture Show* (Reed, Cannon & Johnson, 1975) began life as a stageplay (produced on Broadway by Joseph Papp in January 1975), and is the story of a black poet and writer whose son has taken to writing exploitative films.

    Rhinestone Sharecropping (I. Reed Books, 1981) is perhaps based in part on Gunn's experiences in the film industry. It is narrated by screenwriter Sam Dodd, who is hired to write the script for a film on the life of a football player. Much of the novel is taken up with his and his father's memories and the reality of his marriage and life on the verge of poverty. During a script conference that seems contrived, Dodd is fired. The title is Dodd's wife's description of working for the Hollywood industry.

JOYCE HABER (1932–93) was America's last great gossip columnist, succeeding Hedda Hopper at the *Los Angeles Times* in 1966 and remaining with the newspaper until 1975, when she quit to write her only novel, *The Users* (Delacorte Press, 1976). In reviewing the book, *Time* described Haber as "Hollywood's No. 1 voyeur," and the book became a number-one bestseller on the lists of both the *New York Times* and the *Los Angeles Times*. *The Users* is the story of a Hollywood hostess and social climber named Elena, who loves gossip and whose troubles include an early pornographic film in which she stars which has been acquired by a Mafia figure, as well as a husband with writer's block. The book is described as a roman à clef, and one can only wonder to what extent the characters are based on Haber and her former husband, film and television producer Douglas Cramer. Among the Hollywood crowd mentioned in the book, but not involved in the plotline, are Milton Berle, Truman Capote, Doris Day, Cary Grant, Gregory Peck, Rex Reed, Barbra Streisand, and Gore Vidal.

PETER HAINING (born 1940). *The Hollywood Nightmare: Tales of Fantasy and Horror from the Film World* (Taplinger, 1970) is an anthology of short stories with Hollywood-related themes, with an introduction by Christopher Lee: "The Prehistoric Producer," by Ray Bradbury; "The Plot Is the Thing," by Robert Bloch; "The Shadow on the Screen," by Henry Kuttner; "Return to the Sabbath," by Tarleton Fiske; "A Wig for Miss Devore," by August Derleth; "The Man Who Wanted to Be in the Movies," by John Jakes; "The Perfect Plot," by Frank Fenton; "Death Double," by William F. Nolan; "Booked Solid," by Ray Russell; "The Hollywood Horror Man," by Boris Karloff; "The Casket Demon," by Franz Leiber; "The New People," by Charles Beaumont; "Gavin O'Leary," by John Collier; "Fade Out," by Avram Davidson; "Montage," by Richard Matheson; "Technical Adviser," by Chad Oliver; "The Screen Game," by J.G. Ballard; and "Death Warmed Over," by Ray Bradbury.

RICHARD HALAS was the pseudonym of Eric Knight (1897–1943) (q.v.). The hero of *You Play the Black and the Red Comes Up* (Robert M. McBride, 1938) moves from Oklahoma to California when his wife deserts him. He becomes involved with two women and is accused of killing one of them. Sentenced to death, he is saved when a movie mogul friend commits suicide and confesses to the murder. *The Times* (January 15, 1938) commented, "Although every character in this book by any ordinary standards is crazy the book itself has a curious air of reality; and there is a quickening of interest and even drama, which the rough and deliberately casual style only partly obscures, and a sincere pathos at the end to which this mannerism is splendid contrast."

FRANKLIN HALL. *Ben Turpin, Private Eye* (Aran, 1985) has the cross-eyed comedian solving the 1922 murder of director William Desmond Taylor. Well, why not — no one else has yet been able to accomplish this satisfactorily.

ROBERT LEE HALL (born 1941). *Murder at San Simeon* (St. Martin's Press, 1988) is great fun, a carefully constructed mystery novel written with a good sense of period (the early 1930s) and knowledge of the workings of William Randolph Hearst's castle. Marion Davies throws a party, and among the assorted guests are at least two men with a grudge against Hearst, one of whom may be plotting to kill the newspaper tycoon. Gossip columnist Louella Parsons investigates, determined to save her mentor, but it is Hearst himself who ultimately unravels the mystery. Among the nonfictional characters who play a part in the story are Charlie Chaplin, Marie Dressler, Jean Harlow, Hedda Hopper, Herman J. Mankiewicz, and Adela Rogers St. Johns. Presumably Mankiewicz is there gathering data for his 1941 script collaboration on *Citizen Kane*. As a further tribute to that film, a globe with a snow scene plays a crucial role in the plot, a globe almost identical to that which falls from Kane's hand as he utters the word *Rosebud*.

WILBUR HALL. There are references to the motion picture industry in *Mr. Jory* (Ziff Davis, 1947), the story of the title character who comes to Los Angeles for his health, becomes involved in the oil industry, profits in real estate, exposes graft at city hall, etc., etc., etc.

BRETT HALLIDAY was the pseudonym of David Dresser (1904–77). *Kill All the Young Girls* (Dell, 1973) begins with actress Kate Thackera trying to kill studio head Larry Zion while he is in Florida, attending a meeting of the stockholders of Consolidated-Famous Pictures. Mike Shayne is hired by Zion's son to protect his father by keeping a close watch on Thackera, who is almost immediately killed in a bomb explosion. Shayne learns of an earlier death — of Zion discovery Keko Brannon — and he meets with publisher Oscar Olson, who is trying to take over the studio. After another murder and a number of shootings, the novel reaches its climax at the shareholders' meeting, at which Zion is exposed as Thackera's killer and Zion's daughter-in-law as the murderer of Brannon.

The character of Brannon is perhaps loosely based on 20th Century–Fox contract star Marilyn Monroe. Zion is obviously Darryl F. Zanuck. The historical backgrounds of both men are similar, and like Zanuck, "Zion's one endearing trait is that he always believes his current bed companion has great box-office potential. The idea is: if *he* wants to ball her, so will his audience." Despite the explicit violence and the promise (unrealized) of lurid sex, this is unquestionably a tedious read.

RICHARD HALLIDAY (1905–73) was a producer and critic of stage and films as well as a novelist. His first book, *Fanfare* (G.P. Putnam's Sons, 1929), is the story of an ambitious mother who promotes her daughter into a Hollywood star but, ultimately, cannot prevent her from marrying the man she loves. "In many ways an arresting novel, *Fanfare* marks the debut of a fresh and vigorous talent," wrote Lloyd Morris in the *New York Herald Tribune* (September 15, 1929). "The most obvious merit of Mr. Halliday's work is its abundant vitality. Its vitality apart, *Fanfare* possesses at least three major merits. One is narrative interest; read purely as story, this novel enlists and retains the reader's attention. Another merit, more important than the talent for narrative, is powerful and convincing characterization. A third merit of *Fanfare* is novelty of material."

CHARLES HAMBLETT has written two show business biographies, *Who Killed Marilyn Monroe?* (1966), reprinted as *The Hollywood Cage: Who Killed Marilyn Monroe* (1969), and *Paul Newman* (1975). *The Crazy Kill: A Fantasy* (Sidgwick & Jackson, 1956) is a roman à clef based on the filming of *Moby Dick* (1956), with the director here called John Simpson (John Huston), the star Gregory Pinch (Gregory Peck), the location the Budgerigar Islands (the Canary Islands), and the film *The White Whale*. And just in case there is any doubt in the reader's mind, the novel opens with an introduction by John Huston, who talks of becoming friendly with author Hamblett while shooting *Moby Dick* in Ireland and the Canary Islands.

DIANA HAMMOND. *Sweet Lies* (Bernard Geis, 1979) chronicles the making of a European feature film, *Lovers and Clowns*, and its French director, Italian leading lady, and British rock star leading man. When English producer Ian Spencer is forced to move the location shooting from southern France to a Swiss ski resort, relationships spin out of control. A helicopter crash kills off a number of the novel's principal players. "Like a good B feature at the Bijou— firm and, in spite of all the trashy goings-on, moderately involving" was the opinion of *Kirkus*.

DAVID HANDLER. Veteran ghostwriter Hoagy Hoag, accompanied by his basset hound, Lulu, travels from New York to Hollywood to help boy wonder director Matthew Wax write his autobiography in ***The Boy Who Never Grew Up*** (Doubleday, 1992). Wax is in the middle of an unpleasant divorce from his actress wife, Pennyroyal Brim, whose autobiography is currently being ghostwritten by Cassandra Dee. Brim is determined to gain control of her husband's studio, named Bedford Falls after the town in *It's a Wonderful Life*, and sell it to Norbert Schlom, president of Panorama City. The novel becomes a murder mystery when Brim's lawyer is killed, but nothing can stop Hoag's wisecracks, nor the author from overextending his story.

JACK HANLEY. *Star Lust* (W. Godwin, 1934) is identified by Carolyn See as a Hollywood novel. The book was reprinted by Grayson Publishing in 1949.

WILLIAM HANLEY (born 1931). In *Mixed Feelings* (Doubleday, 1972), the homosexual husband of a Broadway producer's daughter writes a novel about his marriage and asks his wife's lover, a Broadway director, to direct the movie version.

DAVID HANLY. When an American film crew goes to Ireland in search of the "real" Ireland in *In Guilt and In Glory* (William Morrow, 1979), the tourist office bureaucrat who escorts them must decide between the traditional and the modern Ireland.

EDWARD HANNIBAL (born 1936). In his second novel, *Dancing Man* (Simon & Schuster, 1973), Hannibal examines the life of a New York-based filmmaker who goes to live in his late grandfather's home on Cape Cod, and finds direction in his life—confronting the present through the past—by making a documentary on the old man.

JOSEPH HANSEN (born 1923) is noted for a series of mystery novels featuring insurance investigator Dave Brandstetter, published between 1970 and 1991. Brandstetter just happens to be gay, and virtually all of Hansen's novels feature gay characters and gay situations. Brandstetter also happens to work in Los Angeles, but his place of residence and business brings him into little contact with the film community. From the first Brandstetter novel, *Fadeout* (Harper & Row, 1970), we do know that he likes the films of Carl Th. Dreyer and D.W. Griffith, but he has never attended a film screening in the course of the series. *Skinflick* (Holt, Rinehart and Winston, 1979) has Brandstetter investigating the murder of a right-wing bigot who is a partner in a film equipment rental company and a pornographic film enterprise. The non–Brandstetter novel *Backtrack* (Foul Play Press/The Countryman Press, 1982) is narrated by teenager Alan Tarr, who is trying to determine whether the death of his actor father, Alan Tarr, was suicide or murder; one of the main characters is a homosexual Hollywood agent. An actor, Oliver Jewett, is the central character in *Job's Year* (Holt, Rinehart and Winston, 1983); he looks back over his life and loses his role in a television soap opera. In *Steps Going Down* (Foul Play Press/The Countryman Press, 1985), a hustler commits two murders in order to retain the love of a self-centered actor/beach bum. *Living Upstairs* (Dutton, 1993) is the story of a gay love affair set in Los Angeles during the Second World War. It is of minor interest in that one of the secondary characters, Richard Sheridan Ames, was a real person, a theater and film critic who wrote for *Rob Wagner's Script* and other publications.

JIM HARMON (born 1933) has written a number of works on popular culture, including *The Great Movie Serials* (1972), *Nostalgia Catalogue* (1973), and *The Great Television Heroes* (1975). *The Celluloid Scandal* (Art Enterprises, 1961) is one of a series of novels with a Hollywood background identified by Carolyn See as "semi-pornographic." No other information is available.

SANDRA HARMON. Told in flashback, *A Girl Like Me* (E.P. Dutton, 1975) has a nameless narrator who marries a producer of animated film, becomes a magazine writer in Hollywood, and writes a successful screenplay based on one of her articles on women's problems. Through it all, she is incapable of having a successful relationship.

MacDONALD HARRIS is the pseudonym of Donald Heiney (born 1921). An elegant writing style cannot mask the reality that *Screenplay* (Atheneum, 1982) is derivative, in need of structure, and heavily padded. Alys, the young and wealthy narrator of the novel, is persuaded to rent a room in his house to a strange and elderly filmmaker named Julius Nesselrode. Alys discovers that Nesselrode produced silent films, and one day he goes with his lodger to an abandoned Los Angeles movie theater, steps with him behind the screen, and finds himself in a Culver City movie lot of the 1920s. Enamored of the leading lady, Moira Silver, whom he meets there, Alys begs Nesselrode to take him back behind the screen, where the producer will feature him in movies. Back in the past, Alys learns from Moira that neither can escape to the present. "They own us," she tells him. "Once we're in pictures we belong to them." But Alys remembers how he came to be in the past, and brings Moira with him to the present, only to discover that in passing through the screen, she ages (as in James Hilton's *Lost Horizon*). Alys and Moira settle down together, with the former discovering that Moira remains his love, aged as she may be.

Alys first discovers silent films at screenings at the Los Angeles County Museum of Art, and the author/narrator provides a distinguished commentary on the medium:

> For me, the world of the silent film was another world than our own—an artificial and synthetic world in which there existed another life parallel to our own and yet different—a world where other physical laws operated so that impossible athletic feats could be performed and devastating accidents happen without harm to the victim—where even the laws of psychology and character were different, where there was a freedom, an invulnerability, a kind of zany marionette behavior that made everything simpler and less complex than life in our real world of three dimensions.

TIMOTHY HARRIS (born 1946) is a novelist and screenwriter. His mystery *Goodnight and Goodbye* (Delacorte Press, 1979) concerns a private eye obsessed by a beautiful woman who is also a drug addict and a liar. When the sleazy screenwriter whom she marries is murdered and a valuable script disappears, she is the obvious suspect.

HARRY HARRISON (born 1925). With more than a passing nod to H.G. Wells, this prolific science fiction writer tells of a twentieth-century time machine in *The Technicolor® Time Machine* (Doubleday, 1967). Invented by Professor Hewett, this machine seems a boon to the near-bankrupt Climactic Studios. It can ferry movie crews back and forth in time, permitting producers to film real Vikings in the year 1000 and thus cut down on the cost of extras, costuming, and sets. It's a filmmaker's dream, but dreams can also become nightmares.

WILLIAM S. HART (1864–1946) was a prominent stage actor who became the foremost cowboy film star of the silent era. He began his screen career with *His Hour of Manhood* in 1914 and ended it in 1925 with *Tumbleweeds*. Hart published his autobiography, *My Life—East and West* in 1929.

    Told Under a White Oak Tree (Houghton Mifflin, 1922) bears the writing credit "by Bill Hart's Pinto Pony, edited by his master William S. Hart." The illustrations are by James Montgomery Flagg. This slim volume—a mere 51 pages—is intended for young readers. The pony invites a group of children to join him under the white oak tree at Hart's Newhall, California, ranch, and tells them a series of stories of his and Hart's work together on screen. It is a charming and intelligent book, one that must once have given pleasure to both children and their parents. That it will not appeal to a modern generation is more the fault of today's society than of the writing style.

KATHRYN HARVEY is a pseudonym. ***Stars*** (Villard Books, 1992) is about Star's, a health resort in Palm Springs to which come an aging and fading movie star and a handsome screenwriter/producer, and about which lingers the spirit of silent screen star Marion Star, who disappeared in 1932 following the murder of her director husband. A lot happens in the course of the four days during which the story takes place, including the reappearance of Miss Star and assorted romance and mayhem, none of it worthy of much attention. "Slick but suspenseless . . . a lackluster attempt," wrote *Kirkus* (March 1, 1992).

ERIC HATCH (1902–73). ***Good Old Jack*** (Little, Brown, 1937) is a comedy about Hollywood director John ("Good Old Jack") Halcombe, who loses his money and ends up as president of a Central American republic. "It is the sort of outlandish fun in which Eric Hatch and Hatch fans delight," commented the reviewer in the *New York Times* (April 4, 1937).

LOUISE PLATT HAUCK (1888–1943). ***Juliet, Inc.*** (Grosset & Dunlap, 1939) is the name of a dress shop, whose owner feels overly responsible for his foster sister, the mother of whom had been hanged for a crime of passion. The foster sister marries Juliet's fiancé, enjoys a successful Hollywood career, and then tries to kill herself.

GENEVIEVE HAUGEN. ***Women with Wings: A Novel of the Modern Day Aviatrix*** (Ganesha Publishers, 1935) is identified by Carolyn See as a Hollywood novel.

ERNEST HAYCOX (1899–1950). A stunt flying ace in Hollywood gets involved in a murder mystery in ***Rough Air*** (Doubleday, Doran, 1934). The reviewer in the *New York Times* (November 4, 1934) commented, "It is written in slangy lingo and a clipped, staccato style appropriate to the subject, and some of the many characters are realistic enough, after their fashion. After all the talky talk that has gone before, the last fifth of the yarn develops a murder mystery that becomes fairly exciting. But, all in all, it's hardly worth the price."

ALFRED HAYES (1911–85) wrote a number of major screenplays, including *Paisan* (1949), *Clash by Night* (1952), and *Island in the Sun* (1957). *My Face for the World to See* (Harper, 1958) is written in a terse style. It begins with a Hollywood screenwriter rescuing a starlet from the water at a beach party. Only after they become lovers does he recognize her vanity and self-destructiveness. The novel reaches its climax when the writer learns that his wife is on her way to Los Angeles. "One feels on finishing it that one has dug deeply into this sad little world of human self-delusion," commented Anne Ross in the *New York Herald Tribune* (February 2, 1958). "A weightier novel, a greater assortment of characters and incidents, could not have added more."

MARY-ROSE HAYES. *Amethyst* (Dutton, 1991) begins in New York in 1979 as four teenagers, Vera, Jo-Beth (J-B), Arnie, and Saint meet for the first time. It soon becomes apparent that Vera loves Saint, Saint loves J-B, and Arnie loves Saint. Eventually Vera creates a popular feminist comic strip character; Saint gets married, inherits a trust fund, and gets imprisoned in Mexico on drug charges. Saint is released from jail thanks to the efforts of wealthy Hollywood producer Victor Diamond in return for the screen rights to Vera's comic strip, in which J-B and Arnie are to star. The film begins shooting in Mexico, and it is obvious that Diamond has a hypnotic hold over J-B, who has been impregnated by Vera's doctor. Diamond is a ruthless character who kills everyone who gets in his way; he is also Saint's father. Diamond reveals to Saint that his plan is to marry J-B and then have Saint make her pregnant, Diamond himself being impotent. No explanation is offered as to how the impotent Diamond could be Saint's father, and so it is no surprise when later it transpires that he is not. Saint, therefore, feels no remorse when Diamond is killed by a crazed Mexican. J-B marries her doctor friend. Arnie comes out of the closet. And Saint marries Vera. According to the publisher, this book is "in the bestselling tradition of Sidney Sheldon and Judith Krantz." Certainly it owes little to reality fiction.

FRÉDÉRIQUE HEBRARD. *The Month of September* (Little, Brown, 1957), translated from the French by Irene Ash, is the bittersweet love story of a painter who realizes that her husband, François, has fallen in love with an Italian movie star, Sandra Tiepola, whose biography he is translating. Only when the book is completed does the painter understand the actress's importance to both her husband and her daughter.

ANDREW HECHT. *Hollywood Merry-Go-Round* (Grosset & Dunlap, 1947) straddles the dividing line between fiction and nonfiction, being nothing more than a collection of gossip items—some relatively amusing—which may or may not be true. The book contains an introduction by Bob Hope and is illustrated by Leo Hershfield.

BEN HECHT (1893–1964) was a prolific screenwriter (1927–64), an occasional director, and the author of 16 plays. Of his 22 novels, only one, *I Hate*

Actors! (Crown, 1944), is a Hollywood novel. It is a detective story with some of the same satirical humor that Hecht employed in his two most personal films, *The Scoundrel* (1935) and *Spector of the Rose* (1946). The central character is agent Orlando Higgens, who resolves the question of who murdered three of his clients, all of whom were leading men in the Empire Studios production of *Sons of Destiny*. *I Hate Actors!* was reprinted in 1946 by Bartholomew House under the title *Hollywood Mystery!*

WILLIAM HEGNER (born 1928). *The Idolaters* (Trident Press, 1973) is loosely based on the life of Marilyn Monroe. The central character is raped as a teenager, becomes a successful screen star, marries a baseball player and a prize-winning playwright, but kills herself because she cannot become pregnant or fully return a man's love.

MEL HEIMER (1915–71). *West Wind* (Trident Press, 1964) is a roman à clef based on the life of Minnie (Elizabeth Taylor) and Richard (Richard Burton), who are starring in the most expensive costume film ever made in Rome. Minnie's husband arrives in Italy trying to break up the affair, resulting in her taking an overdose of sleeping pills. The husband refuses to permit a divorce, claiming that Richard is homosexual. The latter murders the husband and then dies in a plane crash while leaving for South America. When both Richard and Minnie receive Academy Awards, the latter receives both Oscars. "The characters are just like living people," commented *Kirkus* (June 15, 1964).

A Family Affair (Trident Press, 1965) is a roman à clef based very loosely on the life of Bing Crosby, here called Gordie Harris. One of his sons is a stage director, while the other is a mental case; Harris's wife commits suicide. "The dialogue is unbelievably atrocious," wrote *Kirkus* (October 18, 1965).

HAROLD HELVESTON. *Maid in Hollywood* (Harper & Davies, 1940) consists of a series of letters to Philomene from Kate, who has just arrived in Hollywood and is staying at the Hollywood Girls' Club (Hollywood Studio Club), described in great detail. Kate recounts her efforts to break into films, her dates, and her first Christmas in the film capital. It is tedious satire, lacking in originality. The book is illustrated by Ed Benedict.

MAXINE HERMAN. *Forced Feedings* (M. Evans, 1979) is the story of Off Off Broadway actress Natasha Dawn Finn, whose convoluted life includes endless auditions, attempts to deprogram her cult-crazed father, and relationships with a makeup artist and an avant-garde film director. It was the first novel of an actress and psychotherapist.

JOHN HERMANSEN (1918–73). *The Waxman Production* (Harper & Row, 1973) is the story of Magnus Colorado Waxman, a half–Indian, half–Jewish romantic from Los Angeles who decides to make a film in Yuma, Arizona. As he explains to the local newspaper reporter, "My idea is to shoot a pilot of a pilot, using local talent and local staff. I have the money to make a super-eight presentation which will run thirty minutes, maybe more. From that I'll promote my pilot. We aren't using a star. All the actors are free, and we'll shoot only exterior scenes."

MICHAEL HERR (born 1940). *Walter Winchell* (Alfred A. Knopf, 1990) is a work of prose fiction that began life as a screenplay (the author co-wrote the script for Stanley Kubrick's *Full Metal Jacket*) and reads as such. The story of gossip-monger, newspaper columnist, and radio broadcaster Walter Winchell (1897–1972), the book opens in 1943 at New York's Stork Club, Winchell's favorite night haunt, with the arrival of owner Sherman Billingsley. It concludes in the mid–1960s, with the closure of the Stork Club and the end of Winchell's influential reign as a purveyor of gossip. The book flashes back to Winchell's beginnings in vaudeville with Gus Edwards, and attempts to capture in print both Winchell's power and his nostalgic weakness for his early years. Aside from Billingsley and Winchell, other real-life characters in the "novel" include Damon Runyon, Hedy Lamarr, Bernarr Macfadden, Ed Sullivan, Josephine Baker, and Roy Cohn.

EDWARD HARRIS HETH. A wealthy and beautiful nymphomaniac writer deserts a literary agent in New York for a Hollywood career as a screenwriter in *We Are the Robbers* (Harper, 1947). "Readable, rentable and expendable," opined *Kirkus* (October 29, 1947).

PATRICIA HIGHSMITH (1921–95) was a superior mystery writer whose most famous work, *Strangers on a Train* (1949), formed the basis for the 1951 Alfred Hitchcock film of the same name. *The Tremor of Forgery* (Doubleday, 1969) concerns an American writer, Howard Ingham, who comes to Tunisia to work on what proves to be an abortive film project. While there he develops a close, nonsexual relationship with a gay Scandinavian man and is haunted by the possibility that he may have accidentally killed an elderly Arab thief. This is not a mystery per se but rather a study of moral dilemmas.

OSCAR HIJUELOS (born 1951) received immediate critical success with his first novel, *Our House in the Lost World* (1985). His second novel, *The Mambo Kings Play Songs of Love* (1989), won the Pulitzer Prize and was filmed in 1992. Hijuelos's third novel, *The Fourteen Sisters of Emilio Montez O'Brien* (Farrar, Straus & Giroux, 1993), is a sprawling family saga, spanning some one hundred years, and encompassing the lives of Irish photographer Nelson O'Brien, his Cuban wife, Mariela Montez, and their 15 children. Perhaps because only one of the children is male, the novel is told from a feminist viewpoint. Love and sex are the predominant elements, with son Emilio's career in Hollywood of secondary importance, as is his father's career as the manager of a movie house. "Hijuelos has reinvented the multigenerational family saga, using a conventional literary form to dramatize reality at its most instinctual, nonverbal level," wrote Bill Ott in *Library Journal* (February 1, 1993). *Kirkus Reviews* (February 1, 1993), however, found the novel "fat but flat," while *Publishers Weekly* (February 1, 1993) wrote, "Hijuelos loses his grip on the story, with a formal omniscient narration overwhelming what at times seems to be the older sister Margarita's point of view."

JAMES HILTON (1900–54) is best known for his novels *Lost Horizon* (1933) and *Goodbye Mr. Chips* (1934), both of which have been twice filmed. He began writing for the screen in 1936, with his best-remembered screenplay being for *Mrs. Miniver* (1942). A dinner party is the setting for *Morning Journey* (Little, Brown, 1951). Egotistical Paul Saffron marries actress Carey Arundel. He leaves her for a career as a producer of German films. After World War II, there is evidence that he was a Nazi collaborator. Carey's second marriage is destroyed by Saffron, and she returns to the screen in order to help him. Saffron ruins any possibility the pair have of success by attacking the industry, but Carey continues to stand by him. "Strangely, it doesn't jell," wrote E.J. Fitzgerald in the *Saturday Review of Literature* (March 17, 1951). "I think the reason is that Mr. Hilton never really accepts the shopworn quality of his basic material. A careful craftsman, he has supplied all his characters with names and addresses, birth places, backgrounds, and conversation. But he has failed to bring them alive as the human beings he obviously intended them to be."

AL HINE (born 1915). *The Birthday Boy* (Charles Scribner's Sons, 1959) is Jerry McMann, who, in his fiftieth year, looks back on his work in public relations in Florida, New York, and Hollywood. Barbara Klaw in the *New York Herald Tribune* (March 22, 1959) hailed this as a "very readable first novel," while the reviewer in *The New Yorker* (April 11, 1959) thought it "all right in an all-wrong way."

RICHARD HINKEL. *Two Deaths Must Die* (Fawcett, 1954) is identified by Carolyn See as a Hollywood novel.

BURT HIRSCHFIELD (born 1923). *Acapulco* (Arbor House, 1971) is the location site for a Hollywood production, with a money-hungry producer, his film actress/mistress, and a director who wants to leave the world of commercial filmmaking. *Fire in the Embers* (Avon, 1972) is the story of self-indulgent writer Mike Birns whose aim is to reach the top of his profession in Hollywood.

ERNEST HOBERECHT (born 1918). With the background of fraternization between Americans and Japanese after the Second World War, *Tokyo Romance* (Didier, 1947) is the story of a war correspondent who falls in love with a Japanese actress. Her studio will not countenance marriage. "The story ought to make the Japanese think very highly of American war correspondents, but what it will make them think of our fiction writers one would rather not consider," commented the reviewer in *The New Yorker* (September 13, 1947).

LAURA Z. (Zametkin) HOBSON (1900–86). *The Celebrity* (Simon & Schuster, 1951) of the title is novelist Gregory Johns, whose book is by chance the monthly selection of the Best Selling Book Club. His reaction to fame, including a period in Hollywood during which his novel is filmed, is the subject of *The Celebrity*. "The story is told with a meticulous calm, a careful understatement which makes it possible for the book to tread close to caricature without losing touch with reality. Mrs. Hobson has not misplaced the ability—so admirably revealed in *Gentleman's Agreement*—to share with the reader her rage at human idiocy without permitting him to take his eye or his mind from a vitally exciting story," wrote D.M. Mankiewicz in the *New York Times* (October 21, 1951).

SANDRA HOCHMAN (born 1936). *Happiness Is Too Much Trouble* (G.P. Putnam's Sons, 1976) is the story of Lulu Cartwright, a lawyer, comedy writer, and pornographer, who becomes the head of the world's largest film studio as a result of "a freak of computerized technology." Benefiting from Lulu's newfound stature is a hustler and stud named Dumbo, who had been an out-of-work extra. The novel provides a parody of Hollywood corporate types, the money men who never see the films.

FREDERICK HOLLANDER (1896–1976), also known as Friedrich Höllander, was a prominent German-born composer of film music who first came to fame in 1930 with his score, including "Falling in Love Again," for *The Blue Angel.* He wrote scores for many Hollywood films, such as *100 Men and a Girl* (1937), *The Farmer's Daughter* (1940), *Foreign Affair* (1948), and *Born Yesterday* (1951). He returned to Germany in 1956. *Those Torn from Earth* (Liveright Publishing, 1941) is Hollander's first and possibly only known novel. It opens in Berlin with the burning of the Reichstag and follows the paths of four refugees, not all of them Jewish. One is a prominent conductor who obtains work in England, visits Hollywood, and then briefly returns to Germany to visit a friend in a concentration camp. Another is a filmmaker who seeks employment initially in Paris and then moves to Hollywood. A third leaves for Palestine, where he opens an ice cream parlor before becoming involved in Yiddish cinema. Of Hollywood, Hollander writes, "Hollywood. Most obstinate little scrap of earth on this hemisphere and not to be catalogued. It's not: LIKE, and it isn't: THE OPPOSITE OF. Best definition yet: it's different." He describes the film community's search for talent in Europe:

> Every year Hollywood instigates a wholesale bargain drive in Europe, and sends its shoppers on a tour with large market baskets. The pricelist, which they carry with them, and to which they must strictly adhere, does not boast any exaggerated figures. However, the brief glimpse they offer into the grab-bag, filled with Hollywood tinsel, justifies and hallows any discount. They are not always fortunate in their catch for great genius, but manage most of the time to find a fair percentage of smaller, virile talent wriggling in their nets.

Those Torn from Earth is at times wordy and overblown, but it is also a powerful novel, evidence that Hollander could have been as great a writer as he was a composer. The book is also a plea for the world, particularly the United States, to take note of what had happened to German Jews and to the country's intelligentsia. "God, how many more must be crucified before this world be delivered," asks Hollander. The novel opens with a preface by Thomas Mann, who writes, "It is a splendid novel, new, tense with life, courageous, and artistically entertaining, written in a visible, vigilant, and colorful English, in the rhythmical charms of which one can sense the musicianship of the author."

E. NILS HOLSTIUS. *Hollywood Through the Back Door* (Longmans, Green, 1937) is a semiautobiographical novel, involving a recording industry executive named Ed Hamilton who comes to Hollywood in the guise of a sailor who has missed his boat. He takes cheap lodgings in the downtown area of the city, which seems obsessed with crime and religion. He learns the intricacies of the Los Angeles transportation system and visits Aimee Semple McPherson's Temple. A fall and hospitalization puts an end to the charade, and the narrator begins meeting Hollywood celebrities at the Trocadero, talks music composition with Jimmy McHugh, visits actor Bruce Cabot at RKO, and experiences what it is like to work as an extra. He offers insights on the Hollywood scene, the community's fixation with *The Hollywood Reporter*, and its reaction to the death of producer Irving Thalberg. Hollywood personalities abound on every page, and the author discusses the attitude of those in Los Angeles to the Nazi menace in Germany, noting, "Hollywood, now that the Nazi regime operates in Germany, is the only 'country' which the Jews can call their own."

HUGH HOOD was the pseudonym of John Blagdon (born 1928). After 15 years of success on screen, Rose Leclair is miscast in a musical comedy in *The Camera Always Lies* (Harcourt, Brace, Jovanovich, 1967). The film is reedited to emphasize a minor player, Charity Ryan, who runs off with Leclair's husband. Leclair tries to kill herself with sleeping pills. She meets and marries a French director, Jean-Pierre Fauré, who takes her to Europe and a new career. "The plot is contrived; the people caricatures, and the writing is amateurish and dull," complained the reviewer in *Library Journal* (August 1967).

LAURA LEE HOPE is a pseudonym created by Edward Stratemeyer (1862–1930), a prolific children's novelist who employed various ghostwriters to work on books based on his plot outlines. He also wrote as Victor Appleton (q.v.). The following is a complete listing in chronological order of Hope's film-related children's novels; specific subject matter is indicated after each entry:

> *The Moving Picture Girls; Or, First Appearances in Photo Dramas* (Grosset & Dunlap, 1914). The novel introduces Alice and Ruth DeVere, "The Moving Picture Girls," who here help their actor father, who has lost his voice, obtain work in silent films and themselves become screen performers.

> *The Moving Picture Girls at Oak Farm; Or, Queer Happenings While Taking Rural Plays* (Grosset & Dunlap, 1914). (The New York–based Comet Film Company shoots on location in New Jersey.)

> *The Moving Picture Girls Snowbound; Or, The Proof on the Film* (Grosset & Dunlap, 1914). (On location for winter filming in New England.)

> *The Moving Picture Girls Under the Palms; Or, Lost in the Wilds of Florida* (Grosset & Dunlap, 1914). (As did many early companies, the New York–based Comet Film Company spends the winter months filming in Florida.)

> *The Moving Picture Girls at Rocky Ranch; Or, Great Days Among the Cowboys* (Grosset & Dunlap, 1914). (Filming a Western production on location.)

> *The Moving Picture Girls at Sea; Or, A Picture Shipwreck That Became Real* (Grosset & Dunlap, 1915). (Filming in the West Indies.)

ROBERT SYDNEY HOPKINS. Subtitled "A Novel about the Cannes Film Festival," *Riviera* (William Morrow, 1980) introduces a variety of characters all of whose lives will be affected by what happens at the world's leading film festival. A studio head comes to Cannes determined to form a breakaway studio, out of the control of the conglomerate that owns his present organization. A fading actor has acquired the script for a film in which he wants both to star and to direct. A retired but legendary star comes to Cannes determined to renew her career following the mysterious death of her producer husband. All become involved in a hostage situation, in which the festival director's mistress is an accomplice. The actor dies, but the star eventually decides to make her comeback in a film produced by the studio head, who gets financial backing from the man behind the conglomerate. *Riviera* is a turgid thriller with far too many characters to make it riveting entertaining for the casual reader. The author, who was living in the south of France at the time he wrote the novel, provides this valid commentary on the festival: "The French press was fond of believing that the Festival in former times had been a miraculous but accidental marriage of art and glamour. Not quite. From the beginning it was a carefully managed exercise in public relations, a Festival designed by the French government with the encouragement of a tourist-conscious city of Cannes as a glossy advertisement in self-promotion."

LEONORA HORNBLOW (born 1920). *Memory and Desire* (Random House, 1950) is a study of a romance between a Hollywood screenwriter and an attractive young girl; at its close the man returns to his wife and to other affairs. In the *New York Herald Tribune* (March 26, 1950), John Gunther wrote,

> The minor characters are, it seems to me, better drawn than the major. Sue, the hostess (truly an enchanting character), and Jean, the punctual nymphomaniac, come vividly alive. Mrs. Hornblow has a polished talent for describing sensitively landscape, light, the sky, flowers, or hotel furniture. Her taut, springy dialogue has charm ... like all first novels, this one has defects. Perhaps it is glib in spots and strains too much for effect. Mrs. Hornblow's next will, I imagine, be much better. Even so, *Memory and Desire* is a remarkably spirited and competent performance.

WENDY HORNSBY introduced San Francisco–based documentary filmmaker Maggie MacGowen in *Telling Lies* (E.P. Dutton, 1992). MacGowen comes to Los Angeles, where she discovers that her sister, a former sixties radical, has been shot. The heroine's background helps partially in MacGowen's investigation, but otherwise the mystery novel's primary focus involves the current status of former sixties radicals. Hornsby deserves praise for realistic dialogue and a depressing picture of the poor and homeless in Los Angeles.

Social conditions among the disenfranchised of Los Angeles also form the background for *Midnight Baby* (E.P. Dutton, 1993), in which MacGowen is making a documentary on "a broad range of child-raising experiences." She is assisted by a UCLA film instructor named Guido.

Maggie MacGowen makes her third outing in *Bad Intent* (E.P. Dutton, 1993), in which she is making a film on inner-city life.

TAMARA HOVEY. *Among the Survivors* (Grossman Publishers, 1971) is the story of Christine Mull, who goes from Bryn Mawr to Greenwich

Village, where she falls in love with an Off Broadway playwright. Her mother is married to a successful Hollywood screenwriter but loves another screenwriter, an alcoholic, who falls in love with Christine.

JAMES A. (Arch) HOWARD. The true and tried story of a Hollywood actress blackmailed for her early, pre-stardom participation in a pornographic film forms the basic plotline of *Die on Easy Street* (Popular Library, 1957).

MAUREEN HOWARD (born 1930). *Expensive Habits* (Summit Books, 1986) begins with celebrated writer Maggie Flood's being felled by a serious heart condition, which provides her with an opportunity to make a close examination of her life. She must come to terms with the loss of a private life in return for a public name. One of her plays is adapted for the screen, and the film's director, Sol Negaly, becomes her lover. The Hollywood segment is but a minor part of a refreshingly original and well-written novel, the fifth from Maureen Howard.

RICHARD G. (Gibson) HUBLER (born 1912). The life story of pioneering Hollywood producer Nick Sonnenberg is told in flashback in *The Shattering of the Image* (Duell, Sloan & Pearce, 1959). "This is an amalgamation of every Hollywood novel ever written with all too usual characters (lady gossip columnists, white-haired boys, egomaniac actors, eager ingenues, foreign directors, money-men from the East, successful restauranteurs, cameramen, etc.), settings and situations—and then some in the way of violent and shocking episodes and unpleasant characters," reported *Kirkus* (January 23, 1959).

TOM E. HUFF (born 1938). *Marabelle* (St. Martin's Press, 1980) is a roman à clef based on the life of Tallulah Bankhead, beginning with a neglected childhood in Alabama and ending with fame in New York and Hollywood.

EUGENE HENRY HUFFMAN. *How Am I Civilized* (Wetzel Publishing, 1930) is the autobiography of African American Ras-Taferi Hounin-Kounin, who writes in extreme black dialect about his efforts to acquire "white" speech and thus "better" himself. He recounts his adventures in various parts of the world, including Hollywood, where he works as a cook to a movie mogul and is seduced by screen siren Theda Baraly. *How Am I Civilized* was reprinted in 1975 by AMS Press.

ROY HUGGINS (born 1914) wrote a number of screenplays before making a considerable name for himself as a writer, director, and producer in television. Among his many accomplishments, he produced the pilot episode of "77 Sunset Strip"; he produced "Maverick" and "Alias Smith and Jones"; and he created "The Fugitive." The California-based writer for a national magazine finds himself suspected of his wife's murder in *Lovely Lady, Pity Me* (Duell, Sloan & Pearce, 1949). Several members of the Hollywood community play roles in the novel, including a gossip columnist. "While there are some fast-moving moments, the whole thing doesn't add up to more than just average," wrote Elizabeth Bullock in the *New York Times* (September 11, 1949).

BABETTE HUGHES. With a background of Broadway and Hollywood, *Magic Penny* (Rinehart, 1948) is the story of playwright Dick Chapman who owns a magic penny enabling him to overcome imaginary fears. A heart attack makes him realize that the only thing he needs to fear is death. Failure and love are irrelevant fears, and so he is able to discard the magic penny. "The major fault lies in a complete lack of charm. If Chapman were less self-absorbed, less egotistical, less cold, his plight would more truly enlist our sympathy. As it is, his gropings seem unwarranted, false, and bothersome," commented C.M. Brown in the *Saturday Review of Literature* (March 13, 1948).

DOROTHY B. (Belle) HUGHES (born 1904). *Dread Journey* (Duell, Sloan & Pearce, 1945) is a suspense novel about a film actress doomed to die in order that her director can groom a successor. The four people who know his intentions are powerless to prevent the crime in this "frightening story" (*The New Yorker*, September 15, 1945). The central character in *The Big Barbecue* (Random House, 1949) is beautiful and lazy 18-year-old Ariadne Pontuis, who dreams of a life in Hollywood. In an effort to make her dream reality, she persuades her parents to take her to New Mexico, where she plans to snare millionaire Justinian Hrobel. Barbara Bond in the *New York Times* (February 27, 1949) found this "a light-hearted, blandly amusing story."

GABRIELLE HUGHES. *Trade Secrets* (Pinnacle Books, 1982) are numerous on a film studio lot, and when a vice president of the company is murdered, many come to light.

RUPERT HUGHES (1872–1956) was well known in his day as a writer of both novels and plays, together with a three-volume biography of George Washington, published in 1926, 1927, and 1929. As *Newsweek* (September 17, 1956) commented at the time of Hughes's death, "He turned out 100 novels and over 600 shorter pieces, collecting bad reviews but big money." Rupert Hughes was a familiar figure in Hollywood, at his zenith in the 1920s and 1930s, writing for the screen, occasionally directing, and selling many works for film adaptation. He was also the uncle of Howard Hughes. In 1922 Hughes founded the Authors Club of Hollywood, and his devotion to the film community was absolute. *Souls for Sale* (Harper, 1922) was an attempt by Hughes to depict Hollywood as just as much a regular American community as any other, undeserving of the criticism leveled at that time. The story involved the daughter of a minister who runs away to Hollywood, becomes a movie star, and discovers that it is her religious background rather than the film industry that is responsible for the unhappy moments in her life. In 1923 Hughes produced, directed, and adapted the novel for the screen, for Goldwyn release, and starring Eleanor Boardman, Mae Busch, Barbara La Marr, and Richard Dix. A second novel by Hughes, *City of Angels* (Charles Scribner's Sons, 1941), also has a Hollywood theme, as a lifeguard who saves the wife of a well-known businessman from drowning is briefly discovered for the movies.

WILLIAM BRADFORD HUIE (1910–86). *Kirkus* (January 2, 1951) subtitled *The Revolt of Mamie Stover* (Duell, Sloan & Pearce, 1951) as "a-whoring we will go." Its central character is a contest winner who fails to find fame and success in Hollywood and decides to become a professional prostitute. The novel covers the years 1939 through the end of World War II. "Probably a bum for public libraries," concluded *Kirkus*. A highly sanitized version was filmed by 20th Century–Fox in 1956, directed by Raoul Walsh, and starring Jane Russell, Richard Egan, and Jean Leslie; Mamie is here a dance hostess who invests heavily in real estate.

GARDNER HUNTING (1872–1958). The year 1926 was the first in which the talking film seemed a commercial possibility, thanks to Warner Bros., the Vitaphone, and the John Barrymore vehicle *Don Juan*. In *The Vicarion* (Unity Press, 1926), the author looks to the future, to Santa Monica, California, in 1931, and an invention that combines the motion picture and radio.

LEE HUTCHINGS. The adventures in Hollywood of a young man from Pennsylvania are documented in *Hollywood and Vine* (House of Field/Doubleday, 1946).

ANGELA HUTH (born 1938). On a six-month trial separation from her husband, Clare Lyall moves in with a young film director named Joshua in *Somehow I Had to Find a Brass Band* (Coward-McCann, 1970). She has befriended an elderly woman named Mrs. Fix, who likes brass bands, and when she dies, Clare decides a fitting tribute would be a brass band at her funeral.

ALDOUS HUXLEY (1894–1963) holds a significant place in both British and American literature as a novelist, poet, playwright, and literary critic. The financial potential in screenwriting led him and his wife to Hollywood in the fall of 1937, and during the next ten years he was involved in the writing of four feature films: *Pride and Prejudice* (1940), *Jane Eyre* (1941), *Madame Curie* (1943), and *A Woman's Vengeance* (1947).

He also wrote two novels using the environment of southern California and the medium of film: *After Many a Summer Dies the Swan* (Harper & Row, 1939) and *Ape and Essence* (Harper & Row, 1948). The first is a fictionalization of the life of newspaper tycoon and occasional film producer William Randolph Hearst, here called Jo Stoyte, whose castle, modeled after San Simeon, is located in the San Fernando Valley. Stoyte's "daughter-mistress, child-concubine," based on Marion Davies, is here named Virginia Maunciple. Huxley had originally called her "Dowlas" but realized that that name was a little too close to Marion Davies's birthname of Douras. Aside from Stoyte and Maunciple, the other two central characters in the novel are a friend of modest means named William Propter and a personal physician-in-residence named Dr. Sigmond Obispo. (Coincidentally, the town closest to Hearst's castle of San Simeon is San Luis Obispo.)

It may well be that Orson Welles was influenced to make *Citizen Kane* (1941) as a result of reading *After Many a Summer Dies the Swan*. His first meeting with Aldous Huxley was in July 1939 at a party celebrating the novel's completion.

Narrated by an unidentified man, presumably a screenwriter, *Ape and Essence* has screenwriter Bob Briggs coming across a rejected script called "Ape and Essence," written by a William Tallis. Briggs visits the ranch located just north of the San Gabriel Mountains above Los Angeles, given on the script as the writer's address, only to discover that Tallis had died six weeks earlier. With interpolations by the narrator, the script of "Ape and Essence" is then presented to the reader, and it is a tale of Los Angeles in 2108, following World War III and a nuclear holocaust. Explorers from New Zealand arrive at the city and discover it to be a cultural and ethical wasteland in which society has broken down. One of the explorers, the timid Dr. Alfred Poole, escapes the city with the only woman still capable of love, and on their way through the desert the couple comes across the tombstone of screenwriter William Tallis, 1882–1948.

For more information on the writer's involvement with Hollywood and the film industry, see Virginia M. Clark, *Aldous Huxley and Film* (Scarecrow Press, 1987) and David King Dunaway, *Huxley in Hollywood* (Harper & Row, 1989).

JOE HYAMS (born 1932) has a thorough inside knowledge of the film industry and has coauthored books with Edith Head, Peter Sellers, and Billie Jean King; he has also written two biographies of Humphrey Bogart: *Bogie* (1966) and *Bogart and Bacall* (1976). In 1964 he married actress Elke Sommer. *The Pool* (Seaview Books, 1978) is a social oasis surrounded by the Beverly Hills Hotel. Here, Jere Kazin, founder of World Studios, wages a corporate battle to save the studio for his son and successor.

Murder at the Academy Awards (St. Martin's Press, 1983) is illustrative of Hyams's familiarity with the inner workings of the film industry. The characters are one-dimensional, the dialogue artificial, but one has no alternative but to read the book in a single sitting. It opens with the discovery that some of the ballots for the Academy Awards have been tampered with. When producer Eva Johnson heads for the stage to pick up her Oscar for Best Picture, the audience is shocked that she has won and even more shocked when she drops down dead. It transpires that a tiny bomb has been placed in her body, hidden in a pill, detonated when the theme music for her film, played as she walks up on stage, reaches a particular high note. The tampering with the ballots, as presented here, is a far more reasonable proposition (undertaken by Johnson's boyfriend) than the producer's contrived death. The detective in charge of the case visits an aging gossip columnist at the Motion Picture and Television House and Hospital, and when she is similarly murdered, he is able to identify the killer, which he does at the columnist's funeral. It just so happens that Johnson's father testified before the House Un-American Activities Committee, and that the son of one of the men innocently named by the father was working for the producer. He killed her in revenge for his father, and the gossip columnist for publishing the names of the innocent victims.

SUSAN ISAACS (born 1943). *Magic Hour* (HarperCollins, 1991) begins with the murder of film producer Sy Spencer in the affluent East Coast resort of East Hampton. As the investigation proceeds, it becomes apparent that the intended murder victim was his leading actress, with whom he had been having an affair but who was also ruining his film. Investigating the murder is a local policeman, Stephen Brady, whose colorful past includes time in Vietnam and fights against drug and alcohol addiction. Author Isaacs works hard at getting inside Brady's psyche and narrating the story from the point of view of a tough yet sensitive cop, but, all in all, the story lacks intensity and in the early stages borders on the tedious. Also, the identity of the killer is obvious to the reader long before Brady is able to figure it out.

The author does have a firm handle on the work of a production unit on location, and explains her title: "It's a term of cinematography. The time after dawn or before dusk. Enough light for shooting, but there's a fineness, a tranquility to it—magical light. You have to work fast, because before you know it, the enchantment is over, but while it's there . . . you can get something beautiful."

CHRISTOPHER ISHERWOOD (1904–86) was a highly regarded novelist, playwright, and screenwriter; also, as he indicated in *Contemporary Authors*, "I was a born film fan," and his interest in all aspects of the motion picture influenced his career and life as much as did his homosexuality. Isherwood began as a screenwriter in his native England with *Little Friend* in 1934. His other films include *A Woman's Face* (1941), *Rage in Heaven* (1941), *The Loved One* (1965), *The Sailor from Gibraltar* (1967), and *Frankenstein: The True Story* (1972). His 1946 book *The Berlin Stories* was adapted for the stage as *I Am a Camera* (1951) by John Van Druten. Both the stage play and the book formed the basis for the Joe Masteroff, John Kander, and Fred Ebb musical *Cabaret*, first produced on stage in 1966 and filmed in 1972. The third and most important of Isherwood's autobiographies is *Christopher and His Kind, 1929–1939*, published in 1976.

Christopher Isherwood appears as himself in **Prater Violet** (Random House, 1945). He is a screenwriter and friend of an Austrian-Jewish film director who comes to England, and Imperial Bulldog Pictures, to produce a film about a girl who sells violets in Vienna's Prater. When the film is completed, the Austrian leaves for a career in Hollywood. In the *New York Times* (October 28, 1945), Walter Bernstein wrote, "The simplicity of the plot is deceptive. This is a complex work, operating on more than one level. It is not merely a fable of the artist in relation to a commercialized mass medium. It deals with the relation of man to other men and to the world around him." Writing in *The New Yorker* (November 10, 1945), Edmund Wilson commented, "*Prater Violet* is one of his longish short stories, which resembles the episodes in *Goodbye to Berlin* and keeps up the same high level of excellence. It is perhaps a little more dramatic and more of a deliberate historical parable than the earlier stories were." In *The Nation* (November 17, 1945), Diana Trilling wrote, "It is a book written in the author's own person, yet utterly without ego; it is a novel about movie writers which is yet a novel about the life of every serious artist; it is a book without a political moral, but a profound moral-political statement; it is gay, witty, sophisticated, but wholly responsible."

Another Isherwood novel that perhaps belongs here is **Down There on a Visit** (Simon & Schuster, 1962). Quasi-autobiographical, the book consists of four long stories, the last of which is set in California and deals primarily with its central character's homosexual activities. Writing in the *New Republic*

(April 16, 1962), Stephen Spender described *Down There on a Visit* as "probably Isherwood's best novel."

DONALD JACK (born 1924). *Me Bandy, You Cissie* (Doubleday, 1979) is the fourth in a series of novels featuring Canadian World War I flying ace Bartholomew Bandy. Here he escapes from Russia after being captured by Bolsheviks, falls in love with Cissie Chaffington en route to New York, and stars in a silent flying drama epic.

HEINRICH EDUARD JACOB (1889–1967). *Blood and Celluloid* (Ray Long & Richard R. Smith, 1930) is a curious novel anticipating later international disputes. When a German film company goes to Sardinia to film a bandit and his hideout, the French discover that the hideout is a local institution maintained as a tourist attraction, and they decide to make their own film on the subject. Eventually, it is up to Mussolini to sort the matter out.

NAOMI JACOB (1884–1964) was a former British actress who began a prolific writing career in the mid–1920s. *Fade Out* (Macmillan, 1938) is a romantic melodrama about an intense love triangle. British writer Martin Sharrett loves actress Julia Pinto, but she has fallen in love with her stepfather, Alex Verschoff. The story is played out against a background of the British film industry (Julia is starring in a film for the fictional British Filmtones) and the London stage, on which Julia is appearing in Martin's first play. Since the characters have few realistic qualities and the book often reads like a second-rate Noel Coward drama, readers will find it all rather irrelevant. Indeed, the film background and the film-related title ultimately have nothing to do with the storyline.

THORNWELL JACOBS (1877–19??). *Drums of Doomsday* (E.P. Dutton, 1942) is a very conservative novel, featuring the Reverend John Roderick, minister of the Presbyterian Church in Atlanta. After seeing a film in which actress Maria Rodrigues seems to be appealing directly to him for help, Roderick leaves the church and begins a campaign to expose "New Deal" politics, which he believes are bringing doom to America. In Hollywood, he discovers that Rodrigues is his cousin, and he begins a campaign to reform members of the film community.

JOHN JAKES provides the introduction to *Hollywood Kills* (Carroll & Graf, 1993), a collection of short stories and one novella that use Hollywood as their setting, selected by the staff of *Mystery Scene*. The novella is *Death Out of Focus*, by William Campbell Gault (q.v.). Among the 13 short stories are "Starstruck," by Jon L. Breen; "The Movie People," by Robert Bloch; "How Come My Dog Don't Bark?" by Ron Goulart; "The Man Who Wanted to Be in the Movies," by John Jakes; "The Girl with the Hungry Eyes," by Fritz Leiber; "Find the Woman," by Ross Macdonald; and "Under the Hollywood Sign," by Tom Reamy.

DON JAMES (born 1905). *Hollywood Starlet* (Monarch Books, 1962) is one of a series of novels with a Hollywood background, identified by Carolyn See as "semi-pornographic." No other information is available.

RUSSELL JANNEY (1884–1963). *The Miracle of the Bells* (Prentice-Hall, 1946) is one of those inspirational novels without a single redeeming quality. It is a "joyous novel" about the four days and nights in a small Pennsylvania town when the church bells did not stop ringing (a hideous thought to anyone who welcomes sleep, not to mention peace and quiet). The miracle of the bells takes place as a result of Hollywood agent Bill Dunnigan's efforts to draw attention to an unreleased film starring Olga Treskovna. "I would like to say something pleasant about his book," wrote John Broderick in *Commonweal* (October 14, 1946), "but the only thing I can think of at the moment is that [Janney] has written the kind of novel about Catholics and Catholic ways usually described as fit reading for the entire family." The novel was filmed in 1948 for release by RKO, directed by Irving Pichel, and starring Fred MacMurray and Valli in her second American production.

WILLIAM JEFFRIES is the pseudonym of novelist Jeffrey Wilds Deaver. In the mystery *Shallow Graves* (Avon, 1992), alcoholic filmmaker John Pelham is reduced to working as a location scout. While scouting in upper New York State, he discovers he is far from popular with the local inhabitants — indeed they would like to see him dead.

John Pelham returns in *Bloody River Blues* (Avon, 1994), in which he is scouting the location for an adventure feature in Maddox, Missouri. An innocent errand for a case of beer leads to his being chased by gangland killers, the local police, and the FBI. "Although the book works technically, reading a tale so replete with unpleasantness is still no picnic," commented *Publishers Weekly* (June 14, 1993).

J.G. JÉHU. *The Half Englishman: The Thrill and Joy of the Silver Screen* (Wetzel Publishing, 1927) is often identified as a Hollywood novel. Despite its title, the book has nothing to do with films or filmmaking, but rather is the story of a sheik's son who is sent to England for education and becomes "The Half Englishman."

THOMAS JEIER and JEFFREY M. (Miner) WALLMAN (born 1941). *The Celluloid Kid* (Doubleday, 1984) is cowboy and occasional bank robber Matt Bishop, who comes to southern California and becomes involved in the early film industry. When he is accused of dynamiting a number of construction sites, he is forced to clear his name.

OWEN FOX JEROME was, as far as can be ascertained, the pseudonym of Oscar Jerome Friend (1897–1963), although some sources claim that Friend was the pseudonym and Jerome the real name. The unlikable star of a remake of *The Last Command* is killed on the set in *The Five Assassins* (Thomas Bouregy, 1958). The title refers to the four chief suspects and to the star, who accidentally poisons himself with chemicals intended to kill a fellow actor and his wife's first husband.

NORA JOHNSON (born 1933) wrote the 1958 novel on which the film *The World of Henry Orient* is based. While living in Europe, Maggie, the central character in *Love Letter in the Dead Letter Office* (Dial Press, 1966), discovers that her Hollywood director father, Simon Otis, has disinherited her. She returns to the United States in an attempt to understand her life. "The tour on which Miss Johnson conducts her readers is more rewarding than its destination," commented Martin Levin in the *New York Times* (May 1, 1966).

VELDA JOHNSON. *House Above Hollywood* (Dodd, Mead, 1968) is a gothic mystery-romance in which a young woman seeks the truth behind the death of her father, a novelist and screenwriter. She goes to work as a companion and secretary to a former silent screen star whose biography her father was working on immediately prior to his death. The father's career bears a passing resemblance to that of F. Scott Fitzgerald.

ADRIENNE JONES (born 1915). There are Hollywood references in *A Matter of Spunk* (Harper, 1983), in which the author recounts what happened when her parents in Georgia separated and she and her sister and her mother came to California to settle in a Theosophist colony just as the Depression began.

CAROLYN JONES (1933–83) is perhaps unfairly remembered mainly for her performance as Morticia on the television series "The Addams Family" (ABC, 1964–66), whereas she was in fact an intelligent actress of both screen and stage, whose films include *House of Wax* (1953), *Invasion of the Body Snatchers* (1956), and *Marjorie Morningstar* (1958). She wrote two novels, *Twice Upon a Time* and *Diary of a Food Addict* (Grosset & Dunlap, 1974). *Twice Upon a Time* (Trident Press, 1971) is the grim story of a film actress who tries to make it on Broadway and is involved in a series of meaningless sexual encounters before being able to put her public and private life in order.

HAZEL WYNN JONES is a former British continuity girl or script supervisor; her heroine Emma Shaw has a similar occupation, and the thesis for the two novels featuring her is that Shaw's longtime job has provided her with the ability to see and remember things that the casual observer might not notice.

Emma Shaw and her husband, Hal, were introduced in *Death and the Trumpets of Tuscany* (date and publisher undetermined), in which a mysterious sequence of murders takes place during the shooting of a historical epic in Rome. The filming of another historical drama, this time in the small Italian town of San Bigio, is the background for *Shot on Location* (Collins, 1990). Hal and Emma are now separated and the latter has become a documentary director, but she is persuaded by Hal to take over the script supervisor's duties on the film he is producing. Soon the boyfriend, "Jud the Stud," of the leading lady and an extra are murdered. The solution lies in Jud's earlier life when he had infected a young girl with the AIDS virus. Despite the introduction of the AIDS theme, the novel is old-fashioned in style, with clumsy, unrealistic dialogue suggesting a certain prissiness on the part of the author. Also, although the author's background supposedly provided her with a thorough knowledge of the film industry, her depiction of a Los Angeles–based conglomerate, uninformed on the filmmaking process, is unrealistic to the point of sheer silliness.

JEROME JONES. The title character in *Ambition's Woman* (M. Evans, 1981) is Lady Anthea Harrington, a Broadway star who meets her aristocrat husband while filming in England, and when he and her son die, she returns to the United States to be the television star host of a cooking show.

ERICA JONG (born 1942). *How to Save Your Own Life* (Holt, Rinehart & Winston, 1977) is a sequel to its author's 1973 bestseller, *Fear of Flying*. Heroine Isadora Wing leaves her psychiatrist husband, and the novel concludes with her making love to a 26-year-old screenwriter, Josh Ace, at the Beverly Hills Hotel. Contemporary reviewers were generally unenthusiastic.

WILLIAM JOVANOVICH (born 1920). *Madmen Must* (Harper & Row, 1978) begins in 1940 as Serbian American John Sirovich graduates from college. Not knowing what to do with his life, Sirovich tutors the son of a movie star and obtains a job as a screenwriter at RKO. With the U.S. entry into the World War II, he joins the navy.

HOWARD (born 1940) **and SUSAN KAMINSKY** (born 1937) also write as Brooks Stanwood. *Talent* (Bantam Books, 1989) provides a look at a major Hollywood agency, Universal Talent Management, founded and headed by Gus Morton. It begins as Morton's niece and heir apparent Allison Morton begins her first day on the job and must deal with her uncle's mistress, a top agent with her own agenda, and a financial jackal and his son who have their own plans for U.T.M. Presumably it is nothing more than coincidence that the once most powerful of all Hollywood talent agencies, MCA, founded by the legendary Jules Stein and spearheaded by the equally legendary Lew Wasserman, should in 1962 have taken over Universal Studios, becoming MCA/Universal. Lengthy but lightweight.

STUART M. KAMINSKY (born 1934) is a film academic who is responsible for two series of mystery novels. The better of the two features Moscow police Inspector Porfiry Rostnikov, and began in 1981 with *Rostnikov's Corpse*. Since it takes place during the Moscow Film Festival, one of the volumes in that series, *Black Knight in Red Square* (Charter Books, 1984), does have a film-related theme. The second series is predominantly film-related in that it features a somewhat sleazy Hollywood private eye, Toby Peters, who is generally helping a Hollywood celebrity solve a personal crime problem. The books are set in the 1930s or 1940s, and while author Kaminsky makes good use of his knowledge of film history, they are lightweight in content.

The Toby Peters series began in 1977 with *Bullet for a Star* (St. Martin's Press), featuring Errol Flynn. It was followed by *Murder on the Yellow Brick Road* (St. Martin's Press, 1977), concerning Judy Garland and the Munchkins from *The Wizard of Oz*; *You Bet Your Life* (St. Martin's Press, 1978), involving the Marx Brothers; *The Howard Hughes Affair* (St. Martin's Press, 1979); *High Midnight* (St. Martin's Press, 1981), featuring Gary Cooper; *Catch a Falling Clown* (St. Martin's Press, 1981), featuring circus clown Emmett Kelly; *He Done Her Wrong* (St. Martin's Press, 1983), featuring Mae West; *Down for the Count* (St. Martin's Press, 1985), featuring Bela Lugosi; *The Man Who Shot Lewis Vance*

(St. Martin's Press, 1986), featuring John Wayne and Charlie Chaplin; *Smart Moves* (St. Martin's Press, 1986), featuring Albert Einstein and Paul Robeson; *Think Fast, Mr. Peters* (St. Martin's Press, 1987), featuring Peter Lorre; *Buried Caesars* (St. Martin's Press, 1989), featuring Dashiell Hammett; *Poor Butterfly* (St. Martin's Press, 1990), featuring Leopold Stokowski; *The Melting Clock* (St. Martin's Press, 1991), featuring Salvador Dali, and *The Devil Met a Lady* (Mysterious Press, 1993), featuring Bette Davis.

Kaminsky has also written a number of film-related nonfiction works: *American Film Genres: Approaches to a Critical Theory of Popular Film* (1974), *Clint Eastwood* (1974), *Ingmar Bergman: Essays in Criticism* (1975), *John Huston, Maker of Magic* (1978), *Coop: The Life and Legend of Gary Cooper* (1980), *Basic Filmmaking* (1981), and *Writing for Television* (1988). For a number of years, he has been a professor at and director of the Florida State University Conservatory of Motion Picture, Television and Recording Arts at the Asolo Center, Sarasota, Florida.

FRANK KANE (1912–68). Private detective Johnny Liddell, in the company of coroner Doc Morrissey, solves the murder of a Hollywood idol in *About Face* (Samuel Curl, 1947). The *Saturday Review of Literature* (July 26, 1947) considered that this novel had "an interesting central idea—with sound factual basis—completely surrounded and engulfed by tawdry tough stuff." In *Bare Trap* (Ives Washburn, 1952), Liddell is hired to find the missing son of a former movie star.

GARSON KANIN (born 1912) has been a director, producer, screenwriter, and playwright. His best films as a director are *The Great Man Votes* (1939) and *The True Glory* (1945). His best films as a screenwriter are *A Double Life* (1948), *Adam's Rib* (1949), and *It Should Happen to You* (1954). His novels are rather standard fare, with the second far and away the best and the best known, *Moviola*, a cheap excuse for a retelling of Hollywood history.

Cast of Characters (Atheneum, 1969) is a collection of short stories of Hollywood and Broadway characters. "The glamourous good old days are presented in a genteel, but cynical manner," wrote Genevieve Zahrt in *Library Journal* (May 15, 1969).

In 1940, on a visit to the Motion Picture Country House, Kanin, the narrator of *One Hell of an Actor* (Harper & Row, 1977), meets an old actor who tells him of John J. Tumulty (1849–1930), a flamboyant stage star who dominated the theatrical scene in San Francisco. The book recounts Kanin's efforts through the next three decades to piece together and understand the complex life of the actor, including his career in silent films, through the man's associates and his son, a Hollywood director. Real-life characters, including Ruth Gordon, George Cukor, Tom Powers, and Ethel Barrymore appear as themselves in this original and entertaining work, which combines fact and myth, biography and invention.

When an Arab conglomerate decides to acquire Farber Films from its 92-year-old founder, B.J. Farber is given an opportunity to reminisce in *Moviola* (Simon & Schuster, 1979). He talks of meeting Thomas A. Edison, assisting D.W. Griffith and Mack Sennett, becoming a vice president at M-G-M, the "Fatty" Arbuckle scandal, the arrival of Garbo in Hollywood, the search for Scarlett O'Hara in *Gone with the Wind,* Joan Crawford's seduction of David O. Selznick, and the death of Marilyn Monroe. As *Kirkus* so aptly put it, "It has the grim ring of truth."

Smash (Viking Press, 1980) is a roman à clef that also has that same grim ring of truth. The plotline concerns the birth of a musical show, here called *Shine On, Harvest Moon* (the life of Nora Bayes), but in actuality *Funny Girl* (the life of Fannie Brice), which Kanin directed on Broadway. The star, presumably based on Barbra Streisand, is not nice.

KAREN KARBO. *Trespassers Welcome Here* (G.P. Putnam's Sons, 1989) consists of a series of commentaries on Los Angeles life by various newly arrived Russian émigrés, all of whom have come together at the Department of Slavic Languages and Literatures of an unidentified college. One of the individuals is a former Soviet film star, Tanya Zlopak, who tries to interest director Solly Stein in hiring her for his latest film but only attracts his attention when she runs in front of his car. She takes advantage of his insistence on driving her to the doctor: "In Los Angeles to drive anywhere is forty-five minutes. Forty-five minutes I have now to speak to Solly Stein." The author makes use of the narrative form to offer some biting observations on life in Hollywood versus life in Moscow. It is difficult to know which place seems the more attractive.

RICHARD KARLAN (born 1919) is both an actor and a writer. The central character, Harrison Royle, in Karlan's second novel, **Pageant Faded** (Bobbs-Merrill, 1972), is very obviously based on Orson Welles: "He was the handsome boy-wonder of stage and screen—director-actor-writer-producer-genius—who spent Hollywood's millions making films—only to be regurgitated by the industry after a string of box-office failures." Royle returns from tax exile in Italy to appear on a New York television variety show, similar to the "Ed Sullivan Show." While in New York, he is approached by Charlie Bay, a director at the poverty row Blue Eagle studios, controlled by his brother, Alex, to appear in a cameo role in *The Trial of Captain Black.* (In 1948 Orson Welles directed and starred in *Macbeth* for poverty row production company Republic, and while any similarity between Blue Eagle and Republic is purely coincidental, it is worth noting that Republic's logo was, and is, an American eagle.) In order to hire Royle for the part, Bay has sold his shares in Blue Eagle but is hopeful that the film will prove prestigious enough to improve his Hollywood directorial image. Unfortunately, Alex Bay is being forced out as head of the studio, replaced, at the insistence of the new majority shareholder who happens to be Royle's former financial partner, by Harrison Royle. Royle is told that his first order of business is to close down production on *The Trial of Captain Black.*

Ultimately, Harrison Royle, with considerable selfishness, walks away from the production job, from his troubled teenage son in Hollywood, from all that the American film industry represents, to return to Rome, and continue trying to raise money for his own, oft-delayed, highly personal film.

Richard Karlan is adept at blending fact and fiction. For example, just as Welles was heavily involved in Shakespearean films, Harrison Royle makes *The Life and Times of William Shakespeare.* Rather like Welles, Karlan's hero is interested only in self; he feels only a momentary tinge of conscience over Charlie

Bay's losing not only his film but also his savings. Creditors and tax collectors are irrelevant in the hero's all-consuming desire to finish his film. The only friend he has, who loves him as much as he loves it, is his dog. Unfortunately, while the story is impressive, the dialogue often reads false. Somehow, the author has failed to capture the speech patterns of 1970s Americans, and his picture of the Hollywood film industry lacks bite—it's a dirty business, but not presented with as much filth as really clings to it.

WAYNE KARLIN (born 1945). *The Extras* (Henry Holt, 1989) are Ezra Brenner and Maryam Halim, a Jew and an Israeli Arab, who meet during the shooting of a film in the Israeli desert in 1976. The primary theme in the novel is the politics of peace versus war.

JILLIAN KARR is the pseudonym of Jan Greenberg (born 1942) and Karen A. Katz. *Something Borrowed, Something Blue* (Doubleday, 1993) is the passionate, romantic story of four women, one of whom is Hollywood superstar Ana Cates, married to a handsome senator.

HERBERT KASTLE (1924–87). *The Movie Maker* (Bernard Geis, 1968) is a story of miscegenation. The title character, Nat Markal, plans a Hollywood epic, *The Eternal Joneses*, which will trace a family and its slaves from 1812 to the present. The set is constructed at a secret location and is to be burned down as a publicity stunt. Markal falls in love with one of the leading players, a Eurasian woman, who later reveals that she is black. Subtitled "A Novel of Southern California," *Ladies of the Valley* (Arbor House, 1979) chronicles the lives of a group of filmmakers—writer, leading lady, producer, and screenwriter—who have joined forces to produce a film "in the tradition of *Last Tango in Paris.* . . . They meet to make a movie; they progress to heights and depths of human passion seldom chronicled in word or on film."

DAVID A. (Allan) KAUFELT (born 1938). *The Wine and the Music* (Delacorte Press, 1981) is a family saga that begins in a nineteenth-century Polish shtetl and ends with the U.S. entry into World War II. Bessie Meyer becomes a star of the Yiddish theater, and with the aid of a wealthy lover she is able to bring her three brothers to the United States. One of them, Max, becomes a producer of Westerns at Great Western Moving Pictures, Inc., in Hollywood.

ELIZABETH D. KAUP. *Repeat with Laughter* (Appleton, 1948) has a storyline familiar to anyone who has ever seen the musical *Evergreen*. Forty-nine-year-old Nellie Gail has been a stage favorite since the 1890s. She poses as her own daughter to become a Broadway star and 20 years later is a major Hollywood performer. "It isn't an important novel but it is an enjoyable one," opined George Freedley in *Library Journal* (March 1, 1948).

MARVIN KAYE (born 1938) features New York businesswoman Hilary Quayle and her male secretary, Gene, who happens to have a private detective's license, in *The Laurel and Hardy Murders* (E.P. Dutton, 1977). At the time he wrote the novel, Kaye was president of the New York chapter of the Laurel and Hardy fraternal organization, the Sons of the Desert, and as his hero, Gene, is also an officer, author Kaye reprints both the Constitution and the Guidelines to Decorous Behaviour (By-Laws) in the book. The plotline involves the murder of a particularly unpleasant and shoddy comedian at a Sons of the Desert meeting, together with the breakup of the tenuous relationship between Quayle and Gene after she discovers that women are not eligible for membership in the New York chapter (or "tent") of the Sons of the Desert.

Perhaps members of the Sons of the Desert will enjoy this novel; it will appeal to few others for the storyline is ridiculous and the characters, even for film buffs, seem overdrawn and unrealistic in the extreme. Many readers will identify the murderer long before the author chooses to reveal him. The murder of the talentless performer was, of course, "a parting gesture to the art of comedy."

ELIA KAZAN (born 1909) directed his first stage play in 1935 and his first Hollywood film, *A Tree Grows in Brooklyn*, in 1945. He won directorial Oscars for *Gentleman's Agreement* (1947) and *On the Waterfront* (1954). He became much despised for naming names to the House Un-American Activities Committee in 1952.

The Understudy (Stein and Day, 1974) is the story of actor Sidney Castleman (born Schlossberg) and his former understudy and current protégé, Sonny, who cannot escape from the relationship. The novel is heavily laden with well-known stage and screen names. Contemporary reviewers were not particularly enthusiastic. "This is a roman à clef, but so badly written and so dull that one doesn't care whom the characters are modeled after. The entire book is a prose junk heap," wrote Sammy Staggs in *Library Journal* (March 1, 1975). For *The New Yorker* (January 27, 1975), "There is just enough excitement in this show-biz cops-and-robbers adventure blockbuster to tease you on to the end, but not enough to enable you to overlook its slickness, its sentimentality, and its made-for-the-movies underpinnings."

H. (Henry) R. (Reymond) F. (Fitzwalter) KEATING (born 1926) began writing a popular series of novels featuring Bombay police Inspector Ganesh Ghote in 1964 with *The Perfect Murder*. The thirteenth mystery, *Filmi, Filmi, Inspector Ghote* (Crime Club/Doubleday, 1977), has Ghote investigating the murder of screen star Dhartiraj at Bombay's Talkiestan Studios, despite a plea to his superior that he is "not at all knowing the *filmi duniye* . . . I am not at all a film-world person." Both Ghote and the reader pretty soon learn a great deal about Bombay's bustling film industry. The inspector prepares to arrest the perpetrator of the crime, actress Nilima, at the Filmfare Awards Night, but she instead chooses suicide, "a fitting *filmi* ending." As with all the Inspector Ghote novels, this one is entertaining and evocative of India, but at the same time, the reader is left with the awkward question that were it not for the exotic background, would any of the volumes in this series be that praiseworthy?

DAY KEENE (died 1969). Hollywood is the background for two murders in the mystery novel *Framed in Guilt* (M.S. Mill/William Morrow, 1949).

CLARENCE B. (Budington) KELLAND wrote many short stories and novels, the best known and also first of which was *Scattergood Baines* in 1921. Archibald Cloyd, an authority on Napoleonic history, is helping a company on location in Arizona make a film on the subject in *Archibald the Great* (Harper, 1943). Through his male secretary and a woman with whom the latter has fallen in love, Cloyd uncovers a gangster who is hiding tires needed for the war effort. "Here is Mr. Kelland again with another snappy, up to the minute story, full of eccentric characters.... The plot is practically perfect with respect to suspense and news value," wrote Charlotte Dean in the *New York Times* (May 9, 1943).

Kelland's short story "Stand-In," published in *The Saturday Evening Post* (February 13 to March 20, 1937), was filmed by Walter Wanger Productions in 1937, under the direction of Tay Garnett, and starring Leslie Howard, Joan Blondell and Humphrey Bogart. The story concerns the potential sale of a film studio and the remaking of a drama as a comedy.

JANE KENDALL (born 1952). *Miranda and the Movies* (Crown, 1989) is the type of book for teenagers that parents think they *ought* to read. Set in the midteens, the story concerns a young girl who finds employment with the American Moving Picture Company at Fort Lee, New Jersey, working for director Charles James Tourneur. There was a well-known director named Maurice Tourneur who worked for the World Film Corporation at Fort Lee, and the name change is difficult to understand, as is the name of the fictional company, in reality the name of a film company of the period, formed in Chicago and later headquartered at Santa Barbara, California.

ADAM KENNEDY. *Just Like Humphrey Bogart* (Viking Press, 1978) is the story of an expatriate American in Paris, Duffy Odin, who gets acting jobs in foreign films because he looks just like Humphrey Bogart. He's a nice guy and the book makes pleasant reading.

JAY RICHARD KENNEDY. *Prince Bart: A Novel of Our Times* (Farrar, Straus & Young, 1953), the story of 39-year-old actor Bart Blaine's striving for his old success after a heart attack, was not particularly well received by the critics. *Time* (March 20, 1953) complained that Kennedy lacked Philip Wylie's literary stature and wrote worse than Kathleen Winsor. One of the few good reviews came from William Hogan in the *San Francisco Chronicle* (March 8, 1953): "Hollywood probably won't make a picture from the book, the way it reads now. But even withered down, it would make a good one. It would surely make an interesting one if Kennedy's detailed report on the struggle for survival in this crazily competitive Hollywood setup were left in."

DAVID KENT. *A Knife Is Silent* (Random House, 1947) is a mystery involving screenwriter Steven Wall, working on a film on the history of Haiti on an island off the Carolina coast when the leading lady is murdered. "Haitian high jinks, and a fairly slow routine of questions and answers amplify a mono-murder of rather simple proportions," reported *Kirkus*.

SOPHIE KERR. In *Love Story Incidental* (Rinehart, 1946), 17-year-old Ann Linton journeys from a small Midwestern town to Hollywood for a reunion with her screen star father, whom she last met when she was four. She quickly becomes disillusioned both with her father and Hollywood, recognizing all that is shabby in his career. "Flimsy, feminine fare," wrote *Kirkus* (March 1, 1946).

EVELYN KEYES (born 1919) is a familiar name if not a particularly recognizable face on screen since the late 1930s, and is best known for her work in *Gone with the Wind* (1939), *Here Comes Mr. Jordan* (1941), and *The Jolson Story* (1946). She has published two volumes of autobiography, *Scarlett O'Hara's Younger Sister* (1977) and *I'll Think About That Tomorrow* (1991). *I Am a Billboard* (Lyle Stuart, 1971) is a roman à clef based on Keyes's life; here she is called Christabelle Jones. "Though the book deals with such salable topics as child molestation and various homosexual and heterosexual shenanigans, the characters are one-dimensional, the writing unprofessional, and the whole a performance that most libraries can do without," commented L.W. Griffin primly in *Library Journal* (January 1, 1972).

TABITHA KING (born 1949). The two protagonists in *The Trap* (Macmillan, 1985) are a screenwriter who is enjoying fame as a result of a post–Vietnam action film he has written and his wife. She takes her four-year-old son to the couple's Maine summer cabin to consider a possible separation, and while there she is terrorized and raped by two teenage brothers.

TERENCE KINGSLEY-SMITH (born 1940) has his mystery novel *The Murder of an Old-Time Movie Star* (Pinnacle Books, 1983) alternate between 1935 and the present as the hero-narrator, a hard-boiled Hollywood private eye named Pete McCoy, relates how he discovered that the director-husband of "America's Little Girlfriend," Mary Callendar, was a bigamist back then, and has returned to murder those who tried to dispose of him and his secret. *The Murder of an Old-Time Movie Star* is not a great title, nor is it a great book, but the author does devise one very original plot twist, having Mary Callendar be a female impersonator but one who likes women, as opposed to her husband who likes men. The Mary Callendar character is obviously based on Mary Pickford. Greta Garbo makes a brief cameo appearance, and presumably the author is trying to tell his readers something by having director George Cukor employ a male, homosexual secretary. He creates a fictitious major Hollywood producer in Aaron Selig, but gives him the last name of one of the film community's first producers, Colonel William N. Selig.

WILLIAM KINSOLVING. *Born with the Century* (G.P. Putnam's Sons, 1979) is the story of Scottish immigrant Magnus MacPherson and his empire-building activities. As part of a long-winded plot, Magnus has an affair with an ex-prostitute and rising Hollywood star.

GEORGE KIRGO. *Hercules: The Greek Story* (Abelard-Schuman, 1958) is the tale of child star Dickie Dickinson in the 1930s and 1940s. As an adult he marries his former costar Betty Lou Manly, and the two decide to star in an epic production of *Hercules*.

JAMES KIRKWOOD (1930–89) was the son of silent screen stars James Kirkwood and Lila Lee, and the author of a number of books and plays. The central character in *There Must Be a Pony!* (Avon Books, 1960) is a precocious teenager named Josh, who comes to live with his film star mother Marguerite Sydney, who had been confined to a mental institution following the decline of her career. Just as a comeback seems probable, the actress rails against contemporary Hollywood. A charming real estate tycoon, Ben Nichols, comes into both Josh's and Marguerite's lives, bringing stability with a television pilot for Sydney and acting as a father figure for the boy. Ultimately, this is a rather tedious and tiresome story of a Hollywood childhood. It was adapted in 1962 as an unsuccessful stage play for Myrna Loy, and a television adaptation was aired by ABC on October 5, 1986, as the network's "Sunday Night Movie," starring Elizabeth Taylor and Robert Wagner.

ROBERT B. KIRSCH (1922–80). In *In the Wrong Rain* (Little, Brown, 1959), a Hollywood agent has an affair with a mentally disturbed teenager who dreams of becoming a movie star. Their vastly differing ages make the romance impossible, and the agent returns to his wife.

ELINOR KLEIN and DORA LANDEY. Public relations man Geoffrey Costigan is at the height of his career in *Dazzle* (G.P. Putnam's Sons, 1980) when "the syndicate" demands that he repay an old debt. They are financing a motion picture and want Costigan to oversee the production. When, halfway through the shooting, "the syndicate" demands major changes in the script, tempers on the set reach an all-time high.

NORMA KLEIN (1938–89). *Domestic Arrangements* (M. Evans, 1981) is the story of a remarkable New York family. Amanda Engelberg is an actress, well known for appearances in television commercials and soap operas. Her husband, Lionel, is a prominent documentary filmmaker. Daughter Tatiana, who narrates the novel, is a 14-year-old nymphomaniac who has just starred in her first feature film, which includes a "tasteful" nude scene. Tatiana's sister, Cordelia, is a 16-year-old with an identity crisis and a desire to emulate her sibling.

NORMAN KLEIN. Althea Turtill, the heroine of *She Loves Me* (Farrar & Rinehart, 1933) marries Hollywood newspaper reporter Ben Cotter. He was no great provider but he was the man she wanted and she was satisfied. "This novel is essentially vulgar," complained the reviewer in the *New York Times* (March 26, 1933). "Though they are no doubt authentic types, Althea and 'lover' are not the sort of people one enjoys either to read about or to meet."

HENRY KLINGER (died 1980) created an Israeli detective named Shomri Shomar. In *Lust for Murder* (Trident, 1966), the detective is called upon to watch over an American film star on location in Israel for *The Tower of Babel*, and also to solve two murders.

MAX KNEPPER. *Sodom and Gomorrah: The Story of Hollywood* (End Poverty League/author, 1935) contains a preface by Upton Sinclair, creator of the End Poverty in California (EPIC) campaign of 1934. The book is an attempt to document the truth about Hollywood in a seminovel form, with a demand that federal regulations be introduced to control the worst excesses of the industry in terms of its treatment of individuals. It points out that "Henry Ford may be a calloused, narrow man, but his private life, as far as morality is concerned, is irreproachable." The same cannot be written of the studio executives. This is a fascinating volume, but one that is hard to locate and should be reprinted.

CLIFFORD KNIGHT (1886–19??) was a prolific mystery writer. *The Affair of the Fainting Butler* (Dodd, Mead, 1943) was the thirteenth novel to feature amateur detective Huntoon Rogers, a professor of English at UCLA. The title character works for screenwriter and novelist Jennifer Janeway, a poisoned pill intended for whom is swallowed by her secretary. In *The Affair of the Corpse Escort* (David McKay, 1946), Rogers must uncover the killer of a studio employee whose body is discovered in a coffin on its way from Kansas City to Hollywood. The supposedly empty coffin was being accompanied by a film star to promote her latest film, titled *The Corpse Escort*.

ERIC KNIGHT (1897–1943) was born in Yorkshire, England, and gained the nickname of "The Flying Yorkshireman," the title of a collection of his novellas, published in 1936. He worked as a film critic for a number of minor U.S. newspapers in the 1930s and was briefly in Hollywood as a screenwriter. Prior to his death in a plane crash, Knight worked with Frank Capra on wartime documentaries. British film historian and critic Paul Rotha edited a volume of his letters: *Portrait of a Flying Yorkshireman: Letters from Eric Knight in the United States to Paul Rotha in England* (Chapman & Hall, 1952). Knight's most famous novel is *Lassie Come Home* (J.C. Winston, 1940), which formed the basis for the Lassie films and television series.

    The Flying Yorkshireman (Harper, 1938) documents the adventures in Hollywood of Sam Small, who learns to fly like a bird and thus is a success on the screen. The book was reprinted by Harper in 1942 as *Sam Small Flies Again: The Amazing Adventures of the Flying Yorkshireman*.

    See also **RICHARD HALAS.**

BILL KNOX (born 1928). *The Hanging Tree* (Crime Club/Doubleday, 1984) is the eighteenth mystery novel to feature Detective Superintendent Colin Thane. Here, he uncovers a multimillion-dollar video piracy operation in Glasgow, involving films yet to be released in the United States.

ARTHUR KOBER (1900–75) was a playwright, screenwriter, and columnist, who was at one time married to Lillian Hellman. His pieces frequently appeared in *The New Yorker*, and 17 of the 18 stories in *That Man Is Here Again* (Random House, 1946) are from that publication; the eighteenth is from *Redbook*. The book is a collection of short stories relating to Hollywood agent Benny Greenspan in the late 1930s and early to mid-1940s. Following each short story, Kober relates a real-life event similar to that which took place in fiction. The book also contains a useful introductory essay on the subject of the Hollywood agent.

MICHAEL KORDA (born 1933) is the son of art director Vincent Korda (1897–1979) and the nephew of producer-director Alexander Korda (1893–1956). Since 1958 he has been editor-in-chief at Simon & Schuster.

Charmed Lives: A Family Romance (Simon & Schuster, 1979) is a novel based on the lives of Alexander, Vincent, and Zoltán Korda, based in part on Karol Kulik's 1976 biography of Alexander Korda. Jean Strouse in *Newsweek* (November 5, 1979) described the book as "a first-rate entertainment," while *The New Yorker* (November 12, 1979) stated, "His writing is simple and lively; the characters are fully realized; and both the comic and tragic aspects of the Kordas' dazzle emerge in the telling."

Queenie (Linden Press/Simon & Schuster, 1985) is very loosely based on the life and career of actress Merle Oberon (1911–79), and tells the story of the rise to fame of the Anglo-Indian Queenie Kelley, from her early life in Calcutta to her glory years in Hollywood as movie star Dawn Avalon. Like Queenie, Merle Oberon was what used to be described as a "half-caste," and like Queenie, she married a legendary, Hungarian-born film producer. In the novel, he is named David Konig, while in real life he was Alexander Korda (to whom Oberon was married from 1939 to 1945). Queenie's first love is a photographer named Lucien Chambrun, whose character may be based on Oberon's second husband, cinematographer Lucien Ballard. Queenie begins her film career in England, coming to Hollywood to star in a *Gone with the Wind*–like epic for a producer with a penchant for memorandum writing. The similarity to David O. Selznick is only cursory in that both he and *Gone with the Wind* are also mentioned in the book. Queenie is every bit as ruthless as those around her, as her need for self-protection forces her to deny her ethnic background (as did Merle Oberon) and keep hidden other areas of her past life, even from the man whom she married after Konig's death. Though she suffers considerable humiliation and emotional torment, Queenie is, in many respects, quietly calculating and not particularly likable.

Queenie is a hefty tome (more than 600 pages in length), and its author displays a thorough knowledge not only of the history of filmmaking in Britain and the United States, but also of café society in both countries. It is neither as lurid nor as titillating as other Hollywood novels of the period.

Curtain (Summit/Simon & Schuster, 1991) is a roman à clef based on the lives of Sir Laurence Olivier and Vivien Leigh, here called Robert Vane and Felicia Lisle. The book chronicles Vane's homosexual relationships with Randy Brooks (Danny Kaye) and critic Guillan Pentecoste (Kenneth Tynan). Vane's rivals in the British theatrical scene are gay Philip Chagrin (John Gielgud), and eccentric Toby Eden (Ralph Richardson). As *Kirkus* notes, "Once you forgive yourself, it's riveting."

The Immortals (Poseidon/Simon & Schuster, 1992) is the story of Marilyn Monroe's affairs first with President Kennedy and later with Bobby Kennedy. Monroe's love nest shared with Peter Lawford is bugged by J. Edgar Hoover. "Almost no event in it is unfamiliar, though its great garden of sex-play springs largely from imagination," wrote *Kirkus* (July 15, 1992). "It's a pretty tacky novel," commented *Booklist* (August 1992). "The theme it rests on is this: as JFK's star ascended, MM's descended, and as their stars crossed, heat was definitely generated. Korda understands politics as well as fatal attraction, so his fiction is several notches above your basic steamy romance—but still rigorously formulaic."

PETER KORTNER (1924–91) was a television writer and producer in Hollywood, working on "Playhouse 90," "The DuPont Show," and "The Farmer's Daughter." Like the hero of his novel, he left Hollywood for London because of "the drift towards extremism in politics and towards mediocrity in television." Kurt Heller, the central character in *Breakfast with a Stranger* (St. Martin's Press, 1975) is the son of a major German screen star who left the country when the Nazis came to power and settled in Hollywood, where she was never able to revive her career. Her son became a story editor, producer, and writer, working primarily in television until he came to England. Heller is also homosexual, living with his lover, Dennis, in an apartment immediately beneath that of an American married couple, Nancy and Bob. When Dennis goes away for the weekend, Kurt begins an affair with Nancy, which continues until she becomes pregnant. Kurt is enthusiastic at being a father, but Nancy realizes that life with him would be a mistake, leaves Bob, and returns to the United States. The novel closes with Kurt's reaffirming his relationship with Dennis. A fine novel notable for its witty dialogue, *Breakfast with a Stranger* tells of Kurt's Hollywood years in flashback as he tries to deal with the present but consistently lets his mind wander.

JUDITH KRANTZ (born 1927) is an immensely popular, best-selling writer whose books are unlikely to be mistaken for literature. *Scruples* (Crown, 1978) is the story of a Beverly Hills fashion boutique, founded by Billie Ikehorn. Her second husband is an Italian film producer, and the novel, in part, concerns itself with the making of an Academy Award–winning film. The story continues in *Scruples Two* (Crown, 1992), picking up in 1978. Vito Orsini wins the Oscar; Billie Ikehorn is pregnant but she miscarries and divorces when Orsini cheats on her. "Pure delicious fun," reported *Kirkus*. *Princess Daisy* (Crown, 1980) is the story of Princess Marguerite Alexandrarna Valensky, "Daisy," whose father was White Russian Prince Stash Valensky, and whose mother was film star Francesca Vernon.

STEVE KRANTZ. *Laurel Canyon* (Pocket Books, 1979) is a well-known Los Angeles roadway, snaking across the Santa Monica Mountains and joining the San Fernando Valley community of Studio City with West Hollywood. It is a community within itself known for its mix of hippies and tolerant Hollywood types. The heroine of this lurid melodrama, Stevie Tree, lives in a house off the Canyon, which once belonged to the man who taught her how to love and who was murdered as a consequence of his drug dealing. As the novel opens, Stevie is witness to the drug overdose death of a movie producer's daughter, with the drugs provided by an aging actor, Morgan Oliver, who was sexually involved with the girl and with whom Stevie had once a torrid affair.

The talent agency, International Artists, for which Stevie works, attempts to cover up the circumstances of the death to protect its clients (including Oliver and the producer), and the novel is concerned with Stevie's efforts to have the truth revealed, as her rise to success within the agency is documented. *Laurel Canyon* provides a vivid account of the power of talent agencies within the film community, as well as a more loving report on the coffee shop at Schwab's Pharmacy, which once stood at the junction of Laurel Canyon and Sunset Boulevard. Along the way, there is frequent and explicit sex, patronizing commentary on a smattering of homosexuals, and the obligatory child molestation of the heroine. *Laurel Canyon* is first-rate Hollywood sensationalism, with the socially redeeming feature of exposing the sleaze factor within the film industry's talent agencies.

HARRY KURNITZ (1908–68). Although film related, *Invasion of Privacy* (Random House, 1955) takes place in New York and involves the East Coast representative of a Hollywood studio and a female screenwriter, whose murder script, halfway through production, is too close for comfort to the story of a real, unexplained killing. Kurnitz hung around with Frank Sinatra, Sammy Davis, Jr., and Peter Lawford, and was known as "The Court Jester of the Rat Pack."

RON KURZ (born 1940). *Black Rococo* (M. Evans, 1975) is the name of a movie theater that has deteriorated past pornography to black exploitation films; it is managed by 29-year-old Clifton Praeger. The latter organizes a "Superdude Day" to honor Superdude actor Lorenzo Jones, and when violence breaks out, he barely escapes with his life.

MAURICE L. (Lincoln) KUSELL and M.S. MERRITT. *Marquee Ballyhoo: An American Novel* (A.H. Chamberlain/Overland-Outwest Publications, 1932) is the story of Texas tent-show performers Erol Brothers and Dusteen Frawley, who marry on stage. When film star Katherine Reno comes to Texas on location with the Pinnacle Motion Picture Company, she meets Erol and persuades him to come to Hollywood, which he does, deserting Dusteen. He changes his name to Earl Kelton and marries Katherine Reno. Dusteen has a child, comes to Hollywood, and confronts Katherine, but that same day Erol is killed while making a World War I flying picture. The novel contains a glossary of tent-show and film terms.

JOHN LAHR (born 1941) is a noted critic and the son of comedian Bert Lahr. *The Autograph Hound* (Alfred A. Knopf, 1973) is the cautionary tale of an obsessive fan who aggressively collects autographs, and, in pursuit of his hobby, works as a busboy at a trendy New York restaurant much favored by celebrities. The stream of consciousness is positively orgasmic in *Hot to Trot* (Alfred A. Knopf, 1974). George Melish is an ABC television executive and the son of an independent Hollywood producer (who was once closely associated with Tyrone Power). Following the breakup of his marriage, Melish spies on his wife and her new lover, a rock 'n' roll singer, and reviews his life through his various sexual encounters since his teen years. One of Melish's early television successes had been programming a season of Rita Hayworth films, during which the actress reminisced about her career, and Hayworth figures prominently in his sex fantasies.

ROSALIND LAKER is the pseudonym of Barbara Ovstedal. *What the Heart Keeps* (Doubleday, 1984) is "a well-written tale of star crossed romance in the vital point of the early 1900s." While waiting to leave from her native Liverpool for Canada in 1903, 14-year-old orphan Lisa Shaw meets Norwegian Peter Hagen at the docks. The novel is the story of Peter's search for Lisa, who marries a man interested in the operation of movie theaters. One of the girls whom Lisa befriends in Canada is Minnie, who later becomes a Hollywood star.

GAVIN LAMBERT (born 1924) edited *Sight and Sound* in his native England from 1950 to 1956. He scripted and directed *Another Sky* in Morocco in 1956, and his later screenplays include *Sons and Lovers* (1960), *The Roman Spring of Mrs. Stone* (1961), *Inside Daisy Clover* (1965), and *I Never Promised You a Rose Garden* (1978). He has written a number of nonfiction works on Hollywood: *On Cukor* (G.P. Putnam's Sons, 1972), *GWTW: The Making of "Gone with the Wind"* (Little, Brown, 1973), *The Dangerous Edge* (Grossman Publishing, 1975), and *Norma Shearer: A Life* (Alfred A. Knopf, 1990).

The Slide Area: Scenes of Hollywood Life (Viking Press, 1959) is narrated by an English-born Hollywood screenwriter. As in similar books by Gavin Lambert, the narrator is sexually ambivalent—or perhaps he is just a typical product of an English public school. The book consists of six separate stories, and despite the subtitle, only two relate to the film industry and most take place outside the confines of Hollywood, generally in Santa Monica or other beach-front communities. "The Closed Set" is the story of the making of the latest film featuring Julie Forbes, who would appear to be modeled after Joan Crawford. She is domineering toward her director but loved by the film crew, each of whose names she remembers and all of whom she greets in a friendly fashion. Her young son, Timmy, was witness to the death of one of her lovers in an empty swimming pool and, as a result, can obtain whatever presents he wants from her. The central figure in "Dreaming Emma" is Emma Slack from Galena, Illinois, who finds out the hard way what she must do to become a star named Delia Blow in Hollywood.

Inside Daisy Clover (Viking Press, 1963) is the journal of the child star of the title, chronicling her life as she becomes a star in her teens, marries a homosexual, has an illegitimate child, and then retrieves her stardom. "It is superbly written and fast-moving," wrote Arthur Marx in the *Saturday Review of Literature* (April 27, 1963). "Its dialogue is witty and stiletto-sharp; it is sexy but nor pornographic; and it contains not one stereotyped Hollywood character." In 1965 Alan J. Pakula and Robert Mulligan produced a screen adaptaion of the novel for Warner Bros. release, directed by Mulligan, and starring Natalie Wood, Christopher Plummer, Robert Redford, and Roddy McDowall.

The pointlessness and sheer irrelevancy of life in Hollywood is well captured in *The Goodbye People* (Simon and Schuster, 1971), which, equally, has little import. It comprises three short character studies: the first of Susan Ross, a model who married a film producer, now deceased, who becomes more and more remote and eventually disappears into a marriage with a multibillionaire, obviously modeled after Howard Hughes; the second of a bisexual drifter; and the third of a young woman who lives in the lodge of the former home of a legendary movie star who appears to have become a ghost before her time. It is difficult to know who is the most self-indulgent, Gavin Lambert or the characters he has created.

Running Time (Macmillan, 1983) covers the years 1919–82 and is told in the form of diary entries by Elva Kaye and commentary thereon by her daughter, Baby Jewel. Kaye brings Jewel to Hollywood (on the train they meet Theda Bara) to become a child star. The pair visits D.W. Griffith on the set, and he encourages Baby Jewel, who is signed by a poverty row producer named Sid Gordon, to star in a series of kiddie comedies as a Sherlock Holmes character. Kaye meets William Desmond Taylor, becomes his lover, and is introduced by him to cocaine. When he drops her, she kills him, but is never suspected of the crime because no one knows of her connection to the director. Kaye flourishes as a businesswoman, and Jewel's career prospers at M-G-M, where she meets a Mickey Rooney–type actor with whom she has her first affair and whom she later marries and divorces. Kaye becomes devoted to Louis B. Mayer, and the two have a natural affinity for each other, and Kaye later tries to save the studio after Mayer has been dethroned. Jewel's career suffers when she becomes an adult; she is signed to a contract by Howard Hughes, but all that does is prevent her from working. When Kaye's cosmetics company decides to sponsor a television series, Jewel is the star, and the two women are surprised to discover that Sid Gordon is the producer. He reminds them that there is a close similarity between B movies and television. Following her mother's death, Jewel is awarded an honorary Oscar, and a gay film buff writes a book on her.

Gavin Lambert obviously knows his film history, but was it really necessary to cram quite so much of it into this novel? Practically every major incident in film history is included here. The relationship between the two women is well handled, as is that between Jewel and the Mickey Rooney character, with the two remaining close despite the divorce. The ending is refreshing, with Jewel's receiving death threats, which come to nothing—at least as far as the last page. All in all, impressive but long-winded.

SPEED LAMKIN (born 1927). Narrated by a magazine writer, *The Easter Egg Hunt* (Houghton Mifflin, 1954) tells the stories of the unfaithful wife of an assistant producer and the alcoholic wife of an aging millionaire who wants to be a movie star. James Hilton in the *New York Herald Tribune* (February 28, 1954) wrote, "Mr. Speed Lamkin's *The Easter Egg Hunt* is a James M. Cainish novel about the seamier side of Hollywood, called for purposes of geography 'the tense, glittering, eager world of Beverly Hills.' Those who have lived in Beverly Hills without finding it tense, glittering, eager or even a world, will read Mr. Lamkin's story with no more incredulity than one about Peoria or Park Avenue. ... Mr. Lamkin writes as if he had no time to lose, and handles both plot and character with a great deal of skill."

DORA LANDEY *see* **ELINOR KLEIN and DORA LANDEY**

ABBE LANE enjoyed a minor film career but is better known as the band singer with and later wife to Xavier Cugat (whom she divorced in 1964). Not surprisingly, her novel *But Where Is Love?* (Warner Books, 1993) is the story of New Yorker Julia Lehman whose career is tied to a celebrated Latin bandleader named Paco Castell. The latter is obsessive and cruel, organizing his wife's career to her detriment but to his satisfaction. As the publisher's blurb on the dust jacket states, the details are "too authentic to be fiction." Unfortunately, there are too many details, with page after page filled with minutiae and irrelevances. The reader feels no sympathy for the central character, who seems only to have herself to blame for a troubled life, and the behavior of her parents is impossible to understand. Undoubtedly the most interesting portion of the book concerns a visit to Hollywood by Lehman and her mother when Lehman is invited to make a screen test for Howard Hughes. The manner in which the two women are treated, if indeed it is true, paints a fascinating portrait of the industrialist and studio owner. After taking on the arduous task of reading *But Where Is Love?* one can only wonder why Abbe Lane simply did not decide to write her autobiography; at the same time one is only too aware that it would be equally badly written and, ultimately, the story of a woman whose name and career mean very little in the 1990s.

TAMAR LANE (1895–19??) was a Los Angeles–based film journalist who edited and published *The Film Mercury* from 1924 to 1933, and also wrote three film-related works of nonfiction: *What's Wrong with the Movies* (1923), *Hollywood and the Movies* (1930), and *The New Technique of Screen Writing* (1936). His novel *Hey Diddle Diddle* (Adelphi Press, 1932) begins in the office of producer Jake Mandelbaum of Mastodon Pictures. The New York sales staff is there to tell him that the films of leading man Roland Gillette (John Gilbert) are not selling. With the advent of talkies, Gillette's audience has discovered that the romantic actor "has got a squeaky voice that sounds like a piccolo player calling to his mate." Prop man Larry Duffy punches Gillette when he catches him trying to assault sexually a bit player, Anne Richards. When Gillette becomes overdemanding he is fired, and Mandelbaum decides to make Duffy a star. But as his status grows, Duffy in turn becomes arrogant, and when Anne Richards is starred opposite him, it is obvious who has the greater following. Duffy is now fired, replaced by Gillette, who has learned humility. It is time for Duffy to learn his lesson, which leads to his being reunited with Richards. A subplot involves a banking group taking over the studio. All in all, a parody that is not particularly witty or entertaining.

RUTH LANGAN (born 1937). *All That Glitters* (HarperCollins, 1994) is a romantic novel about the rise to fame and fortune of singer Alexandra Corday. She is obsessed with her work until she meets handsome filmmaker Matt Montrose, whose career is as high powered as her own.

NOEL LANGLEY (1911–80) was a novelist and playwright who wrote the scripts for many major M-G-M films, including *Maytime* (1936), *The Wizard of Oz* (1939), *Ivanhoe* (1952), and *The Prisoner of Zenda* (1953). His best-known play, with Robert Morley, is *Edward My Son* (1948), for which he also wrote the 1948 screenplay.

In *Hocus Pocus* (Methuen, 1952), narrator Pearl O'Hara explains how her boyfriend-agent tricked a producer into signing her to a contract, and provides far from complimentary descriptions of Hollywood's producers, directors, writers, and stars. The book is dedicated to "The Boys on the Black List."

JOE R. LANSDALE

JOE R. LANSDALE (born 1951). Subtitled "A B-Movie with Blood and Popcorn, Made in Texas," *The Drive In* (Bantam Books, 1988) begins by introducing four Texas buddies whose favorite occupation is to visit the Orbit, a six-screen drive-in movie theater. On one fateful night there, just as Cameron Mitchell is about to use an industrial nailer on a young woman he had been spying on in the shower, a meteor or comet flashes by. A black ooze now surrounds the drive-in, and any patron attempting to fight his or her way through is eaten alive. As the author comments, "There was this B-string god and he was making a movie. He didn't have the power to make the Big Movie, so he just borrowed some people (us) and a setting (the drive-in) and made do with that." Civilization quickly breaks down within the complex, as two of the four men are fused together as one to become the Popcorn King. Only after the other two are crucified does the comet reappear and the ooze disappear. As the last two buddies leave the theater, the world outside has obviously aged. *The Drive In* is a highly original work that at times becomes overwhelmed in allegory, but it remains a book primarily for aficionados of fantasy and science fiction.

RING LARDNER, JR.

RING LARDNER, JR. (born 1915), won two Academy Awards for his screenplays for *Woman of the Year* (1942) and *M*A*S*H* (1970); his other scripts include *Meet Dr. Christian* (1939), *Cloak and Dagger* (1946), *Forever Amber* (1947), and *Cincinnati Kid* (1965). He appeared before the House Un-American Activities Committee in 1947, was convicted of contempt of Congress, and, as one of the Hollywood Ten, served ten months in federal prison from 1950 to 1951. That time in American history is recalled in *The Ecstasy of Owen Muir* (Cameron & Kahn, 1955), a satire on American politics during the McCarthy era. One of the people with whom the title character comes into contact is Monsignor Stephen A. Frasso, a Roman Catholic prelate who appears frequently on both television and in films. This "right reverend star" is presumably based on Bishop Fulton J. Sheen. The group, Catholic Action Council Against Communism and Creeping Socialism (CACACACS) is perhaps loosely modeled after the Motion Picture Alliance for the Preservation of American Ideals (MPAPAI).

LAWRENCE LARIAR

LAWRENCE LARIAR (born 1908). Set in an animation studio, *He Died Laughing* (Phoenix Press, 1943) has two new employees, who have created the comic strip character of "Dr. Ohm," investigate the murder of director Mark Richmond while he is at a private screening of a "Benny the Bear" cartoon. "Mr. Lariar is a refreshing change from the earnest whodunits," opined Will Cuppy in the *New York Herald Tribune* (July 25, 1943). "He is at his best, probably, when just kidding around or reporting the casual antics of Hollywood's case histories, drunk or fairly sober."

CHARLES LARSON (born 1922). When a Hollywood film editor is murdered, his homosexual brother is implicated in *Muir's Blood* (Doubleday, 1977). The producer/director, Nils Blixen, investigates the killing.

JESSE L. LASKY, JR. (born 1910), was the son of pioneer producer Jesse L. Lasky, the man who ran Paramount Pictures with Adolph Zukor. He was also a novelist, a television writer, and screenwriter, whose films for Cecil B. DeMille included *Union Pacific* (1936), *Reap the Wild Wind* (1941), *Samson and Delilah* (1950), and *The Buccaneer* (1958). His autobiography, *Whatever Happened to Hollywood?*, was published by Thomas Y. Crowell in 1974.

While it is unquestionably overwritten, **Naked in a Cactus Garden** (Bobbs-Merrill, 1961) is better than most books of its type. The setting is a testimonial dinner for Hollywood producer Rex Godwin, and as his various colleagues and relatives gather they remember the part he played in their lives. Godwin comes across as a tough and aggressive filmmaker who has used people but has also stood by them. The most aggrieved person there is a part-time waiter whose script was stolen by one of Godwin's contract writers, now dead, and presented to the producer as her own. The waiter believes Godwin stole the script and plans to kill him that night. Godwin's career is in decline, and one of the guests, the head of his former studio, will decide whether to allow Godwin to proceed on a new film. As luck would have it, he is the one shot by the waiter. Godwin does not appear to be modeled specifically after any Hollywood producer, least of all Jesse L. Lasky, but there are elements in his character that make him seem similar to Cecil B. DeMille.

JONATHAN LATIMER (1906–83). In *Black Is the Fashion for Dying* (Random House, 1959), writer Richard Blake, director Josh Gordon, producer Karl Fabro, and star Caresse are involved in the reworking of a film script. When the unsympathetic star is murdered, Josh Gordon is determined to identify her killer. "The Hollywood scene in slick, sharp scrimmaging," reported *Kirkus* (October 16, 1959).

ARTHUR LAURENTS (born 1918) was a successful novelist and screenwriter when he published his first novel, *The Way We Were* (Harper & Row, 1972). Because of a wartime romance, committed Communist Katie Morosky abandons her role in the party and marries Hubbell Gardner. The latter is a novelist and is called to Hollywood, only to find himself blacklisted during the McCarthy era as a result of his wife's former activities. The witch-hunt causes the dissolution of the couple's marriage. *The Way We Were* was filmed in 1973 by Rastar Productions for Columbia release, directed by Sydney Pollack, and starring Barbra Streisand, Robert Redford, and Bradford Dillman.

LEW LAURIA (born 1904). *Let the Chips Fall* (Radco Publishers, 1946) is concerned primarily with the radio industry in Hollywood, and the author appears as one of the book's characters. The central figure is New York radio actress Teresa Drake, who decides to continue her career in Hollywood, where she is promoted by program director Dick Randall, who has fallen in love with her.

RICHARD LAYMAN (born 1947). One should not lip-read at the movies as one deaf young woman discovers in *Out Are the Lights* (Warner Books, 1982). Reading lips while watching a late-night movie, she makes the blood-chilling discovery that the murders on the screen are for real.

FANNIE H. (Heaslip) LEA. When actress Malou's aviator lover is killed in *Happy Landings* (Dodd, Mead, 1930), she determines to become a star of sound films in Hollywood. She meets and falls in love with another aviator, Ted Traill, and the couple star together on screen. "The author wins a measure of distinction in her novel by picturing Hollywood without the usual frills accorded it by fiction writers," commented the reviewer in the *New York Times* (June 8, 1930). "She does not paint it as a den of iniquity or as a land of fantastic glamor but as a very busy corner in a work-a-day world."

VIRGINIA LEDERER. *Married at Leisure* (Doubleday, Doran, 1944) is a love story involving minor Hollywood actress Marilyn and her five-year effort to marry Chubb, who is overly attached to his grandmother.

BERNIE LEE has written three mystery novels featuring amateur husband-and-wife sleuths Tony and Pat Pratt: *Murder at Musket Beach* (Donald I. Fine, 1990), *Murder Without Reservation* (Donald I. Fine, 1991), and *Murder Takes Two* (Donald I. Fine, 1992). Tony works in the film and television industry; in the second novel he is a location manager for a Japanese television company, and in *Murder Takes Two*, he is in London directing a television commercial.

GYPSY ROSE LEE was the professional name of Rose Louise Hovick (1914–70), the best known of American burlesque stars who also enjoyed a career on screen, television, and the legitimate stage; her life story was the basis for the 1959 musical *Gypsy*. She wrote two mystery novels, *The G-String Murders* (Simon & Schuster, 1941) and *Mother Finds a Body* (Simon & Schuster, 1942), both of which she narrates as a burlesque stripper, and both of which were, in reality, ghostwritten by popular mystery novelist Craig Rice (the pseudonym of Georgiana Ann Randolph, 1908–57).

JAMES LEE. The title character in *Hollywood Agent* (Macaulay Company, 1937) is Joe Flowers, whose life is devoted to keeping his client, the glamorous if unintelligent screen star Mary Merriwhether, in the public eye and out of public escapades.

RICHARD HENRY LEE was a pseudonym. After inheriting a vast sum of money, illiterate factory worker Fanny Dopass goes to Hollywood and from there writes a series of unintelligent letters home in *Nights and Daze in Hollywood* (Macaulay Company, 1934). Despite being swindled, seduced by a gigolo, and kidnapped, Fanny remains oblivious to what is happening to her and writes only of how thrilled she is by Hollywood.

GENE LEES (born 1928). *And Sleep Until Noon* (Trident Press, 1966) is the story of a piano player who becomes a pop singer and later a movie star.

After living the life of a playboy, he eventually realizes that one cannot "sleep until noon" forever and so returns to his wife and child.

ERNEST LEHMAN (born 1920) is a major Hollywood screenwriter whose credits include *Sabrina* (1954), *Sweet Smell of Success* (1957), *North by Northwest* (1959), *The Sound of Music* (1965), *Who's Afraid of Virginia Woolf?* (1966), and *Hello Dolly!* (1969).

Farewell Performance (McGraw-Hill, 1982) is a skillfully crafted and entertaining novel of intrigue and humor. Teddy Stern and Howard Bluestern are identical twins. Teddy is a hard-drinking second-rate actor. Howard is the president of a film studio. Howard has a medical problem, and in order to pass a physical needed to obtain a company life insurance policy, he asks Teddy to take his place. While the two brothers have temporarily exchanged identities, Howard is murdered. Teddy discovers and hides the body and continues the subterfuge with the aid of Howard's secretary, with whom he begins an affair. Teddy alternates being Howard and himself while trying to decide how to dispose of the body and thus return to being only Teddy. As various characters become involved in the act, including Howard's gay houseman and the insurance company executive, the murderer steals the body, disposes of it in the ocean, and also kills herself. By now, Teddy has come to enjoy being Howard, and the implication at the novel's close is that he will continue to play both roles, continuing his career as an actor and helping improve Howard's image as a producer. The urge to go for farce as Teddy impersonates Howard must have been strong, but the author plays it surprisingly straight. Only the gay houseman seems overdrawn.

JAMES LEIGH (born 1930). *Downstairs at Ramsey's* (Harper & Row, 1968) is narrated by a retired Hollywood film actor, Victor Ramsey, who discovers that he can hear everything that goes on in the apartment he rents out downstairs in the house that he owns. The narrator's previous life is irrelevant to the novel, which is concerned with the relationship between one of the men in the apartment and a 15-year-old girl who has moved in.

ELMORE LEONARD (born 1925) has written a handful of minor screenplays—*Stick* (1985), *52 Pick-Up* (1986), and *The Rosary Murders* (1987)— and a number of best-selling novels, among which is *Get Shorty* (Delacorte Press, 1990). It concerns a small-time gangster from Miami who comes to Hollywood and "cons" a producer and others into agreeing to make a film of his life story, while at the same time disposing of a couple of his colleagues who have gotten in his way. The novel, which is dedicated to producer Walter Mirisch, "one of the good guys," is mildly amusing. The author obviously has a good knowledge of how Hollywood types take meetings and promote script ideas, but the story pales in comparison with the later *The Player*. The *Atlanta Journal-Constitution* claims that *Get Shorty* "does for Hollywood what Tom Wolfe's *Bonfire of the Vanities* did for New York City." One can only assume that paper's critic had in mind the movie version of *Bonfire*.

CHRISTOPHER LEOPOLD. *Casablack* (Doubleday, 1979) is not strictly a Hollywood novel but is noted for informational purposes. Intended as a sequel to the 1941 film *Casablanca*, it depicts the central characters in a more realistic and far less idealistic fashion.

ELLIOTT LEWIS (1917–91). As its title indicates, ***Bennett #2: Dirty Linen*** (Pinnacle Books, 1980) is the second mystery novel to feature Los Angeles ex-cop private eye Bennett, a series that owes a debt to the pulp fiction of yesteryear. Here, Bennett awaits the arrival at an art gallery of Christine Walker, a four-times married Hollywood sex symbol, when she is found dead. Bennett, who knew and loved her, is determined to prove she was murdered.

LANGE LEWIS is the pseudonym of Jane Lewis Brandt (born 1915). In *Meat for Murder* (Bobbs-Merrill, 1943), a police officer uncovers the murderer of set designer Earl Falkoner, killed in his pseudocastle in Hollywood. The book is notable for its eccentric characters, including a man who talks to a werewolf, a midget, and a religious cultist. "Plenty of local color, raft of exotic characters, believable sleuth, and speedy doings all the way," reported the reviewer in the *Saturday Review of Literature* (November 6, 1943). "A tough screwball—but entertaining," opined *Kirkus* (November 24, 1943). When novelist and screenwriter Victoria Jason's director-husband dies after eating poisoned sugar, she is forced to defend herself against a charge of murder in *The Birthday Murder* (Bobbs-Merrill, 1945). It just so happens that her new novel is about a wife poisoning her husband. The novel was reprinted by Garland in its "Fifty Classics of Crime Fiction, 1900–1950" series.

PATRICIA LIBBY. *Hollywood Nurse* (Ace Books, 1962) is identified by Carolyn See as a Hollywood novel.

GODDARD LIEBERSON (1911–77) was the highly regarded head of Columbia Records. His one and only novel, ***Three for Bedroom C*** (Doubleday, 1947), chronicles the amusing adventures of a college professor who is forced to travel, due to circumstances beyond his control, from Chicago to California in a shared Pullman bedroom with a movie star, her daughter, and their pet dog. "The A.T. & St.F. should be as content with his book as the bus companies were, some years ago, with that equally delightful film, *It Happened One Night*," wrote Nancy Ladd in the *New York Times* (February 2, 1947). The novel was filmed in 1952 by Brenco Productions for Warner Bros. release, directed by Milton H. Bren, and starring Gloria Swanson, James Warren, and Fred Clark.

MARK LINDQUIST (born 1959). The first-person narrative of ***Sad Movies*** (Atlantic Monthly Press, 1987) is heavy with angst, relieved by occasional wry humor and an existentialist (and literal) trip. Zeke writes publicity copy for a sleazy Los Angeles production company named Big Gun Films. His extracurricular sexual activities lead to his actress girlfriend's planning to leave him, but after a journey up the coast and the adoption of a puppy, the relationship seems once again to be relatively secure. The novel is at its best in describing the lifestyle of those who follow a routine of sex and drugs on the beachfront at Venice, California.

DAVID L. LINDSAY. *Heat from Another Son* (Harper & Row, 1984) pits a Houston, Texas, homicide detective against a business tycoon who funds Salvadoran death squads and owns an extensive library of filmed violence.

ELIZABETH LININGTON (1921–88) wrote as Lesley Egan, Dell Shannon, and others. Under her own name, she wrote a series of mystery novels featuring Sergeant Ivor Maddox and his wife, Detective Sue Maddox, of the Hollywood precinct. The film industry does not generally enter into the plotlines except in a casual fashion. For example, in *Consequence of Crime* (Crime Club/Doubleday, 1980), there is a knifing in a movie theater and a television star is murdered.

LAYNE LITTLEPAGE. In *Murder by the Sea* (Crime Club/Doubleday, 1987), Vivienne Montrose, Carmel-by-the-Sea resident and Hollywood star of the 1940s, is to play the lead in a summer theater production of *A Classic Case of Murder*. When one of the other actresses in the cast is murdered, Montrose turns detective.

M. (Myran) JAY LIVINGSTON (born 1934). *The Prodigy* (Coward, McCann & Geoghegan, 1978) is prescient in its depiction of the world of the 1990s as represented by the killings of the parents of the Menendez brothers and the anti–child abuse rantings of Roseanne Arnold. A Malibu–based filmmaker is offered a position teaching film production at an Ohio high school. The students there need his help in producing a film on child abuse. They are also involved in blackmailing abusive parents and punishing them with blinding, mutilation, death by burning, and the like.

ARNOLD LOBEL (1933–87). *Martha the Movie Mouse* (Harper & Row, 1966) is a charming tale told in verse for young children about a homeless mouse who finds refuge in a movie theater. But when she frightens the female patrons, she is ejected, only to return triumphant when one of the projectors breaks down and she goes on stage to entertain the audience.

DAVID LODGE (born 1935). "To the pictures! To the warm embrace of Mother cinema. Where peanut shells are spread before your feet, and the ice-cream cometh!" cries out student Mark Underwood in the early pages of *The Picturegoers* (MacGibbon & Kee, 1960). The novel chronicles a few months in the lives of Underwood and other habitués of the Palladium Cinema in a working-class London suburb. The characters are influenced by the films they see on the screen and by their strict or loose adherence to the Catholic Church. Each goes through a period of despondency but ultimately ends up smiling— even the cinema manager finds rehabilitation for the failing audiences at his theater by booking a rock 'n' roll film.

David Lodge has captured the essence of filmgoing in Britain in the 1950s. The kids wait outside asking adults to take them in to a film for which adult accompaniment is required. A young boy finds a stranger's hand on his knee. A teenager slashes the seats. Usherettes show people to their seats, and female attendants come around selling choc ices. The author demonstrates a brilliant and often witty ear for the reactions of those in the audience. Upon seeing the credit "Color by Technicolor," the parish priest wonders for "he had always throught colour was by Almighty God!" The audience reaction to *Bicycle Thief* (*Bicycle Thieves* in the novel and in the United Kingdom) is predictable:

"Queer sort of ending."

"Well, I thought he would get his bike back after all that performance."

"Sort of left you in the air. You know."

"Not bad I s'pose, but it brought you down a bit."

"All those foreign voices, it got on my nerves."

"Bloody wops."

The Picturegoer was reprinted in 1993 by Penguin Books with an introduction by David Lodge, in which he discusses the writing of this brilliantly perceptive novel.

STEPHEN LONGSTREET (born 1907) is a prolific novelist who was also active as a screenwriter—*Uncle Harry* (1945), *The Jolson Story* (1946), and *The Helen Morgan Story* (1957), for example—and writer of radio programs. In **The Beach House** (Henry Holt, 1952), Hollywood producer Mike Zelsmith decides to make a highly commercial feature film in order to finance an artistic one. The politics of talent agencies is the theme of **The Flesh Peddlers** (Simon & Schuster, 1962), as a minor employee with the COK (Company of Kings) agency tries to move upward, is fired, and, subsequently, gets a better job with a newly formed agency. **Wheel of Fortune** (Pinnacle Books, 1981) is the story of two Jewish families who emigrate to the United States in 1892, start their new lives in Chicago, and then move on to Colorado and California, all the while facing poverty and anti–Semitism. Part of their story deals with the early years of the film industry in Los Angeles. **Golden Touch** (Pinnacle Books, 1982) has a similar storyline and may possibly be the same book reprinted under a new title.

Stephen Longstreet is often identified as a pseudonym of Philip Wiener; all his novels in the Los Angeles Public Library system, for example, are catalogued under the name Wiener. As Longstreet points out, this is a mistake that originated with the H.W. Wilson Company back in the 1950s. Stephen Longstreet is not a pseudonym, and he does not write under the name of Philip Wiener.

ANITA LOOS (1893–1981) was one of the United States' best-known screenwriters in large part thanks to her extraordinary powers of self-promotion, often at the expense of her husband, John Emerson. She began her career as a teenager after successfully submitting a script for *The New York Hat* (1912) to director D.W. Griffith. Her films include *The Struggle* (1931), *San Francisco* (1936), *The Women* (1939), *Susan and God* (1940), and *The Pirate* (1948). She wrote a number of books on Hollywood, including two unreliable autobiographies: *A Girl Like I* (Viking Press, 1966) and *A Cast of Thousands* (Grosset & Dunlap, 1977).

Loos enjoyed phenomenal success with the publication of *Gentlemen Prefer Blondes: The Illuminating Diary of a Professional Lady* (Boni & Liveright, 1925). It became a stageplay and a musical, and was filmed as both a silent picture and a talkie. The successor volume, **But Gentlemen Marry Brunettes** (Boni & Liveright, 1928), is a collection of short stories which has Lorelei Lee and her companion, Dorothy, in Hollywood.

A Mouse Is Born (Doubleday, 1951) is written in an irritatingly "cutesy" style, complete with typos (Cinegog for Synagogue, and so forth), and supposedly narrated by siren Effie Huntriss, "Hollywood's Chief Exponent of Sex." As she lies in bed contemplating the birth of her first child, the star decides to write the story of her life for the young one, the mouse's enjoyment. She tells of her three marriages, her rise to stardom following her first appearance in a nudie film, and the discovery of her long-lost mother, to whom she is introduced in front of a studio head who has to be modeled after Louis B. Mayer. The novel is illustrated with a series of drawings by Pallavicini, showing Effie in her best-known roles.

No Mother to Guide Her (McGraw-Hill, 1961) is a mildly amusing satire on Hollywood, but obviously Edmund Wilson had lost all his critical faculties when he described it, on the dust jacket, as an "intrepid satire . . . the Hollywood novel with most teeth in it." Elmer Bliss and his mother live in Hollywood, a community whose greatest booster is Bliss through his newspaper columns and radio broadcasts. When a sensational murder trial threatens to damage the reputation of star Viola Lake, through the exposure of her diaries, Bliss gets himself appointed "czar" (rather like Will Hays) to protect both Hollywood and Miss Lake, with whom Bliss has become enamored despite warnings from his mother. The novel is narrated in flashback by Bliss after he has learned that Lake has become a resident of the Motion Picture Country Club (a somewhat unnecessary name change for the Motion Picture Country House, which, for reasons unknown, Loos moves from Woodland Hills to Van Nuys). The novel ends with Bliss's reunion with Lake, whom he asks what lessons she has learned from her misspent life. Her reply, "If I had it to live over again, I wouldn't bob my hair!"

MARY LOOS is related to Anita Loos and relatively well known in Hollywood circles. *The Beggars Are Coming* (Bantam Books, 1974) is the story of movie mogul Simon Moses, from the silent era through the present, with the emphasis on his power struggles with his son-in-law Fergus Austin. The book provides a potted, popular history of Hollywood filmmaking.

ERNEST LOPEZ. *His Awaking: A Romance of Manila and Hollywood* (Wetzel Publishing, 1929) is identified by Carolyn See as a Hollywood novel.

JAMES LORD's second novel, *The Joys of Success* (John Day, 1958), is one of the more outrageous satires on the film industry. Hollywood director Walter Estrin is determined to produce a classic, and he seizes the opportunity when Jack Noakes is injured in a car crash. While in shock, Noakes is persuaded to sign a waiver to have his leg amputated—and the operation is filmed. However, when Noakes dies, Estrin is left with an unfinished masterpiece. "This novel is apparently meant to be satiric and succeeds only in being clumsy," wrote *The New Yorker* (February 15, 1958).

PETER LOVESEY (born 1903) is a prolific British mystery novelist, noted for the series featuring Victorian Detective Cribb and the more recent books with Albert, "Bertie," Prince of Wales, as the hero.

For an English writer of fiction, Lovesey displays considerable knowledge of early American film history and southern California geography in **Keystone** (Pantheon Books, 1983). Set in 1915, the novel has an English vaudevillian, Warwick Easton, arriving at Mack Sennett's Keystone Studios and being hired to play one of the Keystone Kops. He is romantically attracted to a would-be actress, Amber Honeybee, and becomes involved in solving the mystery of who murdered one of the Keystone Kops during the shooting of a comedy on a roller-coaster ride. The story is well-crafted and has a good period quality, although the author is forced to use conversations between the central characters to explain early filmmaking techniques and identify film personalities such as Mack Sennett and producer Thomas H. Ince. Other real-life participants in the story include Roscoe "Fatty" Arbuckle, Minta Durfee, Mack Swain, Slim Summerville, Chester Conklin, Harry Gribbon, Alice Davenport, and Del Lord. Leading ladies Mabel Normand and Mae Busch are also heavily featured, and the author makes good use of the historical legend that the former broke off her engagement to Mack Sennett after finding the producer in bed with Mae Busch.

HAYNES LUBOU was a pseudonym and the author of *Reckless Hollywood* (Amour Press, 1932) is female. This is rather a sordid and explicit romantic novel about the life of a Hollywood extra, Petty Love, who is introduced on the set of a film, directed by the dictatorial and abusive R.B. De Lacey (obviously Cecil B. DeMille). The story follows Love as she discovers the reality of life for a Hollywood extra—next day's work is contingent upon sleeping with the assistant director tonight. Love meets, and loses her virginity to, a stunt flyer named Dan Eagan, but because of his drinking and a physical assault upon her, she returns to New York, leaving a new job she had acquired in Hollywood as a fan magazine writer. Penniless in New York, Love enjoys partying and the sex that follows—gripped, as the author puts it, by "sex-fever." On her return to Hollywood, she sleeps with an assistant director who had once tried to rape her, thus assuring she can work tomorrow.

The dust jacket for this novel proclaims, "The author knows what she writes about and pins it down with sharp realism. If you know your Hollywood you'll recognize her. You'll gasp at her courage, and you'll marvel at the skill with which she has been able to trap so much of Hollywood into her vivid book."

A number of Hollywood stars are mentioned in passing, including William Bakewell, Mary Brian, and Robert Montgomery. Amusingly, at a party one of the guests makes reference to another Hollywood novel of the day, *Queer People*, noting, "Everyone who owned or could rent a typewriter went into seclusion as soon as *Queer People* came out." *Reckless Hollywood* goes *Queer People* one better by making explicit reference to homosexuals in Hollywood—"They're Mr. and Mrs. God according to the sex, and you can't be sure of *that* in this town"—and like the predecessor novel, acknowledges a certain star's need for frequent abortions.

ANNA M. LUCAS. *Tangled Lives: A Novel in Three Parts* (Buechler Publishing, 1941) is "dedicated to those victims of circumstances whose weaknesses have proved their strength." It is sophomoric in extreme, features some of the most florid dialogue ever found on the printed page, and has not one redeeming quality to make it worthy of resurrection. It begins with a dance at Cranby College, to which student Pete Lanahan has invited two dates, Mary Louise Cordes, from his hometown, and movie star Gloria Merton, who is visiting the college for some inexplicable reason. Lanahan's best friend, Robert Kessler, helps extricate him from the problem by escorting Mary Louise, and the inevitable happens. Kessler marries Mary Louise and Lanahan marries Gloria. Lanahan is something of a feckless youth, and while on location with his bride in Hawaii he has an affair that results in the birth of a baby girl. Kessler takes care of the child and mother in Boston, where he is living with his wife. Mary Louise suspects that the child is Kessler's, but eventually Lanahan confesses the truth to Gloria and the two fly out to Boston for a confessional with Kessler and Mary Louise and also to adopt the child. So novel, apparently, was airline travel in 1941 that four pages are devoted to a description of the trip. Gloria quits the film industry, explaining to her director, "Sometimes . . . a woman must choose between two big things in her life. A great gift is given to us, we are told, for the benefit of others. But mine is not such a great gift. There are many who can take my place. But I have another gift of which you never dreamed, the gift of motherhood. It has been the biggest cross in our married life that we had no children. God willed otherwise."

BETTY WEBB LUCAS. In *Bright Moonlight* (Gramercy Publishing, 1947), Holly Cameron and Michael Stephens meet on the boat carrying both from Europe to New York and are attracted to each other. However, Holly is the daughter of glamorous movie star Jill Cameron, who cannot admit to having a daughter as beautiful as and of the age of Holly. When Jill goes to Hollywood, Holly accompanies her as her secretary. On arrival in Los Angeles, a publicist who is attracted to Holly warns Jill what the film industry can do to an ego, but Jill is uninterested in what the man has to say. She dates the head of the studio, but he makes advances to Holly. Jill refuses to believe that Holly is innocent, thinking she is trying to steal the executive from her, and Holly returns to New York. There she becomes a stage actress and learns that her mother has been jilted by the studio head. Holly is cast in a play, anonymously written by Michael Stephens. When he returns from Hollywood where he has been looking after Jill, he declares both his authorship of the play and his love for Holly. *Bright Moonlight* is in many respects a typical romance but one that boasts an unusual and original storyline.

BOB LUCAS. *Naked in Hollywood* (Lancer Books, 1962) is one of a series of novels with a Hollywood background, identified by Carolyn See as "semi-pornographic." No other information is available.

RICHARD A. (Allen) LUPOFF (born 1935). *The Bessie Blue Killer* (St. Martin's Press, 1994) is the first hardcover novel to feature white insurance adjuster Hobart Lindsey and his black homicide detective–lover, Marvia Plum. Here, Lindsey's employer has written a $100 million insurance policy covering the filming of *Bessie Blue*, a feature about the U.S. Air Force's all-black World War II flying corps, the Tuskegee Airmen. Just as filming starts on location at an airport in Oakland, California, a black janitor is murdered.

Emily Melton in *Booklist* (March 15, 1994) described this as "a fun, funny, fascinating read."

MARK LEE LUTHER (1872–19??). *Presenting Jane McRae* (Little, Brown, 1920) is the story of the title character who falls in love with a young civil engineer but marries a film director, Arthur Gault. He helps develop her career as a screen actress, but she realizes the marriage was a mistake. Even Gault's death during World War I cannot completely free her from marital obligations. "An agreeable little comedy of life not without serious import also," commented *Outlook* (August 4, 1920). "Very long and not very interesting," was the opinion of the reviewer in the *New York Times* (July 18, 1920). "Some of the motion-picture parts of the book are not unentertaining, while of the characters Arthur Gault is by all odds the best, at times becoming a real human being." The novel was illustrated by James Montgomery Flagg.

In collaboration with Lillian C. (Cape) Ford, Luther also wrote a series of mystery novels featuring private detective Arthur Ranleigh. In *The Saranoff Murder* (Bobbs-Merrill, 1930), a Russian-born film star is murdered in her Beverly Hills mansion while her guests view a film in her private projection room. In *Card 13* (Bobbs-Merrill, 1930), a famous screenwriter is killed on his front lawn with his own revolver.

GAVIN LYALL (born 1932). *Shooting Script* (Charles Scribner's Sons, 1966) is a typical suspense thriller, entertaining but with an unconvincing plot-line. Former RAF fighter pilot Keith Carr is working in Jamaica. He and his plane are hired by an actor-producer making a film on location. The plane is confiscated on a flight to a nearby right-wing republic. Carr is then ordered to acquire an aging bomber and agrees to make a bombing raid on the republic to help a revolutionary uprising. The raid is financed by the actor-producer in part because funds he has frozen in the country will be freed by the new government. The bombing raid is relatively successful, but the plane is damaged. The actor-producer turns up and, with Carr and a female lawyer with whom Carr is having an affair, escapes in the flyer's grounded plane. Because the film is being funded with Eady Money, some time is spent explaining to the reader how the British government funds "British" films through that project.

MARY LOUISE MABIE. *The Root of the Lotus* (Charles Scribner's Sons, 1938) is the story of an uneducated orphan who becomes a Hollywood star and brings tragedy to all she comes in contact with, in particular her three husbands. The second is a composer whom she really loves, and the third a producer who commits suicide after learning of her continued love for the composer. Lisle Bell in the *New York Herald Tribune* (August 7, 1938) considered the reading of this novel "rather like watching a motion picture abandoned by the director and somehow assembled by a delirious cutter."

ANNE McALLISTER. Handsome, rugged screen star Joe Harrington can, and does, make love to any women he wants, but for reasons unclear, in *Starstruck* (Harlequin, 1985) what he wants is Liv James, a Madison, Wisconsin, reporter and divorcée with five children. For equally unclear reasons, she does not want him, and when she does decide to go to bed with him, just about everything gets in the way of that happening, including her former husband, her children, who come down with chicken pox, and then Joe, who contracts the same disease! Joe Harrington is not only a film star but also an environmentalist and peace activist—they don't come any finer than Joe—and it is only at the conclusion of a visit to Vienna, where Joe is speaking on world peace to an international convention, that his and Liv's relationship is consummated. Even then the relationship is rocky because Joe will not commit himself to marriage, but all comes out right in the end, and the couple settles down to domesticity in Madison. That city's gain is obviously Hollywood's loss.

ED McBAIN is the pseudonym of Evan Hunter (born 1926), who came to fame in 1954 with his novel *The Blackboard Jungle*. McBain is best known for the more than forty novels featuring the men and women of the 87th Precinct in the mythical city of Isola (New York). *Downtown* (William Morrow, 1989) is a bright and breezy work, in which the central characters are not the usual members of the 87th Precinct but an out-of-town businessman, Michael Barnes, and an eccentric and beautiful female Chinese chauffeur. When Barnes's wallet is stolen and he is set up as a murderer in New York on Christmas Eve, the chauffeur helps him track down the responsible parties, principal among whom is a film director who needed a corpse to help promote his latest production. The director's idea was to have the body be found with the arms clasping the novel on which his film was based, and with the publicity over Barnes's arrest further helping a film for which a bad critical reception was expected. There are numerous and humorous quirks and turns to the plot, with many film-related allusions, including a nightclub at which everyone dresses as a character from the film version of *The Wizard of Oz*; also, the chief villain, whom the hero thought of as a woman, uses the last line from *Some Like It Hot*, "Nobody's perfect."

CAMERON McCABE was the pseudonym of Ernst Julius Bornemann (born 1915), a German-born writer who worked as a film editor and screenwriter, was associated with John Grierson at the National Film Board of Canada, headed the film section of UNESCO, and ended his career teaching sexology. *The Face on the Cutting Room Floor* (Victor Gollancz, 1937) has been described by Julian Symons as "the detective story to end all detective stories," and it is certainly a highly original, if rather implausible, work. Narrated by McCabe, the story is about a young actress found dead in the editing room after the studio head has ordered McCabe, the head of editorial, to remove all her scenes from his latest production. Subsequently, the leading man is murdered. An eccentric Scotland Yard detective discovers that the death of the actress was a suicide, but the actor was murdered, out of jealousy, by McCabe. The latter ends the novel with his acquittal and his subsequent murder by the detective. In an epilogue, a casual acquaintance analyzes McCabe's novel and the press reception of it. On his way to deliver the proofs to the publisher, he meets a second actress with whom McCabe was in love. She reveals that McCabe committed suicide in order to have the detective tried, convicted, and executed for his murder, and she then shoots the acquaintance.

The novel was reprinted by Gollancz in 1974, and at that time published in the United States by Doubleday. In keeping with such an extraordinary novel, in 1974 the publisher had to admit that it did not know the identity of the author. The 1986 Penguin reissue includes a history of the novel and an interview with its author.

VICTOR MacCLURE. *Death on the Set* (J.B. Lippincott, 1935) was the fourth novel to feature aristocratic Chief Inspector Archibald Burford of Scotland Yard. Here, he investigates the murder of a director at the Titan Studios. The suspects are two actresses, an actor, and a publicist, all as regal as the inspector. This entertaining, if dated, novel ends with the revelation that the dead man is not the director but his double, with whom the former had been involved in criminal activities, and he was killed by the director. The novel's characters include a studio manager, "obviously of Hebraic ancestry," who murders the king's English.

Death on the Set was first published in the United Kingdom in 1934 by George G. Harrap. The novel was filmed in 1935 as *Death on the Set* (released in the United States as *Murder on the Set*) by Twickenham Films, under the direction of Leslie Hiscott, and starring Henry Kendall, Eve Gray, and Garry Marsh.

VINCENT McCONNOR's Chief Inspector Darniot returns to Paris in *The Paris Puzzle* (Macmillan, 1981) and is called in to investigate the murder of Hollywood star Alex Scott, whose body is found on a rain-soaked Right Bank street.

JAMES McCOURT (born 1941). *Kaye Wayfaring in "Avenged"* (Penguin, 1984) consists of four short stories. The title character is a major screen star, and while shooting four death scenes, she examines her life, including a Southern childhood and marriage to the son of the heroine of McCourt's previous novel, *Mawrdew Czgowchuz* (1974).

HORACE McCOY (1897–1955) enjoys a small cult following thanks in large part to his 1933 novel *They Shoot Horses, Don't They?* (which was filmed in 1969). A newspaper editor and short story writer, McCoy came to Hollywood in 1931 with the ambition to pursue an acting career. Unemployed as an actor, he began writing screenplays, selling his first, *The Luxury Girl*, to Columbia in 1933. Two years later, McCoy published his first novel, *They Shoot Horses, Don't They?*, the story of two Hollywood extras participating in a Depression-era dance marathon. Five additional novels followed, and McCoy remained active as a screenwriter until his death.

I Should Have Stayed Home (Alfred A. Knopf, 1938) is the plaintive cry of Ralph Carston, a young man from Georgia, lured to Hollywood for a screen test and (like the young McCoy) lingering there in the hope of being discovered: "I hadn't stayed home, I was here on the famous boulevard, in Hollywood, where miracles happen, and maybe today, maybe the next minute some director would pick me out passing by..." Ralph shares a bungalow court apartment with another screen hopeful, Mona Matthews, and across the court lives a third hopeful, Dorothy Trotter, who kills herself following an escape from prison, where she had been sent on a shoplifting charge.

The three are innocents in a predatory jungle, but Ralph and Mona survive and remain relatively unharmed, despite the efforts to bed Ralph of the nymphomaniacal Mrs. Smithers. They learn something of Hollywood's ways from a drunken and disillusioned publicist, Johnny Hill, who quits his job at Universal after the studio bends to the demand of the German consul and censors the scenes of German militarism from its 1937 production *The Road Back*.

On one of his nightly rambles through Hollywood, Ralph comes upon a small park at De Longpre and Cherokee, and muses in front of a statue there of Aspiration, "erected in memory of Rudolph Valentino." When photographers want a shot of Dorothy's corpse with "the Instrument of Death," Mona puts a handful of movie magazines in Dorothy's hands: "That's what really killed her. . . . Go ahead—show the world an authentic picture of Hollywood."

The novel offers a realistic portrait of Hollywood in the late 1930s. While much takes place here, very little happens to the innate decency of Ralph and Mona. The reader may despise some of their attitudes—such as Ralph's antagonism toward blacks—but will empathize with their situation. Hollywood is the source of their troubles in life, but the solution lies in their own hearts and souls.

McCoy's earlier work, ***They Shoot Horses, Don't They?*** (Simon & Schuster, 1935), is often cited as a Hollywood novel, but while it is true that the participants in the dance marathon are failed Hollywood performers, the story is more a study of the Depression-era phenomenon of dance marathons. Here, the marathon takes place in Santa Monica, and the girl asks her partner to shoot her, which she prefers to continuing with her miserable life. At one point, in the early 1950s, Charlie Chaplin acquired the screen and stage rights, planning to have Norman Lloyd direct the production. Nothing came of the project, and in 1969 the story was filmed by Palomar Pictures International, under the direction of Sydney Pollack, and starring Jane Fonda, Michael Sarrazin, Gig Young, Susannah York, and Red Buttons.

FINLEY McDERMID was, as far as can be ascertained, the pseudonym of Archibald G. (Gordon) McDonell (born 1905), who wrote mystery novels under various assumed names. The title of ***Ghost Wanted*** (Simon & Schuster, 1943) refers to the practice in Hollywood of authors having ghosts, just as stars have stand-ins. When a blackmailer is murdered, Lieutenant Bernal tracks down the killers. "Almost every person in the book has a secret that might ruin his or her career if it becomes known. Little by little, as the investigation proceeds, these secrets are revealed to the reader, and the suspense mounts from page to page," commented Isaac Anderson in the *New York Times* (May 23, 1943).

GREGORY McDONALD (born 1937) began writing the series of mystery novels featuring Maurice "Fletch" Fletcher in 1974. The fifth in the series, ***Fletch's Moxie*** (Warner Books, 1982) has Fletch on a movie set in Florida when Hollywood agent Steve Peterman is murdered. Fletch's girlfriend, Moxie, was Peterman's client and is the principal suspect in his murder. The plot is somewhat illogical, and there is preachment on the evils of the film industry.

JOHN D. MacDONALD (1916–86) was the author of more than sixty novels, including 21 featuring hardboiled detective Travis McGee and published between 1964 and 1985. *Free Fall in Crimson* (Fawcett Gold Medal, 1981) has McGee involved in an investigation to uncover the murderer of wealthy businessman Ellis Easterland. His son, Ronald, believes the death was connected with his father's will since the death allowed Easterland's second wife to inherit. She is having an affair with director Peter Kestner, who had some success with a couple of biker movies. Her inheritance is funding Kestner's latest epic featuring hot air balloons. One of the stars of Kestner's biker movies has murdered Easterland, and is now working in porno movies made by Kestner and starring teenage Iowa girls from the location where the hot air balloon film is being shot. The local residents attack the film crew, killing Kestner and others. The biker escapes and goes on a killing spree, murdering three women, one of whom is an actress who had helped McGee. The biker is eventually shot, and when the hot air film is released, Kestner is recognized as a genius. When asked how this could be, McGee's buddy Meyer explains, "How, in these days of intensive communication on all levels, can you tell talent from bullshit? Everybody is as good and as bad as anybody wants to think they are." The identity of the murderer is revealed much too soon—less than halfway through the novel—the plot is convoluted, and the storyline far from realistic. It all makes one wonder why John D. MacDonald should have become such a cult writer.

ROSS MACDONALD was the pseudonym of Kenneth Millar (1915–83). *Archer in Hollywood* (Alfred A. Knopf, 1967) collects together three novels featuring Macdonald's private detective hero, Lew Archer. In his foreword, Macdonald writes,

> If California is a state of mind, Hollywood is where you take its temperature. There is a peculiar sense in which this city existing on film and tape is our national capital, alas, and not just the capital of California. It's the place where our children learn how and what to dream and where everything happens just before, or just after, it happens to us. American novelists have a lover's quarrel with Hollywood.... My lover's quarrel with Hollywood began at the age of seven when, on successive Saturday afternoons in my uncle's theater, I formed a precocious attachment to Pearl White. The quarrel and attachment have since taken more devious forms, as you can see if you read these three novels.

The Moving Target (Alfred A. Knopf, 1949) has Archer hired to find a kidnap victim. His investigation leads to his uncovering a gang that is smuggling illegal aliens into the country, one of whose members is Fay Estabrook, a former silent screen star now working as a supporting player. Estabrook's career and the film industry have nothing to do with the storyline, although Archer does pay a visit to Universal City and watch a feature being shot, making reference to "the evil which hung in studio air like an odorless gas." Macdonald describes *The Moving Target* as "a story clearly aspiring to be a movie," and expressed no surprise that the 1966 Warner Bros. adaptation, *Harper*, directed by Jack Smight, and starring Paul Newman as Archer and Shelley Winters as Fay Estabrook, followed the story virtually scene by scene.

The search for a missing girl in *The Way Some People Die* (Alfred A. Knopf, 1951) leads Archer to a drug ring. One of the killers in the story, and also one of the victims, is a handsome but unemployable actor. In *The Barbarous*

Coast (Alfred A. Knopf, 1956), Archer is in pursuit of a missing wife. She has become a Hollywood actress involved with the head of a studio, and the company's security people use illegal means to prevent Archer from finding her.

JAMES McELROY (born 1930). *Lookout Cartridge* (Alfred A. Knopf, 1974) concerns a stolen, avant-garde film made by two Americans living in England, Dagger DiGorro and Cartwright. The novel is narrated by the latter, whose diary of the film's shooting has also disappeared, apparently because both it and the film reveal something about American intelligence operations in the late 1960s and early 1970s. *Lookout Cartridge* is written very much in the style of an experimental film; it is difficult to read and understand, repetitive, and occasionally lucid. The reader must have patience, and also a knowledge of the elements involved in documentary filmmaking and day-to-day life in London.

J. (Joseph) P. (Patrick) McEVOY (1895–1958) introduced his cartoonlike showgirl character Dixie Dugan in *Show Girl* (1928). Dixie returned in *Hollywood Girl* (Simon & Schuster, 1929), in which she has come to Hollywood seeking a career in talkies and also marriage to a millionaire. The story is told through straight narrative, correspondence, extracts from *Variety*, and so on. The novel was filmed in 1930 as *Show Girl in Hollywood* by Warner Bros., directed by Mervyn LeRoy, and starring Alice White, Jack Mulhall, and Blanche Sweet.

Critics were enthusiastic about *Hollywood Girl* but found it inferior to the original novel. The *New York Times* (November 24, 1929) wrote, "The book is amusing, filled with Hollywood madness and Hollywood slang, but it lacks the easy, hilarious fun of *Show Girl.*" The *Saturday Review of Literature* (November 30, 1929) commented, "Mr. McEvoy is a master of the day's idiom, a genius in the juggling of the pointed topicality. Five years from now *Show Girl* and *Hollywood Girl* will need a glossary; to-day, however, they are quite first class and should on no account be missed by the alert-minded citizenry."

In *Society* (Simon & Schuster, 1931), Dixie Dugan's marriage to millionaire Teddy Page (whom she met in *Hollywood Girl*) has come to an end. However, Dixie has learned a lot from being a member of society, and she is able to use that knowledge to advantage when she returns to Hollywood. The novel takes the same form as the earlier work. "Mr. McEvoy has found many things to laugh at in society, and if his point of view is neither fresh nor penetrating his method of putting it into a book still contains a good deal of amusement," commented the *New York Times* (October 11, 1931). The *Saturday Review of Literature* (November 21, 1931) was less enthusiastic: "To those who have followed him since *Show Girl*, Mr. McEvoy has always meant humor and bite. The ridiculous and the sharply ironical were always blended. But here the irony has wilted and the humor become worn. If it were not nearly unbelievable, we should think that *Society* was written for the delectation of those who regard Bailey's Beach as holy ground and who read the society columns in the tabloids."

WILLIAM McFEE. (1881–1966). *Spenlove in Arcady* (Random House, 1941) has the title character retiring to a farmhouse in Connecticut, where he meets and marries Perdita Ducoy. The latter has a daughter by a former husband who was a Hollywood screenwriter.

MARGARET GIBBONS MacGILL. In *Hollywood Star Dust: A Love Story* (Chelsea House, 1936), Peggy Rooney leaves New York for Hollywood with the promise of a screen test, but the film company goes bust before she gets there. Her boyfriend, David Whitelaw, follows in the position of secretary-companion to Opal Orth, a wealthy and beautiful young woman who plans to break into films. As one might suspect, there is immediate animosity between the two women. On a gambling ship, David accidentally kills another man in a fight, but Opal pays to hush up the matter. Peggy's talents are recognized, and she goes off on location to the mountain resort of Idyllwild to star in the film version of a play written by David. It is a success, and back in New York Peggy and David are reunited. The story has a ludicrous plot coupled with unbelievable characterizations, including an extraordinarily naive leading man.

JILL McGOWN. *Murder Movie* (St. Martin's Press, 1990) is an entertaining and enthralling mystery novel from a British writer who is one of the best of the younger exponents of the genre. It concerns a series of murders among a film crew on location in the west of Scotland, and the principal characters include a straight leading man who is loved by a gay leading man who, in turn, is loved by the film's gay screenwriter. Great fun!

KEANE McGRATH. Against a background of New York, Mexico, Hollywood, and Europe, a cabaret dancer, Colandra la Mara, becomes a movie star in *Hollywood Siren* (William Godwin, 1932).

DON McGUIRE. The unlikely scenario of an actor and a comedian running against each other for the governorship of California is presented in *1600 Floogle Street* (Holloway House, 1967). The corn of the campaign is equally matched by the literary style of the novel.

RICHARD McKAYE. *Portrait of the Damned* (Twayne Publishers, 1954) has strong religious overtones, plus some discussion of blacklisting, as the son of a preacher writes a biblical feature, *Kingdom Come*. He is bothered by a physical attraction to the producer's wife and a story reader, and by the sexuality he is required to engender in the script. In despair, the man sets fire to the sets and decides to martyr himself in the flames.

MARY MacLAREN (1896–1985) was a moderately successful leading lady in silent films from 1916 to 1924. She ended her life in poverty, and just before she died was the subject of considerable publicity in a new role as a "bag lady." A vanity press book, *The Twisted Heart* (Exposition Press, 1952), is presumably a roman à clef, telling the tragic tale of an actress who unknowingly marries a homosexual man. MacLaren's knowledge of homosexuality appears somewhat slight. The novel contains this rather extraordinary statement: "This book was edited by, and dedicated to—James M. Cain."

ALISTAIR MacLEAN (1922–87). *Bear Island* (Doubleday, 1971) is located in the Arctic Ocean, and to it is sailing a film crew planning to film second unit and background shots for an upcoming production. Also on the ship are members of the board of directors of Olympia Productions. When three people on the ship die and four become seriously ill from food poisoning, the ship's doctor turns detective. "A leisurely diagnosis is provided by Marlowe, Olympia's doctor, who unravels a mind-boggling tangle of embezzlement, blackmail, international burglary, triple-agentry and double-eyed villainy," wrote Martin Levin in the *New York Times* (November 14, 1971). "The entire mishmash still seems incredible."

LARRY McMURTRY (born 1936) has an interest in film, evident in his writings on the subject in *American Film* magazine. *The Last Picture Show* (Dial Press, 1966) is primarily a study of small-town sexuality in Texas, with the local movie theater playing a strategic role in the story. The book was filmed in 1971 by Columbia Pictures, directed by Peter Bogdanovich, and starring Cloris Leachman, Cybill Shepherd, and Jeff Bridges.

Somebody's Darling (Simon & Schuster, 1978) is narrated by its three principal characters: a 37-year-old woman who has achieved some success with her first film; her friend, a 63-year-old hack writer for television; and her lover, a former All-American football player and would-be producer. "Mr. McMurtry's characters are real, believable and touching, his prose has life and immediacy and he is a very funny writer," commented Jonathan Yardley in the *New York Times* (November 19, 1978).

CLAIRE McNAB. In the third mystery to feature lesbian police Inspector Carol Ashton, of Sydney, Australia, *Death Down Under* (Naiad Press, 1990), McNab has her heroine investigating a series of ritual killings of women, while Ashton's lover, Sybil Quade, is serving as on-set tutor to a couple of young actors appearing in a film with the novel's title. The identity of the serial killer is linked to the film in this well-written book intended for a lesbian audience but deserving of a mainstream readership.

DORA MACY was the pseudonym of Grace Perkins (Mrs. Fulton Oursler). *Public Sweetheart No. 1* (Farrar & Rinehart, 1935) is narrated by chorus girl turned screen star Violet Chester. Despite her fame and success, she cannot find happiness in five marriages and with a crippled sister. According to the *New York Times* (September 22, 1935), "The book is a highly colored, sensationally jazzed-up version of anybody's off-hand idea of the life of a dancer and film star—down to the last detail of lonely mother, crippled sister, hopeless love, heaps of jewels, Hollywood mansion, and ungrateful friends."

DAVID MADDEN (born 1933). *Bijou* (Crown, 1974) is set in 1947 and is the story of 13-year-old Lucius Hutchfield, whose family is pathetic, and who works as an usher at the Bijou Theatre. He falls in love with Raine, who is an amalgam of all his filmic heroines from Merle Oberon to Gene Tierney and Linda Darnell. "This is a funny, absolutely uncompromising novel about the stuff our dreams were made of, in the days when we still had dreams," wrote *Kirkus*; to Charles Shapiro in the *New Republic* this was "an important novel."

MICHAEL MAGUIRE (born 1945). *Scratchproof* (St. Martin's Press, 1976) is a mystery novel, introducing Simon Drake, a freelance agent for the

British Turf Security Division. For reasons not entirely plausible, he is hired to investigate various threats being made against a legendary actress, Catherine Forrest, who is making her comeback in a film she is also financing. The reader is introduced to the workings of a British film studio through the eyes of Drake, who is an innocent in this arena, and the book's denouement takes place at the deserted studio at night. The book is as much for racing enthusiasts as film buffs since there is a secondary horse-racing theme and the actress also breeds racehorses. In that one dog, two racehorses, and one stag are killed as part of the plot, this is not a novel for animal lovers.

BILL MAHAN (born 1930). The title character in *The Moviola Man* (Doubleday, 1979), written by Mahan in collaboration with his sister Colleen, is 45-year-old Sam Wilder, a superb editor, working in television with his assistant, Tom Ryan. Wilder's marriage is breaking up at the same time he is falling in love with a young actress named Erika. He accepts a position as director of a television pilot with Ryan as his assistant, and also helps his teenage stepson, Jerry, obtain a job as a gofer at the studio. The stepson has gotten into bad company with an older man who is a film pirate, stealing prints of films and television programs and selling them not only to collectors but also to foreign markets. Jerry agrees to steal prints from the studio but is caught by Ryan, whom he accidentally kills. After Jerry's arrest, Wilder decides that he does not want to continue as a director but returns to film editing for an American working in England. At the novel's close, Wilder is united, while on vacation in Wales, with Erika. The novel provides what would appear to be a first-hand account of what is involved in editing; the moviola is, of course, the editor's primary tool. But unfortunately what begins as an intriguing look at the life and work of an above-average Hollywood technician quickly degenerates into a second-rate overdrawn melodrama.

The Boy Who Looked Like Shirley Temple (St. Martin's Press, 1980) is a jolly and entertaining work, with no great literary merit but a good period feel. In the 1930s, the author was a child star in the "Jones Family" series of films featuring Spring Byington, and there is a photograph of him at the time on the book's front cover. The title character is Billy Boyce, who moves to Culver City from Washington during the Depression. By sheer good luck he is hired to play the youngest member of the family in a series of films being made by Olympic Studios, but his disgust with a film career, his use of foul language, and his misbehavior with the leading lady and mistress of the studio head lead to his being fired after one film. However, his older sister Helene has befriended a former star and former mistress of the same man, and the ex-mistress bribes the studio owner into paying her and Helene to suppress an autobiography. Not too much time is spent on the brief period in which Boyce is a child star, with the first third of the novel detailing how he and Helene help raise money for the family by selling lima beans and recycling empty bottles.

NORMAN MAILER (born 1923). *The Deer Park* (G.P. Putnam's Sons, 1955) is the story of two men who meet by coincidence and at the same time come to decisions—the meeting taking place at Desert D'Or, a new city in the California desert. One man is Charles Eitel, a successful director of artistic films who is encountering tax and political problems as a result of the House Un-American Activities Committee investigations. The other is Sergius O'Shaugnessy, who narrates the novel and is a would-be writer. Both men have affairs, Sergius with a Hollywood star, and come to decisions regarding their careers. Also in the book are two Hollywood producers, presumably based on Louis B. Mayer and David O. Selznick. Reviewers were mixed in their reactions to Mailer's third novel. "One would waste no time with this novel if it did not come from Norman Mailer" was the opinion of Dudley Nichols in *The Nation* (November 5, 1955). John Brooks in the *New York Times* (October 16, 1955) found it "studded with brilliant and illuminating passages." "One would have thought it would be a difficult job these days to write a scandalous book about Hollywood, but Mr. Mailer has given it a determined try," wrote Hollis Alpert in *Saturday Review* (October 15, 1955).

GLADYS MALVERN (died 1962). *Hollywood Star* (Julian Messner, 1953) is the third in a series of books for teenage girls about ballet dancer Gloria Whitcomb. Here, she comes to Hollywood to make a film based on the life of Pavlova. "The contrast between her misery as an actress and her supreme confidence in the dance sequences is too extreme to be credible. Otherwise, the story develops logically and dance enthusiasts will enjoy the exposition and the problems, excitements and the hard work of a ballerina in Hollywood," wrote Norma Kramer in the *New York Times* (June 28, 1953).

WOLF MANKOWITZ (born 1924) is a British writer, known for screenplays such as *A Kid for Two Farthings* (1954), *Trapeze* (1955), and *The Day the Earth Caught Fire* (1960), and for plays that include *Expresso Bongo* (1958) and *Pickwick* (1963). His fifth novel, *Cockatrice* (G.P. Putnam's Sons, 1963), is at once a witty yet ironically bitter account of one man's struggle in and against the British film industry. The central character, Danny Pisarov, is personal assistant to producer Arno Borian. The latter has always refused Danny a credit on any of his films. Over a Christmas period Danny decides to become his own producer, acquiring, with the help of Borian's name and money, a script, a supporting cast, and a leading lady in the shape of a French actress whom Borian has discovered. Only as he is about to raise the initial funding does he learn that the actress is in serious condition after trying to kill herself. Despondently, he returns to Borian's apartment, only to find the producer in bed with his ex-girlfriend and reading Danny's script, which the hapless assistant has no alternative but to pretend he had acquired for Borian.

As to the novel's title, Mankowitz explains, "The Cockatrice was a fabulous, serpent-like monster, hatched against nature out of the egg of a cock. It consorted with basilisks and satyrs, and its breath was deadly, its glare fatal to human beings. It has always seemed to me an appropriate heraldic beast for the film industry."

D. KEITH MANO (born 1942). *Take Five* (Doubleday, 1982) is a novel strictly for fans of the author. It concerns Simon Lynxx's efforts to raise money to make a surrealist film—and also to make a girl named Merry—in which he is aided by a group of actors. In acknowledgment of the author's absurdist humor, the novel is paginated in reverse.

M. (Margaret) S. (Sharp) MARBLE. *Everybody Makes Mistakes* (Rinehart, 1946) is narrated by Hollywood press agent Red Kennedy, who comes under suspicion when one of his clients goes over to another press agent and promptly shows up dead.

MELISAND MARCH. Witches, mediums, and veterinarians are just some of the characters who show up in *Mandrake Scream* (Mason/Charter, 1975), in which an unemployed Hollywood screenwriter dabbles in ESP and the occult. His wife is having an affair with his attorney, and then the latter's wife dies. The screenwriter's wife is the next to go, and when a vet's widow rejects the screenwriter in favor of a German shepherd, the dog starts acting strange.

ALAN MARCUS. *Of Streets and Stars* (Houghton Mifflin, 1963) provides a panoramic view of Hollywood, with its virtually plotless storyline concerning a maladjusted screenwriter and his attempt to write a film on displaced persons. "It is laid in Hollywood, although it is not really a Hollywood novel," wrote the reviewer in *Time* (February 22, 1963). "It has to do with a dozen or so people whose lives touch one another only momentarily and tangentially . . . for a few moments they stand illuminated in the light of understanding." In *Library Journal* (January 1, 1963), Dorothy Nyren commented, "At its best, Mr. Marcus's novel recalls Nathanael West; at its worst, it sounds like a sentimental B picture." The novel was first published in a limited edition in 1960 by Manzanita Press.

THOMAS MAREMAA (born 1945). *Studio* (William Morrow, 1978) presents an extraordinary view of the life and work of a production executive as its narrator, Tony Schwartz, discusses in stream-of-consciousness style the development, production, and postproduction of a major motion picture. The film, which bears the same title as the novel, is the story of a group of terrorists taking over a studio and holding hostage various of its employees, including Alfred Hitchcock and the studio head, here called Jake Steinman. The studio in the film and where Schwartz works is very obviously Universal; not only does Hitchcock have offices here, the *Psycho* set is here, and, like Universal, the studio has a black and a white tower. There is also much of Lew Wasserman in the character of Jake Steinman. Just as Universal requires its executives to wear jackets and ties, much is made in *Studio* of the "Suits," the men behind the scenes who run the studio and give orders to the creative staff, the "players." Aside from Hitchcock, who, as in one of his films, makes a cameo appearance, the other "real" characters in the shooting of *Studio* are leading man Robert De Niro and cinematographer Vilmos Zsigmond.

The speed is frenetic in the storytelling as Schwartz displays elements of a film buff—he likes Clint Eastwood because "he shoots people better than any other actor I know"—a workaholic, and a psychotic. At times, he is given to fantasy, and at the novel's close it is difficult to know whether he has really taken over the studio or whether it is part of his highly active imagination.

FRANCES MARION (1887–1973) was a prolific Hollywood screenwriter who began her career in 1915; her films include *The Wind* (1928), *The Big*

House (1930), *The Champ* (1931), *Dinner at Eight* (1933), and *Camille* (1937). She published her autobiography, *Off with Their Heads*, in 1972.

Minnie Flynn (Boni & Liveright, 1925) is a cautionary tale about a beautiful but relatively untalented young girl propelled to stardom by her director and then taken in by sycophants, public relations people, and the public. She quickly returns to obscurity. "Miss Marion writes with a facile pen and her novel, although trite and somewhat sensational, is nevertheless well done," wrote the *New York Times* (May 31, 1925). "This book is a fine performance," commented the *Saturday Review of Literature* (May 30, 1925), "kept well in hand, almost austere in its restraint, safely avoiding the pitfall of nastiness for its own sake, yet dealing without squeamishness with things that under less skillful handling would be merely repulsive, and always keeping the elements of the story in a due proportion. Its narrative is fluent, orderly, developing inexorably to the final tragedy that one foresees from the start."

DON MARQUIS (1878–1937). The pretentious novelist hero of *Off the Arm* (Doran, 1930), Hugh Cass, divorces his lowbrow wife; he goes off to Hollywood to supervise the filming of his latest novel and she returns to waitressing. Later, Cass is shocked to discover that she has become a famous star and is engaged to her director. "Not a remarkable work of fiction; nobody will read it twice," wrote H.W. Boynton in *Saturday Review of Literature* (June 14, 1930). "But a great many people will read it once with pleasure and profit, and this is more than can be said of most novels that pull a long face and make a great display of literary earnestness."

ARNOLD MARROW. *Sweet Smell of Lust* (Art Enterprises, 1962) is one of a series of novels with a Hollywood background, identified by Carolyn See as "semi-pornographic." No other information is available.

G. WILLIAM MARSHALL. In *The Deal* (Bartholomew House, 1963), a producer of European art films, noted for his unprincipled methods, signs a contract with a Hollywood leading man. The actor is immoral and requires the producer to rescue him from a number of scrapes until he succumbs to a heart attack.

PETER MARSHALL (born 1946). An amnesiac confuses a film scenario with reality as he climbs from the beach to the promenade of an English seaside resort where a production is being shot in *Ancient and Modern* (Bobbs-Merrill, 1970). Peter Wolfe in the *New York Times* (May 17, 1970) wrote that the novel "claws your nerves like a Jacobean revenge play. Rarely in fiction have human purposes been so dishonored, human flesh so smashed, or human society portrayed so drivingly as a conspiracy of cruel motives."

WILLIAM MARSHALL (born 1944) has written a series of mystery novels centering on the Yellowthread Street police division in Hong Kong. Told in Marshall's typically exciting and breathtaking fashion, *Sci Fi* (Henry Holt,

1981) has the Yellowthread Street police chasing the Spaceman, apparently brandishing a ray gun, but in reality a flamethrower, and causing pandemonium at the All-Asia Science Fiction and Horror Movie Congress in Hong Kong. While not the best of Marshall's novels, *Sci Fi* provides an entertaining introduction to the series.

AL MARTIN (1896–1971) was a prolific screenwriter for both silent and sound productions, primarily B pictures. In *Dog Gone Hollywood* (Martin Publishing, 1930), a dog who has been taken to Hollywood writes about his own experiences as well as those of other dogs with famous masters and mistresses.

MARCIA MARTIN is the pseudonym of Marcio Obrasky Levin (born 1918). *Donna Parker in Hollywood* (Whitman Publishing, 1961) is a novel for teenage girls in which the title heroine spends "that wonderful summer in Hollywood." She even learns about plastic surgery for aging movie stars!

PATRICIA MARX and DOUGLAS G. McGRATH. *Blockbuster* (Bantam Books, 1988) is the comic story of the Mr. Schwerdloff Studio, founded in 1910 by X.Y. Schwerdloff, whose first film, *Folding the Wash*, "is considered a masterpiece of its genre. Film historians cite it as the first time someone sat down and stood up in the same movie." Such is the humor of this novel, told in the form of taped remembrances and memoranda. Following Schwerdloff's death, the studio continually loses money until the founder's two sisters decide to send their idiot brother to close the place down. Instead, he authorizes a disastrous production of *Pilgrim's Progress*, directed by a once-commercial filmmaker temporarily housed in a mental institution. Among the real people supposedly taped for the book, and whose styles of delivery the authors attempt to ape, are Elizabeth Taylor, Liza Minnelli, Pauline Kael, Alfred Hitchcock, François Truffaut, John Ford, Barbra Streisand, and Lillian Hellman.

PAULE MASON. The title character in *Here Lies Georgia Linz* (World Publishing, 1968) phones a London psychiatrist after unsuccessfully trying to slit her wrists. As he analyzes her, she tells about her life and rise to fame as an Academy Award–winning actress. The novel was first published in England in 1967 by William Collins Sons as *The Dark Mirror*.

WHIT MASTERSON is the joint pseudonym of H. Bill Miller (1920–61) and Robert Wade (born 1920). Masterson's *Touch of Evil* (1956) was the basis for Orson Welles's 1958 film of the same title. One of the author's regular characters, Clem Munro, is featured in *The Last One Kills* (Dodd, Mead, 1969). In his search for a missing waitress in a gangland killing, Munro pretends to be a film actor on location in Mexico, shooting *Seeds of Fire*.

GRAHAM MASTERTON (born 1946). *Mirror* (TOR, 1988) begins when a minor Hollywood screenwriter, Martin Williams, purchases a mirror that had hung in the bedroom of eight-year-old child star "Boofuls," murder by his grandmother 50 years earlier. It is "the very mirror that watched him die." It is, of course, also very special, harboring evil, "Hollywood the Other Way Around," in which Boofuls is still alive. Boofuls crosses over and volunteers to star in a film about his life to be scripted by Williams, but the problem is that Boofuls is no longer the male Shirley Temple but rather a child of the devil. His plan is to deliver the world to his father, beginning with Hollywood—surely a little late?—and the dastardly synopsis begins with everyone who sees the new film dying. A total of 144,000 people commit mass suicide at theaters simultaneously presenting the premiere of the film, which at least rids the world of most of the Hollywood crowd. And so it goes on.

HAROLD Q. MASUR (born 1909). The takeover of a movie chain, American Theaters Corps., in *Make a Killing* (Random House, 1964) results in two murders. Because he is a minority stockholder and his aunt controls a major share of stock, Masur's lawyer hero, Scott Jordan, investigates in this mystery, which "moves with the speed of a ticker tape and is tied up tighter than a balance sheet" (*Kirkus*, February 27, 1964).

    The Broker (St. Martin's Press, 1981) is a novel of corporate greed. Conglomerate UMI is determined to take over the venerable but money-losing Arcadia Films Studio in Hollywood. Mike Ryan, chief executive of an investment banking firm, tries to persuade some of Arcadia's shareholders who are holding out against accepting UMI's offer, but after two murders, Ryan begins to have his doubts as to the conglomerate's integrity.

CLAYTON MATTHEW. *Sex Dancer* (Universal Publishing and Distributing, 1962) is one of a series of novels with a Hollywood background, identified by Carolyn See as "semi-pornographic." See quotes the novel: "Every day the doors of Hollywood are battered by hordes of ambition-ridden, sex-driven girls . . . here's the story of one who didn't quite make it." The one in question is an extra who becomes a stripper.

JACK MATTHEWS (born 1925) is not the film journalist of the same name. The central character in *Pictures of the Journey Back* (Harcourt, Brace, 1973) is a reactionary, drunken old cowboy who agrees to drive the daughter of a dying woman to her bedside from Kansas to Colorado. The girl refuses to come without her boyfriend, who insists on filming the journey as a record of conflicts in age and lifestyle, including nude footage of the girl on the Western prairie. "Of particular interest is the frequently employed technique of telling the story as if it were being filmed; this blends well with the young man's attempt to capture the journey on film," commented Lee Sullenger in *Library Journal* (February 15, 1972). "A lazy performance" was the opinion of D. Keith Mano in the *New York Times* (March 11, 1979).

ROBIN MAUGHAM (1916–81). The emphasis in *Behind the Mirror* (Harcourt, Brace, 1955) is on colonists determined to hold on to the European way of life in Africa. This is done through the device of having a British screenwriter come to Africa on behalf of his film company to interview a reclusive ex-diplomat and writer and get his permission to use his name in a film. Ben Crisler wrote in the *New York Times*, "By a more or less deft intermingling of several piquant ingredients, including tag-end British colonialism, African drums, the primitive rituals and taboos of film production chiefs in England (repressed imitators, it would seem, of Hollywood), and finally a dash of politely theoretical perversion, Robin Maugham has succeeded in compounding a small but rather unexpected fiction, which might be described as a sort of instant, ready-mix witch's brew, to be taken without stirring." For *The New Yorker* (April 9, 1955), "Mr. Maugham's short, fast novel starts off with great promise and excitement, but it ends in triviality, although it never ceases to be entertaining."

The Green Shade (New American Library, 1966): While successful British director Graham Hadley is preparing his latest film, he begins a tempestuous affair with 18-year-old Vicky Tollard. He takes her to Morocco, where he is researching locations for the film, and is disturbed by her untidyness, her constant problems with her contact lenses, and, most of all, her affair with a young Moroccan man. When the couple returns to England, she moves in with him and also renews an affair with a former boyfriend, an actor. Eventually he accuses her of being concerned only with herself, and Vicky walks out. In despair, Hadley goes to visit her parents, only to find that Vicky's past has been a lie and that she has returned to Morocco. It is typical Maugham material; here it is heterosexual but the characters might just as well have been gay, particularly in view of the Moroccan connection.

LORRAINE MAYNARD. A novel for the teenage market, *Twinkle, Little Movie Star* (Century, 1927) is the story of child star Vivi Corelli and her costar, a police dog named Scamp.

AMEENA MEER's first novel, *Bombay Talkie* (Serpent's Tail/High Risk, 1994) concerns a young American woman of Indian descent who goes off to India to visit her film star uncle and his family. "The story is woven from the characters' inner monologues and a narrative that describes the seamiest excesses of wealth, poverty, racial consciousness, deception and hypocrisy with the pace and detachment of a journalist," commented *Publishers Weekly* (June 20, 1994).

TREVOR MELDAL-JOHNSON (born 1944). *Always* (Avon, 1978) is a piece of romantic nonsense. A screenwriter in today's Los Angeles becomes obsessed with a beautiful but dead film star of the 1940s. He searches for her in everyone he meets, knowing that she has been reborn, as he has.

JOAN MELLEN (born 1941) is a film professor whose books include *Marilyn Monroe* (1973), *Women and Their Sexuality in the New Film* (1974), *Voices from the Japanese Cinema* (1975), *The Waves at Genji's Door: Japan through Its Cinema* (1976), *Big Bad Wolves: Masculinity in the American Film* (1978), and *The World of Luis Buñuel* (1980).

Natural Tendencies (Dial, 1981) may be semiautobiographical; it is the story of a Jewish woman from the Bronx, an expert in Japanese cinema, who visits Japan for the first time. She begins a strange relationship with a Japanese producer who physically assaults her. At the novel's close, the American has "learned to face a ravaging disease of the psyche and to hold it in check."

DEENA METZGER (born 1936). *What Dinah Thought* (Viking, 1989) is a haunting and dramatic novel of a Jewish-American feminist filmmaker who comes to Israel, fascinated by the Genesis story of Jacob and Leah's daughter who was loved and ravished by a heathen. As she falls in love with a Palestinian activist, she reawakens her biblical ancestress, Dinah, and the lives of these two women become interwoven.

MICHAEL MEWSHAW (born 1943). The plight of the have-nots of the world compared with the haves of the film industry is the basic plotline of *Land Without Shadow* (Doubleday, 1979). A failed artist, Jack Cordell, is hired by an old school friend to work as art director on a film he is making in North Africa. On location, Cordell becomes attracted to a sincere actress, and the two discover there is severe poverty in the country, from which the film company is isolated in its luxury hotel. The two fail to persuade the film executives to complain about the status of the natives, and so set out to make their own film about the situation, and, as a result, become embroiled in a battle between the country's government and its liberation forces.

CAROLYN MEYER (born 1935). *The Luck of Texas McCoy* (Atheneum, 1984) is a novel for a teenage readership and has a background of Western filmmaking.

LAWRENCE W. (Walter) MEYNELL (1899–1989). *The House in the Hills* (Harper, 1938) is an adventure romance in the tradition of Anthony Hope and John Buchan. The heir to the throne of a remote Mediterranean country travels incognito to England and as a result of her beauty obtains work as an actress on a movie set. She is kidnapped by the pretender to the throne, but a character named Baikie rescues her.

ALICE DUER MILLER (1874–1942) was a prominent Hollywood screenwriter of the 1930s; she should not be confused with Alice D.G. Miller. *The Rising Star* (Dodd, Mead, 1937) is the story of a New York society woman who goes to Hollywood to act in films but is unsuccessful. She is embittered when the nurse in whose care she has left her husband and young daughter is accidentally discovered for stardom. Beatrice Sherman in the *New York Times* (February 21, 1939) commented, "Alice Duer Miller writes light fiction with a light and expert hand. She makes even a flimsy story take on a sparkling texture. In *The Rising Star* she writes a Hollywood romance with the emphasis not on life in the cinema city but on the reactions of her main characters to a chance at fame and glory in the movies."

FLOYD MILLER (born 1912). *Scandale* (New American Library, 1961) is a murder mystery set primarily in the movie colony in Palm Springs, where an architect is blackmailed for a murder he believes he has committed.

PATSY RUTH MILLER (born 1904) was a Hollywood actress on screen from 1921 to 1931. She also wrote four plays and was married to screenwriter John Lee Mahin. *That Flannigan Girl* (William Morrow, 1939) is a roman à clef, detailing the rise to fame, fall, and comeback of 34-year-old Hollywood actress Denise Arden, who was born Dora Flannigan in St. Louis. (Patsy Ruth Miller was also born in St. Louis.) Two contemporary screenwriters endorsed the novel. Gene Fowler wrote, "Patsy Ruth Miller is entitled to hosannahs for giving us the first Hollywood novel which does not let the background smother the fine tale she has to tell." Nunally Johnson opined, "A vivid and truthful account of a Hollywood few persons are privileged to know or understand. A first novel of surprising distinction."

WADE MILLER was the pseudonym of Bob Wade and Bill Miller. *Jungle Heat* (Pyramid Books, 1960) is identified by Carolyn See as a Hollywood novel that discusses "the failure of Hollywood ethics as opposed to the verities of British Colonialism."

ELICK MOLL (born 1907). While in Spain, narrator Bradford Scott reads of the death of Tallie Winthrop, and remembers her influence on him as a young writer in Hollywood in the 1930s in *Image of Tallie* (Simon & Schuster, 1964).

PAUL MONETTE (1946–95) is a well-regarded if controversial gay author, whose 1992 autobiography, *Becoming a Man: Half a Life Story*, was widely acclaimed. Monette's first novel is the stylishly written mystery *Taking Care of Mrs. Carroll* (Little, Brown, 1978), which has been erroneously compared to a Hollywood screwball comedy. The title character, the aging Mrs. Carroll, is a wealthy New England widow who dies as the book opens. Her bucolic lover, Phidias (the only straight man in the book), devises a plan to pretend she is alive long enough to have an imposter sign her will, leaving the large estate intact, out of reach of developers and under the care of various charities. Assisting him is Mrs. Carroll's companion, a handsome gay houseboy named David, and David's ex-lover, Rich, who brings the Marlene Dietrichesque film star and chanteuse Madeline Cosquer to the house to pose as Mrs. Carroll. All the players in the story are amoral, and the primary reason they evoke a sympathetic response from the reader is that there is no self-interest in their dishonest acts.

The Gold Diggers (Avon, 1979) is a trite novel with an unbelievable plot and characters. It begins with ex–New Yorker Rita moving into the Bel Air home of lovers Nick and Peter. Their home is the former mansion of silent film producer Dusty Varda and his lover, actress Frances Dean, and Rita discovers a hidden room there in which the producer has stashed his collection of stolen artwork. While Rita busies herself returning the pieces to their rightful owners, Nick breaks off an affair with a hustler named Sam. It just so happens that Sam had also serviced Varda when he was alive, and at the book's climax, Sam breaks into the house to find the producer's treasure, which he had assumed was cash. Although *The Gold Diggers* is set in Los Angeles, the Hollywood theme is less relevant here than in the East Coast story *Taking Care of Mrs. Carroll*.

The Long Shot (Avon, 1981) presents the unlikely partnership of a widow and her husband's male lover's male lover joining forces to uncover the murderer of their respective "spouses." There is no question that supermasculine movie star Jasper Cokes has been found dead in the hot tub with his current lover, Harry Dawes, but Cokes's widow and Dawes's lover, Greg, do not accept the police verdict of double suicide. Greg is an interesting character, making his living forging the signatures of movie stars on photographs and selling them through the mail. Good, perverted fun.

BRIAN MOORE (born 1921). *Fergus* (Holt, Rinehart & Winston, 1970) is the story of Fergus Fadden, who has left his wife and is in Hollywood reworking a script. Here is a typical Moore character searching for identity and a typical slow pace.

PAMELA MOORE (1937–64) was the daughter of an RKO studio executive, Don Moore, who achieved literary fame at the age of 18 when her first book, *Chocolates for Breakfast* (Rinehart, 1956), was published. The novel's principal character is Courtney Farrell, whose parents are divorced and who wants to be an actress. Her only friend at boarding school is Janet Parker, who has a similar ambition. Courtney goes to Hollywood and has an affair with an aging, juvenile, homosexual film actor. Returning to New York, she is introduced to the sordid pleasures of Greenwich Village by Janet, whose later suicide helps Courtney to sort out her life. The youthful approach of the author is what probably gave the novel its initial appeal. Like the character Janet, Pamela Moore also committed suicide.

ALBERTO MORAVIA was the pseudonym of Alberto Pincherle (1907–90), one of the best known Italian novelists of the twentieth century, who also wrote many screenplays and was a film critic from 1944 on. *A Ghost at Noon* (Farrar, Straus, 1955), translated by Angus Davidson, recounts the marital difficulties of a young scriptwriter whose producer is attracted to his wife. The breakup of the marriage is followed by the wife's death. The background careers of the two men are strictly secondary to the relationship between them and the woman. *A Ghost at Noon* was originally published in Italy in 1954 under the title *Il Disprezzo*.

HELGA MORAY. *Carla* (Museum Press, 1954) is identified by Carolyn See as a Hollywood novel.

JOE MORELLA (born 1949) **and EDWARD Z. EPSTEIN** have written a number of popular volumes on Hollywood history. *The Ince Affair* (New American Library, 1978) is a fictionalized account of the death of producer Thomas H. Ince, who became ill while on board William Randolph Hearst's yacht in 1924. Unsubstantiated gossip has suggested that Ince was murdered by Hearst, either because the producer was having an affair with Hearst's mistress, Marion Davies, or because he was mistaken for Charlie Chaplin, who was having an affair with Davies.

AL MORGAN (born 1920). *Cast of Characters* (E.P. Dutton, 1957) uses the backdrop of a premiere at Grauman's Chinese Theatre as the framework for character sketches of six Hollywood types, including a director, a writer, a male star, and an editor. Reviews of this novel, a portion of which was first published in *Playboy*, were mixed. *Kirkus* (July 15, 1957) called it "a bright to brutal form of entertainment." "If one is not looking for the vitals of Hollywood but simply a package of stories in a hardcover *Confidential* style, Mr. Morgan is your boy," wrote Bosley Crowther in the *New York Times* (October 6, 1957). D.R. Benson in the *Saturday Review* (October 5, 1957) described it as "a B quickie—strictly the bottom half of a double bill."

A Small Success (Holt, Rinehart & Winston, 1960) is the story of Academy Award–winning and alcoholic actress Laurie Kane as she costars in the play of the book's title. Playing opposite her is a cowboy star, and the play is directed by one of her former lovers. At the novel's close, the actress retires to marry an accountant, who is a fellow member with her of Alcoholics Anonymous.

To Sit on a Horse (William Morrow, 1964) is the sentimental tale of an ex-vaudeville comedian, Jack Judson, who is dying from Parkinson's disease and the effects of a stroke. The world of the vaudevillian is contrasted with that of the cold and distant Hollywood crowd, as his successful director son refuses to give him a "bit" part in his latest film. Judson dies happy, reviving one of his old vaudeville routines in a 60-second television commercial. "This is a different approach to the story of the broken-hearted clown who must go on with the show," reported W.H. Matthews in *Library Journal* (June 15, 1964), "and although it is basically a tragedy, it is threaded with wry American Jewish humor and occasional laughs."

JOAN MORGAN (born 1905) was a silent film actress in her native England who often worked with her father, director/writer Sidney Morgan; she was also a novelist and playwright. *Camera!* (Chapman & Hall, 1940) provides an entertaining overview of silent filmmaking in the United Kingdom as it recounts the story of a major British star who ends her own life; she is modeled after Lilian Hall Davis, who was active on screen in England from 1918 to 1931.

MICHAEL MORGAN was the pseudonym of C. (Cecil) E. "Teet" Carle (1900–92) and Dean M. Dorn. Carle was a well-known Hollywood publicist, with Paramount from 1927 to 1936 and from 1940 to 1962, and with M-G-M from 1936 to 1940. With Richard Webb, he wrote a remembrance titled *The Laugh's on Hollywood* (Roundtable Publishing, 1985). *Nine More Lives* (Random House, 1947) is one of a number of detective novels written by Carle and Dorn as Michael Morgan. Here, a stuntman named Bill Ryan is accused of murder after the clothes of a woman found dead on the roof of his building are discovered in his apartment.

ANNE MORICE was the pseudonym of English writer Felicity Shaw (1918–89), who wrote a series of 21 mystery novels featuring actress and amateur sleuth Tess Crichton and her Scotland Yard detective husband, Robin Price. Crichton's background was the stage rather than motion pictures, but in *Nursery Tea and Poison* (St. Martin's Press, 1975), one of the central characters is a Hollywood director who retires to an English country house.

WRIGHT MORRIS (born 1910). *Love Among the Cannibals* (Harcourt, Brace, 1957) is narrated by Earl Hortner, the lyricist in a team described as the "poor man's Rodgers and Hart." Earl and his partner, Mac, are brought to Hollywood to work on a musical feature; they each pick up a date, and the four head for Acapulco and self-discovery. "The most recent National Book Award [for *The Field of Vision*] novelist has tossed off a comedy of morals unlike his preceding books and, in its conception and writing, unworthy of them," complained W.T. Scott in the *New York Herald Tribune* (August 11, 1957). "All that has distinguished Wright Morris' novels—his beautiful evocation of America's towns, his deep perception of middle-class people and neighborhoods, his fine sense of our past interwoven in our present—all this is absent. Hollywood can do that to people."

JAMES MORRISON (1888–1974) began his screen acting career with the Vitagraph Company in 1910; he retired from films in 1925, later working on the stage and teaching speech and drama. *April Luck* (G.P. Putnam's Sons, 1932) is the story of a small-town Connecticut girl who runs away to Paris and becomes a dancer on stage. Later, she embarks on a successful career as a Hollywood leading lady, but her dream of a happy love affair never becomes reality.

L. (Larry) A. (Alan) MORSE (born 1945) introduced his Hollywood private eye, Sam Hunter, in *The Big Enchilada*. The second novel, *Sleaze* (Avon Books, 1985), contains enough explicit sex and violence for even the most jaded of readers. The title refers to a porno magazine, whose editor—a woman—hires Hunter to discover who is writing her threatening letters. The plot revolves around an attempt to sell a television network a pornographic film of its latest star. A supporting character is an aging and powerful gossip columnist with lesbian tendencies, who, like all the female characters in the novel, is attracted to Hunter.

JOHN MORTIMER (born 1923) is a distinguished British playwright, novelist, and former barrister who is best known to American audiences as the author of the "Rumpole of the Bailey" series. He worked with the Crown Film Unit during the Second World War, and has contributed scripts to film, radio, and television.

Charade (Viking, 1986) is based on Mortimer's experiences with the Crown Film Unit, as the youthful narrator joins the Action Film Unit in 1944 as an assistant to the director. The latter was a friend of his mother's, and hence the job. The young man watches with naive innocence the behavior of the fellow members of the unit, and also witnesses the death during filming of an unpopular sergeant in a cliff-face exercise. With all the brashness of youth, the young man tries to interest both the unit and the local army officer in the man's death, which he believes was not accidental. He is unable to determine the truth of the matter, but he does realize that he lacks the qualities necessary to become a filmmaker. *Charade* was first published in England in 1947 by The Bodley Head.

Dunster (Viking, 1992) is the type of friend nobody deserves, least of all Philip Progmire, the hero of this novel, who works closely with the head of

Megapolis Television in London. After Dunster has stolen Progmire's wife, he turns his attention to Progmire's boss and insinuates that he committed a serious war crime in Italy. There is no alternative but for a libel suit, in which a jury finds against Dunster. The background of the novel is television, but the head of Megapolis is married to a former British screen star, and there are some amusing comments on her career in films of World War II. *Dunster* is engrossing, and the reader gets some satisfaction at its conclusion when the title character is finally bested, albeit unfairly. It is what Dunster merits and what hero Progmire is entitled to.

FERN MOSK see ANNE TAYLOR and FERN MOSK

JAMES MOSSMAN. Set against a background of Hong Kong, England, and Vietnam, *Lifelines* (Little, Brown, 1971) is the story of four people, a British war correspondent, his film star lover, his wife, and her lover (an American journalist). "A fine, dour novel about different styles of dying," wrote Martin Levin in the *New York Times* (August 15, 1971) of Mossman's second and last novel; the author died prior to its American publication.

PATRICIA MOYES (born 1923) has her ongoing character Chief Inspector Henry Tibbett play only a supporting role in *Falling Star* (Holt, Rinehart & Winston, 1964). The mystery novel is narrated by the overbearing, smug, and pretentious Anthony Croombe-Peters, who has raised the money for a London-based film production and so overly concerns himself with every aspect of the manner in which the money is spent. When the leading man "accidentally" falls under a subway train, production continues thanks to Croombe-Peters's careful concern for insurance. When the continuity girl "accidentally" falls from her apartment window, even Croombe-Peters begins to wonder what is wrong with the production. A third killing, that of the leading man's dresser, leaves Henry Tibbett in no doubt that there have been three murders. It transpires that the continuity girl was engaged in blackmail, and the director, determined to complete the production at all costs, had taken matters into his own hands. Since Croombe-Peters is an amateur as far as film production is concerned, the author is able to use his commentary to explain the finer points of filmmaking. The continuity girl's occupation and need to document every detail of the film project has a strong bearing on the storyline.

ROBERT MULLER. The narrator of *Lovelife* (Hutchinson, 1970) is a British television director who kidnaps his daughter from a failed marriage, engages in a number of affairs, and makes a film attacking his own lifestyle and that of his friends.

DALLAS MURPHY. *Lover Man* (Charles Scribner's Sons, 1987) introduced an unemployed jazz musician named Artie Deemer, who made a living by hiring out his dog, Jellyroll, for television commercials and feature film appearances. Artie is the chief suspect when his ex-lover is murdered. "Initially intriguing, often entertaining, ultimately overstuffed," was the opinion of *Kirkus* (June 1, 1987). Artie Deemer reappeared in *Lush Life* (Simon & Schuster, 1992).

WILLIAM MURRAY. *Fugitive Romans* (Vanguard Press, 1955) is the story of a group of expatriate Americans living in Rome and their relationship to both the native film industry and Hollywood companies shooting on location there. The novel is narrated by a young American public relations man working on an epic titled *Ave, Caesar.* "On a slim foundation, William Murray has managed to erect a creditable, formidable super-structure of satiric observation, nearly all of it extremely comic, much of it telling, some of it important," wrote D.M. Mankiewicz in the *New York Times* (March 27, 1955).

MARY RUTH MYERS (born 1947). Laura Fitzgerald arrives in Hollywood, trying to become a screenwriter, in *Friday's Daughter* (Ballantine Books, 1984), but her mother, a glamorous movie actress named Jessamyn Friday, is jealous of her daughter and attempts to get her blacklisted. Both mother and daughter are in love with the same man, Jake Turner, and when he and Laura are married, Jessamyn is able to manipulate both their lives by financing a production company for Jake.

PHINEAS BARTON MYERS (1888–19??). *Hollywood Murder: A Mystery Romance of California and the Near East* (Exposition Press, 1958) is a complex mystery novel set in 1926 involving Sir Hammond Taylor, whose professions include exploration, membership in the Royal Secret Service, and film direction. While shooting in the southern California desert, he is apparently shot and killed, but after an investigation that leads to drug smuggling in Algeria, it is revealed that the victim was only a look-alike.

VLADIMIR NABOKOV (1899–1977). First published in a different version in the United Kingdom as *Camera Obscura*, **Laughter in the Dark** (Bobbs-Merrill, 1938) is a tale of adultery, outlined on its first page by the author: "Once upon a time there lived in Berlin, Germany, a man called Albinus. He was rich, respectable, happy; one day he abandoned his wife for the sake of a youthful mistress he loved; was not loved; and his life ended in disaster." This novel, which, as Clifton Fadiman wrote in *The New Yorker* (May 7, 1938), combines "Chekhovian lassitude with surrealist degeneracy," is cited by many academic writers as a major Hollywood novel because the woman with whom Albinus falls in love is a cinema usherette, who wants him to finance her career as a movie star. Further, as the critic in *Bénet's Reader's Encyclopedia of American Literature* (HarperCollins, 1987) points out, "The texture of this novel is closely related to cinematographic images and techniques of the 1930s."

Laughter in the Dark was filmed in 1969 for Lopert Pictures release, directed by Tony Richardson, and starring Nicol Williamson, Anna Karina, and Jean-Claude Drouot. The novel was adapted by Edward Bond. Nabokov's relationship to the motion picture is discussed in Alfred Appel, Jr.'s *Nabokov's Dark Cinema* (Oxford University Press, 1974).

R. (Raispuram) K. (Krishnaswami) NARAYAN (born 1906). The highly praised *Printer of Malgudi* (Michigan State University Press, 1957) boasts a central character who decides to produce an epic film and make his town the "Hollywood of India" when the local newspaper goes bankrupt.

RICHARD N. NASH. When successful Hollywood actress Calla Stark receives a threatening telephone call in *Radiance* (Doubleday, 1983), she recalls her past life, rise to fame, failed marriage to a character actor, work for the civil rights movement, and the death of her daughter. When her stand-in/secretary is assaulted, Calla wonders if the attack was intended for her, or whether it is related to the stand-in's relationship with a black cult leader. Calla agrees to star in a film about the cult leader's life, featuring her ex-husband, directed and written by the man with whom she is currently having an affair, and to be filmed in the same Southern location where her daughter was killed. "A verbose, pretentious mishmash that rarely even threatens to be entertaining—notwithstanding a few dollops of show-biz sparkle here and there" was the opinion of *Kirkus*.

RICHARD NEHRBASS. *A Perfect Death for Hollywood* (Harper-Collins, 1991) may be a well-written mystery novel, but its plotline, characters, and dialogue fail to ring true. When the crucified, naked body of a teenage prostitute is found at the base of the Hollywood sign, private detective Vic Eton is asked to investigate by a high-priced hooker who was the girl's closest friend. A second body, that of a wealthy recording industry executive, is also found in a similar position and with similar wounds to the wrists and ankles. The solution involves a legendary Hollywood director who was the recording executive's father-in-law, snuff movies, and the Mafia. The novel does contain a good, short descriptive passage of a walk down Hollywood Boulevard: "past unshaven men slouched alone in doorways or propped against walls, my eyes riveted on the gold stars embedded like fossils in the wide litter-strewn sidewalk, names most people had never heard of mixed among the stars: Colleen Moore and David Selznick, Joseph Schenck and Joan Crawford, Mae Clarke and Cary Grant."

In *Dark of Night* (HarperCollins, 1992), Vic Eton is hired by a film producer to track down his missing daughter.

MARGUERITE NELSON is the pseudonym of Lee Floren (born 1910), a prolific writer of fiction for teenagers. *Jill's Hollywood Assignment* (Avalon Books/Thomas Bouregy, 1958) documents the romantic adventures of a teenage girl in Hollywood. When nurse Cynthia Holden transfers from Lime Valley to Hollywood in *Hollywood Nurse* (Arcadia House, 1963), she gets the opportunity to meet movie celebrities, but when an earthquake strikes Lime Valley, she decides to return and, coincidentally, renews a romance with a local doctor. Nancy Brooker-Bowers wrote, "This light romance for adolescent girls appears to merge the conventional nurse novel motifs with the Hollywood novel genre, but Hollywood seems only a colorful backdrop for the action rather than an integral part of the story."

DAVID NEMEC (born 1938). *Bright Lights, Dark Rooms* (Doubleday, 1980) is a mystery novel featuring Florida writer Richard Barwegan. He comes to New York's Soho district, and as he tries to solve the murder of a female black artist, he becomes acquainted with the area's artists and filmmakers.

JOHN NICHOLS (born 1940), two of whose novels—*The Sterile Cuckoo* (1965) and *The Milagro Beanfield War* (1974)—have been filmed, lives in and writes about New Mexico. *A Ghost in the Music* (W.W. Norton, 1979) is a story of relationships between father and child and between lovers. Forty-eight-year-old Bart Darling is an actor and stuntman who is about to perform a stunt on a B picture which will probably kill him. His pregnant girlfriend threatens to leave him if he continues with the stunt, and, in desperation, Bart turns to his illegitimate son for help. Now 29 years old, the boy must sort out both his feelings for his father and his growing love for his father's girlfriend.

GEOFF NICHOLSON (born 1953). *The Errol Flynn Novel* (Hodder and Stoughton, 1993) concerns an eccentric American producer, Dan Ryan, who comes to England to produce a film on the life of Errol Flynn, based, it would seem, on Charles Higham's biography of the actor and acknowledging Flynn's homosexuality and Nazi proclivities. A young, inexperienced English actor named Jack—who narrates the novel—is hired to play Flynn, and when the film is closed down, he goes to Las Vegas to seek out Ryan and the truth about his background. The novel is great fun, outrageously witty, sexy, and, ultimately, original—rather as Errol Flynn must have appeared to his fans.

HELEN NIELSEN (born 1918). When Omar Bradley Smith returns from Vietnam in *Shot on Location* (William Morrow, 1971), he goes from California to Greece to try to locate a missing director who stole his idea for a television series, and who also stole and made a film star of Smith's ex-girlfriend. "A smooth piece of work . . . urbane and agreeable," commented Newgate Callendar in the *New York Times* (September 12, 1971).

DAVID NIVEN (1909–83) was a Scottish-born, debonair leading man in such Hollywood films as *The Moon Is Blue* (1953), *Around the World in 80 Days* (1956), *Separate Tables* (1958), and *The Guns of Navarone* (1961); his British films include *The First of the Few* (1942) and *A Matter of Life and Death/Stairway to Heaven* (1946). He wrote two well-received volumes of autobiography, *The Moon's a Balloon* (1971) and *Bring on the Empty Horses* (1975), and two novels, *Round the Rugged Rocks/Once Over Lightly* and *Go Slowly, Come Back Quickly*.

Presumably a roman à clef, *Once Over Lightly* (Prentice-Hall, 1951) is the story of John Hamilton, a former English soldier, who comes to Hollywood and achieves success as an actor. He is unable to differentiate between his real self and the Hollywood-created image until he begins a meaningful relationship leading to marriage. The novel was originally published in the United Kingdom under the title *Round the Rugged Rocks*.

Go Slowly, Come Back Quickly (Doubleday, 1981) is the story of Stani Skolimowski, a handsome young man of Polish extraction, who serves with distinction in the RAF during World War II and comes to Hollywood with his girlfriend, Pandora, who is the recipient of a major studio contract. Pandora is well liked by the gossip columnists of the period, but she suffers the indignity of a name change, a costarring role in a Mexican-based feature film whose director and producer are at odds, and an early, disastrous appearance on live television. Stani meanwhile finds his true vocation as a still photographer. The couple is briefly separated when Stani comes upon Pandora having drug-induced sex with the studio head, but the two are soon reunited for an ending in the West Indies, where they survive a hurricane. The hurricane has no relevance whatsoever to the storyline and appears to have been thrown in because of the lack of a dramatic climax to the novel. All in all, the book seems to consist of generally unrelated incidents. Further, although Stani and Pandora come to Hollywood immediately at the end of World War II, much of what happens to them there and in New York appears to take place in the 1950s.

The publisher's jacket blurb states that Stani also becomes a football star, but I seem to have missed that in my reading of the novel. He might be, as the publisher claims, "one of the most engaging heroes of recent fiction," but the novel itself is strictly for the David Niven fans, who will try to find something of the actor in the fictional character.

JOAN LOWERY NIXON (born 1927). "Hollywood Daughters: A Family Trilogy" is intended to chronicle the lives of three generations of mothers and daughters in Hollywood. The first in this series for young adults, *Star Babies* (Bantam Books, 1989), features Abby "Cookie" Baynes who was once the highest-paid child star of the 1930s and now, in 1942, wants to be a star again. Her mother wants her to continue with her little-girl act, but an eccentric neighbor encourages her to create a fresh, new image.

WILLIAM F. (Francis) NOLAN (born 1928). *The Black Mask Murders* (St. Martin's Press, 1994) is the first in a series of mystery novels to feature "The Black Mask Boys," Dashiell Hammett, Raymond Chandler, and Erle Stanley Gardner. The mystery novel is narrated by Hammett, set in Hollywood in 1935, and features an assortment of movie stars and movie moguls in a plotline that owes something to *The Maltese Falcon*. "Of interest as a period piece and for its insider allusions, this is no hard-boiled tale," wrote *Publishers Weekly* (June 20, 1994).

BARRY NORMAN. *The Matter of Mandrake* (Walker, 1968) blends filmmaking and international intrigue as a London reporter tries to prevent a government minister from giving secrets to the Russians during the filming of a biblical epic in Spain. The author is probably the British television personality of the same name.

STANLEY NOYES (born 1924). *Shadowbox* (Macmillan, 1970) is a thought-provoking novel of suspense and violence. Arnie Hale is a part–Cherokee pacifist minister who kills a man in a holdup. Riddled with guilt, Hale sets out for Hollywood, determined to find the man's sister, his ex-girlfriend, who works as a showgirl and "bit" actress. His search leads him into the gangster-infested world of the show business underground, as well as to an encounter with two pathological killers.

AKIYUKI NOZAKA (born 1930). *The Pornographers* (Alfred A. Knopf, 1968) is a witty novel of an Osaka, Japan, pornographer, an endearing individual with a humanist view of the world. He seeks aestheticism and morality in a profession hampered by poor technical facilities, an overbearing cameraman, and actors who will not follow the script. Originally published in Japan in 1966 under the title *Erogotoshi-Tach* by Shinchoosha, *The Pornographers* was translated by Michael Gallagher.

ELLIOTT NUGENT (1899–1960) made good use of his background as an actor, producer, and director in the writing of his first novel, *Of Cheat and Charmer* (Trident Press/Simon & Schuster, 1962). The central character, Myron Myros, is a successful producer/director who must fight with his two partners over a screen remake of *The Little Foxes*, and help save a play featuring his estranged wife. Unfortunately, Myros tries to live his life according to screen fantasy rather than reality; his failure to love ultimately leads to self-destruction. Most reviewers found the novel disappointing, its characters wooden, and the dialogue unrealistic.

DARCY O'BRIEN (born 1939) is the son of George O'Brien, who is primarily remembered as a Western star, and actress Marguerite Churchill, a photograph of whom graces the cover of *Margaret in Hollywood* (William Morrow, 1991). Narrated by its heroine Margaret Spencer, the novel begins, "Back in the days when Shakespeare still meant something to a lot of people, I wanted to be a great dramatic actress. Before I knew it, I was in Hollywood." In fact, the reader has to go a long way with Margaret Spencer before she gets to Hollywood, reliving with her the beginnings of her career in vaudeville in the Midwest at the age of five, acting as a child in Buenos Aires, and her Broadway debut. It is not until the last third of the novel that the heroine arrives in Hollywood (in 1927). Much of the book is taken up with Spencer's overambitious stage mother (who involves her in an oil swindle) and her sexual awakening, with explicit sex between Spencer and a comedy writer, a director, a cowboy star, and others. The book concludes with Margaret Spencer's work in a Western, presumably based on Marguerite Churchill's performance in *The Big Trail*. Despite the graphic sex, *Margaret in Hollywood* is a somewhat old-fashioned novel that leaves the reader wondering just how much of it the author based on his mother's life.

The same question is raised by O'Brien's first novel, *A Way of Life Like Any Other* (W.W. Norton, 1977). Here, a teenager chronicles his life with a Western cowboy father and an actress mother. The parents are divorced, and in the late 1940s and early 1950s, the boy lives first with his mother in Europe and then with his father in Los Angeles. Director John Ford puts in a guest appearance. The novel provides a good portrait of growing up with two somewhat eccentric people and also raises the question of how much a roman à clef this book is. Somehow one hopes that it is pure fiction because it does nothing for the image of either O'Brien or Churchill.

GEOFFREY O'BRIEN (born 1948). The novel *The Phantom Empire* (W.W. Norton, 1993) examines the manner in which the motion picture has affected the way one looks at the world. In *Booklist* (September 15, 1993), Benjamin Segedin wrote,

> Having immersed himself in a sea of celluloid, O'Brien speaks a film language; all his references are to the conventions of film—its archetypal

character, familiar plot twists, and exotic locales. With nearly every breath, he exhales film titles in an outpouring ranging from French classics such as *A Nous la Liberté* to Italian monster flicks such as *Zombie Holocaust*. His original work is a subjective critical-historical survey of cinema, an enchanting prose poem on the flickering image that is ultimately the epic of a hundred years of the moving picture.

LYNDA OBST is a producer and **CAROL WOLPER** a screenwriter. Together they wrote *Dirty Dreams* (NAL Books, 1990), which is primarily the story of two contemporary women in the film industry, one the production head of a major studio and the other her new secretary and would-be screenwriter. Both have problems with the men in their lives, particularly the studio executive, who loses her job because she will not support a sex and bondage movie titled *Dirty Dreams*, which the studio's moneymaking director is determined will be on the production schedule. The novel presents a depressing picture of contemporary film and deal making, but how much of it is true is difficult to know since the writers are extraordinarily sloppy in their presentation. Factual errors outside the motion picture business are perhaps understandable (for example, the authors think rugby is played with a stick), but why are there mistakes in an area with which they are supposedly familiar? Why write of a central aisle in the theater at the Academy of Motion Picture Arts and Sciences, when it has none? It is a minor error, but it throws into doubt the validity of the novel as a whole.

JANET O'DANIEL (born 1921). In 1913 two brothers, Theodore and Leopold Wharton, founded a film company in Ithaca, New York, producing serials for release through Pathé Frères. Their filmmaking activities form the basis for *The Cliff Hangers* (J.B. Lippincott, 1961), which is set in Ithaca in 1914 and primarily concerns director Matthew Hillyer and his work for Lambert Frères. In 1916 the Whartons brought dancer Irene Castle to Ithaca to star in a patriotic serial, *Patria*; here Hillyer brings a dancer named Marian Vance to the company, also to star in a patriotic serial. The novel concentrates on the filmmakers, but subplots involve an effort by a zealous citizen to curb their activities and the murder of the leading man, who has tried to seduce the same citizen's daughter. Janet O'Daniel captures the spirit of the time well; she has a good descriptive sense and brings alive the university town of Ithaca as it was in the teens. Ultimately, however, the plotline is little better than a movie melodrama of the period, a little better but not much more so than the serial that Matthew Hillyer is making.

CONSTANCE O'DAY-FLANNERY is noted for her time travel romances. In *The Gift* (Zebra Books, 1994), she has Hollywood actress Val Manchester, dead some thirty years, return to earth as a guardian angel for a young woman who has problems in her love life and is facing mental collapse.

LILLIAN O'DONNELL (born 1926) has written many mystery novels featuring either Gwenn Ramadge, Mici Anhalt, or New York police Lieutenant Norah Mulcahaney. The last is the heroine of *Pushover* (G.P. Putnam's Sons,

1992), in which a retired and legendary Hollywood star is murdered in her New York apartment and her grandson kidnapped. The O'Donnell mysteries have been praised by some as good police procedurals, but it is difficult to understand from *Pushover* what is so marvelous about Mulcahaney's work as she botches the investigation. The writing is tight and crisp—and a little old-fashioned. The title relates not to the main murder in the novel but to a secondary series of killings in which young women are pushed in front of subway trains. It is a favorite device of O'Donnell to present two disparate crimes and then tenuously (and here very tenuously) link them at the novel's close.

LIAM O'FLAHERTY (1896–1984). *Hollywood Cemetery* (Victor Gollancz, 1935) was based on O'Flaherty's time in Hollywood while director John Ford was filming his 1925 novel, *The Informer*. The book is a roman à clef with the central character an Irish author named Brian Carey who has been hired at $500 a week to help in the filming of a novel by director Bud Tracy (John Ford) and screenwriter Sam Gunn (Dudley Nichols). As John Zneimer writes in *The Literary Vision of Liam O'Flaherty* (Syracuse University Press, 1970), "The book, however, is not primarily about Carey, but a satire on Hollywood and motion-picture making in which the naive and bumbling Carey has been unwittingly involved. The essence of the satire is Hollywood's artificiality, the necessity of 'fixing' everything so that an Irish village in Ireland would never be as convincing on the screen as the Hollywood version of it, and the Irish girl Mortimer [the producer] imports could never be as convincing as the version of her that he has created." In reality, the Irish heroine in *The Informer* is played by British actress Margot Grahame.

JAMES D. O'HANLON was a Hollywood screenwriter who wrote a series of mystery novels featuring former Hollywood extras Jason and Pat Cordry who are now amateur sleuths: *Murder at Malibu* (Phoenix, 1937), *Murder at 300 to 1* (Phoenix, 1938), *Murder at Coney Island* (Phoenix, 1939), *As Good as Murdered* (Random House, 1940), and *Murder at Horsethief* (Phoenix, 1941). Bill Pronzini describes the last as "of such hilarious awfulness that it deserves cult status." In *As Good as Murdered*, Jason Cordry becomes a screenwriter who finds that the screwball comedy he is writing has become reality.

JOHN O'HARA (1905–70) is a noted twentieth-century novelist and short story writer, hailed for the Americanness of his work, as biographer Matthew J. Bruccoli has commented in *The O'Hara Concern* (Random House, 1975). Bruccoli commended O'Hara for the value of his writings as "a record of 3 decades of American life. He knew exactly what he was writing about." Certainly O'Hara was fully conversant with the film industry, both as an observer and as a participant. As early as 1930 he was the movie critic for the *New York Morning Telegraph*, and in 1931 he worked in the New York publicity office of Warner Bros., moving over to RKO the following year. He first came to Hollywood in 1934, under contract to Paramount; in 1937 he was with Samuel Goldwyn and M-G-M, in 1939 with RKO, and from 1939 through 1941 with 20th Century–Fox. In 1945–46 it was back to M-G-M, and in 1955 through 1957 he returned to 20th Century–Fox. O'Hara received credit for his work on *Moontide* (1941),

A Miracle Can Happen (1946), and *The Best Things in Life Are Free* (1955), and was also seen briefly on screen in *The General Died at Dawn* (1936). He never did get to write his proposed screenplay of *The Great Gatsby*, to star Clark Gable, but four of his works were filmed: *Butterfield 8* (1935), *Pal Joey* (1938/1940), *A Rage to Live* (1949), and *Ten North Frederick* (1956).

Of one of the two novels that fit the subject of this survey, **Hope of Heaven** (Harcourt, Brace, 1938), O'Hara wrote, "It's not a Hollywood story, but it is Californian." The book tells the story of a love affair between a Hollywood screenwriter, Jimmy Malloy (the only time O'Hara based a character on himself), and a leftist bookstore clerk, Peggy Henderson. The relationship dissolves when Peggy's father accidentally shoots and kills her brother.

Hope of Heaven was not a major success on its initial release, but it did sell 13,000 copies. In his critical study *John O'Hara* (Twayne, 1966), Sheldon Norman Grebstein commented, "Although the reader learns little about the film industry *per se*, O'Hara does transmit the feel, the mood of Hollywood life as experienced by one of its lower echelons, the second-string film writers."

The second novel, **The Big Laugh** (Random House, 1962), is not as well known as *Hope of Heaven*. It chronicles the life and career of Hubert Ward from poverty in the 1920s through Hollywood stardom 30 years later. The emphasis is on Ward's three marriages, including one to a British actress.

LIONEL OLAY. *The Heart of a Stranger* (New American Library, 1959) is identified by Carolyn See as a Hollywood novel.

D.B. OLSEN was the pseudonym of D. (Dolores) B. (Birk) Hitchens (1907–73). Professor Pennyfeather investigates the murder of a professor's wife and her lover in **Love Me in Death** (Doubleday, 1951), and two of the suspects are a film actress and a director. The setting is southern California. "Professor Pennyfeather is at his engaging and efficient best among all these peculiar types," commented the reviewer in *The New Yorker* (February 17, 1951).

RUSSELL O'NEILL. In a novel that is reminiscent of Thorne Smith at his best, *Jonathan* (Appleton, 1959) finds a Hollywood screenwriter on location in Mexico turned into a horse by a witch whom he has angered. Jonathan, the horse, now becomes the star of a "horse opera," written by Jonathan Cartwright, and is able to take his revenge on the loathsome star, for whom he had written many successful films.

DENISE OSBORNE. *Murder Offscreen* (Henry Holt, 1994) introduces former Hollywood private eye Queenie Davilov, who would like to be a screenwriter but is currently working as a script supervisor. When a horror film producer is murdered at the premiere of his latest attraction, Davilov is hired to find the killer. *Publishers Weekly* (June 27, 1994) praised the novel's "bright and highly charged reality."

O.D. OSBORNE. *Leave Her to God* (Fawcett, 1952) is identified by Carolyn See as a Hollywood novel.

KATHERINE HALL PAGE has created an unusual mystery novel heroine in Faith Fairchild, who runs her own catering business in Aleford, Massachusetts. In *The Body in the Cast* (St. Martin's Press, 1993), a film company comes to Aleford to film on location an updated version of *The Scarlet Letter*, and Fairchild is hired to feed the crew. It is not long before the bean soup is dosed with laxatives and a stand-in is poisoned. Arson and murder follow, and Fairchild is forced to investigate. "Sprightly, with a light dusting of satire and, alas, a heavy dollop of this year's most overused plot complication, child abuse," noted *Kirkus* (October 1, 1993).

DOLORES PALA. *Trumpet for a Walled City* (Harper & Row, 1974) documents the relationship between a star of foreign films and the daughter of a New York Irish American family who took him in when he was abandoned by his parents.

LINDA PALMER. *Star Struck* (G.P. Putnam's Sons, 1981) begins with Abby Tyler's arrival in New York in 1973, penniless, a murderer, but determined to become a writer. She becomes involved with playwright Peter Rossano, and their relationship helps him write a great play. However, on opening night Peter realizes that Abby has fallen in love with agent Julian Karr. With the latter, Abby moves to Los Angeles, where Julian is trying to revive the fortunes of Olympic Studios. (The dust jacket description calls the company Centurion Pictures.) Ambition comes between the two, but after a hefty dose of sex, both straight and gay, all works out for the best with Abby's novel *All Together Now* turned into a brilliant film with a script by the real-life Larry Gelbart. As the publisher so aptly puts it, *Star Struck* is "the story of love striving to survive the temptations of that ultimate aphrodisiac—success."

STUART PALMER (1905–68) wrote 14 novels and three short story collections featuring aging spinster and amateur sleuth Hildegarde Withers. The mysteries were brought to the screen in the 1930s with Edna May Oliver playing the central character. Palmer also worked in Hollywood as a screenwriter, and wrote an additional seven non–Withers books.

In *The Puzzle of the Happy Hooligan* (Crime Club/Doubleday, 1941), Miss Withers is on vacation in Hollywood, when she is approached by an agent who wants her hired by Mammoth Studios to work as a technical adviser on a screen version of the Lizzie Borden story. No sooner does Miss Withers arrive at the studio than one of the screenwriters is murdered, his neck broken without any physical signs of violence. A check with Withers's colleague Inspector Oscar Piper of the New York City Police Department reveals that a similar murder occurred in that city some years ago, committed by an at-large criminal named Derek Laval. Piper comes to Hollywood when it appears that Miss Withers has been murdered, but she is still around and eventually proves that the screenwriter's partner was his killer. "Laval" was a name used by many writers, just as "George Spelvin" is used in the theater, for someone who does not exist. Writers would take advantage of tax laws by "giving" money to the nonexistent Laval and would use his name when stopped for a traffic violation, for example.

There are a number of references to film personalities. The screenwriter is apparently killed by a falling poster of Josephine Baker. Among the actresses rejected by the studio head for the role of Lizzie Borden are Irene Dunne, Myrna Loy, Janet Gaynor, Ann Sheridan, and Olivia de Havilland. Piper discovers "that in real life, Miss Dunne looks smaller than on the screen, while Myrna Loy looks larger, that Miss Greer Garson's beauty cries out for the color camera, that Mickey Rooney and Jackie Cooper are grown up now in some ways, especially as regards blondes."

Cold Poison (M.S. Mill/William Morrow, 1954) is probably typical of the novels in the series. It is lightweight and verges on the ridiculous since it seems extremely unlikely that anyone would accept Hildegarde Withers as a detective or that Inspector Oscar Piper of the New York City police would willingly work with her as a colleague. The Hildegarde Withers novels were published between 1931 and 1969, and by the 1950s *Cold Poison* makes it very obvious that the character is no longer contemporary. The story concerns an animation studio in Los Angeles, where the popular "Peter Penguin" cartoons are produced; four of the workers there receive threatening notes, one is murdered, and Hildegarde Withers and her poodle, Talleyrand, are hired to investigate. The author acknowledges a debt to Walter Lantz, upon whose cartoon creation "Woody Woodpecker" Peter Penguin is apparently based. He explains to the reader the workings of an animation unit within a larger motion picture studio (here called Miracle-Paradox), and Miss Withers offers her views on some Hollywood stars she sees in the studio commissary: "Alan Ladd was not quite as tall but certainly quite as handsome as she had previously imagined, ... Abbott and Costello lunched quietly without throwing any dishes at each other, ... Piper Laurie was a pixie and Esther Williams a sexy madonna."

The non–Withers novel **Rook Takes Knight** (Random House, 1968) features ex-reporter/current private eye Howie Rook, searching for the murderer of former starlet Deirdre Charteris, killed in a hit-and-run incident.

ROBERT B. PARKER (born 1932).

Spenser, Robert B. Parker's Boston-based private detective, heads for Los Angeles in *A Savage Place* (Delacorte Press, 1981) when he is hired to protect a television newswoman who has uncovered evidence of mob infiltration of a major Hollywood studio. After assorted death and violence, Spenser is able brutally to beat the head of the conglomerate controlling the studio shortly after he has ordered the murder of the newswoman. *A Savage Place* is not one of the better Spenser novels, and the author is not completely successful in writing about the Los Angeles scene; for instance, he repeatedly misspells the name of a well-known street and places a fully operating bar on a studio lot, where drinking is generally frowned upon.

HELEN LAWRENCE PARTRIDGE (born 1902).

A Lady Goes to Hollywood: Being the Casual Adventures of an Author's Wife in the Much Misunderstood Capital of Filmland (Macmillan, 1941) is a fictionalized account of the author's life in Hollywood while her husband Bellamy Partridge's 1939 book, *Country Lawyer*, was being filmed. The contemporary press was not too enthusiastic. *The New Republic* (December 22, 1941) opined, "All right if you can stand lady authors who find color in exclamation points, the words 'yummy' and 'scrumptuous,' things to be 'ahed' and 'ohed' over and 'just too dear for words.'"

ERCOLE PATTI (1904–76). *Roman Affair* (William Sloane, 1957), translated from the Italian by Constantine Fitzgibbon, chronicles the affair of an intellectual son of a Roman count and an Italian screen star. The background is the Italian film industry. Anne Ross wrote in the *New York Herald Tribune* (December 8, 1957), "Mr. Patti can make one feel the changing seasons in the Eternal City. He can make one see the spectacle of middle-aged business men dressed in white smocks sitting down before a feast of oxtail in a Trastavere restaurant. He can even make one feel sorry for the hapless and unambitious Anna. But deeper than this he cannot go—his picture is entirely on the surface."

ELLIOT PAUL (1891–1958). *The Black Gardenia* (Random House, 1952) is not up to Paul's usual detective fiction. Here, detective Homer Evans tries to establish the innocence of his young associate, Finke Maguire, in the murder of three members of the film industry. The author devotes too much space to the motion pictures' tourist attractions and folklore. "He's done better," commented the reviewer in *Saturday Review* (January 26, 1952), the reaction of most contemporary critics.

LAURENCE PAYNE (born 1919) is a British novelist who was formerly an actor with the Stratford-upon-Avon and old Vic companies. He has written a series of mystery novels featuring ex–film star turned private investigator Mark Savage.

In *Malice in Camera* (Crime Club/Doubleday, 1985), Savage heads for an unidentified studio at Elstree, where his one-time director Andrew Elliot has received a threatening letter and is becoming increasingly aware that his new production is being sabotaged. Three people are involved in the attempt to destroy Elliot, a fervent anti–Communist. One is his wife; the second is a young actor whose father was named by Elliot when he appeared as a friendly witness before the House Un-American Activities Committee; and the third is the financer of the film, whose granddaughter committed suicide as a result of her treatment in one of the director's productions. Laurence Payne knows well the workings of a modern British studio and brings to life a fascinating collection of backstage characters, from the guard at the gate to the property man. The novel is well plotted, but it would perhaps have been better to build the link to the House Un-American Activities Committee rather than have the principal instigator of the anti–Andrew Elliot brigade be the financer. His granddaughter was untalented, and the director had every right to fire her. The director's motive in naming the young actor's father is less defensible.

ARTHUR PEDERSON *see* **RACHAEL FIELD and ARTHUR PEDERSON**

SAMUEL PEEPLES (born 1917). *The Man Who Died Twice* (G.P. Putnam's Sons, 1976) is "an adventure in time" as a Los Angeles police officer is shot and finds himself propelled back to the 1920s and inside the body of director William Desmond Taylor. He knows Taylor will be murdered on February 1, 1922, and it is the shooting that sends the detective back to the present. Mabel Normand plays a prominent part in the story, but Mrs. Shelby, the mother of actress Mary Miles Minter, is the killer. (Perhaps because Minter was still alive when the novel was published, she is here called Betty Blayne and her mother Mrs. Denker.) Peeples knows film history, but his novel is surprisingly dull. There are no surprises in the police officer's findings, and really his trip back in time was hardly worthwhile.

HUGH PENTECOST is the pseudonym of Judson Philips (born 1903) (q.v.). Pentecost has written two major series of mystery novels, one featuring hotel manager Pierre Chambrun, begun in 1962; and the other featuring public relations director Julian Quist, begun in 1971. *Beware Young Lovers* (Dodd, Mead, 1980) borrows elements from both series as its narrator, Mark Haskell, is the public relations director at a New York hotel that is a home away from home for many celebrities. No sooner does movie star Sharon Brand arrive to participate in a talk show originating from the hotel than her young lover disappears and turns up dead. A second death—of a gossip columnist—occurs during the show's taping.

WALKER PERCY (1916–90) was awarded the 1962 National Book Award for fiction for his first novel, *The Moviegoer* (Alfred A. Knopf, 1961). The book's central character and narrator, Binx Bolling, is a prosperous New Orleans stockbroker whose main enjoyment in life is going to the movies. One of the phenomena of moviegoing is certification: "Nowadays when a person lives somewhere, in a neighborhood, the place is not certified for him. More than likely he will live there sadly and the emptiness which is inside him will expand until it evacuates the entire neighborhood. But if he sees a movie which shows his very neighborhood, it becomes possible for him to live, for a time at least, as a person who is Somewhere and not Anywhere." The thoughts that the movies evoke are interesting to the reader, far more than the novel's irritating Southerners with their speech characteristics and quaint cultural limitations. New Orleans is a foreign land compared to the movies of which Walker Percy writes.

The characters in *Lancelot* (Farrar, Straus and Giroux, 1977) are often compared to film actors, with the title figure, Lancelot Andrewes Lamar, described as similar in appearance to Sterling Hayden. From his room in a mental institution, this scion of a distinguished Louisiana family describes what took place after he discovered that his daughter is not his own. The drama unfolds against the background of the making of a feature film in his ancestral home, a production featuring his wife, who is having an affair with the director. *Lancelot* is a compelling novel, with weighty discussion of the sexes and the differences between North and South. While images of movie stars figure strongly in the narrative, the film production is at best secondary to the novel's storyline.

ELEANOR PERRY (1915–81). Born Eleanor Rosenfeld, Perry began her career as a screenwriter in 1962 with *David and Lisa*, directed by her husband, Frank Perry (the couple was divorced in 1971). Her script for *Diary of a Mad Housewife* (1970) is considered a feminist milestone in film history, and that strong feminist theme is also very evident in *Blue Pages* (Lippincott, 1979), in which a female screenwriter named Lucia is exploited by her director husband, Vincent Wade. "Rarely has a heroine been so put upon by loathsome people," wrote Christopher Lehmann-Haupt in the *New York Times* (May 1, 1979) of this novel, which Perry denied was a roman à clef. The title refers to final script revisions, which are always printed on blue pages.

Perry discussed the novel in Arthur Knight's column, "Hell Hath No Fury Like a Writer Scorned," in *The Hollywood Reporter*, April 20, 1979 (pp. 10–11).

STELLA G.S. PERRY (1877–19??). ***Extra-Girl*** (Frederick A. Stokes, 1929): In her New Orleans convent school, Odile Vaure dreams of movie star Vance Murdock. She goes to Hollywood and obtains work first as an extra and then as a "bit" player. She begins to frequent a popular restaurant, the Montmartre on Hollywood Boulevard, which is described in some detail: "Odile had had so many 'bits' that she was even beginning to be a luncheon habituée of Montmartre . . . that restaurant where the prosperous or seemingly prosperous actors gathered to let the tourists 'get an eyeful' once or twice a week." Eventually, Odile obtains a role in a Vance Murdock feature, and he "discovers" her. But she realizes that her love for him was not the real thing. She decides to commit herself to helping girls who like her come to Hollywood with a dream but no true vocation. She will live in "the *other* Hollywood . . . where the real houses are. And the little real hopes. And the little real people."

The reviewer in the *New York Times* (November 24, 1929) commented, "The situations of the narrative are not unduly exaggerated, but the author's injudicious mixture of sentimental romance and melodrama casts the whole story in an atmosphere of unreality, the principals standing out as grotesque and rather absurd caricatures against the rambling structure of the plot."

ELLIS PETERS is the pseudonym of Edith Mary Pargeter (born 1913) and is well known as the author of the series of twelfth-century mystery novels featuring Brother Cadfael, which began in 1977. In ***Morning Raga*** (William Morrow, 1970), the 14-year-old daughter of a divorced American movie star and a wealthy Indian goes to India for a reunion with her father. When she arrives, she discovers that her father has disappeared and that her mother is dying. A family friend who is working on a film in India takes care of the girl, who is promptly kidnapped. "More a travelogue of modern India, than a novel of suspense," sniffed A.J. Hubin in the *New York Times* (April 21, 1970).

GERALD PETIEVICH (born 1944). ***Shakedown*** (Simon & Schuster, 1988) begins with a successful extortion plot against an aging Hollywood movie star with an unusual sexual appetite, and that sets in motion a chain of events leading to the arrest of a Mafia boss in Las Vegas. A well-plotted thriller. Two previous novels by Petievich, ***To Die in Beverly Hills*** (Arbor House, 1983) and ***To Live and Die in L.A.*** (Arbor House, 1984), contain scenes set in Hollywood, but have no connection to the film industry.

JUDSON PHILIPS (born 1903) is better known as a writer under his pen name of Hugh Pentecost (q.v.). The muder of alcoholic movie star Molly Malone, beaten to death with her own Oscar, in ***The Dead Can't Love*** (Dodd, Mead, 1963) reveals a plot by Hollywood moguls to substitute a stand-in for the real actress, and to keep her under control by having her believe she murdered Malone's husband, when, in reality, it was Malone who committed the crime.

The author is not aware that there was a real film star, active in the silent era, named Molly Malone.

Private detective Peter Styles is featured in a series of Judson Philips novels. In *The Black Glass City* (Dodd, Mead, 1965), he is asked by a friend to come to his Connecticut estate where a film crew is on location and apparently out of control. The title refers to the dark glasses that members of the crew wear.

ANN PINCHOT has served as coauthor on two show business autobiographies, *Weep No More, My Lady*, by Mickey Deans, which told of his life with Judy Garland (1972), and *The Movies, Mr. Griffith, and Me*, by Lillian Gish (1969). The relationship between the two women working on the latter book was obviously not a totally amicable one, and Pinchot used the lives of Lillian and Dorothy Gish as the basis for her novel *Vanessa*. Shortly after the novel appeared, I was at a luncheon party with Lillian Gish, and Ann Pinchot's name came up in the conversation; with pursed lips, the actress commented, "I understand she is now writing pornography."

Vanessa (Arbor House, 1978) is certainly not pornographic, but it is exploitative. Vanessa and Cassandra (Cassie) Oxford are two children who become film stars under the guidance of director Joshua Fodor. Just as Vanessa and Cassandra are modeled on Lillian and Dorothy Gish, Fodor is obviously based on D.W. Griffith, and he is a pedophile. "The typical Fodor actress was thirteen years old and would never age, if she wanted to stay in his company." The younger sister Cassandra is dominated by Vanessa, and when she becomes pregnant is shipped off to Italy to have the child, just as Dorothy Gish went to Italy in the 1920s. Director Fodor is apparently lost at sea off the Florida coast, just as D.W. Griffith was briefly missing during a Florida storm in 1920. Fodor does not die but is found in a comatose state. Like her sister, Vanessa has him moved to Italy, where she takes care of him, assuming the dominant role in their relationship, just as he had once dominated her. Much has been made of Lillian Gish's controlling the life and career of her sister, and here author Pinchot has Cassandra Oxford own a portrait of her sister in the nude, with cashboxes where the breasts should be and an erect penis emerging from her nest of pubic hair.

Less entertaining and less obvious in its characterizations is *52 West* (Farrar, Straus & Cudahy, 1962). The title refers to the address of a New York boardinghouse where artists, musicians, and actors lodged. A group of 1930s boarders gather together in 1961 to help the owner out of her current financial problems, and among their number is an actress who became a starlet after posing in the nude; she contemplates suicide and has some of the same characteristics as Marilyn Monroe.

EVELYN PIPER. *The Stand-In* (David McKay, 1970) is a mystery novel of which Jackie Collins would be proud, but the difference between a Collins book and this one by Evelyn Piper is that, outrageous as the plot may be, it is also fascinating and engrossing. When Bran Collier was a child star at Paramount, his stand-in was Desmond Crossman, but as Bran grew up, Desmond was no longer needed, and, worse yet, his voice did not change with puberty. Desmond's mother decides to use her son's pretty looks and high-pitched voice to advantage and obtains a job for him as a female impersonator in New Orleans.

Eventually, the heterosexual Desmond makes it to London, where a doctor helps him lower his voice. Bran is now married to film star Coral Reid and is frustrated that his career is fading as hers is flowering. When Desmond is inadvertently ridiculed by Coral on the set of her new production in London, he decides to seek revenge, dressing as a nurse and kidnapping her daughter. But the day after the kidnapping, Desmond discovers that the girl is not Coral's daughter but her sister's daughter, who had been standing in for her cousin in the film. Desmond wants to return the girl, but his accomplice wants to kill her and obtain a ransom. In desperation, Desmond kills the accomplice and returns the girl to her mother. The mother recognizes Desmond and goes to nurse him after a suicide attempt. Meanwhile, Coral admits to her sister that the dead accomplice was Bran's father and the father of her child. When it first seemed that it was Coral and Bran's daughter who had been kidnapped, Bran was forced to sell the script of a film, which he wanted to direct and star in, to Coral's current director. Bran now becomes temporarily insane, believing, as does Coral, that he has murdered the accomplice. Desmond determinedly seeks him out at Bran's mother's house, but Bran accidentally shoots his mother and falls to his death from a cliff. Desmond would now appear to be free of the past and able to settle down with Coral's sister and the daughter he had kidnapped, the only two people who know he is a murderer.

It is difficult to believe that 20 years earlier, the same Evelyn Piper wrote *The Motive* (Simon & Schuster, 1950), a mystery novel very much of its day, confused in storyline and with characters who thrive on verbosity. It begins in a New York park, where an eccentric woman, walking her dog at night, finds what appears to be a homeless man, whom she takes home. The homeless man is, in reality, a famous Hollywood movie star, who has been forced quickly to leave the apartment of a female friend and, thus, is not adequately attired. When the woman is murdered, everyone but the movie star appears to have a motive, but it is, of course, the actor who is the culprit. After taking him back to her apartment, the woman tried to bed him, found he was impotent, and threatened to reveal his secret. The other principal character in the story is a Hollywood screenwriter, who shared the apartment with the woman, and returns to New York to try and identify her killer. The Evelyn Piper here is a pseudonym. Could it be that this Piper is not the same as the later novelist of the same name?

LUIGI PIRANDELLO (1867–1936) revolutionized world drama in 1921 with his play *Six Characters in Search of an Author*. Among his less than twenty works to be translated into English is ***Shoot! The Notebooks of Serafino Gubbio, Cinematograph Operator*** (E.P. Dutton, 1926), translated by C.K. Scott Moncrieff from the Italian *Si Gira*. The cinematographer/narrator is a party to the drama in the personal lives of the actors appearing in front of his camera, and those lives are recorded at times in an almost incoherent fashion. Contemporary reviews were mixed. "As a work of art, *Shoot!* is not merely bad, it is impossible," commented Edwin Muir in *The Nation and Atheneum* (February 19, 1927), while L.P. Hartley in *The Saturday Review* (January 29, 1927) found it "abstract, ingenious and a little arid."

JAMES S. POLLAK was a film industry executive who used his background knowledge to good effect in ***Golden Egg*** (Henry Holt, 1946), the chronicle of a Hollywood dynasty. "Pollak is obviously at home in a film studio, and his description of cutting and projection rooms, movie sets and commissaries and the cutters, scriptgirls, grips, and assistant directors gives us an accurate picture of the still not well enough known Hollywood proletariat," wrote Budd Schulberg in the *Saturday Review of Literature* (October 12, 1946). The literary worth of the novel was questioned by no less than Raymond Chandler in the *Atlantic Monthly* (January 1947): "To Mr. Pollak goes the satisfaction and I trust the reward of having written 493 pages of what some persons may regard as absorbing fiction. As a fellow oarsman in the long galley I regret that I may not be numbered among them."

ABRAHAM POLONSKY (born 1910) was a screenwriter who appeared as a hostile witness before the House Un-American Activities Committee in 1951 and was subsequently blacklisted by the film industry until 1967. While not a Hollywood novel per se, *A Season of Fear* (Cameron, 1956) deals with that period in American history as a California engineer, who has signed a loyalty oath, goes as far as burning all the books of his deceased brother-in-law who he is sure was a Communist. The publisher, Angus Cameron, was the former editor-in-chief at Little, Brown, and specialized in publishing books by blacklisted authors. This novel was not reviewed, in part, claims Polonsky, because of the press's fear of the blacklist.

DARRYL PONICSAN (born 1938) wrote *The Last Detail* (1970) and *Cinderella Liberty* (1973), as well as the screen adaptations of both books. *Tom Mix Died for Your Sins* (Delacorte Press, 1975) is a novel about the life of the colorful cowboy star, narrated by Kid Bandera, who supposedly first met Mix in 1904. The book concludes with Bandera's last meeting with the actor, the day of his death, described in a cold and detached, yet grimly emotional style. Ponicsan is a lively writer and aims for accuracy; for example, when recounting Mix's entry into films, he footnotes the page, indicating a 1927 *Ladies' Home Journal* article as the source. The novel is illustrated with photographs from Mix's career and also contains two pages of acknowledgments.

NANCY POPE. *Sentence of Youth* (Doubleday, 1936) examines the effects that the many marriages of a glamorous Hollywood star have on her son and daughter. Happily, the children are of stronger moral fiber than their mother. "As a sympathetic study of childhood and adolescence, the book is most successful in its earlier half. The latter part of Lyn's romance takes on a cinema air of unreality," commented Beatrice Sherman in the *New York Times* (September 13, 1936).

ZELDA POPKIN (1898–1983). Mildred Samuelson narrates *Dear Once* (J.B. Lippincott, 1975), the story of her family. She marries an actor who becomes celebrated for his gangster roles in the 1930s but is blacklisted during the McCarthy era. (The actor is presumably based on John Garfield.) Mildred continues with her life, despite her husband's premature death, determined to help the children succeed.

DARWIN PORTER (born 1937). *Marika* (Arbor House, 1977) is subtitled "a novel about one of the world's most shocking women," and the lady in question appears to be an amalgam of at least three screen legends. The first third of the novel concerns Marika Kreisler's early life in Germany and Poland, her marriage as a child to a Polish count, and her subsequent marriage to an Englishman whom she helps save in Belgium during World War I. When the English marriage turns sour, Marika travels to Vienna to live with her grandmother, whose lover stars her in a film he is making in which she appears nude. When a wealthy industrialist, whose mistress Marika becomes, sees the film, he tries to buy every copy (in an incident obviously borrowed from the early life of Hedy Lamarr). Marika has a child by the industrialist, but he is taken away from her and in later life becomes a transvestite, impersonating his by now famous mother. Marika moves on to Germany, where she meets Walter von Menzel (a character loosely based on Josef von Sternberg), who stars her in his film *Carnival*. As a result of that film's success, both von Menzel and Marika are signed to a Hollywood contract by M-G-M, with Louis B. Mayer making a brief appearance in the novel. In the United States, Marika creates a sensation by dressing in male attire (as did Marlene Dietrich), and (just as did Dietrich in *Morocco*) in her first Hollywood film, *Istanbul*, Marika dresses as a man and sings a love song to a woman. Hitler is entranced by Marika, and she is lured back to Germany, where she is unable to escape. She stars in an anti–Semitic drama, *Judes of Sodom*, is directed by Hitler's favorite female director, Lale Wessely (loosely based on Leni Riefenstahl), and is persuaded to dance nude for the Führer. Only Goebbels knows her secret—Marika is Jewish. He wants her killed, and Marika is able to escape from Germany only by faking her own death.

After the war, Marika is much despised for her anti–Jewish films, but survives thanks to the wealth and affection of an elderly lesbian, who takes care of her and ultimately makes Marika her heir (much as Pola Negri was cared for in later years). A new career opens up for Marika as an international concert star, noted for her ageless beauty and her stunning legs (again the Dietrich element). Her fans are usually gay, and she continues to have her detractors who recall her work in Nazi Germany.

The novel opens with the arrival in New York of Marika's cousin, who promptly disappears, never to return, and ends, very abruptly, with Marika's receiving an honor from the mayor. *Marika* is great fun in that the reader can match various incidents in its heroine's life with actual happenings in the lives of famous stars, but there is perhaps too much space devoted to the prefilm years, and far too little to the postwar years.

RICHARD S. (Scott) PRATHER (born 1921) wrote a series of paperback novels featuring Hollywood private eye Shell Scott, many of which seem preoccupied with nudity. In *The Cockeyed Corpse* (Fawcett Gold Medal, 1964), Scott is sent by a movie producer to a dude ranch in Arizona where a "nudie" titled *The Wild West* is being filmed and where a starlet has been murdered. According to Art Scott in *1001 Midnights* (Arbor House, 1986), the "climactic scene gives rise to that memorable line 'You won't believe this, but that rock just shot me in the ass!'"

THEODORE PRATT (born 1901). *Valley Boy* (Duell, Sloan and Pearce, 1946) is the story of a ten-year-old boy, Johnny Birch, who lives in Studio Village in the San Fernando Valley. The community is presumably named after Studio City, although there is little similarity between the two. Birch is an eccentric child whose best friend is Oscar the Sea Lion. Although there are vague connections between Johnny's neighbors and the film industry, the novel is basically a study of characters, interesting but perhaps a little disappointing in the ultimate inconclusive ending.

Miss Dilly Says No (Duell, Sloan and Pearce, 1945) is the story of 48-year-old Miss Dilly, a meek secretary to a producer at Superior Pictures, whose ambition is to write a screen story. When studios seek frantically to acquire the rights to her "Hollywood Diary," Miss Dilly realizes that reality is far removed from dreams. "A gentle farce on Hollywood foibles that aims to put the cinema circus in its place" was the opinion of *Kirkus* (January 1, 1945).

The Golden Sorrow (Fawcett, 1952) is identified by Carolyn See as a Hollywood novel.

JAY PRESSON (born 1922), also known as Jay Presson Allen, is a well-regarded screenwriter—*Marnie* (1964), *Cabaret* (1972), *Deathtrap* (1986), and others—and television writer—*Family* (1976–80), for example. Her best-known novel is *The Prime of Miss Jean Brodie* (1969), for which she also wrote the screenplay, and her first was *Spring Riot* (Rinehart, 1948). That novel is narrated by Kate Larson who "mothers" two Hollywood actors—Bubba Duncan and Destry March—while her actor-husband is working on the East Coast. A drunken Bubba runs down Destry with his car; she dies, his career is ruined, and he commits suicide. Kate Larson is happy to pack her bags and remove herself and her children from the negative environment of Hollywood. The reviewer in the *San Francisco Chronicle* (January 2, 1949) commented, "*Spring Riot* is filled with Hollywood color—Laurel Canyon, San Fernando Valley, Beverly, Culver, Laguna, Ciro's and so on. It is peopled with the benzadrine and hyper-thyroid set who desire only convertibles. It is supposed to be a mad, gay book with a tragic, bitter ending, and almost as real."

DON and SUE PRESTON. *Crazy Fox* (Prentice-Hall, 1981) is a parody on the Lone Ranger legend which begins in the 1860s. The hero, Jack Knight, vows always to wear a mask until he has avenged his name and captured outlaw John Wesley Hardin. The novel chronicles Knight's various adventures with Wild Bill Hickok, General Custer, Buffalo Bill, and others, until he is playing in a silent Western. Suddenly, the white stallion he is riding carries him over a cliff, and the director asks, "Who was that masked man?"

JACK PRESTON was the pseudonym of John Preston Buschlen. Little else is known of this character, believed to be Canadian, whose contribution to the Hollywood novel, while unacknowledged, was substantial. The only reference to Preston occurs in Jesse L. Lasky, Jr.'s autobiography, *Whatever Happened to Hollywood?* (1975). Lasky describes Preston thus: He "wore loose, worn-out clothing, had a breathless voice and the face of a fragile gargoyle. Hair sparse as mountain grass, live blue eyes, hands that darted in birdlike gestures and a smile warming the whole, wildly enthusiastic thin face. He looked as though he might not have long to live."

Preston hired Lasky, Jr., as a hack writer of novels for the Macaulay Company, for which Preston apparently wrote potboilers. He and his wife owned an apartment building on Vista Street in Hollywood, and took Lasky in as both a writer and a boarder. Preston is described as a "fanatical writing machine," and since the Macaulay Company published numerous Hollywood novels in the late 1920s and early 1930s, information on whose authors is nonexistent, it may be that some of those authors were no more than pseudonyms of John Preston Buschlen.

Preston's most prominent novel, **Heil! Hollywood** (Reilly & Lee, 1939), is a convoluted and badly written effort that defends the film industry, while pointing out some of its excesses, against attacks from anti–Semitic forces, including a semisecret organization (presumably the German-American Bund) and a rabble-rousing Catholic priest (presumably Father Coughlin). In his foreword, the author begins, "I am not a Jew," and goes on to suggest that forces promoting animosity within American society can be defeated by "adoption of the Golden Rule, stream-lined and supercharged.... Persons, nations, races, make such a staggering job of being decent to one another." He continues, "Whatever philosophy this book may have is a product of my association with a World of Others in the melting pot that is Hollywood."

The novel opens as a brilliant, neurotic former studio head, Adolph Merripp, summons six members of the film industry, all of whom he believes to have wronged him in some way, to his house. They sit down together at dinner and the host asks each of the guests to drop a pellet (supposedly medication) in his wine glass. The host toasts his guests, drinks the wine, and dies of strychnine poisoning. The six men, who have been set up by Merripp, would appear to have little to fear, but agitation against them is fomented by anti–Semitic individuals, who also use as ammunition in their anti–Hollywood campaign a second death, that of a Hollywood agent, in which an aspiring actress and a British screenwriter are involved. To fight the forces of anti–Semitism, one of the six, a young Jewish studio executive named Matthew (Matty) Abraham Gallin, convenes a rally at which it is resolved:

> We request the chief executive to name a Commission with full power to act in an investigation of conditions in the motion picture business with a purpose to remove evils that exist and as a guarantee to the people of the nation that no power inimical to the wellbeing of America ever be permitted to find a voice in this great motion picture medium, and that the industry shall now and hereafter consider itself an instrument of public welfare and conduct itself accordingly, in reality and not in word only.

The book concludes with Gallin's marriage to the would-be actress, a Gentile, and his reading to her part of Paul's letter to the Romans, in which the saint asks, "What advantage then hath the Jew? or what profit is there of circumcision?"

While attacking anti–Semitism, the author does not defend the film industry. He is critical of its self-regulating governing body, an organization now known as the Motion Picture Association of America and here given a fictitious name. He paints an unpleasant picture of many studio executives. His hero is the idealistic young producer/executive Matty Gallin, to whom the book is dedicated, and who may perhaps be based on Irving Thalberg, often credited with an undocumented idealistic approach to filmmaking.

Unfortunately, the novel is confused. Is it attacking anti–Semitism or a film industry out of control? The picture the author paints of the industry is a relatively sordid one, and it was that aspect rather than anti–Semitism that contemporary critics noted in their generally negative reviews. Writing in the *New York Herald Tribune Books* (April 23, 1939), Lisle Bell commented, "His scenario takes in all the industry's sins from murder to block booking, covering everything—including the reader—with confusion." Similarly, Robert Gelder wrote in the *New York Times* (April 23, 1939), "Mr. Preston attempts to handle about six times as many people as he has room for. It is obvious that he is familiar with his scene and it may be that Hollywood could stand a housecleaning. Certainly this book contains some mightily disgusting stories. But they are offered as fiction. And judged as fiction this novel is not a success."

Seven years prior to *Heil! Hollywood*, Preston published **Screen Star** (Doubleday, Doran, 1932). The novel may well be considered a precursor to the Jackie Collins style of Hollywood novels, daring enough for its day to have a Hollywood actress find her actor boyfriend in bed with his boyfriend. Simplistic in plot development, *Screen Star* is the story of Hollywood leading lady Lira Morgan. She meets a Canadian rancher named John Massey and, against the wishes of her mother, marries him and moves to his ranch. Before long she tires of the farming life, and Massey does not object when she asks to return to Hollywood. Massey subsequently sells his ranch and buys acreage in Arizona, close enough for his wife to spend the weekends with him.

What lifts the novel above the ordinary are the many obscure Hollywood anecdotes provided by the author and the number of references to real members of the film industry. The book even includes a four-page index to such characters. The novel features a party given by actress Mary Brian, with whom presumably the author was friendly. In an effort to identify Preston/Buschlen, I asked Miss Brian if she had any remembrance of the man—she had none.

J. (Joseph) B. (Boynton) PRIESTLEY (1894–1984). Many works by this major British novelist and playwright have been filmed, including *The Old Dark House* (1932, 1963), *The Good Companions* (1933), *Sing as We Go* (1934), and *An Inspector Calls* (1954).

In **Albert Goes Through** (Harper, 1933), a young English clerk has a crush on a screen star. While on medication for the flu, he passes out in the middle of one of her films; dreams of playing the hero opposite her in a variety of productions, all with the same plot; gets tired of her; and wakes up to realize he is in love with a girl at the office.

A successful English writer who has worked for many years in Hollywood goes to a Cornish hotel to complete a script in **Bright Day** (Harper, 1946). He begins to reminisce about his early life in Yorkshire and meets a woman with the idealism and enthusiasm that he once had. His future is obviously with her and not in Hollywood. The novel was reprinted in 1966 by E.P. Dutton with a new introduction by Priestley.

MANUEL PUIG (1932–90) burst on the American publishing scene with his first novel, *Betrayed by Rita Hayworth* (E.P. Dutton, 1971), translated from the Spanish by Suzanne Jill Levine. Alexander Coleman, writing in the *New York Times* (September 26, 1971), announced that Puig "has written a masterpiece ... a dazzling and wholly original debut." The story is concerned with the filmgoing experience, as the inhabitants of the bleak flatland pampas of the Argentine escape from the boredom and hopelessness of their lives through the movies, responding to what they see on the screen in the 1930s and 1940s films of Rita Hayworth, Shirley Temple, Tyrone Power, and others. The novel is narrated by a boy named Toto, born in 1942. *Betrayed by Rita Hayworth* was first published in Buenos Aires in 1968.

Transformed into both a successful musical and a film, *Kiss of the Spider Woman* (Alfred A. Knopf, 1979), translated from the Spanish by Thomas Colchie, is a relatively simple tale of two men in an Argentine prison. One is a homosexual window dresser named Molina and the other a Marxist student named Valentin. As the prison guards try to make the two betray each other, Molina entertains Valentin by recounting the plots of his favorite Hollywood movies.

As Robert Coover wrote in the *New York Times* (April 22, 1979), "It is Mr. Puig's fascination with old movies that largely provides [the book's] substance and ultimately defines its plot, its shape. What we hear are the voices of two suffering men, alone in the dark, but what we see are panther women and zombies, exotic settings (a lot of finely perceived detail, especially about fashion) and fabulous metamorphoses.... But other than these film synopses, there's not much here."

NINA WILCOX PUTNAM (1888–1962) wrote many books, including *Laughing Through, Being the Autobiographical Story of a Girl Who Made Her Way* (Sears Publishing, 1930). A number of her works were adapted for the screen, including *Sitting Pretty* and *A Lady's Profession* (both 1934).

Just before she leaves New York to work in Hollywood in *West Broadway* (George H. Doran, 1921), actress Marie La Tour is warned by a Greenwich Village anarchist that America is on the verge of revolution. The actress decides to travel across the country to see if America really is in trouble and to preach against Communism. West Broadway is the nickname for the highway that runs from Bowling Green, New York, to the Golden Gate, San Francisco. The critic for the *New York Times* (December 18, 1921) commented, "To an age of literature where 'to amuse' is essentially low brow and 'to depress' the main goal, this book comes like a refreshing breed."

Bonnie McFadden believes she has a Hollywood contract and comes to the film capital from New England in *Laughter Unlimited* (George H. Doran, 1922). Once in Hollywood, she becomes a maid, but her basic honesty and puritan-like decency overcome the evils of the city.

NICK QUARRY. *Till It Hurts* (Fawcett, 1960) is identified by Carolyn See as a Hollywood novel.

ELLERY QUEEN was the pseudonym of Frederic Dannay (1905–82) and Manfred B. Lee (1905–71), and is also the name of the popular mystery writer and amateur sleuth who has been appearing in short stories and novels since 1929; the series continues with a new group of writers. Queen first came to Hollywood in 1938 in *The Devil to Pay* (Frederick Stokes, 1938), in which he helped the confused local police solve a murder that was not related to the film industry. While working in Hollywood in *The Four of Hearts* (Frederick Stokes, 1938), Queen became involved in a notorious film industry feud and also solved a double murder. Again in Hollywood for *The Origin of Evil* (Little, Brown, 1951), Queen investigated a murder instigated by a dead dog's being left on the victim's doorstep. These three novels were gathered together in one volume as *The Hollywood Murders* (J.B. Lippincott, 1957).

PATRICK QUENTIN was the pseudonym of Richard Wilson Webb and Wheeler Hugh Callingham (1912–87). Obsessive son Nickie begins to wonder if his Hollywood screen star mother, Anny Rood, is a murderer in *Suspicious Circumstances* (Simon & Schuster, 1957), when two actresses with whom she is competing for a starring role are murdered. The killer proves to be Nickie's uncle who is in reality his stepfather and who has murdered before in order to help Anny Rood's rise to stardom. "It's all bright and gay and foolish, full of amusing characters (not all of them fictional) and vividly lighted glimpses of show business in Hollywood, Las Vegas and Cannes.... You'll find there's a solid story of suspense and detection underlying the whole charming extravaganza," wrote Anthony Boucher in the *New York Times* (December 15, 1957).

STEPHEN RABLEY. *Future Attractions* (Armada, 1989) is the third, and representative, novel in the "Media Crew" series of books for teenage readers in Britain, featuring a group of media students at London's Portobello Sixth Form College. The students are involved in two projects here: a comparison of media coverage of AIDS in the United Kingdom and the United States, and the saving of the local Gaumont Cinema, scheduled for redevelopment. The latter project brings a thriller-like atmosphere to the novel; the author is also able to dispel some of the myths surrounding the AIDS epidemic and show those suffering from the illness in a positive light. Neither storyline overwhelms the basic plot, which concerns the various relationships among the students, and no neat endings or solutions are offered. The Gaumont is destroyed by fire, and a budding romance between one of the students and an AIDS worker ends in their parting. The writing is professional and engrossing, with the only dissimilarity between the students here and those in real life being the absence of four-letter words and references to drug use.

DOTSON RADER (born 1942). The central character in *The Dream's on Me* (G.P. Putnam's Sons, 1976) is Paul McFarland, a successful screenwriter, whose wife takes their son and leaves him. The wife and son are killed in a car crash, and McFarland seeks out a woman named Jessie whom he met in a bar and with whom he would like to rebuild a relationship.

PAUL RADER. According to Carolyn See, *Big Bug* (Fleming H. Revell, 1932) is "a religious, 'evangelical' work [that] depicts Hollywood as being not only a center of sin but of possible salvation."

IRIS RAINER. *The Boys in the Mailroom* (William Morrow, 1980) offers an intriguing storyline as it follows four young men from the beginnings of their working lives in the mailroom of Hemisphere Studios (obviously based on Universal). There is an amusing incident early in the novel as the boys invent a director and issue memoranda concerning him in order to get "perks" for themselves. One of the four becomes a studio executive, another a record promoter and manager, a third a concert promoter, and the fourth eventually a well-known actor. The book concludes with the shooting death of the last, just after he has achieved stardom, and the remaining three meet at his funeral. It is a bitter ending for what is generally a light-hearted romp.

MILTON M. (Michael) RAISON (born 1903). When Hollywood celebrity Jimmie Melville is found murdered in *Nobody Loves a Dead Man* (Murray & Gee, 1945), the initial reaction is that it was a suicide, although many in the film community welcome Melville's passing. One of the suspects is a New York drama critic, and, in order to prove his innocence, he joins forces with Lieutenant Holden of the Los Angeles Police Department to solve the crime. The *Saturday Review of Literature* (November 24, 1945) described this as a "rather confusing jamboree of crime, cinema cuties, and various varieties of intrigue."

ANNE RAMPLING is the pseudonym of Anne Rice (born 1941), and the pen name is usually used for her semipornographic novels. The narrator of *Belinda* (Arbor House, 1986) is Jeremy Walker, a writer and illustrator of children's books that have formed the basis for both television series and movies. He is seduced by Belinda, a 16-year-old runaway, whose past in Hollywood was intertwined with that of a sex kitten. "Walker's first-person narrative is erotic and strong with bursts of artistic passion, but it's bogged down with detailed background exposition and resolution," wrote Michele Leber in *Library Journal* (November 1, 1986). "And art and truth, as moral issues, take a back seat to eroticism."

ROBERT RAMSEY. *Fiesta* (John Day, 1955) is basically the story of life in a small Mexican town. The central character is servant Antonio who becomes infatuated with movie actress Consuela and moves with her to Mexico City. He finds her as dominating as his former boss, but through a triumph in the bull ring, he is able to return to his native town and marry his sweetheart. "Mr. Ramsey's novel is authentic," commented Lou Tinkle in the *Saturday Review of Literature* (November 12, 1955). "It is not about the author's own experience. It hews to Mexican experience, and the author's experience is sensed only as a conscience at work. This is a reassuring sort of presence."

GREG RANDOLF. In *Sex Goddess* (Neva Paperbacks, 1962), a construction worker has an affair with a Hollywood sex goddess. The two are married. The man has a couple of affairs, but each time he is drawn back to his wife. Noteworthy primarily for the graphic sex scenes.

STEPHEN RANSOME was the pseudonym of Frederick Davis (1902–77). When educational film producer Hugo Sandor is kidnapped while on location in Florida, his assistant, Dick Craig, raises the ransom and solves the crime in **Meet in Darkness** (Dodd, Mead, 1964).

FREDERICK RAPHAEL (born 1931). The central character in **California Time** (Henry Holt, 1976) is a British director named Victor England, who is brought to Hollywood, described as "a city without a center which has spawned a morality without a structure." Nothing appears to bother England as he wanders through love affairs, marriages, studio upheavals, and even a few murders. "Raphael destroys normal plot development and aims for the metaphysical. He fails through sheer boredom and a pervasive cynicism, not to mention an unbearably consistent use of pretentious puns. It's unfortunate: there is an obvious literate intelligence at work, but the entire effort seems dreadfully exaggerated, misdirected, and needlessly obscure," wrote Thomas D. Bedell in *Library Journal* (April 15, 1976).

PHYLLIS RAPHAEL (born 1940). *They Got What They Wanted* (W.W. Norton, 1972) is the story of a well-to-do couple, she an actress and screenwriter, he a producer, whose lives are empty and their marriage a failure. The two basic themes here are alienation and liberation.

HERMAN RAUCHER (born 1928) is the author of *Summer of '42* (1971), as well as writer of the film version (1971) and its sequel, *Class of '44* (1972). His other screenplays include *Watermelon Man* (1970), *Ode to Billy Joe* (1976), and *The Other Side of Midnight* (1977). **There Should Have Been Castles** (Delacorte Press, 1978) is a raunchy and entertaining novel that begins in 1949 when would-be writer Ben Webber comes to New York. The book is narrated alternately by Webber and dancer Ginnie Maitland. Webber obtains work at 20th Century–Fox (where Raucher worked from 1950 to 1954), and he and Ginnie eventually meet after he becomes a successful screenwriter. Their relationship blossoms until Ginnie finds Ben in bed with her mother. Eventually, all ends happily.

SIMON RAVEN (born 1927). **Come Like Shadows** (Blond & Briggs, 1972) is the eighth novel in the "Alms for Oblivion" series, which began in 1964 with *The Rich Pay Late* and ended in 1976 with *The Last Survivors*. Here the central character, novelist Fielding Gray, is hired to revise the script of a film version of *The Odyssey* being shot on Corfu. The film is financed by the Oglander-Finckelstein Trust administered by Montana University, and left-wing student activities at the university lead to demands that the classic be modernized with a social bent; the leading lady, a wicked parody of Vanessa Redgrave, is asked by the university to oversee the production and ensure that it is politically correct. Meanwhile, Fielding Gray becomes greedy, tries to blackmail the producer, using his old over the actress, and ends up incarcerated in an institution run by the Greek junta. He is eventually rescued by his publisher.

Simon Raven is one of Britain's great, and relatively undiscovered, contemporary novelists, with a fine ear and eye for the class system and its product. His characters are always fascinating and often sexually ambiguous. The "Alms for Oblivion" novels are linked by these characters who have, as Raven points out, many commonalities: "Soldiers, dons, men of business, politicians, writers and plain shits are drawn, in the main, from the Upper and Upper-Middle Classes," and for each the author has a curious blend of affection and contempt. While *Come Like Shadows* stands in its own right, true enjoyment of the Fielding Gray novels can be obtained only by reading the series in sequence.

CHARLES RAY (1891–1943) was a major star of the silent screen, specializing in youthful bucolic roles. As his ego grew, so did his determination to appear in more sophisticated parts. Audiences rejected Charles Ray's new image, and by the late 1920s his career was in considerable decline. The actor probably financed the following book in an effort to keep his name in front of both Hollywood producers and the public. The stories in *Hollywood Shorts: Compiled from Incidents in the Everyday Life of Men and Women Who Entertain in Pictures* (California Graphic Press, 1935) are not badly written, nor are they particularly entertaining or exciting.

In "Once a Baby," a director needs a baby for a movie scene. A star double is hurt in "The Double's Cross." A dramatist follows the talkies to Hollywood in "A Writer's Carp." A sick mother and a desperate need give a father the courage to pretend he is a "Stunt Man." The phrase "Sans Tarte" confuses the makers of slapstick comedies. "Adieu Hollywood" is a suicide's note. An animal trainer tries his hand at "Chickens." "The Stand-In" reveals Charles Ray is "just a girl with makeup on, never to be photographed." M-G-M means Mighty-Good-Mice to "The Studio Cat." An English actor is cut from a film in "Vanity." A "Sour Puss" becomes a comedian. A producer deals with Will Hays in "Tarzan Clutches." In "a Jump into Prominence," an actress jumps to her death and receives more publicity than she did when she was alive. "Exit Alley" has a little man asking for an autograph. "Gorgeous" is the name of an actress promoted by a high-powered publicist. "It Stinks" is the outburst at a scenario conference. An actor elopes with an unknown from Hoboken in "Glamor Afar." "An Old Spanish Custom" involves the making of a Spanish-language film. In "Outward Bound" an author tries to sell a story to a producer. A preview audience dislikes a film in "Quickie." "Hearty" has a boxing theme. A scene is reshot in "Sound and Silence." While waiting for a call from central casting, an actor counts "Windows." In "An Actress and How" a girl from Indianapolis says she wants to be an actress in "the worst way" and so is sent to Hollywood. "Unseen Faces" reveals the dialogue from various booths in a Hollywood café at 4:00 A.M. A prominent actor offers a woman a lift in his car in "As Told at the Masquers Club." The surprise in "Murder at the Studio" is that the actor the audience suspected at the start really did it. "Screwy" is a reference to screenwriters who provide actors with screwy dialogue.

CLAIRE RAYNER (born 1931). *Shaftesbury Avenue* (Weidenfeld and Nicholson, 1983) is the tenth novel in "The Performers," a family saga that began in 1973 with *Gower Street*. Set in 1919, the story involves shell-shocked Theo Caspar, who is persuaded to become a screen actor by director/producer Letty Lackland. The novel's climax has Casper coming to terms with his homosexuality and realizing the irony of his being mobbed by lovesick female fans. The coverage of the British film industry is slight, despite an acknowledgment to British film historian Rachael Low, and the novel's chief originality in the area of motion pictures is to embrace as a principal character a female director at a time when none was active in British film production. The storyline is very much in the style of a "Masterpiece Theatre" drama, and undemonstrative; even Casper's sexual preference, which is soon obvious to the reader, is discussed in veiled terms, and the word *homosexual* is not once mentioned.

JOHN RECHY (born 1934) gained immediate prominence in 1963 with the publication of his first novel, *City of the Night*, and its agonizing vision of homosexuality. The tragic life of Marilyn Monroe is rehashed in *Marilyn's Daughter* (Carroll & Graf, 1988). When her supposed mother, a one-time Hollywood starlet, dies, Normalyn Morgan discovers a letter claiming her real mother was Marilyn Monroe. She travels to Hollywood, determined to recreate the secret lives of Monroe and the woman she thought of as mother, Enid Morgan. As this extremely long novel progresses, the possibility emerges that Normalyn's father is Robert Kennedy, and a strange teenage cult group obsessed with Hollywood scandals becomes interested in Normalyn's quest. Ultimately, she realizes that the most important truth of all is that "Norma Jean" be allowed to rest in peace.

IONE REED *see* **ROSE GORDON and IONE REED**

TOMLIN REED. *Call Me Mistress* (Midwood Publications, 1948) is one of a series of novels with a Hollywood background, identified by Carolyn See as semipornographic. No other information is available.

ARTHUR J. (John) REES (1872–1942). *Tragedy at Twelvetrees* (Dodd, Mead, 1931) is a mystery novel involving the murder of an English woman in a film studio housed on a residential property (not that unusual in Britain). The killing was apparently accidental, but that is not revealed until a considerable amount of scandal has been unearthed.

ARTHUR BENJAMIN REEVE (1880–1936) collaborated on the scripts of many early serials featuring Ruth Roland, Houdini, and others. Many of his Craig Kennedy mystery novels were also filmed. In *The Film Mystery* (Harper, 1921), the detective Kennedy investigates the murder of movie star Stella Lamar in front of the camera. The author provides a first-hand impression of silent filmmaking.

ADRIAN REID. A 54-year-old British screenwriter becomes infatuated and has an affair with his 14-year-old goddaughter in *The Goddaughter: A Romance* (Rawson Associates, 1977). The screenwriter's wife is a costume designer.

RON RENAUD. Eric Binford, the antihero of *Fade to Black* (Pinnacle Books, 1980), is the ultimate movie buff. He lives with his wheelchair-bound aunt in Venice, California, tapes movies on television all the while, collects 16mm prints, and is a habitué of Larry Edmunds Bookstore. "In his room and in the movie theatre were the only places where Eric felt he truly belonged, where he was among real friends and family. The movies had raised him, taught him all he knew. Just like Peter Sellers in *Being There*. Almost." The constant nagging of his aunt, whom it transpires is really his mother, leads to Eric's pushing her and her wheelchair down the stairs, in imitation of Richard Widmark in *Kiss of Death*. He meets a Marilyn Monroe look-alike, whom he stalks, while killing various people who have hurt him in one fashion or another. The climax of the novel takes place at Grauman's Chinese Theatre. Eric has brought Marilyn the look-alike there while he is in the guise of the James Cagney character, Cody Jarrett, in *White Heat*. Standing on the roof of the theater, he is brought down in a hail of sharpshooter bullets, his last words being, of course, "Top o' the world, Ma!" The novel was filmed in 1980, under the direction of Vernon Zimmerman, with Dennis Christopher as Eric Binford.

JEANE RENICK. *Always* (HarperCollins, 1993) features Marielle McCleary, who desperately wants a baby, and movie star Thomas Saxon, who decides that he will be the perfect sperm donor. There used to be a phrase, "Only in the movies..." Perhaps it should be changed to "Only in the romantic novel..."

MACK REYNOLDS. *This Time We Love* (Monarch Books, 1962) is one of a series of novels with a Hollywood background identified by Carolyn See as semipornographic. No other information is available.

CHARLES REZNIKOFF (1894–1976). *The Manner Music* (Black Sparrow Press, 1977) is set during the Depression and is the story of a musician in Hollywood and New York whose talents are unrecognized during his lifetime. The book contains an introduction by Robert Creeley, and the manuscript was found in the author's papers after his death.

HARI RHODES (born 1932). In *The Hollow and the Human* (Vantage Press, 1976), a Chicago journalist is assigned to interview a group of successful black actors and actresses in Hollywood, and gradually becomes personally involved in their lives.

JODI RHODES. *Winners and Losers* (Jove, 1983) has as its heroine a Hollywood producer named Erin Connolly who at the age of 30 sees her lover shoot himself. In flashback, Connolly examines her life: separation from her husband and son in favor of a Hollywood career, one lover after another to help build that career, an Oscar, a Porsche, and the inevitable cocaine addiction.

CRAIG RICE was the pseudonym of mystery novelist Georgiana Ann Randolph (1908–57), who ghostwrote three novels attributed to Hollywood personalities. For Gypsy Rose Lee, she wrote *The G-String Murders* (Simon & Schuster, 1941) and *Mother Finds a Body* (Simon & Schuster, 1942); and for George Sanders, she ghosted *Crime on My Hands* (Simon & Schuster, 1944). In 1942 she introduced two characters, Ringo Biggs and Handsome Kusak, who were street photographers, in *The Sunday Pigeon Murders*. Started by Rice and finished after her death by Ed McBain (pseudonym of Evan Hunter, born 1926),

The April Robin Murders (Simon & Schuster, 1958) has the two men in Hollywood, investigating what really did happen to "old" movie star April Robin.

ELMER L. (Leonard) RICE (1892–1967). *Voyage to Purilia* (Cosmopolitan, 1930) is a satire on the film industry. The novel takes readers on a plane trip to Purilia, which would appear to be a Hollywood creation where the inhabitants behave in a standardized fashion and in accord with an impersonal voice, the Presence. They have no digestive or reproductive organs, and the act of marriage results in a blissful smile and total annihilation. "Unfortunately, the hackneyed devices of producers at Hollywood do not provide enough material for 288 pages of sober irony, and Mr. Rice did not make us laugh," wrote the critic in *Saturday Review* (September 13, 1930).

DONNA RICHARDS. *Hollywood Lesbian* (France Books, 1963) is one of a series of novels with a Hollywood background identified by Carolyn See as semipornographic. No other information is available.

MORDECAI RICHLER (born 1931). Jacob "Jake" Hersh is a successful Jewish film and television director, living in London with his wife and children in *St. Urbain's Horseman* (Alfred A. Knopf, 1971). His problem is that he feels he should have been involved in conflicts and causes, such as the Spanish civil war, Korea, and Vietnam, like his cousin, but when he does try to get involved, there is only disaster. As L.J. Davis wrote in *Book World*, this is "a book about getting older and making compromises and missing chances that will never come again."

HOWARD RIGSBY (born 1909). Hollywood star Laura Robbins seeks seclusion at a northern California inn in *Calliope Reef* (Doubleday, 1967). A Hollywood producer with contract in hand pursues; accidents, murders, and international intrigue follow.

SIMON RITCHIE is the pseudonym of Simon R. Fodden (born 1944). In *Work for a Dead Man* (Charles Scribner's Sons, 1989), Ritchie's maverick detective, J.K.G. Jantarro is hired by Hollywood producer/director Alan Laki to find out how his wife managed to spend a quarter of a million dollars in a few weeks. When Laki is discovered dead, Jantarro loses a client but has a new job— finding his killer.

STU RIVERS. *The Casting Couchers* (Art Enterprises, 1961) is one of a series of novels with a Hollywood background, identified by Carolyn See as semipornographic. No other information is available.

HENRY H. ROBBES. Members of the Hollywood social set face the typical problems of jealousy and marital disputes in *Hollywood Episode* (Dorrance, 1946).

HAROLD ROBBINS is the pseudonym of Harold Robin (born 1916), who describes himself as "the best novelist alive." That title is largely based on his sales figures, with more than 250 million of his books in print, *The Carpetbaggers* alone having sold more than 8 million copies.

The Dream Merchants (Alfred A. Knopf, 1949) is the story of Johnny Edge and his financial backer, Peter Kessler, and their rise from nickelodeons in Rochester, New York, to short filmmaking in New York, and feature film production in Hollywood. It is the first in Robbins's Hollywood trilogy, which was to continue with *The Carpetbaggers* and *The Inheritors*. *The Carpetbaggers* (Simon & Schuster, 1961) concentrates on five characters: Jonas Cord, an industrialist whose interests include film production; Rina Marlow, a film star whom Cord wants to marry; Nevada Smith, who had taken care of Cord as a child and has been a Western star in silent films; David Woolf, Cord's partner in film production; and Jennie Benton, whom Cord is building up as a star after her earlier career as a Hollywood hooker. The novel was filmed by Joseph E. Levine for Paramount release in 1964, directed by Edward Dmytryk, and starring George Peppard, Alan Ladd, Bob Cummings, and Martha Hyer. *The Inheritors* (Trident/Simon & Schuster, 1969) presents the story of San Benjamin, who is trying to make a name for himself in films, and Steven Grant, who makes it big in television. Much of the novel concerns itself with the latter's activities with various ladies in various beds.

Where Love Has Gone (Trident/Simon & Schuster, 1962) is a roman à clef based on the killing of gangster Johnny Stompanato by Lana Turner's daughter, Cheryl Crane, in 1958. Here, the mother is a sculptor, the Stompanato character is having an affair with both the mother and the daughter, and it is the mother whom the girl is trying to kill.

The Lonely Lady (Simon & Schuster, 1976) is JeriLee Randall, a massage parlor hostess, starlet, and topless dancer, who writes an Academy Award–winning screenplay. The novel is dedicated to Jacqueline Susann.

The Storyteller (Simon & Schuster, 1986) documents the rise to fame of a budding writer, from Brooklyn in 1942 to Hollywood. David Finkle in the *New York Times* (January 26, 1986) suggested as more appropriate titles "The Draft Dodger," "The Pimp," or "The Best-Selling Author."

LES ROBERTS (born 1937) has authored a series of mystery novels featuring Saxon (no first name given), a Hollywood actor who moonlights as a private investigator. Saxon was introduced in **Not Enough Horses** (St. Martin's Press, 1987), in which he uncovers the murderer of a bit actor and part-time male prostitute. *Not Enough Horses* was followed by **An Infinite Number of Monkeys** (St. Martin's Press, 1987), **A Carrot for the Donkey** (St. Martin's Press, 1989), **Snake Oil** (St. Martin's Press, 1990), and **Seeing the Elephant** (St. Martin's Press, 1992).

NORA ROBERTS (born 1950) is a prolific romance novelist. In **Captivated** (Silhouette, 1950), screenwriter hero Nash Kirkland thinks self-proclaimed witch Morgana Donovan would be a perfect "resource" for his next horror film. With such a silly notion on Kirkland's part, how could romance or bewitchment not be far behind?

VIRGINIA ROBERTS is the pseudonym of Nell Marr Dean (born 1910). **Nurse on Location** (Avalon Books/Thomas Bouregy, 1958) is the story of nurse Patricia Taylor, ministering to a Hollywood film crew on location in Fiji. She gets involved with native superstition when her medicine fails to save the life of a local child.

JILL ROBINSON (born 1936) is the daughter of Hollywood producer/ writer Dore Schary, and has written two autobiographical works, *With a Cast of Thousands: A Hollywood Childhood* (1963, as Jill Schary) and *Bed/Time/Story* (1974). Her family background must, presumably, have influenced Robinson in the writing of *Perdido* (Alfred A. Knopf, 1978). The title refers to one of the stately homes of Hollywood where narrator Susanna Howard lives with her parents—the father is a major Hollywood producer with his own studio—and grandmother. Early in the story, which begins in 1950 and ends a decade later, the teenager discovers that she is, in reality, the illegitimate daughter of handsome leading man Jackson Lane. She enjoys one wonderful day in his company, and when abruptly he leaves Hollywood, she crosses the country in search of him. A second meeting is brief as he rushes to catch a plane to Europe, but in the novel's final pages, the two are reunited. Along the way, Susanna's actoruncle is forced to leave the United States and work abroad as a result of accusations by the House Un-American Activities Committee; he dies in Europe. His daughter Val, Susanna's best friend, is killed in a car crash at almost the exact moment Susanna is having a sexual encounter with Val's husband. Her parents are forced to sell Perdido, and Susanna has a son by an unhappy marriage to an old boyfriend, whose father was once also the head of a studio.

In ironic and wry fashion, Robinson tells what it is like to be a Hollywood daughter with a famous studio head as a "father." In the early stages of the novel, there are many witty comments, a suggestion, for example, that Rhonda Fleming should be put in all of Rory Calhoun's movies, which would then be run in Azusa. Gilbert Roland and Cesar Romero appear briefly together playing polo, and of the latter Val says, "Notice how the smile moves by itself, not the attention, but just the smile—like a searchlight." Ethel Barrymore puts in an appearance at a funeral: "She wheezes, but with elegance, as though she had inhaled the dust of one hundred thousand velvet theatre curtains from the real stages where she used to act before she was a movie star."

At one point, a friend of Susanna mentions that she has delivered a remarkable parody of what the public would expect the Hollywood child to say, and this is a valid comment on the first third of the novel—but what a brilliant parody it is. Unfortunately, the book makes an abrupt turn and gets relatively serious in the search for Susanna's father and in a surprisingly frank and explicit discussion of a marriage in which the husband has lost interest in sex. The first third is strictly a Hollywood novel, but the remainder is something else—a work of literary worth.

MARTHA ROBINSON. *Continuity Girl* (Robert Hale, 1937) begins with the author's description of British film production in the 1930s, explaining, "This book has for its background a British film studio under the conditions I have briefly sketched as having existed generally during 1932 to 1935, and still existing (sad to relate) in most of the independent companies in England to-day. Against this background I have attempted to record my impressions as a continuity girl in a strange world where, though everything is synthetic, the individuals are still real—and earnest." A continuity, or script, girl vouches for continuity in a film by recording the particulars of each shot and assuring that details match from scene to scene, and while *Continuity Girl* is supposedly a novel it is really little more than an autobiographical sketch by Martha Robinson, documenting her work with various minor British film personalities, including Anthony Kimmins, Ivar Campbell, John Baxter, Frank Launder, Will Fyffe, and Ralph Ince. Just as the author seems unsure whether she is writing a novel or an autobiography, she is equally uncertain as to her readership—adults or children.

CLARISSA ROCK. *Only Make Believe* (W.W. Norton, 1980) is a romantic novel set in the Hollywood of the 1920s, with references to many personalities of the decade.

PHILLIP ROCK (born 1927) is the son of Joe Rock, who began as a comedian in silent films and later became a minor producer in Hollywood and England. *Flickers* (Dodd, Mead, 1977) begins in 1920 with Warren Harding's election as president and ends shortly after Harding's death. From vaudeville, con man Earl Donovan, fat comic Billy Wells, and ingenue Mae Pepper come to Hollywood. Donovan marries Doll Fairbaine, a major Hollywood star obviously based on Mary Pickford, whose brother Niles (based on the much-maligned Jack Pickford) is a wastrel. Wells is teamed with a prominent comedian named Tom Pipp, and he pays to bring out Mae Pepper, with whom Pipp falls in love but who has an affair with Donovan. Because of an oil-related scandal, producer Vardon Bolling loses control of his studio, and Donovan is appointed its new head. Doll Fairbaine finds God and ends her career. The story is told through the use of flashbacks and an oral history with Donovan in later years, in which he more than exaggerates the truth. The novel is highly entertaining and offers a fairly realistic portrait of silent filmmaking.

VINGIE E. (Eve) ROE (1879–1958). *Monsieur of the Rainbow* (Doubleday, Page, 1926) is Monsieur de Bon Coeur, an aged Frenchman, who roams around California playing his accordion and searching for the end of the rainbow. At the book's close, he has brought together a screen star and an ex-soldier, and has himself been signed to a film contract.

MARTHA ROFHEART. *The Savage Brood* (Thomas Y. Crowell, 1978) is the saga of the Savage theatrical family, beginning in London in 1536 with strumpet Moll Savage. In the early years of the twentieth century, Sammy Savage, little more than a boy, finds work in the fledgling film industry and is soon starred in a series of comedies as "Spotless Sam." His son J.P. becomes a leading man on screen in the 1940s after an apprenticeship in the theater. Later J.P. is named by the House Un-American Activities Committee. The novel closes in London in 1978.

DAVID ROGERS. The two central characters in *Somewhere There's Music* (St. Martin's Press, 1977) are Don Vestry and Tudi Taylor. The former is a hack screenwriter in Hollywood and the latter a would-be popular singer. The two meet in the Catskills, where Don is to write a novelization of Tudi's life. The novel is written and becomes successful, and Don is offered a teaching position in Ohio; he wants Tudi to join him, but she will not give up her dream of stardom. An overlong romance, but better than many of the genre.

GARRET ROGERS is an attorney who ran, unsuccessfully, for mayor of Los Angeles in 1961. His novel *Scandal in Eden* (Dial Press, 1963) won the first award in literature from the state bar of California. It is deserving of other awards and wider recognition. Influenced by the 1921 rape-murder trial of Roscoe "Fatty" Arbuckle, the novel is set in the late 1920s and concerns a similar trial, in which a stout comedian named Archibald Forbes, and better known as The Feeb, is accused of inserting a piece of ice in the vagina of a minor Hollywood actress and semiprofessional prostitute, resulting in her aborting and subsequently dying of septicemia. The story is told from the viewpoint of defense attorney Mark D'Andor, who had known the murder victim and is slowly sinking into alcoholic stupor. The novel moves backward and forward in time, telling D'Andor's story as he successfully defends The Feeb. When the trial is over, D'Andor learns that the Feeb did indeed assault the woman, as he had always suspected, but had used an item taken by the murder victim from D'Andor's house. D'Andor is accidentally killed, and, in a surprise and perhaps almost unnecessary ending, it is revealed that he was not who he claimed to be.

The author is a first-rate storyteller with a keen sense of cynicism—he describes the studio head as having "impeccable taste for the genuinely vulgar"—and he has made his central character, attorney D'Andor, a sympathetic one. D'Andor fights for his client not because he believes he is innocent but rather because he does not believe in the death penalty. His years of caring in an objective way for the slain actress lead him to seek out the truth but not necessarily to consider it of relevance in the murder trial. The killing of the girl leaves the reader unmoved, but Mark D'Andor's death seems an unfair and hurtful tragedy. When the reader learns that D'Andor is an imposter, the boy in a tale told by the attorney who saw his father publicly executed, it is a secret one feels was better left hidden. Allow us to remember D'Andor not as a charlatan but as a decent human being in a community and a profession where such people are few and far between. *Scandal in Eden* is a powerful, entertaining, yet disturbing novel.

ROSEMARY ROGERS (born 1932). *The Crowd Pleasers* (Avon 1978) is a curious mix of romance and intrigue and does not work in either category. As romantic fiction it is turgid. As a thriller it is overly complicated and impossible to accept. The central character is the wealthy daughter of an American industrialist. She divorces her Washington, D.C., husband for sexual incompatibility, meets a handsome and roguish actor at the local theater, comes to London, becomes a model, and reignites her love affair with the actor. The couple, along with assorted and ill-matched characters, head for an island off Big Sur in California, and to a mansion once owned by the woman's grandparents. Here, they are making a feature film with overly realistic scenes of rape and torture. The actor at first appears to be a member of the Mafia and working as an agent for Castro, but in reality he is a true American, working for the CIA. It is the lawyer-husband who is the traitor. In view of the amount of sex in which the actor indulges, it is difficult to understand how he could be loyal to anything or anybody, but in the end he and the woman are reunited for good in Spain, where the actor promises to keep her permanently pregnant so she will not look at another man.

FRANK ROONEY. When a beautiful Hollywood actress is assaulted in *The Great Circle* (Harcourt, Brace & World, 1962), her friends, lovers, and enemies examine their involvement in an effort to figure out the identity of her attacker.

ELLIOTT ROOSEVELT (1910–90) wrote a series of mystery novels featuring his mother, Eleanor Roosevelt, beginning in 1984 with *Murder and the First Lady*. Mrs. Roosevelt was a movie fan and often invited Hollywood celebrities to the White House and to the Roosevelt home at Hyde Park. It is not surprising, therefore, that one of Elliott Roosevelt's books should be peopled with a group of Hollywood personalities.

Murder at Hobcaw Barony (St. Martin's Press, 1986) takes place at Bernard Baruch's South Carolina estate. Of this friend of presidents, Dorothy Parker once commented there were only two things in the world she could not understand: the theory of the zipper and the function of Bernard Baruch. Mrs. Roosevelt is Baruch's houseguest, along with Tallulah Bankhead, Humphrey Bogart, Joan Crawford, and Darryl F. Zanuck. Also present is a fictional Hollywood producer and a fictional Hollywood leading lady. When the former is murdered, Mrs. Roosevelt investigates and uncovers a decidedly shady past. She and her fellow guests are so repulsed by the past activities of the murder victim that they permit his murderer, the fictional Hollywood star, to go free, and even thwart Walter Winchell's attempts to uncover what is going on at Hobcaw Barony.

The plotline involves the supposed pornographic film that Joan Crawford made before becoming a star, and of which the fictional producer has obtained a copy. Tallulah Bankhead wanders around the house in the nude, and Crawford and producer Darryl F. Zanuck enjoy a brief sexual relationship. It is those aspects of the novel that hold the reader's attention. Otherwise, the dialogue is often wooden, and the characters lack depth. Unfortunately, with so many real-life film people present, it is very obvious to the reader that the murderer has to be a fictional character.

ROBERT ROSENBERG's Jerusalem detective Avram Cohen comes to Los Angeles in *The Cutting Room* (Simon & Schuster, 1993), at the request of a childhood friend with whom Cohen was in a concentration camp. The friend is now a prominent producer, and his latest work concerns Cohen's activities in the camp and immediately following World War II. When Cohen arrives, the friend is dead, a supposed suicide. Other deaths follow, including that of a gossip columnist, as Cohen discovers that the film was to expose a Nazi currently living in the United States, who has purchased the studio backing the production in order to prevent the film's release. A well-written novel but far from believable, particularly in its depiction of the workings of contemporary Hollywood.

OLGA ROSMANITH. *Picture People* (Doubleday, 1934) documents the rise to stardom of Viennese actress Josepha, who is brought to Hollywood by a well-known Austrian director. "Unlike the normal run of Hollywood novels," wrote the reviewer in the *New York Times* (August 12, 1934), "the book contains a number of plausibly drawn characters, is told in respectable diction, and excludes from its pages the traditional orgies as well as malicious parodies of the industry's bosses. Altogether, it is a very fair and credible movie novel indeed."

PAUL ROSNER. *The Princess and the Goblin* (Sherbourne Press, 1966) is the dramatic story of the rise to fame of Maureen Covillion, who comes to Hollywood in 1938. She becomes a second-string star, specializing in roller-skating pictures (!) and is taken under the wing of major star Josie Miller, who also becomes her lover. In 1944 Maureen leaves Hollywood, and by 1962 she is the reigning star of Broadway. It is the same old tale of loss of innocence and the desperate search for fame, but at the same time it is always eminently readable, with its author throwing in a fair sprinkling of Hollywood names of the 1940s.

JOANN ROSS. *Secret Sins* (St. Martin's Press, 1990) is a typical Hollywood novel of the 1990s, set in the period 1972–81, and providing the reader with an adequate quantity of eroticism and fantasy. The principal characters are studio head Joshua Baron, his two daughters, Leigh and Marissa, handsome Matthew St. James and his long-time and worthless buddy Jeff Martin, real estate agent Tina Marshall, and her Hollywood agent husband Corbett. Tina and Leigh persuade Matthew to become an actor, but soon he is busy writing and directing his own films. Because she is not his natural daughter, Joshua Baron has no time for Marissa, who gets involved in the world of drugs and pornography and marries Jeff Martin. Matthew marries Leigh, but they are divorced after she causes her father to have a stroke when she confronts him with her memories of his sexual abuse of her as a child. Marissa divorces Jeff and, pregnant, marries Matthew. When her father dies, Leigh becomes the studio head and eventually agrees to produce Matthew's screenplay exposing corruption within a studio. A former actor turned politician, who has ties to the Mafia and drug dealing and is Marissa's biological father, tries to halt the production, but in the end fails. Marissa is murdered by Jeff, and Matthews remarries Leigh, who promises they will have children together.

WALTER ROSS. *The Immortal* (Simon & Schuster, 1958) is the story of 24-year-old movie idol Johnny Preston told through a series of interviews with the men and women who seduced him. It begins with a mob scene at Preston's grave following his death in a plane crash. "The old story of the uncouth, foul-mouthed opportunist climbing rough-shod (albeit in this case with tennis shoes) to fame and fortune and seeking an elusive 'something' beyond these has been told before with, it might be noted, less clinical detail, fewer four-letter words and more insight," commented critic Judith Crist in the *New York Herald Tribune* (May 25, 1958).

ELIZABETH ROSSITER. *The Lemon Garden* (Carroll & Graf, 1991) is an uneasy mix of romance and mystery. British actress Joanna Fleming is on location in Italy, when she is involved in a car accident and loses her memory. As she seeks to uncover the mystery of what happened the evening of the accident, it is obvious that somebody (or somebodies) is trying to kill her. The solution lies in a murder that she saw happen when the film's director killed a female journalist whom he had raped while a Nazi officer. Just as the storyline hardly rings true, neither does the author's depiction of the actress, her actor lover, or the director.

THEODORE ROSZAK (born 1933) describes *Flicker* (Summit Books, 1991) as "a secret history of the movies," but it might also be described as an intellectual film buff's fantasy trip, as its author demonstrates a phenomenal knowledge of film history coupled with a florid imagination. The book's narrator is Jonathan Gates, a 1970s film student and later film professor who first begins his screen education at a Los Angeles repertory theater run by a strong-willed woman who provides her own program notes for the productions she shows and later becomes a film critic (and who is obviously loosely based on Pauline Kael). In bed with his mentor and while involved in various bouts of sexual athletics, Gates is lectured on the art and history of the motion picture. The narrator becomes fascinated with a German-born schlock filmmaker named Max Castle, who apparently died in 1941. Uncovering a treasure trove of the director's films, Gates discovers subliminal images in the features, and as he researches Castle's background he learns of an ancient Christian religious cult that has apparently used the motion picture to its own ends. As he is drawn deeper and deeper into an investigation of the cult's activities, Gates realizes too late that the organization has also been studying him.

Flicker is a long novel (almost 600 pages), and one that will appeal primarily to film buffs and connoisseurs of the fantasy genre. The author demonstrates an extraordinary knowledge of motion picture theory and history, but ultimately the basic premise of the book is indefensible. The idea of the subliminal textual images that Castle and the cult supposedly interjected into their films is not practical, since even one frame of film when projected is visible to the naked eye.

MARC RUBEL (born 1949) captures well the language and culture of the 1950s in *Flex* (St. Martin's Press, 1983), set in 1958 in the Muscle Beach area of Santa Monica. It is a complicated mystery novel involving a missing teenager and serial killings, with which a powerful Hollywood agent and his client, a prominent male star, are in some ways involved. In an effort to confront the star, the book's hero pays a visit to the Samuel Goldwyn Studios, where he sees Goldwyn, director Otto Preminger, and actor Sidney Poitier, and talks with actress Dorothy Dandridge. *Flex* is entertaining but at times a little too confusing, with an overload of characters, including a doctor barred from the RKO lot for his overfriendly provision of drugs to the acting fraternity, and there are simply too many things happening at the novel's Fourth of July climax.

BERNICE RUBENS (born 1923). *Go Tell the Lemming* (Washington Square Press, 1984) is a novel of loss and self-loathing, as London film editor Angela Morrow bemoans the two-year loss of her film producer husband to a young mistress. After a series of one-night stands, she is murdered by a man who picks her up in London's West End.

BERTA RUCK (1878–1978) was a prolific British romantic novelist who began her career in 1914 with *His Official Fiancée*, and was married to novelist Oliver Onions (aka George Oliver). At least three of her books contain film-related themes.

　　Star in Love (Dodd, Mead, 1935) is a Welsh actress, Jane Richards, who is given the opportunity to play Marie Antoinette on stage. The play closes prematurely, but later the same role on screen is offered to the actress. In *Handmaid to Fame* (Dodd, Mead, 1939), Terry Gray is chosen by the fiancée of England's leading film star, Val Lavery, to be his secretary, because she was the least attractive of the three applicants. However, Terry helps write a play that brings the actor new fame. *Shining Chance* (Dodd, Mead, 1944) has English girl Millie Saunders reluctantly taking the place of a rising American movie star named Dawn Morrow, only to discover that she and Dawn are twins!

SALMAN RUSHDIE (born 1947). *The Satanic Verses* (Viking, 1988) is one of the most discussed novels of our time but possibly, in comparison with its fame, one of the least read. It begins with the blowing up of a hijacked jumbo jet over the English Channel and the falling to earth from the plane of Saladin Chamcha and Gilbreel Farishta. The latter is "the biggest star in the history of the Indian movies" who "had formed the habit of being transported from set to set on the great D.W. Rama lot by this group of speedy, trusted athletes, because a man who makes up to eleven movies 'sy-multaneous' needs to conserve his energy."

MARTIN RUSSELL (born 1934) is a British mystery writer who needs to limit his activities to areas with which he is familiar. *Unwelcome Audience* (Walker, 1986) demonstrates a total lack of knowledge about film production, with equally shaky familiarity with Los Angeles, U.S. presidential politics, and the Los Angeles Police Department. The novel is narrated by London-born actress Angelica Browne, who has returned home to star in a film that will, she hopes, change her image. She is blackmailed by her ex-husband over photographs showing her and a U.S. presidential candidate in a sexual situation. For some reason, the actress believes publication of these photographs will damage her career, even though she has previously appeared nude on screen. Instead of going to the police and putting an end to this tedious story, the actress tries reasoning with her husband. He is allowed to visit her parents and even have access to the set on which she is working. When he is killed, regrettably much too far into the novel, the actress becomes one of the suspects, along with her father, sister, and the producer of her film. Ultimately none of them is revealed as the murderer. Upon her return to the United States and a blossoming future in films, the actress is approached by a representative of the now-elected president, demanding that she not publish the story of her one-night stand with him.

Despite her previous concern that nothing be revealed of this escapade, the actress now decides it is time to go public. If only she had felt that way before her poor ex-husband got murdered and the unsuspecting reader got involved in this pathetic tale!

PAMELA REDFORD RUSSELL (born 1950). *Wild Flowers* (Harper & Row, 1982) is the saga of six daughters, each named for a wildflower and born in the 1930s to a depressing couple from Kansas. "Neurosis-filled," wrote *Kirkus*. "Owes a bit to Joyce Carol Oates and a great deal to Harold Robbins," commented *Library Journal*. One of the daughters, Holly gots to Hollywood, becomes a story editor, and falls in love with a writer. The rest endure less happy lives.

RAY RUSSELL (born 1924). *The Colony* (Sherbourne Press, 1969) is a series of relatively unrelated incidents in the life of screenwriter Clayton Horne. He gives up his job as senior editor at a Chicago magazine (the author was formerly executive editor of Chicago-based *Playboy* magazine) and flies to Hollywood, sitting next to film-star-to-be Lovey Dovey. The major story involves an associate producer named Rudy Smith, whose two girlfriends are stolen away from him by actors owning the same lavender-colored Rolls Royce; Rudy wreaks revenge on the car. There is a lecherous agent named Avery Bletch, who interviews his female clients in the nude. A number of the chapters relate to the vagaries of life as a screenwriter, with Horne sharing center stage with fellow writer Chet Montague. The latter kills himself, and nobody but Horne understands what is meant by Montague's self-written epitaph:

> Friends I am resting
> Under this stone,
> Cool, unprotesting,
> Kingly, alone,
> Younger than wisdom,
> Older than youth,
> Ugly as unadorned truth.

There are some genuinely amusing incidents, such as when Horne tries to persuade a recalcitrant producer that a title with four *z*'s in it is unacceptable—no theater owner in America has that number of *z*'s available for the marquee. An actress auditioning for agent Bletch does a series of impersonations, beginning with Marilyn Monroe, and moving down the scale through Bella Darvi, Terry Moore, and Linda Christian, and ending with Laurence Harvey. Perhaps because one of the central characters, Rudy Smith, is English, Ray Russell's writing makes one think of an updated version of P.G. Wodehouse on Hollywood. Several chapters on *The Colony* appeared previously in *Playboy*.

PAUL RUSSO. *Stag Starlet* (Tower Publications, 1961) is one of a series of novels with a Hollywood background identified by Carolyn See as semipornographic. No other information is available.

DON RYAN. The narrator of the surrealist novel *Angel's Flight* (Boni & Liveright, 1927) is newspaper reporter Will Pence, who gathers material for his daily column from both the unknown and the famous, including a director who bears a striking resemblance to Erich von Stroheim. The title is taken from the historic railroad that ran an uphill city block in downtown Los Angeles and was long ago demolished. In *The Nation* (January 25, 1928) James Rorty wrote, "An interesting and readable novel. If one were a movie magnate one would be tempted to buy the rights to *Angel's Flight*, call it *The Prodigal of Babylon*, and make a lot of money. But as for Mr. Ryan, one wonders why he doesn't write something really nasty about Los Angeles—something tolerant, appreciative, and only incidentally contemptuous. His talent, one feels, is adequate to the task; it might prove to be a good book. And the Angelenos would never know they had been bitten."

The central character in ***Roman Holiday*** (Macaulay Company, 1930) is Hollywood dancer and comedienne Diana Hunter. After the war, Hunter, who is sophisticated and has a taste for highbrow literature, marries her soldier lover, but he commits suicide. She moves to New York, and under an assumed name directs a highly acclaimed screen version of Spengler's *Decline of the West*—and dies. In *The Nation* (February 19, 1930) F.T. Marsh wrote, "There is much in this audacious book that seems to this reviewer quite absurd; and there are some things about the extraordinary and fascinating heroine that seem to him incredible. But this is the most interesting novel ever to have come out of Hollywood. It could never have come from anywhere else. That is its curse as well as its significance."

J.M. RYAN. *The Rat Factory* (Prentice-Hall, 1971) is a wicked parody of Walt Disney and labor conditions at the studio. Disney is here called Wade Simpson—"I am not a boss in the usual sense of the word. I am more like a god"—who makes "Sappy Sonata" (Silly Symphonies) cartoons, the first of which was *Rowboat Billie* (*Steamboat Willie*), introducing the character of Ricky Rat. Simpson's agents scour the country for young men to work at the studio for less than poverty wages. Simpson, a despotic, egotistical employer, is quite willing, in order to prevent pilfering, to fire the entire staff. The novel presents a frightening and surrealistic view of Los Angeles, where police brutality is the norm and anything unpleasant, such as an earthquake, is not reported in the newspapers for fear of scaring away Easterners. To add to the surreal quality, the time period in which the few weeks of the story take place is very confusing, relating to actual events as early as 1934 and as late as 1939. The principal character is a young man from Bozeman, Montana, named Ambrose. He obtains employment at the studio, finds lodgings at a nudist colony in the former set of *The Hunchback of Notre Dame*, and eventually stands up for his rights when after working days and nights without pay to finish a film, his salary is cut to zero, his girlfriend deserts, and his father, fired by the postal service, moves in. The book ends with Ambrose entering a Marine Corps recruiting office.

BJORN ROBINSON RYE (born 1942). In *A Feast of Pikes* (Bobbs-Merrill, 1976) a New York screenwriter who is separated from his wife comes to London and becomes involved with an English aristocrat and his actress-girlfriend in making a film that has the same title as this novel, set in Greece. There, they become involved in helping an aging actress locate her son.

FLORENCE RYERSON and COLIN CAMPBELL CLEMENTS. *Shadows* (Appleton-Century, 1938) is "a well-constructed crime puzzle" (*New York Times*, August 5, 1934) about a young Hollywood screenwriter who solves a murder.

FRANÇOISE SAGAN. *Kirkus* wrote of this author's one Hollywood novel that "Mlle. Sagan always gets by with very little, [and] hasn't overextended herself in this one." Much the same opinion was expressed by Norman Rosen in the *New York Times* (November 10, 1968), who wrote that *The Heart-Keeper* (E.P. Dutton, 1968) was "a puzzle—a book that does not work, that baffles us with its self-contradictions, that resembles the author's best work to the point of parody." The story, as translated by Robert Westhoff, is of a middle-aged female screenwriter who takes in a young man as a protégé. The young man's plan is to murder everyone who has ever hurt his lover, beginning with her two ex-husbands.

LEONARD ST. CLAIR (1916–86). *Obsessions* (Simon & Schuster, 1980) is principally concerned with a Russian émigré's determination to kill all those involved in the murder of the czar's family. His son is involved during the 1940s and 1950s with a movie star named Erin Deering. The plot heats up when Erin decides to marry one of the czar's killers.

MADELON ST. DENNIS. *The Death Kiss* (Jacobsen Publishing, 1932) begins on a Hollywood film stage, when an actor is murdered with a gun supposedly containing blanks. The novel was filmed in 1932, for 1933 release, by KBS, under the direction of Edwin L. Marin, and starring David Manners, Adrienne Ames, and Bela Lugosi.

ADELA ROGERS ST. JOHNS (1894–1988) was the preeminent chronicler of Hollywood lore and legend in the 1920s and 1930s; she also wrote the occasional screenplay and had a number of her short stories (notably "A Free Soul" and "The Single Standard") adapted for the screen. She began writing for *Photoplay* in 1919 and contributed stories on most of the Hollywood greats, although generally she was inclined to be more interested in legend than fact. St. Johns was the daughter of criminal attorney Earl Rogers, and she wrote a 1962 biography of him; she published her own autobiography, *The Honeycomb*, in 1969.

The Skyrocket (Cosmopolitan, 1925) tells the conventional Hollywood story of Sharon Kimm, who is "skyrocketed to glory and a place among the stars." Before finding ultimate happiness with the right man, "she goes the way of desire, vanity and debt." "At best a commonplace yarn, verging at times upon the ridiculous," commented the *New York Times* (June 7, 1925), while the *Boston Evening Transcript* (May 16, 1925) wrote, "A tale of this kind might breed discontent by arousing yearnings in restless youth but doubtless it will escape disapproval where a sincere and earnest play such as 'Desire Under the Elms' did not." The novel was filmed in 1926 by Celebrity Pictures for Associated Exhibitors release, directed by Marshall Neilan, and starring Peggy Hopkins Joyce, Owen Moore, and Gladys Hulette.

JEANNIE SAKOL (born 1928). Dorrie Bridges is an unusual creature, a gossip columnist who prints only the truth in *Hot 30* (Delacorte Press, 1980). So when she disappears on her thirtieth birthday and her body is subsequently discovered in the ruins of her burned-out beach house, a newspaper reporter named Lou Dexter decides to investigate among the beautiful people of Hollywood, Beverly Hills, and Malibu, all of whom were featured in Dorrie's column.

RICHARD SALE (1911–93). Bacteriology plays a prominent role in *Lazarus #7* (Simon & Schuster, 1942), whose hero and narrator is bacteriologist Dr. Steve Mason. Four citizens of Hollywood are dead, including a famous actress, and the studio wants a verdict of suicide. The studio doctor has been experimenting with bringing dogs back to life (each is called Lazarus), and the doctor is killed. But he is revived long enough to reveal that the murderer is an actress who has been killing to prevent exposure of the fact that she has leprosy. Highly entertaining! "The motive, which is probably unique, ties in perfectly with the general atmosphere of Hollywood as the author has pictured it. There is romance in the story as well as crime, and both have the accepted Hollywood touch," wrote Isaac Anderson in the *New York Times* (March 22, 1942).

When Hollywood star Kerry Garth's double is murdered in *Benefit Performance* (Simon & Schuster, 1946), the actor's agent persuades Garth to pretend to be the double in order to capture the killer. "Fast, funny, and not as confusing as it sounds" was the opinion of the reviewer in *The New Yorker* (May 11, 1946).

The Oscar (Simon & Schuster, 1963) documents the ruthless methods by which one nominee seeks to win an Academy Award. As *Kirkus* so aptly put it, there are "days awash with liquor and nights noxious with sexuality," as Frankie Fane engineers bad publicity about his fellow nominees.

GEORGE SANDERS (1906–72) was a suave and cynical leading man on screen in Britain, the United States, and elsewhere, from 1936 until his death by suicide. He appears as himself in *Crime on My Hands* (Simon & Schuster, 1944), investigating the death of an extra while a film titled *Seven Dreams* is on location in the desert. His knowledge of the plots of various crime movies helps Sanders uncover the murderer. "Lots of fun and a sufficiency of bloodshed," wrote Isaac Anderson in the *New York Times* (October 8, 1944). Simon & Schuster published a second crime novel by Sanders, *Stranger at Home*, in 1946. Writing in the *San Francisco Chronicle* (August 11, 1946), Anthony Boucher noted, "This is so far a cry from the flip first Sanders novel that it is hard to attribute them to the same typewriter." He was correct. *Crime on My Hands* was ghostwritten by Craig Rice and Cleve Cartmill, while *Stranger at Home* was ghostwritten by Leigh Brackett.

DOUGLAS SANDERSON. A screenwriter becomes involved in blackmail and murder because he was too drunk to prevent his starlet-wife from driving her car off a cliff in *Catch a Fallen Starlet* (Avon, 1960). Nancy Brooker-Bowers comments, "The Hollywood community is shown here as united in a giant conspiracy to preserve outward respectability at all costs, despite its actual corrupt nature."

NICHOLAS SANDYS. *Starset and Sunrise* (Sheed & Ward, 1951) is a cloying melodrama, dripping with religious fervor. The narrator is Marjorie Chatham, the daughter of gypsies, educated in a convent, who becomes a movie star thanks to sexual relationships with various men. At the novel's close, she returns to the convent and dies of tuberculosis while preparing to play the part of a nun on screen. The Catholic periodical *Commonweal* (September 21, 1951) was most enthusiastic: "Sandys has drawn freely on his considerable experience as an actor for the rich background of this novel. One of its merits is the satisfying subtlety with which his own contempt for the politics, strut and false grandeur of the movies shines through Marjorie's enthusiastic account."

WILLIAM SAROYAN (1908–81). *Rock Wagram* (Doubleday, 1951) was only the third novel by Saroyan, primarily noted for his short stories and plays. He worked for M-G-M in the 1940s and wrote two screenplays based on his own works, *The Good Job* (1942) and *The Human Comedy* (1943). *Rock Wagram* begins in 1950 as its title character looks back on his life from the time he has discovered tending bar in Fresno, through his success as a film star and marriage to a New York socialite. There are obviously elements of Saroyan's own life and his own failings here.

SUSAN SAUNDERS (born 1945). *The Movie Mystery* (Bantam Skylark, 1987), illustrated by Thomas Sperling and Sara Kurtz, is one of the so-called plot-your-own-stories novels for teenage readers. The reader is asked to make his or her own choice to determine the outcome of an adventure during the making of a movie.

TEO SAVORY (1907–89). *A Penny for His Pocket* (J.B. Lippincott, 1964) is a very English novel, which opens in a working-class home in London's Camden Town, where Tom Loving lives with his mother, a former British music hall star. During World War II, Tom is injured by falling masonry, and a concussion makes him "simple-minded." He falls in love with a ballet dancer named Miranda, and she persuades him to become a film actor. Through a misunderstanding, Tom goes to Hollywood, and while there hears from Miranda that she is going to marry a munitions baron. Tom returns to Camden Town, indifferent to his career and in search of a meaning to his life. "It has been a long time since so many enchanting characters have been gathered together in one book," wrote E.P.J. Corbett in *America* (March 28, 1964). "The narrative is cleverly interspersed with snatches of folk songs and music-hall ballads and excerpts from travel guides, which serve as a chorus-like commentary on the passing scene. It will be a shame if this delightful novel is neglected. Talent like Miss Savory's deserves a wide audience." The book was originally published in the United Kingdom under the title *A Penny for the Guy*.

CHARLES SAXBY wrote three mystery novels with Hollywood subject matter. *Death Over Hollywood* (E.P. Dutton, 1937), coauthored with Louis Molnar, concerns the murder of a Hollywood gossip columnist; the likely suspect is appearing in a film currently in production, and the assistant studio manager is anxious that the sheriff not make an arrest until the feature is completed. In *Death Cuts the Film* (E.P. Dutton, 1939), a mystery writer is traveling on a yacht with two competing female movie stars and the crew of a feature film, based on the writer's novel, about to be shot off the Mexican coast; when one of the stars goes overboard, the writer approaches the murder as he would one of his mystery novels. A young and handsome leading man becomes involved with the agents of the Axis powers in *Out of It All* (E.P. Dutton, 1941).

ALMA SIOUX SCARBERRY (1899–1990). *Puppy Love: A Hollywood Romance That Hit the Front Page* (Grosset & Dunlap, 1933) is an extraordinarily complex romance whose plotline would surely delight any Harlequin romance reader or writer. The principal character is Curt Little who is involved in the field of Hollywood finance. He meets Mary Sawyer, an 18-year-old working as a costume designer. He believes that Mary's father had an affair with his wife and forced him to leave home and change his name. In revenge, he plans to marry Mary and treat her badly. Just as he and Mary are about to elope, Mary's ex-boyfriend arrives on the scene and takes her away. At the novel's conclusion, it is revealed that the boyfriend is the financier's son and that the wife was not unfaithful.

SUSAN FROMBERG SCHAEFFER (born 1941). *First Nights* (Alfred A. Knopf, 1993) is told in narrative form by two women, the Garboesque reclusive screen star Anna Asta and her housekeeper for two decades, Ivy Cook. The similarity between Asta and Garbo is obvious, with Asta born in Finland rather than Sweden. Just as Garbo had a doomed love affair with leading man John Gilbert, here Asta has an affair with actor Charles Harrow. The novel opens with a prologue by Asta's director, Anders Estersen, but upon whom he is based it is difficult to tell, certainly not Mauritz Stiller, who brought Garbo to the United States and is here called Max Lilly. While the lives of Anna Asta and Ivy Cook might seem at variance, the author gradually builds a common link between the two in a novel that is stylish and elegant, but, at over 600 pages, tends at times toward the pretentious.

MARGARET SCHERF (1908–79). *The Beaded Banana* (Crime Club/Doubleday, 1978) features Scherf's regular heroine, Dr. Grace Severance, and the small Montana town of Summerhill, where a film company is on location. The presence of the crew complicates investigation of the murder of a former Las Vegas casino owner. The title refers to a creation by a member of the film company, a black man in a white fur hat, who explains, "In Hollywood this is very big. Any kind of fruit covered in beads."

MAXINE SCHNALL (born 1934). After winning a million dollars in a civil lawsuit, the heroine of *The Broadbelters* (Evans/J.B. Lippincott, 1970) goes after fame by writing an exposé of a mother and daughter in the film industry who marry the same movie executive.

RAYMOND L. SCHROCK and EDWARD CLARK. *Broken Hearts of Hollywood* (Jacobsen-Hodgkinson, 1926) is based on the 1926 Warner Bros. feature film of the same title, directed by Lloyd Bacon, and starring Patsy Ruth Miller, Louise Dresser, and Douglas Fairbanks, Jr. The daughter of a former screen actress wins a beauty contest and comes to Hollywood, where she meets her male counterpart. Both fail their screen tests, the daughter is arrested in a raid on a wild party, and her friend performs a dangerous stunt in order to raise the bail money. The girl is able to obtain a film part in which her real mother plays her screen mother. When the film is completed, the latter kills the man who led her daughter astray, and at her trial, the daughter is able to save her mother.

BUDD SCHULBERG (born 1914) is probably the best known person associated with the genre of the Hollywood novel, not simply because he wrote two of its finest examples, but also because he has commented often in print on other representative books and has supplied introductions for the reprints of some of them. As the son of B.P. Schulberg, one-time head of production at Paramount, and also as a screenwriter of note, Budd Schulberg was well qualified as a Hollywood novelist. His autobiography, *Moving Pictures: Memories of a Hollywood Prince*, was published by Stein & Day in 1981.

Sammy Glick is the quintessential Hollywood type, created by Schulberg as the central character in his novel ***What Makes Sammy Run*** (Random House, 1941). The story of Sammy Glick is told by Al Manheim, a theatrical reporter who first meets Glick when his newspaper hires the ferret-faced youth as an office boy. Glick insinuates himself as the paper's radio commentator and then, using a script written by the pathetic Julian Blumberg, talks himself into a job as a Hollywood screenwriter. Manheim pays two lengthy visits to Hollywood, studying Glick's rise to power as a Hollywood producer. He views Glick almost as if he were a social phenomenon: "I decided that the history of Hollywood was nothing but twenty years of feverish preparation for the arrival of Sammy Glick." Glick is not without talent; it is just that he does not want to use it except in a negative fashion as he claws his way to the top, using everyone around him. He is not lazy but hard-working and self-engrossed. Ultimately, Glick marries the daughter of the financial head of the studio, only to find that she has used him and made him as vulnerable as everyone else in the Hollywood hierarchy.

While documenting the rise of Sammy Glick, the author, through his alter ego, Al Manheim, considers the situation of Jews in America, most notably as Manheim visits Glick's mother and brother on New York's Lower East Side and learns about his childhood and early years. Additionally, the novel discusses the efforts of screenwriters to unionize through the Screen Writers Guild, and Glick's betrayal of it.

Carolyn See suggests that Sammy Glick is a combination of Jerry Wald and Norman Krasna, and that Julian Blumberg is based on the brothers Julius and Philip Epstein. Schulberg has maintained that Glick is not based on any specific Hollywood character, although his creation certainly offended many in the community. After reading the book, Louis B. Mayer is said to have commented, "You know what we should do with him? We should deport him!" "I had written about Sammy Glick because I had been brought up among Sammy Glicks, and I had used Hollywood as a background because Hollywood was my hometown, until I exchanged palm trees for pine trees, the only community I knew," states Schulberg.

"This novel is brilliantly effective because it is completely of this time, expressing the beliefs and hopes that begin to stand out in this period, marked in it by the threat of complex defeat," wrote Robert van Gelder in the *New York Times* (March 30, 1941). "The book carries on its jacket the recommendations of the author of *This Side of Paradise* and of the author of *Appointment in Samarra*. It does not come up to either of these first novels, yet it is unquestioningly one of the most interesting and promising first novels to appear in several years." *The Saturday Review of Literature* (March 29, 1941) commented, "This Hollywood novel is straight from the 'tough' school of *I Can Get It for You Wholesale* and *Pal Joey*. It is not quite as remorseless as the first title and it does not have O'Hara's humor but it has qualities of its own sufficient to make one cry frantically for the Flitt, long before the skillful climax comes off."

In *The New Republic* (March 31, 1941), Otis Ferguson wrote, "Budd Schulberg is one of the very few to approach Hollywood with understanding and grim tolerance, and his writing has clean workmanship... It is not one of the most dramatic novels, partly because of this serious analysis and single purpose; but partly because the actual evolution of the character is less believable than the character himself... On the whole *What Makes Sammy Run?* elbows out most of the trash that has been piling up since this crazy capital of a special world became a thing to write and wonder about."

"This is Mr. Schulberg's first novel, and he is more concerned with saying what he sees and feels than with how he says it, and that is as it should be," wrote H.P. Lazarus in *The Nation* (April 19, 1941). "The book is uneven; the first part is badly written and developed; there is too much of the paltry patois of small-story sophistication and typewriter chatter. One finds a paucity of expression, and the snappy conversation is at times oh so nugatory. But each of these charges is controverted as one turns the pages, and it is a pleasure to watch the author write through and past what really is his 'first novel' to find his own form and content."

Schulberg's contemporaries were most enthusiastic. F. Scott Fitzgerald wrote, "It is a grand book, utterly fearless and with a great deal of beauty side by side with the most bitter satire." Similarly John O'Hara commented, "Here is a fine book and with it its author now stands up there with the good writers of our day." Dorothy Parker defended Schulberg's reliance on a Jewish antihero, pointing out, "Those who hail us Jews as brothers must allow us to have our villains, the same, alas, as any other race."

What Makes Sammy Run? was adapted for television and seen on NBC in 1960 with Larry Blyden in the title role, and adapted as a Broadway musical in 1964, starring Steve Lawrence.

The fiftieth anniversary edition of the novel, published by Random House, includes an introduction by Budd Schulberg, two short stories, "What Makes Sammy Run" and "Love Comes to Sammy Glick," originally published in *Liberty* prior to the novel's creation, and an afterword, "What Makes Sammy Keep Running," originally published in *Newsday* (August 2, 1987).

The Disenchanted (Random House, 1950) is very much a roman à clef, but far more of a literary effort than those novels usually saddled with that description. Hollywood producer Victor Milgrim hires junior writer Shep Stearns to work with Manley Halliday, a former major American novelist of the 1920s, on the script for a college picture. Manley is an alcoholic and has a wife with mental problems. He is also financially insolvent. The two men are ordered to fly east and then proceed to a New England college where the movie is to be set. Halliday gets steadily drunk and engrossed in past remembrances, including that of a Hollywood party. He disgraces himself on arrival at the college, where Milgrim is hopeful of receiving an honorary degree, and the producer orders both writers to return to Hollywood, via New York. In New York, Halliday becomes seriously ill, is hospitalized and dies. The entire story is based on Schulberg's assignment to write the script for the 1939 Walter Wanger production of *Winter Carnival*. Stearns is Schulberg, Halliday is very obviously F. Scott Fitzgerald, Milgrim is Walter Wanger, and the college is Dartmouth. Wanger did attempt, unsuccessfully, to promote an honorary degree for himself, and just as here a professor asks that Wanger arrange for the college to receive a collection of scripts to be housed in its library and named in the producer's honor, Dartmouth did promote a script collection—but named it after Irving Thalberg.

James M. Cain reviewed the novel in the *New York Times* (October 29, 1950) and commented, "The book is so good that one curious point must be made in regard to it. Scott Fitzgerald, in his lifetime, certainly did not lack recognition. Whether he was quite the genius, the sweet prince of narrative prose, that Shep seems to think, may be a moot point, for many will take exception to him, particularly on the score of workmanship. But he carved out a niche for himself, and he still sits in it, for many do him reverence, even now." In the *Saturday Review of Literature* (October 28, 1950), Hollis Alpert wrote, "The book has a strangely disjointed effect upon one. You believe on one level and disbelieve on another. Part of this may be due to Mr. Schulberg's failure to convince you of Halliday's past greatness.... I have the feeling that it is the magnitude of the project, perhaps too large for a man of Mr. Schulberg's talents and experience, which has, in the long run, defeated him."

HENRY SCHWARTZ. *Albert Goes to Hollywood* (Orchard Books, 1992) is one of a series of children's books for four- to seven-year-olds, written by Schwartz, illustrated by his daughter Amy, and featuring a pet dinosaur named Albert. Here the MOGO Studios in Hollywood decide to film the story of how Albert was found in Baja, California, by eight-year-old Liz Bradford. Albert becomes a star and puts his footprints in the cement at Grauman's Chinese Theatre.

DORIS SCHWERIN (born 1922). Leanna, a concert pianist, and Grisha, a Russian filmmaker, meet in the Paris of the 1930s in *Leanna* (William Morrow, 1978). The couple continue their separate careers, first in France and then, as a result of World War II, in the United States. Their son, Tony, lives with his mother, but after attaining a successful career as a television producer, he commits suicide.

ETHEL SEXTON. *Count Me Among the Living* (Harper, 1946) is the psychological study of a young woman's mental disintegration, from her birth on a Hawaiian plantation to her total insanity in Hollywood at the age of 21. "An extremely careful piece of writing, but an unsuccessful one," was the opinion of the reviewer in *The New Yorker* (April 27, 1946).

STEVE SHAGAN (born 1927) is a screenwriter, the script of whose first novel, *Save the Tiger* (1973), was highly praised. *City of Angels* (G.P. Putnam's Sons, 1975) features a detective with a strong moral code who is forced to face reality—in the form of pornographic movies, the Mafia, and illicit sex—as he tries to uncover the killer of a teenage girl.

City of Angels was Shagan's second novel. *A Cast of Characters* (Simon & Schuster, 1993) is his seventh. The initial plot device is original, even if it is obvious to most readers what the ultimate outcome will be. The writing style is entertaining and often amusing, and the novel as a whole makes relaxing and intriguing reading. In partnership with a Mafia kingpin, various executives at Gemstone Pictures devise what appears to be a masterly scam. An outsider will launch a takeover bid for the studio, raising the value of its shares. At exactly the right moment, the executives will sell their stock and the takeover bid will be rescinded. In order to persuade stockholders to accept the tentative offer, the head of production authorizes the making of an epic film about the Spanish civil war, which he anticipates will be a disaster thanks to a temperamental cast and crew that include drug addicts, alcoholics, sex maniacs, losers, and has-beens. As the reader might expect, the film is an artistic success. Learning of the scam, the producer/writer of the film arranges a private screening of the incomplete production for critics Gene Siskel and Roger Ebert, who both give it a "thumbs up." Ultimately, the executives in on the scam come out on top, for the film's estimated profits will bring in just about as much money as their scheme would have, had it succeeded. Shagan's knowledge of the film industry permits his writing a lengthy and accurate account of preproduction and production of a film shot on location in Spain.

DIANE K. SHAH (born 1945). *As Crime Goes By* (Bantam Books, 1990) is the second mystery novel to feature Paris Chandler, "legman" for gossip columnist Etta Rice at the *Los Angeles Examiner*. Her father is a movie executive and her mother a former actress, and the recently widowed Chandler drives around in a chauffeur-driven Bentley and lives with her housekeeper in Pasadena. (Her chauffeur is a would-be actor.) The year is 1947, and Chandler becomes involved in the murder of a starlet, who is one of a number of kept women of a prominent director. The Black Dahlia case vaguely intrudes, as does Chandler's inability to handle the death of her husband and a relationship with Rice's other legman. Diane K. Shah has a splendid ability to recreate period atmosphere, and the novel is intelligently written, although the solution to the crime comes across as somewhat unsatisfactory.

MELVILLE SHAVELSON (born 1917) is both a writer and a director. His first novel, *Lualda* (Arbor House, 1975), begins with an Italian starlet asking Hollywood director Steven Berman for a part in his latest film in return for sex. The couple begins a 20-year relationship, during which time Berman helps her get a visa and an abortion. "As improbable as a Thurber fantasy and far less entertaining" was the opinion of Joyce W. Smothers in *Library Journal* (February 1, 1975).

DIANA SHAW. *Gone Hollywood* (Joy Street Books/Little, Brown, 1988) is a novel for young adults, in which teenage sleuth Carter comes to

Hollywood, where her father is directing a popular television show. The star has vanished and her disappearance may be linked to a series of unsolved murders.

IRWIN SHAW (1913–84) was a novelist, playwright, and screenplay writer (*Talk of the Town*, 1942; *Desire Under the Elms*, 1958; and others). His most popular novel, *Rich Man, Poor Man* (1970), formed the basis for the first television miniseries.

John Andrus, an ex-actor and a NATO worker in Paris is begged by a Hollywood producer to help with a film being made in Rome in *Two Weeks in Another Town* (Random House, 1960). After two weeks of drama and passion, Andrus returns to his wife and family, disillusioned but willing to answer the producer's call again if necessary. "An old-fashioned novel. It has a plot, action, a reasonable degree of suspense, and a set of characters whose proceedings, while not exactly ordinary, remain within shouting distance of possibility," commented Phoebe Adams in *Atlantic Monthly* (February 1960). The novel was reprinted by Dell in 1978, and filmed in 1962 by M-G-M, under the direction of Vincente Minnelli, and starring Kirk Douglas, Edward G. Robinson, and Cyd Charisse.

Evening in Byzantium (Delacorte Press, 1973) is a study of producer Jesse Craig, once powerful but now middle aged and feeling the strain of failure as he attends the Cannes Film Festival. "Mr. Shaw is an expert teller of tales, and if his latest is a bit reminiscent of *Two Weeks in Another Town*, no matter. It entertains" — this was, again, the opinion of Phoebe Adams in *Atlantic Monthly* (May 1973).

SIMON SHAW is a professional British actor who has written two mystery novels featuring the delightfully amoral actor Philip Fletcher, who has no compunction about murdering anyone who stands in his way. Fletcher was introduced in *Murder Out of Tune* (Crime Club/Doubleday, 1988), wherein his high regard for his own talents do not prevent his losing an agent and a current girlfriend and being ignored by producers. Only by disposing of a mediocre rival actor does Fletcher gain a part he considers rightfully his in a BBC television production. Fletcher is up against much the same problem in *Bloody Instructions* (Doubleday, 1992). Here, a second-rate movie star has the title role in a stage production of *Macbeth*, while Fletcher is relegated to playing Banquo. Happily for Fletcher, both the movie star and a critic who trashed his performance are murdered—the only problem is that Fletcher was not responsible and must track down the killer.

DOUGLAS SHELDON. *The Rainbow Men* (Doubleday, 1975) presents the love stories of two men. The first is an American B-17 bomber pilot based in England during World War II. The second is his son, a young actor, whose success on the London stage leads to a major screen role in Hollywood. The author, whose first novel this was, is a London actor whose films include *Ryan's Daughter*.

SIDNEY SHELDON (born 1917) was a successful screenwriter—*The Bachelor and the Bobby-Soxer* (1947), *Easter Parade* (1948), *Annie Get Your Gun*

(1950), *The Buster Keaton Story* (1957), *The Birds and the Bees* (1965), and others—before achieving greater fame as a popular novelist. Sheldon's third novel, *A Stranger in the Mirror* (William Morrow, 1976) indicates that the author has a solid knowledge of filmmaking as he moves his story from such diverse locations as Schwab's drugstore and the Cannes Film Festival. This is the story of a third-rate comic, Toby Temple, who becomes successful after discovering how to denigrate his audience, and Josephine Czinski, from a small Texas town, who tries to sleep her way to the top in Hollywood. The two marry. "Think of it as Caesar's Palace poolside reading," wrote *Kirkus*, "a combo of de luxe tastelessness and shamelessly readable bestsellmanship."

JAMES SHERBURNE (born 1925). *Poor Boy and a Long Way from Home* (Houghton Mifflin, 1984) is a witty and entertaining novel—*Library Journal* (July 1984) described it as "an enjoyable combination of popular history and relaxed storytelling"—primarily concerned with the American labor movement between 1909 and 1912. The central character is Glen Hatton, who is involved in various misadventures in Spokane, San Francisco, Fresno, and Los Angeles. In the last city, he works as a stuntman and cinematographer for an idealistic director named Gebhardt.

R. (Robert) C. (Cedric) SHERRIFF (1896–1975) was a novelist (1930–73), playwright (1928–49), and screenwriter (1933–56). The best-known play of this accomplished British writer is *Journey's End* (1928), filmed in 1930; his most important films are *The Invisible Man* (1933), *Goodbye, Mr. Chips* (1939), *That Hamilton Woman* (1941), *Odd Man Out* (1947), and *The Dam Busters* (1955).

Another Year (Macmillan, 1948) is a curious work that at first sight might appear to have nothing to do with Hollywood. It is the story of a Church of England vicar, who, with his wife and daughter, leaves a pleasant country parish, in late middle age, because of a desire to take care of the needs of the poor in London's East End. Nothing seems to go right for Mr. Matthews, the vicar, until he helps a group of youngsters organize an amateur dramatic presentation. A Hollywood producer attends the show and signs the vicar's daughter to a Hollywood contract. The family makes the trip to Hollywood, where Matthews is persuaded to play his daughter's father on film. The production company decides not to sign the girl to a contract but does want Matthews. However, when he returns to his parish, he realizes how much he has been missed, and decides that he belongs there.

Yes, the story is quite preposterous, and ends abruptly without a full explanation of the consequences of Matthews's decision for his family and for the parish. But there is considerable charm and appeal to the story, despite its shortcomings and the author's surprisingly sympathetic and totally unrealistic view of the Hollywood film community. If only film industry personnel could be as nice as R.C. Sherriff depicts them!

JAMES SHERWOOD. *Stradella* (Grove Press, 1967) is an experimental novel concerning a young man's love for an aging beauty queen and Hollywood star. The book was originally published by Olympia Press (Paris) and the New English Library (London) in 1966.

LEE SHIPPEY (1884–1969) was a novelist and editor of the "Lee Side o' Los Angeles" in the *Los Angeles Times* from 1927 to 1950. *The Girl Who Wanted Experience* (Houghton Mifflin, 1937) is not a Hollywood novel per se but a murder mystery that ends up as a farce. It is set in the small town of Ourville, close to Los Angeles and, unfortunately, too close to Hollywood and the contamination that it inflicts on the world. Maxine Tuyler is the girl of the title, and Hollywood gossip and intrigue affect various townspeople thanks to Maxine's attempts to get what she wants. "The characters are puppets moved about to fit the intrigue," wrote the reviewer in the *New York Times* (January 10, 1937). "Nobody will very much mind what happens to any of them, though they go through some pretty lively antics. The best part of this thinly dramatic novel is an alien chapter which has somehow crept into it—a lively short story about a sanctimonious preacher who was inveigled into taking a long shot on the races."

The central character in *If We Only Had Money* (Houghton Mifflin, 1939) is Richie Marlet, a small-town writer of magazine and newspaper stories, perhaps based on its author. A Hollywood producer reads one of Richie's stories in a Western magazine and signs him to a contract. Richie, his wife and daughter move to Hollywood, only to discover that whatever income they earn—and more—is immediately spent, as the children are sent to boarding school, they eat at expensive restaurants, and purchase a car and a ranch. Richie's wife learned "that Hollywood must always be acting, always thinking of how the public will be impressed, even at the funerals of its dearest." Richie's uncle, Frank, who had earlier helped him pay his debts, kills himself after Richie inadvertently forgets to repay some of the money, and when their daughter is kidnapped, Richie and his wife decide that Hollywood is not for them.

Despite this summary, *If We Only Had Money* is a rather joyous and entertaining novel of Hollywood life. The author points out that the only nonfictional character is Grover Jones, who is assigned to work with Richie Marlet on a script: "Grover bounced in. Jones was so full of bounce that he did everything bouncingly." The author recounts the amusing story of how Douglas Fairbanks, Sr., furnished his library at Pickfair. His houseboy measured the shelves and was then sent to buy 42 yards and 16 inches of books. When asked what kind, Fairbanks replied, "Five or six yards of red ones, and enough blue and green and yellow and the other colors to look well. But don't get any black ones."

AARON SHIRLEY. *Body of a Young Woman* (Kozy Books, 1961) is one of a series of novels with a Hollywood background, identified by Carolyn See as semipornographic. No other information is available.

IRVING SHULMAN (1913–95) wrote *Harlow: An Intimate Biography* (1964) and *Valentino* (1967), and also a number of minor screenplays. Several of Shulman's books are set in Hollywood, but the only novel with a film-related character is *The Velvet Knife* (Doubleday, 1959), which is narrated by novelist and scriptwriter Dick Fleming. He is helped to Hollywood by a New York promoter who is obsessed with America's most popular singer.

SIMONE SIGNORET (1921–85) was a prominent French actress, whose films include *La Ronde* (1950), *Les Diaboliques* (1955), *Room at the Top*

(1958, for which she won an Academy Award), *Ship of Fools* (1965), *Is Paris Burning?* (1966), and *Madame Rosa* (1977). Her autobiography, *Nostalgia Isn't What It Used to Be*, was published in the United States in 1976. Signoret's first and only novel, **Adieu Volodya** (Random House, 1986), translated by Stanley Hochman, was first published in France in 1985. It is an evocative and descriptive tale of a group of Eastern European Jewish émigrés in Paris from 1925 through the end of World War II. Two of the women become dressmakers and are soon involved in providing costumes for the French film industry. There is some commentary on the films of the period, but the emphasis is more on the lives of the various characters, their loves, their dealings with the political climates of the day, and their relationships with each other. There are times when one wishes one knew a little more about French politics, but on the whole this is a moving and often amusing novel.

DIANA SILBER (born 1936). Four friends, who have known each other since college, find that secrets from the past can come back to haunt them in **Confessions** (Bantam Books, 1990). One of the four is a successful Hollywood screenwriter who has returned to New York for the opening of her first stageplay off Broadway. She becomes mentally deranged and is murdered by an old friend, just one of the acts of violence with which each woman is threatened.

MEL SILVERSTEIN (born 1940). Andrea Crawford is a film director in **Conspiracy of Silence** (Doubleday, 1980), but her profession is not particularly relevant to the story. When a surgeon discovers a cancerous growth in Andrea's breast, she sues her former doctor, who failed to diagnose the problem. None of that doctor's colleagues will testify against him, and when the surgeon who did spot the cancer bears witness on her behalf, he is fired from his position and spurned by the medical community.

GEORGES SIMENON (1903–89) began writing his series of novels featuring Inspector Jules Maigret of the French Police Judiciaire in 1931 with *Prètr-le-Letton/Maigret and the Enigmatic Left*. **The Heart of a Man** (Prentice-Hall, 1951) was first published in France in 1950 as *Les Violets Vert*. It is the story of Maugin, a legendary French actor of stage and screen who, at the age of 59, is told he must slow down. He retires to the south of France but returns to Paris for one last fling—and dies. "A dissection that is precise in both medical and emotional pathology, this is overlaid with the specter of death and despair," commented *Kirkus* (June 25, 1951).

In **Maigret's Pickpocket** (Harcourt, Brace & World, 1967), translated by Nigel Ryan, the detective meets a thief with a dead wife and seeks the killer within the French film industry. The novel was first published in France in 1967 as *Le Voleur de Maigret*.

JOHANNES MARIO SIMMEL (born 1924). While in a Roman clinic, a former child star named Jordan relates the "bad and wicked" story of **To the Bitter End** (McGraw-Hill, 1970). His artistic temperament and desperation to make a comeback lead to drugs and filmmaking in Hamburg. The novel was translated from the German, *Bis zu Bitteren Neige*, by Rosemary Mays.

CLIVE SINCLAIR (born 1948). *Bed Bugs* (Allison & Busby, 1982) is a collection of short stories, including one about Mickey Mouse being assassinated at Disneyland, and another concerned with Jewish immigrant filmmakers in Hollywood.

MURRAY SINCLAIR (born 1950) has written a series of mystery novels featuring screenwriter and part-time sleuth Ben Crandel. He was introduced in *Tough in L.A.* (Black Lizard Books, 1980), in which he had to track down the killer of a former prostitute who had refused to star in a porno film and in whose death Crandel was implicated. A human body is found in the La Brea tar pits in *Only in L.A.* (A&W, 1982), and later Crandel must contend with the kidnapping of his adopted son and basset hound, and a demand that he rewrite a script by a legendary Hollywood writer. Neo-Nazis figure prominently in *Goodbye L.A.* (Black Lizard Books, 1988), in which Crandel's adopted son becomes a punk rocker and a *Los Angeles Times* reporter disappears. In all three novels, the city of Los Angeles plays a leading role in the drama.

HOWARD SINGER's novel *Wake Me When It's Over* was filmed by Hollywood in 1960. In *The Devil and Henry Raffin* (Funk and Wagnalls, 1967), the young minister of the title writes a thesis on the Dead Sea scrolls which a Hollywood producer acquires to film as *The Sword and the Scroll*. Raffin meets the star, a sex symbol who is surprisingly respectable, the two marry, and Raffin leaves his church. She helps him restore integrity to the film.

JUNE FLAUM SINGER (born 1933). *Star Dreams* (M. Evans, 1983) begins on the afternoon of the 1970 Academy Awards presentation, at which gossip columnist Beebie Tyler is to receive an honorary Oscar. She is visited by a young journalist from Omaha, Nebraska, and relates to her the story of two sisters, Kiki Devlin and Angela du Beaumond. Aside from the unlikelihood of any gossip columnist's receiving an Oscar, it must have been an awfully long afternoon, and surely any author would know that in 1970, the Academy Awards were presented in an auditorium, not at a banquet style gathering. The two girls are born in New Orleans; after being caught in flagrante delicto with their aunt, their father runs off to Hollywood to become a minor B picture leading man, later moving to Europe as a "kept man" of various aging and wealthy women. The two sisters remain friends throughout their lives, as Kiki becomes a film star and Angela marries a politician who becomes the governor of California and later is wed to a powerful magnate. Despite many problems, which are often resolved with oral sex, the two sisters survive, both nominated for an Oscar in 1970, both ultimately losers but winners in that they are reunited with their father.

Kiki, whose screen career begins in 1950, has sexual encounters with three famous men: Errol Flynn (who "was so filled with booze that his performance suffered"), Clark Gable ("she would never ever reveal to anyone that the King was not absolutely regal in bed"), and Howard Hughes ("whoever billed Howard Hughes as one of the world's great lovers was either its biggest liar or had never gone to bed with him"). Part of the story takes place at Grace Kelly's wedding to Prince Rainier of Monaco, where an unsavory multimillionaire becomes obsessed with Angela, later making her an international star.

A Daphne du Maurier heroine might dream of returning to Manderley, but Buffy King, the heroine/narrator of *The Movie Set* (M. Evans, 1984) dreams of returning to Ohio State University, where she met her husband, Todd, and began friendships with a group of women who ultimately wind up in Hollywood. Buffy and Todd make a fortune in Ohio, building shopping malls, and then Todd moves on to Hollywood, where he buys a studio and names it after his wife. Hollywood contaminates everyone in the Ohio group, even good-hearted Todd, who is drugged and seduced by the female companion of a rock star who just happens to have syphilis. Todd infects Buffy, and she is forced to abort her fourth child. She and Todd live together in name only until virtually the last page when Buffy learns the facts behind Todd's one night of infidelity.

If portions of the plot might read as if lifted from *Damaged Lives* or some other VD classic of the past, the author does deserve praise for a (at times) brilliant parody of Hollywood life and mores—if only one could believe that the author is aware she is indulging in parody. She does offer a tasteless portrait of a Howard Hughes character, living at the top of a Las Vegas hotel, and also provides an amusing glimpse at the attitudes and behaviors of the staff at the Beverly Wilshire Hotel.

The President's Women (Crown, 1988) is the story of Judith Stanton and her determination that her son, Rud Tyler Stanton, become president of the United States. One of the erstwhile president's women is his great-aunt, a movie star named Carlotta Collings.

"Grandly silly" (according to *Kirkus*), *Brilliant Divorces* (William Morrow, 1993) chronicles four such separations in the life of the English daughter of a barmaid, who begins married life with the homosexual son of a British lord. Her third husband is an actor and the fourth is a movie mogul. Told in flashback form, 1943 to the present, *Brilliant Divorces* is brilliant bestseller fluffery.

CHARLIE SMITH. *Chimney Rock* (Henry Holt, 1993) is a Hollywood saga with literary pretentions. Growing up in a Hollywood movie family, Willie Blake falls naturally into the role of a rising screen actor. At the same time, he must deal with a monomaniacal producer father, who drove his younger son to suicide, destroyed his wife's career, and is now carrying on a liaison with Willie's wife, actress Zebra (Kate) Dunn. The novel reaches a climax when Willie discovers that his wife is pregnant with his father's child. "The stream-of-consciousness sentences are occasionally ponderous and confusing, and Will's philosophical ramblings are sometimes repetitive," wrote Emily Melton in *Booklist* (April 1, 1993), "but this book is so full of originality, raw power, great pain, and terrible beauty that it makes mere quibbles of what might be serious defects in another, less brilliant novel."

LADY ELEANOR FURNEAUX SMITH. *The Spanish House* (Doubleday, 1938) is a colorful romantic novel about gypsy Paris Faa, who lives in both Belgium and Spain. One of the characters she meets is a Hollywood movie star.

HARRY ALAN SMITH (1907–76). *Mister Zip* (Doubleday, 1952) is a burlesque on the Hollywood Western, in which Midwesterner Clifford

Humphrey is transformed by Hollywood into cowboy star Mister Zip. Disappointed by what he finds in the film capital, Humphrey sets out in company with a sidekick character actor to find the real West. "As a story to be read just for fun, *Mister Zip* is quite successful," wrote Irving Babow in the *San Francisco Chronicle* (February 12, 1952). "But on another level also, with its many sharp insights into the social psychology of our national character, the novel is a revealing document. Of course this unpretentious novel has no such 'serious' purpose, but in reading of the process by which a highly puerile young man becomes a national hero, one wonders what Hollywood and the advertising man have wrought." To the reviewer in the *Saturday Review* (January 26, 1952), "*Mister Zip* starts out as satire—in the strictly collegiate sense—and ends up with a burlesque of the Western movie that is supposed to have you in stitches. Unfortunately, not even Mr. Smith can be funnier than a Western movie."

DAVID SNELL (born 1942) is an actor and writer whose thriller *Lights, Camera ... Murder* (St. Martin's, 1979) is entertaining but outrageously unbelievable. New York actor Osgood Bass has a new screen role, as leading man to Selena Carpenter. She also hires him as a semibodyguard because she believes someone is threatening her life. After Bass is nearly shot, beaten up, and otherwise harassed, he discovers that she and a female friend have been getting their kicks by terrorizing him. But no sooner does the truth come out than Selena is killed on the film set. It transpires that the producer and a colleague are making two films; one is the legitimate drama and the other is a pornographic snuff film, in which the more erotic love scenes between Bass and Carpenter will be used as well as footage of her death during a rape sequence. Just as Bass is about to be killed as part of the snuff film, he is rescued by his agent.

LAURENCE SNELLING (born 1933). A screenwriter tries to solve two murder cases in *The Heresy* (W.W. Norton, 1973), when a murder is committed on the set of a film he has written whose plot concerns the unsolved killing of an American in Paris in 1940.

CAROL SNYDER (born 1941). *Ike & Mama and the Once-in-a-Lifetime Movie* (Coward, McCann & Geoghegan, 1981) is a charming story for children, set in the Bronx in 1920. Ike Greenburg and his friends sneak into a screening of *Broken Blossoms* without paying. His mother insists the children must put matters right; Ike goes to watch D.W. Griffith shooting on location, is hired as an extra, and earns enough money to take his entire family to see Griffith's *Way Down East*.

JERRY SOHL (born 1913). *The Resurrection of Frank Bòrchard* (Simon & Schuster, 1973): Frank Bòrchard, a successful Hollywood producer, survives a heart attack, but, unable to cope with his existence, he runs away to die. Bòrchard meets a couple of seekers of cosmic consciousness, passes through various altered states, and is eventually strong enough, both mentally and physically, to survive a heart bypass operation. I can only agree with Maya Lauberstein of the American Pharmaceutical Association, writing in *Library Journal* (February 1, 1973), "Frank Bòrchard died and was resurrected. So what?"

MARIO SOLDATI (born 1906). *The Malacca Cane* (St. Martin's Press, 1973), translated from the Italian by Gwyn Morris, is apparently semi-autobiographical. A "plodding novel of self torture" (*Library Journal*, September 15, 1973), this is the story of aristocratic Emilio who seeks in vain for a love similar to that he felt as a child for the working-class Piero. A marriage of convenience leads to Soldati's obtaining a job in the Rome film industry. The novel closes with Piero's daughter killing Emilio on her father's grave.

BRAD SOLOMON's (born 1945) first novel, *The Gone Man* (Random House, 1977), features private detective/actor Charlie Quinlan, who is hired to find Jamie Stockton, the drug-addicted alcoholic son of movie and television mogul Ethen Stockton and his ex–movie star wife. Quinlan thinks he has found Jamie dead, but it is only an actor impersonating the son. Contemporary reviews were not enthusiastic.

Jake & Katie (Dial Press, 1979) is the tale of a sadomasochistic relationship, as the mysterious Katie takes over the life and career of failed Hollywood actor Jake. She gets him jobs and then systematically sets out to destroy his career. "The good stuff here—much terrific dialogue and some very convincing glimpses of the foul life of a non-star TV-and-film actor—may compensate for the undue length and the ugly transparency of the romantic/sadistic/masochistic goings-on," wrote *Kirkus*.

TERRY SOUTHERN (born 1926) is an eminent screenwriter—*Dr. Strangelove; or, How I Learned to Stop Worrying and Love the Bomb* (1964), *The Loved One* (1965), *Easy Rider* (1969), and others—and novelist, whose work in both media is noted for its satiric quality. *Blue Movie* (World Publishing, 1970) might be considered a follow-up to Southern's 1958 satire on pornography, *Candy*. The target here is the film industry, with a Hollywood producer deciding to make the ultimate pornographic movie, *The Faces of Love*. The film is to be shot in Liechtenstein, which will have the exclusive right to screen the film for ten years, and while the film is in production its cast and crew indulge in every known sexual act. "A tasteless, kinky book," was the opinion of David Dempsey in the *New York Times* (September 13, 1970).

NORMAN SPANRAD (born 1940). *Passing Through the Flame* (G.P. Putnam's Sons, 1974) owes something to the Woodstock rock festival. Jango Beck is a producer in the recording division of a major Hollywood studio. An evil genius, who plans to take over the studio, he is determined to profit from his idea to make a film about a rock festival in the California desert by controlling the drug concessions. "There are enough sex scenes to make even the most prurient celibate, and some very silly writing," sniffed Susan Beth Pfeffer in *Library Journal* (December 15, 1974).

MURIEL SPARK (born 1918). *The Public Image* (Alfred A. Knopf, 1968) is a short novella set in Rome, and concerns the relationship between a film actress, Anna Christopher, and her playwright husband. After many years of obscurity, she has at last become a star, but her husband arranges an orgy in her apartment while committing suicide in a deliberate attempt to destroy his wife's image. "Brilliantly crafted, with the new breed of hollow men and women in amber," commented *Kirkus*.

CECILY SPAULDING. *From This Day On* (Arcadia House, 1942) is a somewhat tiresome novel about Hallie Singleton's love for actor Eric Adams. He is not successful either in Hollywood or in New York. Eventually, he joins the RAF and is killed, and Hallie is free to marry his brother.

DOROTHY SPEARE (1898–1951). The title *The Road to Needles* (Houghton Mifflin, 1937) is a reference to a small town on the Arizona side of the border with California, where trains from Los Angeles to Chicago stop to pick up water. The story here is of a New England woman who comes to Hollywood to work as a screenwriter, marries a drunken playwright, and, her dreams shattered, takes the road to Needles. "*The Road to Needles*, with a multitude of subsidiary plots, is readable, and there are many details sufficiently accurate to make any reformed Hollywood writer smile," wrote Phil Stong in *Saturday Review of Literature* (February 13, 1937). "The general social picture of the writer's life in Hollywood is, however, untrue and unjust so far as this reviewer has been able to observe."

BART SPICER (born 1918). As its title suggests, *Festival* (Atheneum, 1970) takes place at the Cannes Film Festival, where American publicist Ethan Allen Chapin is officially promoting a film by a respected veteran Hollywood director and unofficially publicizing a low-budget production from a blacklisted filmmaker friend. Chapin's son and a group of left-wing students disrupt the festival, and no Palme d'Or is awarded that year.

KAREN STABINER. *Limited Engagements* (Seaview/Simon & Schuster, 1979) features a female director, Rae Drummond, and screenwriter, Phoebe, who are trying to sell a script that Drummond will direct. Drummond's producer/boyfriend is not interested, being heavily involved with his ex-wife's activities. When the boyfriend leaves the studio to become an independent producer, Drummond is able to sell her script package to his successor. Here is a feminist viewpoint, coupled with a solid knowledge of contemporary Hollywood.

DAVID STACTON (1925–68) was known for his historical novels when he wrote his first book with a contemporary theme, *Old Acquaintance* (G.P. Putnam's Sons, 1964). Urbane and witty, the novel describes the reunion of two old friends at a film festival in Luxembourg. Charlie is an acclaimed novelist who is sitting on the festival jury, while Lotte is a famous singer and actress (obviously modeled after Marlene Dietrich; she even sings "Falling in Love Again"). Charlie brings with him a young and kept male lover named Paul, and Lotte has a similar female companion named Unne. Nothing much happens aside from a great deal of brilliant dialogue, and Paul and Unne falling in love and getting married. There is some extremely entertaining commentary on the types of films usually screened at film festivals:

> There is the magnificent Czech film which probably is magnificent, if you could just see it, for all the red filter photography.... It will get the prize

unless the Polish film wins instead. The Polish film is exactly the same, except that it takes place in a sewer. At the end of the Polish film the hero emerges from the sewer, takes a look around, and then goes back down it again. In Central Europe it is always groundhog day. All you see is the lid fitting back on again, in the middle of an empty street. This represents life. If the Poles are feeling cheerful this year, a water truck goes by. This represents hope and shows the eternal continuity of things.... The U.S.S.R. has sent along a film completely free of propaganda, but you won't see it, because at the last moment it was withdrawn because it was completely free of propaganda.... The Finns have sent a nature film, about winter, very long; the Swedes an adaptation from Strindberg, even longer; and the French, as usual, are being French."

AUDREY STAINTON. *Sweet Rome* (Holt, Rinehart & Winston, 1982) begins in the 1950s when Mike Donato, an English-born star of Italian films, is arrested and convicted for the murder of public relations gossipmonger Beppe Palazzo. Released 20 years later, Donato determines to track down Palazzo, who he does not believe is dead. A pleasant mix of humor and background information on the Italian film industry.

FRANCESCA STANFILL. *Wakefield Hall* (Random House, 1993) is a romance of intrigue as journalist Elizabeth Rowan follows the instructions in the will of beloved actress Joanna Eakins and attempts to write her biography. There is more to Eakins's character than might appear on the surface.

JOHN STANLEY *see* KENN DAVIS and JOHN STANLEY

D. STAPLETON was the pseudonym of Dorothy Stapleton and Douglas Stapleton. The central character of *The Crime, the Place and the Girl* (Arcadia House, 1955) is press agent Peter Hack (perhaps a little joke there?), who is sent by his studio, Loeb Films, to locate an attractive young woman with star potential who appears at a Hollywood premiere. When he does find her, he discovers that she has been accused of murder and he must prove her innocence.

JIMMY STARR (1904–90) began his career as a gossip columnist in 1924 with the *Los Angeles Daily Record*; from there he moved to the *Los Angeles Herald*, where he remained until 1962. He wrote silent title cards and scripts for a handful of films, and also appeared in a few features. *365 Nights in Hollywood* (David Graham Fischer, 1926) consists of a series of short stories with a pretence of being literary art and running a total of 365 pages. The first edition was limited to 1,000 signed and numbered copies, and one story is a polite putdown of director Fred Niblo. The book was filmed in 1934 by Fox, directed by George Marshall, as a vehicle for Alice Faye.

Set against a Hollywood film industry background, *The Corpse Came C.O.D.* (Murray & Gee, 1944) has newspaper reporter Joe Medford solve two murders. Columbia filmed the novel in 1947, under the direction of Henry Levin, with George Brent and Joan Blondell. In *Three Short Biers* (Murray & Gee, 1945), three tiny coffins are delivered to a Hollywood studio, and shortly thereafter three midgets are murdered. Joe Medford investigates.

NEVILLE STEED. *Die Cast* (Weidenfeld and Nicholson, 1987) is the second mystery novel to feature antique toy dealer Peter Marklin, and it is one of the most entertaining volumes in the series. A Hollywood actor by the name of Lana-Lee Claudell comes to Marklin's native Dorset. When her husband is murdered, the prime suspects have an alibi; they were watching *Sleuth* on television. As an example of the influence of the motion picture on the literary world, when a butler shelters Marklin from the rain under an umbrella, he is described as doing a Gene Kelly act.

DANIELLE STEEL (born 1947) is noted for her romantic novels featuring the rich and powerful, generally formulaic, but never ceasing to have strong reader appeal. More than 125 million copies have been sold of the novels that she first began writing in 1973 with *Going Home*, and *Crossings* (1986), *Kalaidoscope* (1990), and *Fine Things* (1990) have been adapted as television miniseries.

Family Album (Delacorte Press, 1985) is the story of the 40-year-old marriage of screen star Fay Price and shipping magnate Ward Thayer. After countless personal and financial struggles, Fay becomes "the most important female director in the world," and also manages to save the marriage and the couple's joint fortune.

Danielle Steel tries to answer the questions, what is a star, and what does stardom really mean, in *Star* (Delacorte Press, 1989). Here, 14-year-old Crystal Wyatt discovers that events can conspire to lead her to Hollywood and stardom. Of course, the heroine also has the help of a beautiful singing voice and a love for a man who belonged to another.

DANIEL M. STEIN. In *Wall of Noise* (Crown, 1960), a young racehorse trainer finds himself socially out of his depth when a California millionaire hires him to train a newly acquired racehorse. The millionaire's wife just happens to be an ex–movie star.

DANIEL STERN. *Miss America* (Random House, 1959) is narrated by Peter Shaw, a musician who provides title character Catherine Forester with the security that she needs. After winning the Miss America contest, Forester goes to Hollywood and has an affair with a man who promises to produce a film in which she will star.

Final Cut (Richard Seaver/Viking Press, 1975) is described by its publisher as about the power brokers and corrupters who control filmmaking; writer James Jones calls it "a scary picture, it makes a sort of Last Tycoon of the Seventies." Yet, in hindsight, the novel seems oddly dated, a far cry from the harsh corporate world of filmmaking in the 1990s. It is the story of Ezra Marks, who regards President Kennedy as his mentor, has made a few educational films, and is wooed to Hollywood by an executive with King Studios. When he arrives at the studio, he meets its aging, crippled, and despotic head, Lothar Kleinholz, and discovers that the man who hired him has been dismissed and is involved in a fierce proxy battle with Kleinholz for control of the studio. Kleinholz has only two films in production: one is a documentary on a rock festival, and the other an Italian independent feature. There are problems with both. The director of the documentary will not permit his film to be cut or viewed prior to completion.

The Italian drama has a homosexual director and a homosexual, aging British actor, both of whom are in love with the production's young male discovery. Ezra Marks's job is to promote both films, but, through his actions, inadvertently, the young male lead in the Italian film is murdered by the studio publicist. In addition to dealing with his guilt, Marks must consider his position in the fight for control of the studio. The outsider's view of studio politics has its interest, but the character of Ezra Marks evokes little or no empathy on the part of the reader.

B. (Burton) E. (Egbert) STEVENSON (1872–1962). An American film company heads for Egypt to produce a feature based on the last line in a poem by William Ernest Henley, "When I Was a King in Babylon and You Were a Virgin Slave" *(Echoes, 1872–1889)*, in *A King in Babylon* (Small, Maynard, 1923). An Egyptologist from the Metropolitan Museum of Art is a member of the crew, using the expedition as an excuse to return to his excavation. The leading man is affected by sunstroke and believes he and his costar are reincarnations of a king and his favorite buried 4,000 years earlier in the tomb. Events suggest that the reincarnation theory may be true, and the novel ends with the couple riding off into the desert. The story is narrated by the cinematographer.

SYLVIA STEVENSON. *The Flowering Aloe* (Henry Holt, 1937) — a "sensitive and delicate book," wrote the reviewer in the *Times Literary Supplement* (March 13, 1937) — is the story of an English widow of 59, determined not to be a burden to her children, who takes up various pursuits in order to fight loneliness. One of the three children works in the British film industry.

FRED MUSTARD STEWART (born 1936). *The Titan* (Simon & Schuster, 1985) is the story of an American tycoon, Nick Fleming, whose life is dominated by desires for power and sex. Among his holdings is a Hollywood film studio.

RAMONA STEWART (born 1922). *The Apparition* (Little, Brown, 1973) is a frightening drama of modern life. The principal characters are an anthropologist and his son, who is making "a quasi-existential documentary." The subject matter includes a suicide, conspiracy, and murder.

PAULINE STILES. *Red Pavilion* (Doubleday, 1936) is the story of handsome British film star Roger Mallard, who becomes popular on both sides of the Atlantic despite being deaf. Beatrice Sherman in the *New York Times* (October 18, 1936) thought the story combined "dignity and romance," while Lisle Bell in the *New York Herald Tribune* (October 25, 1936) considered it "shrill without being exciting, and even more remote from reality than Hollywood is from London."

EDWARD STILGEBAUER (1868–19??). It is difficult to know whether the author or the translator, E.W. Wilson, is responsible for the very heavy hand in the writing of *The Star of Hollywood* (International Fiction

Library, 1929). First published in Germany in 1927, the novel opens with the death from morphine and cocaine poisoning of the "Star of Hollywood," an actress named Rita Aston. The studio doctor determines that her death is accidental, but another drug-related death follows...

JIM STIMSON used his background as a film school graduate and worker in various capacities in film and video production in a series of mystery novels set in the Los Angeles area and featuring Stoney Winston, a willing if not always proficient filmmaker, each of whose jobs usually gets him involved in murder.

Double Exposure (Charles Scribner's Sons, 1985) introduces Winston in his usual situation—unemployment. He is hired to find the missing daughter of a studio executive, and along the way becomes involved in pornographic filmmaking and gay parties. Winston actually gets the opportunity to make a film in *Low Angles* (Charles Scribner's Sons, 1986), when a producer asks him to ghost-direct a low-budget biker movie being shot in the San Gabriel Mountains. He is to help a female director, Diane LaMotta, who resents the interference; the cinematographer is a drunkard; and a series of accidents makes it clear that someone wants the film stopped. This is the best of the bunch and the only novel with considerable description of the filmmaking process. *Truck Shot* (Charles Scribner's Sons, 1989) is entertaining, if implausible, as Stoney Winston takes a job teaching film production at a decaying Los Angeles arts and design college. When the college president is killed in an explosion, Winston becomes involved in a real estate scam and discovers that the president's death was the inadvertent outcome of a student film he was supervising. *TV Safe* (Charles Scribner's Sons, 1991) finds Winston working on a television game show whose female star is receiving threatening letters. She lives with a "nerdy" member of the crew whose specialty is imitating the voices of cartoon characters and whose master's thesis was entitled "Gender Identity in Warner Brothers Cartoons." His comment concerning how often Bugs Bunny gets into drag has more significance than the reader might first suspect. The novel's title refers to the area of a frame of film that will not be cut off if shown on television.

MONICA STIRLING (1916–83). *Ladies with a Unicorn* (Simon & Schuster, 1954) is the story of four women who love one man, an Italian film producer named Anton-Giulio. The background is the Italian film industry, and *Kirkus* (January 12, 1954) considered this "a graceful and worldly entertainment." *The Summer of a Dormouse* (Harcourt, Brace & World, 1967) is the study of the time spent by a movie star in a mental institution; she was committed after a suicide attempt. Stirling wrote the 1965 biography *The Life and Times of Hans Christian Andersen*, and the reviewer in the *Times Literary Supplement* (September 21, 1967) said that the novel "is presumably meant to be something of a modern fairy tale."

ROBERT STONE (born 1937). *Children of Light* (Alfred A. Knopf, 1986) is a stylish novel, but its theme and characters are so depressingly self-absorbed that it has little appeal. Its author writes of a film industry in which everyone is an alcoholic, or a participant in substance abuse, where people do not care for anyone but themselves unless they are paid to take care of others. The love affair between the two central characters is so removed from anything a reader can comprehend that it becomes neither beautiful nor emotionally over-whelming, but sleazy and beneath contempt. The one protagonist is a screen-writer, separated from his wife and children, who journeys to Mexico where a screenplay he wrote is being filmed, with a former lover, Lee Verger, as the star. She is married with children, and as Gordon Walker, the writer, arrives on the set, her husband has just left to take the children to visit his parents. Walker is obviously bad for Verger; he is too self-involved to understand or care, and she is too weak to resist. Those in the film company close to the pair know but do not care, including the young director of the film and his aging father who lives in Mexico (and is perhaps loosely based on John Huston). Verger's death, paral-leling that of the heroine of the film, seems a foregone conclusion long before it happens. It is only regrettable that the author did not decide to take other members of the company along with her. The book contains one curious error, in that the author has Walker and his agent leave Musso and Frank restaurant in Hollywood and then be on a street a couple of miles east of that restaurant's actual location.

PHIL STONG (1899–1957) is best remembered for his first novel, *State Fair* (Century, 1932), which was filmed in 1933, 1945, and 1962. *The Farmer in the Dell* (Harcourt, Brace, 1935) is a study in contrasts as a retired Iowa farmer, Pa Boyer, decides to crash the movies. "Written obviously for the movies, the book combines a series of rollicking incidents, with much bright con-versation. There is never a dull moment, and there are several particularly amus-ing spots," wrote the reviewer in the *Christian Science Monitor* (July 12, 1935). "The characterization is not so superficial as it seems at first, for Mr. Stong has a talent for incisive phrasing. Nevertheless, the accent remains on the action, as in most stories constructed purely for light entertainment." As prophesied, the novel was filmed in 1936 by RKO, directed by Ben Holmes, and starring Fred Stone, Jean Parker, and Esther Dale.

NOEL STREATFEILD (1895–1986) was an English writer responsible for 45 novels and 17 works of nonfiction. The most endearing and enduring of her works are the so-called Shoes Books, all of which have "shoes" in their titles, and which began in 1936 with *Ballet Shoes*. Written primarily for teenagers, but perhaps equally appealing to adults, the 12 novels in the series always feature talented, artistic children.

The sixth book in the series, *Movie Shoes* (Random House, 1949), features the Winter family of London, whose members decide to spend six months in Santa Monica, California, for the sake of Mr. Winter's health, staying with his sister. The middle one of Winter's three children, Jane, is neither par-ticularly polite nor attractive, but on the second day of the family's visit, while walking on the beach, she meets a young director from Bee Bee Studios. He ar-ranges a screen test for Jane, and the girl is cast as Mary in the version of *The Secret Garden* the director is currently filming. The appeal of the book rests largely on Jane's difficult personality and her on-set fighting with a child star who, unlike Jane, is a professional actor.

Movie Shoes is discussed in detail by Noel Perrin in "Cinderella with an At-titude" (*Los Angeles Times Book Review*, January 24, 1993, pp. 2, 5).

FLORENCE STUART. A typical romance, *Happiness Hill* (Arcadia House, 1961) features a young doctor from Tennessee who is named "Mr. Sweetheart." He is brought to Hollywood for publicity purposes, and there he meets screen star Lili Landon. The novel's title is the title of her latest film.

FRANCIS WILLIAM SULLIVAN (1887–19??). *Star of the North* (G.P. Putnam's Sons, 1916): While the Graphic Company is on location in Canada, leading man Paul Temple wanders away from the camp and meets June Magregor, whose father works for the Hudson Bay Company. She returns with him to the camp and becomes the object of affection of both Temple and juvenile Jack Baillie. It seems that June is drawn to the latter, until she realizes his true character when he fails to rescue her while she is doubling for the leading lady and later tries to seduce her. Temple does not reveal that he has a wife who will not divorce him, but June meets the woman when she comes to Canada to find her husband. Luckily for June and Temple, the wife dies in a snowstorm. "The futile past became only an evil dream, and they faced forward together, eager for the new life that opened to them, so glorious and full of promise." The description of location filming does not read true.

LEON Z. (Zaven) SURMELIAN (born 1907). The journey of tubercular Daniel Moore from one institution to another is documented in *98.6°* (E.P. Dutton, 1950). In a private sanatarium, he has a brief encounter with a Hollywood screenwriter. The book manages to blend explicit discussion of various diseases with lurid sexual encounters.

JACQUELINE SUSANN (1921–74) was the Jackie Collins of her day, whose novel *Valley of the Dolls* (Bernard Geis, 1966) was a phenomenal success and spawned an equally popular 20th Century–Fox feature film, *Jacqueline Susann's Valley of the Dolls* (1981), directed by Walter Grauman and starring Catherine Hicks, Lisa Hartman, Veronica Hamel, David Birney, and Jean Simmons. The book is the story of three New York women, Jen, Neely, and Anne. Jen becomes a European sex queen and commits suicide, Neely becomes a Hollywood star, and Anne is successful in television. All three are addicted to sex and drugs, and the title "dolls" are red seconal, yellow nembutal, and emerald green amytal. "For the reader who has put away comic books but isn't yet ready for editorials in the *Daily News*, *Valley of the Dolls* may bridge an awkward gap" was the opinion of Gloria Steinem in *Book Week* (April 24, 1966).

HENRY SUTTON is the pseudonym of David Slavitt (born 1935). *The Exhibitionist* (Bernard Geis, 1967) created considerable controversy when it was first published because of its graphic sexual content. The central character is an unhappy Hollywood star whose marriages and affairs are failures, and whose daughter, also a movie star, suffers similar problems.

PAUL TABOR. *Lighter Than Vanity* (Cassell, 1953) is identified by Carolyn See as a Hollywood novel.

MARY TANNEN (born 1943). *Second Sight* (Alfred A. Knopf, 1988) is the contemporary story of a once affluent Anglo-Hispanic family in a fading New Jersey mill town. One of the family members reads tarot cards, and is approached by the actress girlfriend of a prominent New York film director. After she foresees a couple of accidents that happen to the director, he becomes obsessed with her to the point that, at the book's close, they are married. While the relationship between the psychic and the director is an interesting one, it is not the primary focus of the novel, which intertwines the lives of its various protagonists in a deeply fascinating fashion. *Second Sight* is a first novel that manages to combine the mundane with the exotic, and never loses the attention of the reader.

SYLVIA TATE. Despite its title, *The Fuzzy Pink Nightgown* (Harper, 1956) is not a sex drama but a somewhat predictable mystery novel. An ex-con and his buddy kidnap a Hollywood sex symbol named Laurel Gold. When the two kidnappers have doubts about their escapade, Laurel persuades them to go through with the crime, reasoning that the publicity can only help her faltering career. The novel was filmed in 1957 for United Artists release, under the direction of Norman Taurog, and starring Jane Russell, Ralph Meeker, and Keenan Wynn.

ISABELLA TAVES (born 1915). This author's first novel, *The Quick Rich Fox* (Random House, 1959), has a young, female publicist writing the biography of a has-been actress. The central character in the latter's life is a mysterious invalid, Bert Irving, a former studio head and now the silent partner in a talent agency, who exerts tremendous influence over the actress, two other women, and eventually the publicist. His death frees all four women. *Kirkus* (August 27, 1959) described this as "a curious, mildly interesting story."

ANNE TAYLOR (born 1934) **and FERN MOSK.** The story of *Press On Regardless; or, The Confessions of a Sports Car Addict* (Simon & Schuster, 1956) is told in the form of a series of letters from sports car enthusiast Prudence Trumbull to her mother. She is fired as an assistant costume designer in the film industry and takes to selling and driving fast sports cars in Hollywood. One of her customers is a producer who uses his Oscar statuette for Best Picture as a hood ornament.

ELIZABETH TEBBETS-TAYLOR. Indian detective Joseph Pratt Miles discovers who has murdered a Hollywood actress in an exclusive dress shop in *Now I Lay Me Down to Die* (Arcadia House, 1955).

JAN TEMPEST is the pseudonym of British writer Irene Maude Swatridge, who has written more than 200 romances under various names. Even allowing for the general mediocrity of such books, few if any lovesick maidens can find much to admire in *Short Cut to the Stars* (Mills & Boon, 1949). Teenager Amanda O'Geary persuades her older sister, Louise, that the two of them should seek employment as housemaids at a secluded Cornish mansion, where producer/actor Torre Steger finds a refuge from the harsh realities of public life. Amanda convinces Steger to offer her a screen test, but it is Louise who intrigues the man. The writing is abysmal and the plot ludicrous.

ELSWYTH THANE was the pseudonym of Elswyth Thane Beebe (born 1900). *Remember Today: Leaves from a Guardian Angel's Notebook* (Duell, Sloan & Pearce, 1941) is, as its title suggests, "written" by a guardian angel. The angel's charges are Sierra Thompson and James Montgomery, who meet at the age of 12 and fall in love. They are not reunited until after Sierra begins in a film career in Hollywood and is sent to England to make a feature there. Beebe should have worked as a screenwriter for Frank Capra.

LEE THAYER (1874–1973) wrote a number of mystery novels featuring Peter Clancy and his valet, Wiggar. In *Murder on Location* (Dodd, Mead, 1942), Clancy is at a dude ranch watching a Western being filmed when a murder takes place. "Lives of horse-opera actors get thorough and colorful ventilating in picturesque and slightly tiresome tale, with interesting and cinematic climax" was the description in the *Saturday Review of Literature* (August 22, 1942).

BOB THOMAS (born 1922) has been reporting on film for the Associated Press since 1943. Beginning in 1958 with *Walt Disney: The Art of Animation*, he has authored more than a dozen show business biographies.

The *Flesh Merchants* (Dell Publishing, 1959) is identified by Carolyn See as a Hollywood novel. *Kirkus* describes *Weekend '33* (Doubleday, 1971) as "a melodrama dated from its title onwards." The basic plotline concerns a William Randolph Hearst–like newspaper tycoon who is at his castle in central California over Labor Day weekend, 1933, trying to manipulate four studio heads into giving him control of the film industry. There are many references to Hollywood events and personalities.

LLOYD S. THOMPSON. When Hollywood producer Lucien Cantwell is murdered while attending the premiere of his latest film in *Death Stops the Show* (Crown, 1946), there are many suspects, in view of Cantwell's unpopularity, but ultimately the murder is linked to a group of Nazi extremists. A drama critic helps the police in their investigation.

DAVID THOMSON (born 1941) has written a number of well-regarded nonfiction works on Hollywood: *Movie Man* (Stein and Day, 1967), *The Biographical Dictionary of Film* (William Morrow, 1976, 1981), *America in the Dark: Hollywood and the Gift of Unreality* (William Morrow, 1977), *Overexposure: The Crisis in American Filmmaking* (William Morrow, 1981), *Warren Beatty and Desert Eyes: A Life and a Story* (Doubleday, 1987), and *Showman: The Life of David O. Selznick* (Alfred A. Knopf, 1992).

Suspects (Alfred A. Knopf, 1985) consists of a series of biographical sketches of characters from the great Hollywood films, beginning with Jake Gittes, who was played by Jack Nicholson in *Chinatown* (1974). All of the characters are in some way related so that they are first introduced in the sketch of an earlier character. Critical response was mixed. In the *New York Times* (June 30, 1985), Phillip Lopate wrote, "The book's trick frame may, in the end, provide too shaky a support for such speculations. But if *Suspects* does not always live up to its ambition as experimental fiction, it deserves respect as an endlessly intriguing parody sourcebook on the movies and as a fertile meditation on the trajectory of character." In *The Nation* (July 6, 1985), Terrence Rafferty commented,

> Thomson's notion is that our movies and our stars, all we mean by "Hollywood," are the shining madness of the flat Midwest in the middle of the night, a delirium our national unconscious has managed to push to the edge of the map. This thesis is the big problem with Thomson's novel: first of all, because it is a thesis. (Yes, sometimes it's the critic who's lurking in the poet's style, and the artist is revealed as just a map maker.) Second, because it rests on assumptions that are unsound and even a little unsavory.

DAVID THOREAU. *The Santanic Condition* (Arbor House, 1981) is a story of a cocaine shipment from Mexico to Los Angeles which pits the dealer against a U.S. attorney, whose wife once had an affair with the dealer. A narcotics agent learns of the shipment through a drug-addicted Hollywood starlet.

SABINA THORNE (born 1927). Margo Tarrish, the heroine of *Reruns* (Viking Press, 1981) is the daughter of legendary Hollywood agent Sue Collier. She now lives in Berkeley with her husband and daughter, and when a young girl who stayed briefly at her home is murdered in San Francisco's Haight-Ashbury district, she believes the girl to be the daughter of film and television star Maeve Malone. Tarrish believes that Malone used their friendship to advance her career, and she is obsessed with proving the murdered girl's identity and accusing Malone of child neglect. In so doing, she must take on the Hollywood establishment. "An agreeable patchwork," opined *Kirkus*, "even if it's full of holes—and surefire fascination for anyone with a fierce interest in the by-now-familiar Hollywood child syndrome."

ERNEST TIDYMAN (1928–84) is best known for the seven novels in the "Shaft" series and for the screenplay to *The French Connection* (1971). *Table Stakes* (Little, Brown, 1978) is the story of father and son gamblers. The father is the old-fashioned variety, but after he is killed, the son decides to gamble on the film industry. He gambles on three low-budget productions, marries the daughter of the studio head, and gambles to take over the studio.

MICHAEL TOLKIN (born 1950). The 1992 film version of *The Player* (Atlantic Monthly/Little, Brown, 1988), directed by Robert Altman and starring Tim Robbins, was the type of movie that Hollywood loves—satirical and cutting—but outside the film community interest in the feature was subdued, and in the long run the novel will probably have the greatest and longest-lasting impact. Michael Tolkin's first book, *The Player*, introduces a typical, young, aggressive Hollywood executive named Griffin Mill, a senior vice president and still upwardly mobile. Mill's position, second in command at the studio, is threatened by his boss's plan to bring in a golden boy outsider and by his own fears, brought on by threatening and anonymous messages from a disgruntled writer. Mill goes after the writer he believes is responsible, but picks on the wrong man. Tolkin admirably captures Hollywood morality, where the right table at the right restaurant and taking command at a story meeting are more important than murder to the self-absorbed young executive. As David Bartholomew wrote in *Library Journal* (June 15, 1988), "Tolkin's bemused view of Hollywood is curt and bloodless yet hardly original, but he does have a keen perception of its various battle strategies. There's a happy ending, which the Hays Office wouldn't like, but Hollywood in the 1980s just might."

TOM TOLNAY. Filled with motion picture allusions, *Celluloid Gangs* (Walker, 1990) is a mystery novel in which a reporter, Igor Lopes, is accused of stealing a missing film, *Escape from Monte Carlo* (starring Sydney Greenstreet and Linda Darnell), from the home of a murdered mogul. Igor has never heard of the film, but it is of "historical significance to the members of [a] Cultural Alliance," and sought by his accusers, two rival gangs. As movie stars begin appearing in the text, both Igor and the reader get further removed from reality—and so does the author, assuming the hero can hide a feature film weighing 40 pounds down the front of his trousers. Three people are trampled to death at an Academy Awards presentation. But eventually at the "Big House" all is explained—kind of. As the hero comments, "Obviously, I'd gone to Heaven."

SAM TOPEROFF (born 1933). The *Queen of Desire* (HarperCollins, 1992) is Marilyn Monroe, whose life, in fictionalized form, Toperoff tells through a series of 13 episodes, each prefaced by a created magazine interview: sexual molestation of Monroe at the age of nine; accompanying a friend who is getting an abortion; singing at a Los Angeles nightspot; visiting a plastic surgeon; accompanying Joe DiMaggio to Old-timers' Day at Yankee Stadium; filming a sequence for *The Seven Year Itch* on location in New York; studying at the Actors Studio with Lee Strasberg; being with Arthur Miller and Frank Lloyd Wright; having her hair done in company with Simone Signoret; an attempted seduction by President Sukarno of Indonesia after the British premiere of *The Prince and the Showgirl*; playing poker with John Huston on location for *The Misfits*; visiting her analyst; and watching Madalyn Murray O'Hair on television the night before she commits suicide. The result is a book that reads very well but seems little more than a truncated biography. The author explains that the incidents presented are wholly fictitious, but leaves the reader wondering where fiction ends and reality begins.

MEL TORMÉ (born 1925) has been a popular singer—known as "The Velvet Fog"—since the 1940s; he is the author of the memoir *The Other Side of the Rainbow: With Judy Garland on the Dawn Patrol* (1970) and of the 1955 novel *Dollarhide* (written under the pseudonym of Wesley Butler Wyatt).
   Wynner (Stein & Day, 1978) began life as an episode of the television series, *Run for Your Life*. The novel is semiautobiographical, documenting the life of a jazz singer/musician, Marty Wynner, who, like Tormé, was born in Chicago. His mother helps promote his career and gets work for herself in Hollywood as a minor actress; he sings with various big bands, makes a few films, and marries a lesbian.

CHARLES HANSON TOWNE (1877–1949). *Pretty Girls Get There* (Appleton-Century, 1941) is the story of Marnie McLaughlin, who works in the Bronx and is the main support of her family of five. Eventually, her beauty wins her a place in the film industry as an actress. The book is illustrated by Rafaello Busoni.

PETER TOWNSEND (born 1914) has as his mystery hero Philip Quest, a still photographer blinded in one eye. In *Zoom!* (St. Martin's Press, 1972), Quest is involved in kidnapping and murder as a star of spaghetti Westerns plans to marry the daughter of a wealthy Texan. Sex and violence predominate.

VIRGINIA TRACY. *Starring Dulcy Jayne* (Doran, 1927) is the story of a 17-year-old whose father signs a five-year contract for her with Perfection Pictures of Fort Lee, New Jersey. When Dulcy Jayne fails to retain her popularity, the studio tries to get her to break the contract, but she is able to manipulate them into breaking the contract and is thus able to organize her own company. Prominent in the story are members of the studio scenario department. "This is just another novel, but rather amusing, and entertaining enough to fill an empty afternoon or evening," wrote the reviewer in the *New York Times* (November 20, 1927). "Its faults are those of the amateur, and it has the virtues of its vices. It shows excellent promise, but Miss Tracy should concentrate her next effort on either her business or her dream. Stars are things to direct our course by, not toward, and *Starring Dulcy Jayne* has a way of seeking the empyrean at inconvenient moments."

SHEPARD TRAUBE (1907–83) was a film and theater producer and director, best remembered for his Broadway hit *Angel Street*. His years in Hollywood led to his writing *Glory Road* (Macaulay Company, 1935), which tells the history of the film industry through the eyes of German-Jewish executive Karl Lustig, who came to the United States as a young man in the 1890s. The reviewer in the *New York Times* (May 26, 1935) commented, "Any one familiar with the life stories of several preeminent motion-picture executives—though the name of none is here mentioned—should perceive how closely Karl's character, his struggles and achievements parallel those of the leaders who have in reality built and dominated the industry. Karl is indeed a composite of those noted men, sympathetically portrayed, and the atmosphere of actuality thus imparted to them renders the book far more interesting than if he were conceived purely as a figure of fiction."

MARGARET TRENT. *The Hills of Home* (A.L. Burt, undated) documents the travels of some "young moderns" in the 1920s. They spend a brief period appearing in movies.

JOHN TRINIAN. *House of Evil* (Pyramid Books, 1962) is one of a series of novels with a Hollywood background, identified by Carolyn See as semipornographic. No other information is available.

MILES TRIPP (born 1923). *Some Predators Are Male* (St. Martin's Press, 1985) is a mystery novel whose central character, Neil Pensom, is a film and television production assistant. He is the subject of an elaborate "candid camera" type operation, which is drastically affecting his life. As with all the books of this British novelist, the writing is entertaining even if the storyline is more than a little preposterous.

HENRI TROYAT (born 1911). *One Minus Two* (Ives Washburn, 1938) is a psychological study of three people, an unsuccessful ham actor, his wife, who pampers him, and his son, who becomes a movie star and for whom the wife neglects her husband. When the son's second film is a flop, the father gloats but the wife remains loyal to the young man. The novel was translated from the French by James Whitall, and received the 1936 Prix Femina Américain.

THOMAS TRYON (1925–91) was a Hollywood actor, best known for his leading role in *The Cardinal* (1963), who switched from performing to writing in the late 1960s. He wrote a number of best-selling novels, including *The Other* (1971), which was filmed in 1972. Tryon wrote two books with Hollywood backgrounds, and they are the poorest of his novels. They lack depth and illustrate their author's worth as a film buff rather than his skill as a writer.

Crowned Heads (Alfred A. Knopf, 1976) contains four stories. The first concerns a legendary, Garboesque Hollywood star named Fedora, whose ageless beauty is the result of no secret formula but rather the reality that she had been replaced in her later films by her daughter. It is hardly an original concept. Lorna Doone is a neurotic Hollywood star who goes to a Mexican resort to relax and ultimately to die. Bobbitt is a child star of the 1950s who is unable to come to terms with reality. Willie Marsh is a witty and urbane, aging leading man, who lived with his mother and is presumably based on Clifton Webb. Three young hoodlulms come to Marsh's Beverly Hills home one night and, searching for imagined wealth, murder him. The two men and one woman are sexually involved with each other, and Willie is revealed as a transvestite. While there is something of a homosexual relationship between the two men, there is no indication that Willie is homosexual, but undoubtedly the story is influenced by the October 31, 1968, murder of actor Ramon Novarro by two male hustlers he had invited to his house for sex.

In hindsight it is difficult to understand why the "Fedora" story should have been filmed, but it was, in 1978, under the direction of Billy Wilder and with Marthe Keller in the title role. The film is as forgotten as *Crowned Heads* deserves to be.

All That Glitters (Alfred A. Knopf, 1986) is narrated by actor turned writer Charles Caine, and tells the stories of five disparate Hollywood stars, Babe Austrian, Belinda Carroll, April Rains, Maude Antrim, and Claire Regrett. Each played a part in the narrator's life, and each is linked through a legendary Hollywood agent (and lover) named Frankie Adano. The novel opens with Babe Austrian's funeral. Obviously based on Mae West's life and career, the Babe Austrian story is the most entertaining, with the revelation that she had in fact died some years previously and that a female impersonator had been playing the star for quite some time and was buried in her place. April Rains is probably based on Frances Farmer, Maude Antrim on Mary Pickford, and Claire Regrett quite definitely on Joan Crawford.

The loves and anguish that the various ladies experience becomes tedious after a while, but Thomas Tryon is adept at connecting his stories. A minor episode in one has relevance to another. He also demonstrates skill in presenting what would appear to be five separate lives in chronological order; the narrator is a young boy when the Babe Austrian story begins, and he has experienced a divorce and married Belinda Carroll with the end of the Claire Regrett chapter (the longest in the book). So adept is Tryon at interweaving his stories and the lives of his characters that Claire Regrett begins in the novel as a basically unsympathetic figure but at the book's close has become a gentle, emotionally responsive one.

Thomas Tryon knows all the Hollywood stories and legends and uses them to advantage, but he appears to be writing to an audience of lovesick female movie fans who vanished in the 1960s. Also, for all his knowledge of Hollywood fable, in the opening pages of *All That Glitters* he manages to move the former Desilu Studio from its actual location next to Paramount several blocks west and adjacent to Columbia; further, he moves the body of Valentino from its slot in the Hollywood Memorial Cemetery mausoleum to a solitary crypt.

WILSON TUCKER (born 1914). *The Dove* (Rinehart, 1948) was summarized by *Kirkus* (April 15, 1948) as "far-fetched and erratic doings." The title character is a former silent star of Westerns, whom a Hollywood detective helps recover money and diamonds she had hidden on a movie set.

F.P. TULLIUS. *Out of the Death Bag in West Hollywood* (Macmillan, 1971) consists of a series of letters from a 29-year-old actor, Race Stirling, to a psychology professor. One of the actor's exploits is driving his car through a movie set, and among his idiosyncracies is sleeping in a coffin. His meeting with an eccentric young woman named Bibi leads to his overcoming quite a few inhibitions. Portions of the book were published in *The New Yorker* in 1966 and 1967.

JIM TULLY (1891–1947) was a colorful character and a down-to-earth writer who is totally forgotten today. His early career included prizefighting, circus performing, and newspaper reporting before he had success as a novelist and screenwriter. Tully's 1924 novel *Beggars of Life*, which is perhaps based on his own early years, was adapted by him for the 1928 Louise Brooks vehicle of the same title.

Jarnegan (Albert & Charles Boni, 1926) is a strong novel, telling of Jack Muldoon, who kills a man in a saloon fight, is jailed, changes his name to Jack Jarnegan, and becomes a Hollywood director. The *New York Times* (September 19, 1926) wrote, "*Jarnegan* is a disorderly, vehement and honest novel. Its sincerity is beyond doubt. Its mixture of fantasy, humor, irony and blunt statements of doubtful taste are all essentially part of a chaotic figure. It is a vivid picture of life out of the commonplace. A less distorted perspective might have clarified the book. This would have demanded different treatment. It is Jarnegan's story—and he is amply presented. His story remains a novel for the literary rather than the general reader." In the *New York World* (September 12, 1926), Harry Salpeter wrote, "Jim Tully looks like a pugilist and writes like one. His *Jarnegan*, just published, is that kind of book. It has the breath of life in it and some of its chaos. He writes, not like an angel, but like the very devil, with falls from the grace of prose into gross exaggeration and unprovoked pugnacity." In the *Saturday Review of Literature* (October 16, 1926), Clayton Hamilton commented, "This man is gifted with sincerity, with earnestness, with elemental power. He is afire with a passion for expression which, every now and then, purifies itself into poetry. *Jarnegan* is not a skilful book, for Jim Tully still has much to learn about the craft of authorship; but it contains many sentences and several paragraphs which are not, by any means, unworthy of the masters."

MARGARET TURNBULL (18??–1942) was a prolific novelist (1913–34); a playwright, whose best known work was *Classmates* (1907), coauthored with William C. de Mille; and the author of 44 screenplays, primarily for Paramount, written between 1915 and 1924.

The central character in **The Close-Up** (Harper, 1918) is Kate Lawford, the personal secretary to Tom Crews, Jr., who works for his father's accounting firm and becomes acquainted with an entrepreneur named Howard Carwood. Carwood and Crews take over a film company in Hollywood, here called Mountainside, and persuade Kate to join them in an executive position. Kate has just broken up with her boyfriend, Jeffrey Grace, who is in despair that his attempt to join the Canadian military and fight in World War I has been thwarted by the suspicion of incipient tuberculosis, and so she agrees to go with Crews and Carwood. Once at the studio, Kate is urged to become an actress and is soon the company's leading lady, while Jeffrey joins the Secret Service and is assigned to Los Angeles. By chance, Kate meets Jeffrey but is persuaded not to acknowledge him, while he uncovers two Germans violating American neutrality. It is obvious that Carwood is involved in some way with the Germans, but he is also determined to marry Kate. Just as she has decided to give herself to him, the United States declares war on Germany and Jeffrey reappears. Kate tells him, "I've been a bad, ungrateful girl, but I did love you, studio, people and place. It was all my fault if sometimes I lost the beauty and only saw the defects in the close-up. I'll be content with the long-distance shots now, because I belong to Jeff." When Jeffrey points out that he must enlist, she responds, "I'll share you with my country, but with nothing and nobody else."

The Close-Up is well written and absorbing, and unusual in that its leading lady is shown to have both strength and determination, the earliest novelized example of a female studio executive. The author's knowledge of filmmaking is such that she can write realistically about the work of everyone from an assistant director to a leading player.

JOHN TURNER. *Starlet!* (Pyramid Books, 1961) is one of a series of novels with a Hollywood background identified by Carolyn See as semipornographic. No other information is available.

MARK UPTON is a pseudonym of popular novelist Lawrence Sanders (born 1920). **The Dream Lover** (Coward, McCann & Geoghegan, 1978) is lifted slightly above the typical, run-of-the-mill Hollywood novel in that the bad guy ultimately wins, although it must be admitted that he does have a valid point with regard to the future of Magna Pictures, where the various characters are employed. Eli Hebron is head of production at the studio, nephew to its founder and next in line for succession. The year is 1927, and one of the supervising producers, Charlie Royce, argues passionately for the studio's embracing the new medium of talkies, but Hebron sees it as only a fad. Royce plots with a Boston banker to whom the studio is heavily in debt to bring about Hebron's downfall. Hebron meets and falls in love with a young actress whom he puts under contract; they begin an affair and she moves into his house. Hebron does not realize that the actress is working for Royce and that she is only 15 years old. Rather than face exposure, Hebron is forced to resign from the studio; he then suffers a mental breakdown, and finishes up in an institution where he and his fellow residents produce films in their imagination. The author is deserving of praise for his first-rate knowledge of contemporary slang, and familiarity with stars and productions of the period. No real-life performers actually appear in the novel, but there are references to many, from Esther Ralston and Dagmar Godowsky to Mary Pickford and Clara Bow.

ROBERT UPTON. Seedy, alcoholic San Francisco private detective Amos McGuffin makes his second appearance in *Fade Out* (Viking Press, 1984), in which he is hired by the father of a Hollywood producer who apparently committed suicide by walking into the ocean. McGuffin uncovers a conspiracy involving the producer's actress wife, an actor, a director, and a screenwriter. Perhaps because the author was also a screenwriter, it is only the last who is depicted in a sympathetic fashion. McGuffin stays at the Beverly Hills Hotel, and there is a mildly entertaining description of that establishment. Otherwise *Fade Out* is no encouragement for the reader to demand a third novel in the series.

JEAN URE. Martha and Jesse are opposites who attract in the madcap world of English repertory theater as depicted in *Bid Time Return* (Severn House, 1977). When Jesse goes off to Belgium for a featured role in a film, Martha discovers she is pregnant and plans an abortion, believing free soul Jesse would not want to be tied down by a child. As romantic novels go, *Bid Time Return* is remarkably believable, both in terms of dialogue and plot structure, but that may have more to do with the "unreal" world of the theater about which the author writes than with her skills as a novelist.

RICHARD S. USEM. *The Face Behind the Image; Politics: Hollywood Style* (Exposition Press, 1968) is a satirical novel in which Western star Rex George (Ronald Reagan) and a former movie star turned Las Vegas stripper, Lola LaMange, both run for governor of California on the Republican ticket. Both win and set up rival governments. The novel ends with the separate planes in which they are traveling having a midair collision.

LOUIS JOSEPH VANCE (1879–1933) wrote the screenplays—or, as he points out in his novel, "he's called a continuity writer"—for some nine films between 1915 and 1929, primarily for Thomas H. Ince. None of the characters in *Linda Lee Incorporated: A Novel* (Grosset & Dunlap, 1922) bears any resemblance to Ince, but Vance's thorough knowledge of the filmmaking process is very apparent. The book provides an admirable description of silent filmmaking in the late teens and early twenties, both in New York and Hollywood. The principal character is New York socialite Lucinda Druce, who, tired of her husband Bellamy's extramarital activities and alcoholism, decides to flee to the West Coast and seek a divorce. On the train from Chicago, she meets a Hollywood leading man named Lynn Summerland, and the two gradually fall in love. Persuaded by Summerland, Lucinda comes to Los Angeles, staying at the Hollywood Hotel (described in some detail), and with two society friends decides to form a film company, Linda Lee, Inc., for which she will star under the assumed name of Linda Lee. Bellamy Druce shows up in Hollywood in company with a mysterious woman named Nelly Marquis, whom Summerland warns Lucinda against, claiming she is involved in drugs: "It isn't California, it isn't Hollywood, it's human nature, one sort of human nature. You'll find the same thing going on in every big city; read the newspaper accounts of the campaign against the drug traffic. Only, out here we know more about it, because the studios make it more or less one big village, and it's hard to keep anything quiet, talk will get out..."

After a final confrontation with Summerland, Lucinda discovers that Marquis is his wife. Marquis appears and shoots and kills Summerland. She is about to shoot Lucinda when Bellamy arrives and saves her. Bellamy has been pursuing Lucinda because he still loves her, and the two are reunited at the novel's close.

Linda Lee Incorporated is not a great novel. It was popular reading for its day—entertaining but with a relatively intriguing and original plotline. Modern audiences will learn more about the technique of silent filmmaking from a book such as this than from most film histories. The novel was first published serially under the title of "The Coast of Cockaigne" in an abridged version in *McCall's* magazine in the winter of 1921-22.

CHARLES E. VAN LOAN (1877–1919) was a humorist and journalist,

noted for his short stories with baseball themes. Two of his stories were the basis for feature films starring silent screen juvenile Charles Ray, *Scrap Iron* (1921) and *The Deuce of Spades* (1922), and a couple of his stories—*Buckshot John* and *Little Sunset*—were filmed in 1915 by Hobart Bosworth, who also directed and starred in the productions. Van Loan dedicated *Buck Parvin and the Movies* to Bosworth, "the original Jimmy Montague of the stories, actor, scenario author and director."

Buck Parvin and the Movies: Stories of the Moving Picture Game (George H. Doran, 1919) has as its title character a Western actor who has lived many of the parts he plays, "a moving-picture cowpuncher, acting during every waking moment." All the stories take place at the Titan studios (possibly based on the Selig studios in Los Angeles) and feature director Jimmy Montague. While the stories are dated, they are evocative of the early years of filmmaking in Los Angeles and read almost like scenarios for potential two-reel short subjects.

"The Extra Man and the Milkfed Lion" involves an extra who overacts to impress the actress with whom he is in love, but he succeeds only in making her feel he has spoiled her performance. A polo game is the central theme of "The International Cup." A conceited stage actor who specializes in Western roles tries to make a film Western in "Man-Afraid-of-His-Wardrobe." In "Water

Stuff," a young actress is forced to perform in a water scene after pretending she can swim proficiently. "Buck's Lady Friend" finds the hero losing interest in leading lady Myrtle Manners (who appears in a number of the stories) after meeting Georgine. In "Desert Stuff," Jimmy Montague decides to make "a real desert picture." "Author! Author!" has Titan's head make the mistake of having an author supervise the adaptation and production of his story. In "Snow Stuff," Jimmy Montague is filming a production on location in Truckee and must endure the visit of an efficiency expert. "This Is the Life!" finds the wealthy Mrs. Gribble intent on an acting career; a payoff to director Montague by Mr. Gribble ensures that her screen career is brief.

ERIC VAN LUSTBADER (born 1946). In *Sirens* (M. Evans, 1981), beautiful Hollywood actress Diana Whitney is starred in a feature film involving Arab terrorists holding a group of Americans and Israelis hostage. The role is rather like that of a female Arnold Schwartzenegger, but according to the author, the actress demonstrates immediate Oscar potential and does indeed win the Academy Award for best actress. In the meantime, Whitney is recalling her teenage years and has fallen in love with the film's producer. She, and the reader, come to realize that terrorism is a part of our everyday lives—at least in Hollywood—as the producer terrorizes his lawyer, she terrorizes a studio head, and so on. Terrorism is also behind the killings of a rock star and his wife, both friends of Whitney. "It's only a movie," says the leading man of the film. "But in real life . . . that's where it counts." He then decides to fund Palestinian terrorists. And, of course, at least on the printed page, if not in real life, life does imitate art as the heroine guns down the killer of her friends, just as she had gunned down the leader of the Arab terrorists on screen. The style is flamboyant, and sex scene follows sex scene (there is even an obligatory lesbian coupling), and Whitney, as a teenager, is forced into shock therapy. The terrorist aspect is somewhat overdrawn as the author brings in Palestinians, the IRA, and the Hollywood mafia. The last group appears to be the most worthless, with a cause linked purely to ego.

CARL VAN VECHTEN (1880–1964) was noted for his sophisticated satires on New Yorkers in the 1920s. In that mode, *Spider Boy* (Alfred A. Knopf, 1928) chronicles the career of the author of a Broadway hit who is lured to Hollywood with a contract for a scenario he is neither expected nor allowed to write, and further lured into marriage with a Hollywood star. Contemporary reviews were mixed. "*Spider Boy* would like to be a mad, farcical, nonsensical extravaganza in which the insanities of Hollywood and super-productions and temperamental movie stars and Hebraic entrepreneurs are to be touched off with the neatest of hands. But it is not. It is a wearisome and flat burlesque," commented the reviewer in *The Nation* (September 19, 1928). However, Vincent McHugh in the *New York Evening Post* (September 15, 1928) considered the novel "as gay as a piece of music by Rodgers and Hart."

GORE VIDAL (born 1925) is a celebrated and often controversial novelist, playwright, and essayist. He has also scripted a number of feature films, including *The Catered Affair* (1956), *Suddenly Last Summer* (1959), *Is Paris Burning?* (1966), and *Caligula* (1977).

The title heroine of *Myra Breckinridge* (Little, Brown, 1968) is a transsexual who began life as the gay Myron Breckinridge. Myra arrives in Los Angeles to claim her previous self's inheritance, half ownership of an acting academy and the land on which it stands, belonging to a former cowboy star and Myron's uncle, Buck Loner. Myra takes up a position as a tutor at the academy, rapes one of the male students, Rusty Godowsky, but ends up in bed with his girlfriend, Mary-Ann Pringle. Rusty begins an affair with the sexually rapacious Hollywood agent Letitia Van Allen, and the book concludes with Myra's slowly changing back to Myron as a result of an accident.

Myra Breckinridge is intellectual camp, a novel lost in the fantasy world of Hollywood movies of the 1940s, while paying loving homage to cultist, homosexual film critic Parker Tyler. Almost everything Myra does she considers in terms of how a film star of an earlier decade would have handled the situation. The lengthy chapter in which Myra sodomizes Rusty is pure homosexual fantasy. Throughout, the descriptions of Rusty's clothed body, particularly his buttocks, belong more to the world of the gay novel than female eroticism. The remainder of the book is the work of a film buff who is a little too preoccupied for his own good with creating a semioriginal literary style.

The novel was made into a very unsatisfactory film by 20th Century–Fox in 1970, with Michael Sarne directing, Raquel Welch as Myra, John Huston as Buck Loner, Roger Herren as Rusty, and Mae West as Letitia Van Allen.

Hollywood: A Novel of America in the 1920s (Random House, 1990) is the sixth volume in Vidal's self-described biography of the United States which began with *Burr*. Despite its title, the novel has little to do with Hollywood or filmmaking, but is largely set in Washington, D.C., beginning with Woodrow Wilson's leading the United States into World War I and ending with the death of Warren G. Harding. It is a rambling panorama of real and fictional characters who seem in search of a cohesive plotline. One such character is newspaper publisher Caroline Sanford, who, as Emma Traxler, embarks on a Hollywood career as a producer and leading lady. She meets up with director William Desmond Taylor (whom Vidal quietly labels homosexual) and is one of the last women to see him alive. Vidal accepts the generally held theory that Taylor was murdered by the mother of actress Mary Miles Minter. Aside from Taylor, the only other Hollywood characters who have any significance in the novel are William Randolph Hearst's mistress, actress Marion Davies; Charles Eyton, Paramount studio manager; Douglas Fairbanks; Charlie Chaplin; and Elinor Glyn. Vidal's knowledge of film history is sound, and he mentions many names and films familiar to film buffs and film students, if not the general public. He does, however, take liberties in his chronology, with references to Pola Negri before she would have been known to American audiences, and the Motion Picture Patents Company, which had no relevance to Hollywood during the period in which his story is set.

Myron (Random House, 1974) is the sequel to *Myra Breckinridge* in which the transsexual protagonist is pushed through the television screen on to the set of a 1948 feature film, *Siren of Babylon*, starring Maria Montez. Myra takes control of Myron's body and she tries to save the world from overpopulation by changing the male sex urge. "It is an invidiously amusing camp fantasy," wrote

Time (October 21, 1974). *Myra Breckinridge* and *Myron* were reprinted as a single volume by Random House in 1986.

PETER VIERTEL (born 1920) is the son of director Berthold Viertel and screenwriter Salka Viertel, who worked on many of Garbo's scripts. Peter was also a screenwriter as well as a novelist, and in 1960 he married actress Deborah Kerr. *White Hunter, Black Heart* (Doubleday, 1953) is a roman à clef based on the making of *The African Queen*, with director John Huston here identified as John Wilson. The novel is narrated by Pete Verrill, who had been brought along on the expedition to work on the script when necessary, and is obviously author Viertel. Contemporary reviews were mixed, with A.H. Weiler in the *New York Times* (July 12, 1953) writing that Viertel "probes deeply, though often angrily. It is fascinating, swiftly paced and sometimes moving." *The New Yorker* (August 8, 1953) thought, "The writing is poor, and one is left with the impression that Mr. Viertel overreached himself in his choice of a subject."

The novel was filmed under its original title in 1990 by Malpaso and Rastar Productions, for Warner Bros. release, directed by Clint Eastwood, and starring Eastwood, Jeff Fahey, and Charlotte Cromwell.

HORACE ATKISSON WADE (born 1908). A 21-year-old millionaire, Jack Jarvis, comes to Hollywood and produces an independent feature in *To Hell with Hollywood* (Lincoln MacVeigh/Dial Press, 1931), but the Hollywood establishment makes certain that he is not successful. According to Nancy Brooker-Bowers, "This rather unpleasant novel exhibits obvious anti–Semitic, anti–Negro, and anti–Irish biases."

JOHN WAER. *Jade* (House of Field, 1943) is the name of a would-be actress loved by a Detroit croupier, John Avery, who also loves an Italian statue and another actress, Myra Neilan. Myra goes with producer Al Bowman to Hollywood, where she meets Jade. Avery also goes to Hollywood and writes a novel about Jade, who, it transpires, posed for the statue. Avery marries Jade, and Myra is persuaded to wed Bowman. The novel contains a curious foreword in the form of a letter from William Saroyan, who has not read the novel and suggests that it will be a failure. He was correct.

BRUCE WAGNER's first novel, *Force Majeure* (Random House, 1991), is the outrageous story of Bud Wiggins, a would-be Hollywood screenwriter whose films are never released and if they are, it is without his credit. Wiggins is a young man who earns his living when not writing as a chauffeur, and he daily faces humiliation and contempt as he battles the Hollywood power system, including the Writers Guild of America (of whose arbitration process the author is particularly critical). The first half of the novel is brilliant, the second part, in which the hero comes to terms with his Jewish heritage and deals with the Holocaust, is less appealing. It is almost as if the author is trying to manage too many themes rather than concentrate on the one fascinating topic of the writer in Hollywood.

ROB WAGNER (1872–1942) was a popular and well-regarded Hollywood film journalist who also worked in the film industry as a director and screenwriter. He published an anecdotal book on film history, *Film Folk* (1918), and from 1929 until his death published and edited the magazine *Rob Wagner's Script*, which is comparable to a West Coast edition of *The New Yorker*. (For more information, see Anthony Slide's *The Best of Rob Wagner's Script* [Scarecrow Press, 1985].) ***Tessie Moves Along*** (J.H. Sears, 1928) is the poorly written story of a Bowery waitress who is discovered by a lecherous director and becomes a "bit" player. She moves to Hollywood, changes her name to Vivian Vane, becomes a star, and marries a boxer turned oil man.

FREDERICK WAKEMAN. As he becomes involved with a European actress, a screenwriter is forced to consider the potential effect of a divorce on his wife and children in ***The Fault of the Apple*** (Simon & Schuster, 1961). "With the best will in the world he [Wakeman] is not quite able to give his picture of the film-business the necessary authenticity that, for example, Scott Fitzgerald gave to *The Last Tycoon*," wrote the reviewer in the *Times Literary Supplement* (October 28, 1960). Wakeman is best known for his study of Madison Avenue in *The Hucksters* (1946); *The Fault of the Apple* was his ninth novel.

LESLIE WALKER. *Amazing Faith* (McGraw-Hill, 1988) is set in the Riviera principality of San Sebastian, whose princess was once a Hollywood movie star named Faith Brennan. Princess Faith has helped restore some glamor and respectability to a country whose casinos were controlled by the Mafia. The Mafia is far from happy with Faith's idealism; she survives a manufactured car crash but is killed by the attending physician. The publisher's dust jacket comment is apt: "She traded the tinsel treachery of Hollywood for the deeper corruption of royalty." The similarity of this story to the life of Grace Kelly is obvious, and presumably the author's previous existence as a crime reporter and agent with U.S. Army Air Force Intelligence implies some truth to a work of fiction.

IRVING WALLACE (1916–90). The effect Hollywood can have on a person is the theme of ***The Sins of Philip Fleming: A Compelling Novel of a Man's Intimate Problem*** (Frederick Fell, 1959). A Hollywood screenwriter between assignments and unhappily married meets a young widow who buys his house. Without success, he attempts a physical relationship with her. In ***The Fan Club*** (Simon & Schuster, 1974), four men decide to act out their sexual fantasies by abducting an attractive movie star and taking her to a mountain cabin. She persuades them to demand a ransom for her return, and slowly the four men turn against each other. The not-too-original storyline is much too long and lacks suspense.

PAMELA WALLACE (born 1949). ***Malibu Colony*** (Pinnacle Books, 1980) documents the story of two prominent Hollywood film industry families from 1922 through 1979, from motion pictures and television to rock 'n' roll. Greed, passion, and power are the dominant elements in the saga.

SYLVIA WALLACE. In ***Empress*** (William Morrow, 1980), former movie star Mary Anne Callahan is celebrating the fifteenth anniversary of her marriage to the emperor of Bahrait. Among the guests are Selma Shapiro, head of Hanover Studios, where Mary Anne first became a star, and her former leading man, Doug Braden. The empress intends to announce a divorce from her unfaithful husband and a return to films, but his death and the kidnapping of her sons bring an abrupt change to her plans. "Easy, sleazy reading" was the opinion of *Kirkus*.

JEFFREY M. WALLMAN *see* THOMAS JEIER and JEF-FREY M. WALLMAN

JOSEPH WAMBAUGH (born 1937) is a former Los Angeles Police Department detective (he joined the police in 1960 and resigned in 1974) whose novels, while sympathetic to his former colleagues, often illustrate the worst elements in the force. Wambaugh's first novel, *The New Centurions* (1971), was filmed in 1972 and influenced the making of the television series "Police Story." His best novel, *The Onion Field* (1973), is based on the 1963 murder of an LAPD officer; Wambaugh wrote the screenplay for the 1979 film version.

The Glitter Dome (William Morrow, 1981) features a typical Wambaugh cast of officers; one is impotent and alcoholic, and the other is fighting a battle against early religious training. The two men are assigned to investigate the murder of Hollywood mogul Nigel St. Claire. The killer is the father of a girl who was to be murdered in a snuff film shot in Mexico, with which St. Claire was involved. The title refers to a Hollywood nightclub where police officers routinely drink and relax. The novel was filmed in 1983 for airing on HBO.

DONALD WARD's first novel, *Death Takes the Stage* (St. Martin's Press, 1988), is intended primarily for a gay readership. The central character is a fairly disreputable but lovable Hollywood agent named Jake Weissman, who turns detective when one of the few actors on his books is murdered in a bizarre fashion. The book makes entertaining and amusing reading.

JACK L. WARNER, JR., (1916–95) is the son of the best-known member of the Warner brothers; resumably his novel *Bijou Dream* (Crown, 1982) is based, perhaps only loosely, on his father. It is the story of Hamilton J. Robbins, the head of Robbins International Studio, and begins at the Hollywood Humanitarian of the Year banquet, presided over by George Jessel, at which Robbins is the guest of honor. The novel documents Robbins's life in the film industry, from the nickelodeon days at the turn of the century; how his first wife is unable to satisfy his sexual needs; how a second wife came between him and his son; and how the two brothers who helped build his empire have come to loathe him. Nevertheless, Robbins knows ultimately that he would go through it all again. A deeply felt concern with the central character's Jewish faith runs through the novel, which uses as its motif the Yiddish saying "Better to be a decent human being and not a Jew, than a Jew and not a decent human being." *Bijou Dream* is a long and at times arduous read, but one is left with the strong impression that the author knows from where he writes.

WILLIAM WARNOCK. *Danziger's Cut* (Macdonald, 1986) opens with a quote from Jean Renoir's *The Rules of the Game*, "The terrible thing about this world is that everyone has his own reasons." The relevance of this quote is unclear, as is why the French title of the film is misspelled. The novel proper begins with the purchase of thriller writer Jack Danziger's novel *Enmeshed* by independent Hollywood producer Solly Amsberg. He intends to star Danziger's ex-lover Chantal Camargue and chooses as his director the vicious, beautiful, and sexually ambiguous Christian Kurtz, who surrounds himself with a motley crew known as "The Circus," all of whom are thugs and many of whom dress in drag. Not only does Kurtz savage Danziger's script, he also drugs Chantal and films her in sexually explicit scenes with himself as the leading man. After receiving a brutal beating at Kurtz's hands, Danziger plots a curious revenge. He steals the negative and workprint of the original film, re-editing it to remove the pornographic aspects, and ransoms it to producer Amsberg. Subsequently, Kurtz murders Chantal, but Danziger kills him in a barrel of developing fluid, staging the deaths to make it appear that Chantal had overdosed and killed Kurtz. The novel concludes with the re-edited film winning Oscars for best picture, director, actor, and actress.

Danziger's Cut teeters on the edge of being a titillating drama of sexual perversion and gratuitous violence, but it never quite takes the plunge. Christian Kurtz is like no other Hollywood director, with a body he apparently allows his producer one-time use of in return for the directorial assignment on *Enmeshed*. The hero suffers from a double dose of obsession—for his original novel/script and for his ex-girlfriend.

The plotline contains two major flaws. First, a laboratory generally processes film at night, its busiest time, and no such laboratory would be empty of staff between midnight and 6:00 A.M. when the negative heist takes place. Second, a workprint consists of separate picture and soundtrack elements. While Danziger is presented cutting the picture negative, at no time is there any indication that the soundtrack would need to be cut in sync with the picture. One other minor error: Mulholland Drive in Los Angeles is a semirural road, bordered by expensive homes; it does not, as described here, have any section with offices or restaurants.

L.J. WASHBURN has written a series of mystery novels featuring Lucas Hallam, a retired Texas Ranger and marshal, who arrives in Hollywood in 1915 and becomes a private investigator. He is introduced in ***Wild Night*** (TOR, 1987), in which he is involved in transforming a ghost town into a movie set and protecting the founder of the Holiness Temple of Faith. In ***Dead-Stick*** (TOR, 1989), he is hired to work as a stuntman on the set of *Death to the Kaiser!*, which has been plagued by a series of accidents. ***Dog Heavies*** (TOR, 1990) finds Hallam trying to turn a spoiled New York actor into a cowboy star. The author demonstrates a solid knowledge of early Westerns and peoples her books with many real-life cowboy stars, including William S. Hart, Tom Mix, and Yakima Canutt.

COLIN WATSON (born 1920) is the author of some of the wittiest crime novels, featuring Detective Inspector Purbright and the eccentric English residents of Flaxborough. In ***Blue Murder*** (Eyre Methuen, 1979), a muckraking journalist is about to expose the members of the Flaxborough Camera and Cinematograph Society for the production of pornographic films—in reality, their films are perfectly innocuous but have been doctored to include obscene sequences. When the journalist is murdered, Purbright investigates and discovers that the murderer's activities were related to his sister's participation in pornographic films.

IAN WATSON (born 1943). *Chekhov's Journey* (Carroll & Graf, 1983) is an entertaining work of science fiction that should appeal to readers not usually enthusiastic about the genre. In the contemporary Soviet Union, a film unit is attempting to recreate Anton Chekhov's 1890 historic journey across Siberia to the convict island of Sakhalin. The leading actor is not only playing the author but also believes himself to be Chekhov, through "reincarnation by hypnosis." Unfortunately, as the film progresses, the actor also believes himself to be the captain of a Soviet spaceship plunging, out of control, to Earth in the year 2090.

ROBERT WATSON (born 1925). *Lily Lang* (St. Martin's Press, 1977) is the story of siblings Louis and Lily Lang. He grows up to be a prominent screenwriter and director, and she becomes a movie star. Despite their closeness, Lily eventually retires from the screen and from a symbiotic relationship with her brother for a quieter life "where no heads will turn."

CHARLES WAUGH see MARTIN HARRY GREEN-BURG and CHARLES WAUGH

EVELYN WAUGH (1903–66). *The Loved One: An Anglo-American Tragedy* (Little, Brown, 1948) is the tragic love story of Englishman Dennis Barlow, who loses his screenwriting contract with Metropolitan Pictures, takes a position in a Hollywood pet cemetery, and falls in love with Aimée Thanatogenos, who works as a cosmetician at Whispering Glades Cemetery (obviously modeled after Forest Lawn). The novel is actually a satire not on Hollywood itself but rather on the English colony there, whose members are outraged by one of their own taking a position with a pet cemetery. Waugh got the idea for the novel when he visited Hollywood in 1947, for discussions with M-G-M, which had optioned two of his novels, *Brideshead Revisited* and *Scoop*. While in Hollywood, Waugh took tea with his favorite movie star, Anna May Wong, toured the Disney Studios, and dined with Charlie Chaplin, who gave him a private screening of *Monsieur Verdoux*; Waugh pronounced the film "brilliant."

The Loved One was first published in February 1948 as a special issue of *Horizon* magazine. On American publication of the novel, reviews were surprisingly mixed. In *The New Republic* (July 26, 1948), John Woodburn wrote, "As a piece of writing it is nearly faultless; as satire it is an act of devastation, an angry, important, moral effort that does not fail. *The Loved One* is not outrageous but outraged; sickened but not sickening; its macabre humor is the shocked, protective laughter of the civilized man confronted with the unassimilable horror that permits no other means of rejection." In *The New Yorker*, Woolcott Gibbs commented, "Never before that I can remember has a talent of such austere and classic design been applied to such monstrous vulgarities; never before have the majestic themes of love and death been so delicately perverted to absurdity. *The*

Loved One represents the perfection of an attitude that was first expressed in *Decline and Fall* and *Vile Bodies*. . . . It is certainly a work of art, as rich and subtle and unnerving as anything its author has ever done."

For B.R. Redman in the *Saturday Review of Literature* (June 26, 1948), the novel was "a clever trifle, which will be enjoyed by many readers, and condemned by others as being in the worst of taste." In *The Nation* (July 31, 1948), Ernest Jones wrote, "In *The Loved One* there is no comprehension or control, only a calculated series of shocks."

In 1965 Martin Ransohoff produced the screen version of *The Loved One* for M-G-M, directed by Tony Richardson, and starring Robert Morse, Jonathan Winters, Anjanette Comer, and Rod Steiger.

JOHN VAN ALSTYN WEAVER (1893–1938).

A New York artist, Don Slocum, picks up a cigarette girl in a nightclub in *Joy-Girl* (Alfred A. Knopf, 1932). He helps her to succeed in Hollywood, but then she rejects him for a man with more wealth and influence. "Hollywood is subjected to a fearful roasting in this new novel, a scathing burlesque of the movie industry which, unfortunately, is robbed of full comic effectiveness by the maudlin banality of its true love story," wrote the reviewer in the *New York Times* (June 5, 1932).

LYDIA WEAVER.

Child Star: When the Talkies Came to Hollywood (Viking, 1992) is the story of ten-year-old Joey in Depression-era Hollywood, who becomes child star Little Joey Norman with the advent of talkies. A novel in the children's series "Once Upon America," *Child Star* is beautifully illustrated by Michele LaPorte.

HENRY KITCHELL WEBSTER (1875–1932).

Leda Swan is not Mary Pickford "but the next brightest star in the kinematographic firmament." In *Real Life: Into Which Miss Leda Swan of Hollywood Makes an Adventurous Excursion* (Bobbs-Merrill, 1921), the lady in question discovers life beyond the stages of Hollywood. When she rescues a young man from death beneath the wheels of a truck, she discovers that he is a great violinist also trying to escape from the routine of his career. She has never heard of him, nor he of her. For 24 hours the two experience real life. This mildly amusing novel is illustrated by Everett Shinn.

TERESA WEIR.

Last Summer (Bantam Books, 1993) is a typical romantic novel, involving prim and proper Maggie Mayfield and dissipated movie star Johnnie Irish, as they get together for one hot summer in Hope, Texas.

DAVID WEISS (born 1928).

Justin Moyan (William Morrow, 1965) is the story of the title character, from high school football player in 1944 to Broadway star in 1960. In between, Moyan works in Hollywood films, for which he has little liking. The emphasis is on the stage, and there is a hint of Marlon Brando in Moyan's behavior and attitude.

SHEILA WELLER (born 1945).

Hansel & Gretel in Beverly Hills (William Morrow, 1978) is the tender love story of 54-year-old Lil, a divorced and widowed Hollywood publicist, and a 40-year-old gay hairdresser named Ronald. They care for and support each other in a story about a special kind of love narrated by Lil. The Hollywood connection is slight.

CAROLYN WELLS (1870–1942) was a prolific, popular, but critically unacclaimed mystery novelist. She wrote three books featuring an ex–silent film star named Kenneth Carlisle: *Sleeping Dogs* (Doubleday, Doran, 1929), *The Doorstep Murders* (Doubleday, Doran, 1930), and *The Skeleton at the Feast* (Doubleday, Doran, 1931).

MARVIN WERLIN (born 1929). On the dust jacket of *Shadow Play* (William Morrow, 1976), critic Rex Reed writes, "Film buffs will have a grand time reading this Gothic novel. It contains elements of *Sunset Boulevard*, *The Loved One*, and *Phantom of the Opera*. It is eerily amusing and chillingly perverse, with everything but the camera angles. A total delight." Reed neglects to add that the novel is ridiculously and unbelievably melodramatic. Heroine Christine Glenville arrives at the northern California oceanside mansion of millionaire Max Deveraux, where she is to work as his assistant. On arrival, she recognizes the front of the house as Manderley from the screen version of *Rebecca*. The interior of the house is identical to the sets of various movies: the terrace is from *Death Takes a Holiday*, the library from *Suspicion*. Deveraux lives like Citizen Kane, and his wife spends hours solving jigsaw puzzles in the manner of Susan Alexander. Deveraux is the ultimate movie buff. He even has actors and actresses playing roles in his life, and he has planned to use Christine as the central character in a gothic drama that he is enacting. But Deveraux is not just a sick film buff, he is also a perverted one. He stages scenes from old films, playing out sexual fantasies that would never have been shown on screen. Christine's predecessor was murdered during one such fantasy, killed by Deveraux's supposed niece Leora. After a second murder, Christine and the "decent" members of the household escape with their lives, while the rest perish in a fire set by Leora in a perfect imitation of Judith Anderson in *Rebecca*.

CHARLES WEST. While working as a stand-in for a famous film actor in *Funnelweb* (Walker, 1988), Tom Grant finds a link between two apparently unrelated killings and eventually uncovers the identity of a ruthless killer called Funnelweb. This is the author's second mystery novel set in Australia.

NATHANAEL WEST (1903–40) first came to Hollywood as a screenwriter in 1933, returning in 1935, and from 1936 onward he worked steadily as a writer of B pictures for Republic, Columbia, RKO, and Universal. Unemployed in 1935, he stayed at the Pa-Va-Sed Hotel on North Ivar Street in Hollywood, and it became the model for the San Bernardino Arms in *The Day of the Locust*. West was very much an onlooker in relation to the world of Hollywood, and he peopled his novel with many of the characters he saw in the Hollywood Boulevard area. The money he earned as a writer at Republic helped finance the writing of *The Day of the Locust*, and the poor sales of the book—fewer than 1,500 copies—determined West's continuance as a screenwriter.

Curiously, West and his wife, Eileen, were killed in a car crash on December 22, 1940, one day after the death of F. Scott Fitzgerald. West's screen career is covered in some detail in Tom Dardis's *Some Time in the Sun* (Charles Scribner's Sons, 1976) and Ian Hamilton's *Writers in Hollywood, 1915–1951* (Harper & Row, 1990).

The Day of the Locust (Random House, 1939), West's longest novel, was written over a four-year period. It was influenced as much by the Depression as by his screen career, and deals little with actual production but rather concentrates on the figures on the sidelines of Hollywood filmmaking. The central character, Tod Hackett, is a set and costume designer who is painting "The Burning of Hollywood." In an effort to evoke realism in his painting, Hackett seeks to learn and understand more about his colleagues, particularly his fellow boarders at the San Bernardino Arms. He is attracted to Faye Greener, and by extension becomes friendly with her father, an ex-vaudevillian named Harry Greener. Hackett visits a brothel run by a former silent film actress named Mrs. Jennings, and there views a pornographic film titled *Le Predicament de Marie*. While at Harry Greener's apartment, Hackett meets one of Faye's suitors, Homer Simpson, "an exact model for the kind of person who comes to California to die." Simpson replaces Hackett as the principal character in the novel, as the reader is introduced to him and his lonely and pathetic existence. Meanwhile, Hackett continues to court Faye Greener; her father dies, she becomes one of Mrs. Jennings's girls, and she moves in with Homer. The dividing line between Hollywood filmmaking and reality becomes blurred as Hackett observes the filming of an epic entitled *Waterloo*, visits various Hollywood churches, and goes to a cockfight at Homer's house attended by other characters important to the novel: Earle Shoop, a theatrical cowboy, and Claude Estee. In the final chapter, Homer is killed in a riot at a movie premiere. Denied access to their screen heroes and heroines, the "little people" of Hollywood turn on each other. As Randall Reid wrote in *The Fiction of Nathanael West* (University of Chicago Press, 1967), "The victims turn victimizers. The Burning of Los Angeles is the inevitable vengeance of those who, cheated by life, find that even their dreams have betrayed them."

DONALD E. WESTLAKE (born 1933). Three young men program a computer named Starnap to plan the kidnapping of Hollywood star Sassi Manoon as she attends a film festival in *Who Stole Sassi Manoon?* (Random House, 1969). *Enough!* (Evans/J.B. Lippincott, 1977) consists of two novellas. The first, "A Travesty," concerns a film critic who accidentally kills his girlfriend and is blackmailed by a private detective. Later, the critic solves the murder of a film buff. "Modestly entertaining and meat for movie buffs," opined the reviewer in *Library Journal* (March 1, 1977). In "Ordo," the ex-husband of a teenage bride discovers she has become a Hollywood star, a blonde "Jane Fonda who doesn't nag."

MICHAEL WESTLAKE (born 1942). *Imaginary Women* (Carcanet, 1987) is not so much a novel as an academic exercise in semiotics. Some chapters are written by a woman filmmaker whose company is called Fur Q, while others are written by her cat, who has mastered the art of the computer. The plots of *North by Northwest* and *Touch of Evil* figure prominently in the book, if not in the storyline (if such there is to be found here). *Imaginary Women* is not a book for the weak or unadventuresome.

RUTHE S. WHEELER writes for teenagers in *Janet Hardy in Hollywood* (Goldsmith Publishing, 1935) about the title heroine's experiences as she visits the film capital.

RAOUL WHITFIELD was the pseudonym of Temple Field (1908–45). Set in 1930, *Death in a Bowl* (Alfred A. Knopf, 1931) opens with a fight on the set between director Ernest Reiner and screenwriter Howard Frey. Both men approach Hollywood private eye Ben Jardinn, with Reiner claiming that Frey is trying to kill him and Frey asserting that Reiner is going to frame him. Jardinn takes on both men as clients: "We have a wonderful organization here.... We can handle two angles at one and the same time. By God, but we're efficient!" However, it is not Ernest Reiner who is murdered but his brother, Hans, as he conducts at the Hollywood Bowl and while a plane flies low overhead, its engines covering the noise of the gunshots. Jardinn has many problems with his office staff, and his associate Max Cohn proves to be the killer. And there is something of an anti–Semitic slant in the revelation, with Cohn not only having an obviously Jewish name but also being identified by Jardinn, for no apparent reason, as Jewish. The plot is convoluted, and *Death in a Bowl* is definitely dime novel stuff—but good dime novel writing.

PHYLLIS A. WHITNEY (born 1903) is a prolific romantic novelist, at least two of whose books have film-related themes. In *Listen for the Whisperer* (Fawcett, 1987) Leigh Hollins goes to Norway to find her legendary movie actress mother, Laura Worth. Twenty years before, the director of one of Laura's movies was murdered, and now someone is trying to kill Laura and Leigh. In *Star Flight* (Crown, 1993) Lauren Castle is the illegitimate daughter of two "golden age" movie stars. The young woman travels to North Carolina to confront her father and thereby help understand her husband's recent death. "Overly talky and cluttered," opined *Kirkus* (July 1, 1993).

GEORGE S. WHITTAKER. Not only destiny but also the long arm of coincidence play major parts in *Beggars of Destiny* (Dorrance, 1935). When Hollywood star Sylvia Palmer, owner of Filmarte Studios, is kidnapped by her studio manager, a minor Hollywood star, Paul Burgess, who is in love with her, puts up the money for her ransom. Personal problems in Paul's life, including Sylvia's blindness from an accident, persuade him to go to Hawaii, where he falls in love with Pele, a native girl. Subsequently, Sylvia regains her sight and also goes on location to Hawaii. Paul is stabbed, Sylvia donates her blood to save his life, and the two are married after Pele commits suicide. Successful in Hollywood, Paul and Sylvia both win Academy Awards. Phew!

MARGARET WIDDEMER (18??–1978). *This Isn't the End* (Farrar & Rinehart, 1936) recounts the story of the rise to fame and wealth of a former radio entertainer in the film industry. The breakup of his marriage is, ultimately, to his wife's benefit. "To point the moral, Miss Widdemer has rubbed a little excess black on her blackguard and outfitted her heroine with too much halo, but the story is absorbing, timely and effectively staged," commented Lisle Bell in the *New York Herald Tribune* (January 23, 1937).

IRENE WILDE. In order to help pay the bills, a female writer in Los Angeles teaches young performers on location in **Red Turban** (Liveright Publishing, 1943). The title refers to a mystic of that name whom the woman meets, and the novel contrasts the ideals and poetry of Eastern philosophy with "the speed of the flashing, brilliant life of the moving-picture colony in California."

MARGARET BUELL WILDER was the author of the best-selling novel *Since You Went Away* (1943). Wilder was present in Hollywood during 1944 while the book was being filmed by producer David O. Selznick, under the direction of John Cromwell and starring Claudette Colbert, Jennifer Jones, and Joseph Cotten, and she wrote a fictionalized account of her time there under the title **Hurry Up and Wait** (Whittlesey House, 1946).

ROBERT WILDER (1901–74). *The Sound of Drums and Cymbals* (G.P. Putnam's Sons, 1974) is the story of a Hollywood dynasty, replete with many items of Hollywood history (usually accurate). Only two nonfictional entities play a prominent part in the story, MCA (when it was still a talent agency) and the Garden of Allah. The novel begins with Deke Kincaid's return to Hollywood from military service after World War II. He had been married to the daughter of a prominent studio head and was blacklisted as a result of his leaving her. The father-in-law in question is Louis Bernard, known by the initials L.B., and though the backgrounds are different there is considerable similarity between Bernard and L. (Louis) B. Mayer. Kincaid returns to his wife and the studio, as head of production, and the book follows his progress from the mid-1940s through the mid-1960s, by which time his father-in-law is dead and a conglomerate, working in league with Kincaid's son, is about to take over the studio. The son had headed the studio's television division, called Screen Classics (just as Columbia's television division was known as Screen Gems), and was fired by his father just as Kincaid had been fired by his father.

There is perhaps a little too much historical data in the book, but *The Sound of Drums and Cymbals* does manage to provide what would appear to be an accurate overview of studio production through three decades. Earnestly and intelligently, it documents the end of the studio era and the Hollywood moguls and the beginning of the age of the conglomerates, the demise of films as entertainment and the rise of the social drama and the so-called message film.

HUGH WILEY (1884–19??) wrote a series of novels featuring a black protagonist, Vitus Marsden, of Memphis, and his goat, Lily. In **The Prowler** (Alfred A. Knopf, 1924), Marsden is on the West Coast and trying to break into movies. "Mr. Wiley has created from likable negro virtues and almost as likable negro failings, a very definite piece of characterization indeed. Through all the verbal grotesqueries that give light—albeit at times an artificial light—to his pages there stands out a living soul," commented the *New York Times* (January 11, 1925).

MAX WILK (born 1920), a former television writer, has written a number of books on show business: *The Golden Age of Television* (1977), *Represented by Audrey Wood* (1983, with Wood), *And Did You Once See Sidney Plain? A Random Memoir of S.J. Perelman* (1986), and *Beautiful Morning: The History of Oklahoma!* (1992).

Dust jacket blurbs for **The Moving Picture Boys** (W.W. Norton, 1978) claim it is "the meanest, nastiest, most driving and suspenseful thriller ever written about the gnomes and elves of the silver screen" (Richard Condon) and "a brilliantly incisive novel" (Judith Crist). It is neither, but it is an entertaining and well-plotted work, coincidentally the first novel to use the idea of kidnapping and holding hostage the negative of an as yet unreleased film. The central character is an out-of-work screenwriter, Perc Barnes, who is reduced to giving tennis lessons at a local Los Angeles country club. He is contacted by two ex-cons who want him to write a script based on their lives. Barnes does not consider the concept very original but goes ahead, with some prompting from his girlfriend who also plants various publicity stories about the proposed film. Producer Harry Elbert, whom Barnes actively dislikes, is attracted to the project and hires Barnes to write a script and the two ex-cons to serve as consultants. What neither Barnes nor Elbert knows is that the ex-cons have their own plans, first to gain access to the studio lot, and then to steal the negative of Elbert's multimillion dollar Western production. They take Barnes into their confidence, and, though at first horrified, he agrees after discovering that Elbert is planning to double-cross him. The heist is successful, Elbert pays a million dollars in ransom money, and the two ex-cons leave for Michigan, reminding Barnes that the job can only be successful if all three lie low for a lengthy period. But the screenwriter is nervous about his share, goes to visit the ex-cons, and is followed by an insurance investigator. The latter plans to turn the three men in, but is persuaded by the ex-cons to join the "gang" in return for a third of the money. Barnes returns to Los Angeles and receives an Academy Award for his script, and the two ex-cons decide to pursue the insurance investigator, realizing that he has probably "blackmailed" others into turning over some of their gains to him.

RAMSAY WILLIAMS. The leading character in **Bitten Apples** (McGibbon & Kee, 1960) is East Coast actor Conrad Eldred. With the help of a former roommate, Luke Barney, who is now a Hollywood star, Eldred is able to obtain a featured role in a Western starring Barney, but no sooner does he learn of his big break than he discovers that Barney and Eldred's girlfriend are having an affair. A fine capturing of the joy and tragedy that together have been Hollywood since the film community came into existence.

WIRT WILLIAMS (1921–86). **The Trojans** (Little, Brown, 1966) opens on a crisis during the filming of Globe-International Pictures' production of *Helen of Troy* on a Greek island. The leading lady, Margaret Dayton, has walked off the set and disappeared. The author then proceeds to document, in the first person, the lives of the various principals in the story: the star's husband and the film's writer, Grover Brand; the head of the studio, Sidney Tate; the star's mother, Octavia Dayton; her agent, Nelson Glassgow; the male lead, Mace Garrett; and the film's producer, Howard Sills. Each has known Margaret Dayton at one time or another, and while their stories are interesting, none reveals too much about the actress. The saddest is that of Mace Garrett, who, although terminally ill, is working hard to make enough money to take care of his wife after he is gone. Margaret Dayton's disappearance is ultimately linked to an industrialist whom Sidney Tate once bested, and who is now plotting to take over the studio. The concept is not particularly well presented, nor is the picture of the Armenian moneyman behind the studio, sailing the oceans of the world in his yacht and about to descend on the production.

The author has a sound knowledge of film production and is reasonably well versed in film history, although he is off by four years in his date for *The Great Train Robbery*. He depicts an incident in which agent Glassgow is shot in the thigh after producer Sills finds him in bed with his wife. That is obviously based on Walter Wanger's shooting of his wife Joan Bennett's agent, Jennings Lang, in the groin. There are no other obvious similarities between the fictional characters and Wanger and Lang.

DIXIE WILLSON. *Hollywood Starlet* (Dodd, Mead, 1942) is a novel for high school girls, telling of two who try to break into the movies; one is the winner of a beauty contest, the other is not. "The descriptions of the movie industry are unoriginal but informative and there is a good hard common sense attitude about the difficulties of getting into the movies," wrote E.L. Buell in the *New York Times* (January 21, 1942).

DANA WILSON. *Make with the Brains, Please* (Julian Messner, 1946) is a mystery novel, narrated in the first person, with a Hollywood background. The critic for the *Saturday Review of Literature* (November 16, 1946) thought it "silly," and Anthony Boucher wrote in the *San Francisco Chronicle* (October 27, 1946), "Maybe you can swallow the muddled sentimentality that so often passes for tough-mindedness in fiction. Maybe you aren't tired of sagas of Hollywood sex. Maybe you can even believe in a French hero who complains of his difficulties with American psychology and language but writes in strictly ersatz James Cain. But if you can gulp down all of these elements at once you're a stronger man than I am."

HARRY LEON WILSON (1867–1939) wrote one of the classic popular novels on Hollywood, *Merton of the Movies*, which, though it has not been reprinted since 1923, spawned two film versions (with Glenn Hunter in 1924 and Red Skelton in 1947) and was adapted for the stage by Marc Connelly and George S. Kaufman. The novel was originally serialized in the *Saturday Evening Post*, with which Wilson was closely associated as a humorist from the early years of the twentieth century through 1935. Wilson's writing was as much a part of American humor as that of Mark Twain, and when he died the *New York Herald Tribune* (June 30, 1939) wrote, "Others have attempted loftier flights. But in the air that Wilson breathed he was a master, and the result was not so much a record of the country, its scene, its salient folk, their bedevilment and their victory as the essence of the soul itself. Harry Leon Wilson was America."

The writer had little to do with Hollywood. Unlike many of his contemporaries, he never worked there as a well-paid, underemployed screenwriter.

Only when he was short of money in 1935 did he agree to work briefly at M-G-M as a consultant. In that same year, he expressed outrage at what Paramount had done with its adaptation of his novel *Ruggles of Red Gap*, starring Charles Laughton in the title role. (An earlier version in 1923 had starred Edward Everett Horton.)

He did come to Hollywood in 1920 to "research" *Merton of the Movies* and later noted, "The details of him filled themselves in as I hung around Hollywood studios, watching, listening, for an always entertaining three months. What would be his adventures, his shocks, his tragedies, his triumphs? These movie lots told me day after day, and I tried to put them down. If Merton is real, all the credit to that incredible Hollywood. If he isn't the fault is all mine. No excuse for a writer worth his salt who can't see a dozen characters in that exciting atmosphere. It still excites me. I wish I had Merton to do all over again."

For more information on Wilson and *Merton of the Movies*, readers should study George Kummer's *Harry Leon Wilson: Some Accounts of the Triumphs and Tribulations of an American Popular Writer* (Cleveland: Press of Western Reserve University, 1963), and Lawrence Clark Powell's "Harry Leon Wilson's *Merton of the Movies*," in *Westways* (October 1970), pp. 24–27, 66–67.

Merton of the Movies (Doubleday, Page, 1922) opens with Merton Gill fantasizing that he is hero Buck Benson rescuing Estelle St. Clair from the clutches of the leering Snake Le Vasquez. Merton is an assistant at the Gashwiler Emporium in Simsbury, Illinois, where the only person who understands him is Tessie Kearns, "sedate and mouselike of middle age," who like Merton has her own film-related dream—to become a scenario writer. Nightly, Merton prays, "Oh, God, make me a good movie actor!" and, armed with a diploma from the General Film Production Company of Stebbinville, Arkansas, "certifying him to be a competent screen actor," and with a new name, Clifford Armytage, he arrives in Los Angeles.

After lingering for weeks outside the Holden Studios, Merton is allowed on the lot by a kindly receptionist. Eventually, he is hired as an extra, and, as his money runs out, he takes to sleeping secretly at the studio. There, he discovers that the star with whom he is besotted, Beulah Baxter, has been doubled for the past two years by a "bit" player named Sarah Montague, who has befriended him: "It was the Montague girl who had most thrilled him for two years." She realizes Merton's plight and brings him to the attention of a director who likes his freshness. The director casts the young man in *Hearts on Fire*, which Merton does not realize is a parody of the work of the studio's most popular star.

Offended that he is being treated as a comedian, Merton turns on Montague, and she comforts him with a motherly hug: "It's all right, everything's all right." Merton accepts that he has a "low-comedy face." The novel ends with an interview in *Silver Screenings*, in which it is revealed that Montague and Merton are married, and he admits, "I owe my real success all to her."

What is perhaps most surprisingly about *Merton of the Movies* is that it still entertains after more than 70 years. Its wit and satire have a freshness equal to that seen in Merton by the comedy director. The story of a young boy or girl trying to make good in Hollywood has been told and retold countless times since 1922, but never with such refreshing charm and understanding of the innocence of Midwestern youth.

Wilson returned to a Hollywood theme with *Two Black Sheep* (Farrar, 1931), which was also serialized in the *Saturday Evening Post*, and which liberally borrows ideas from *Merton of the Movies*. This satire concerns a French prince, traveling incognito, who comes to Hollywood with a young woman, posing as a New York society heiress. Both break into talkies, and the Frenchman gets his wish to become an American citizen.

If anything *Two Black Sheep* indicates that Wilson has failed to move with the literary times; despite the reference to talkies, the basic story belongs to a decade earlier. The *Saturday Review of Literature* (December 19, 1931) commented, "The characters have not the memorable warmth of Merton, Ma Pettengill or Cousin Jane, and the extreme naive credulity of the hero, in particular, is nearer to the line of farce and frank absurdity than Mr. Wilson usually allows himself to go. But the story is told with the author's customary skill and is altogether a highly amusing book."

SLOAN WILSON (born 1920). The central character in *Janus Island* (Little, Brown, 1967) is 45-year-old Ben Powers, whose career as a writer for films and television is just about over. He heads for Janus Island off the Florida coast, where a millionaire friend is searching for buried treasure and using a movie company to cover up his activities. Eventually, the millionaire commits suicide.

DON WINSLOW. *Way Down on the High Lovely* (St. Martin's Press, 1993) is a gripping if implausible thriller that begins with its hero Neil Carey's release from three years of internment in a Chinese monastery. He comes to Los Angeles and agrees to help a female Hollywood executive find her young son, kidnapped by her ex-husband. The trail leads Carey to a remote area of Nevada and a white supremacist group.

KATHLEEN WINSOR (born 1919) gained immediate fame in 1944 with publication of her first novel, *Forever Amber* (filmed in 1947). *Calais* (Doubleday, 1979) is in much the same romantic vein. This wordy tome (almost 700 pages) details the rise to fame and fortune of actress Arlette Morgan, née Lily Malone. She becomes a star of stage and screen whose career is pretty much paralleled by that of her husband.

THOMAS WISEMAN (born 1931) was the film critic of the British *Sunday Express* from 1961 to 1964; he also co-wrote the 1974 screenplay for *The Romantic Englishwoman*, based on his 1971 novel. *Czar* (Simon & Schuster, 1965), despite its title, is the story of two Hollywood moguls. One is a businessman with artistic pretentions and the other a former garment worker, and both have the attributes of a number of real-life film industry tycoons. Both have interesting sex lives, and both rely heavily on bankers to finance their careers, from the silent era through the end of the studio era, following the work of the House Un-American Activities Committee. "The dialogue is as banal as the story is predictable," opined *Kirkus*.

HARRY CHARLES WITWER (1890–1929) was a popular novelist and short story writer of the 1920s whose works formed the basis for three feature films of the decade: *The Fourth Musketeer* (1923), *The Great White Way* (1924), and *Alex the Great* (1928). The central characters in his novels usually had sporting backgrounds and spent some time in Hollywood.

Kid Scanlan (Small, Maynard, 1920) is a collection of short stories detailing the adventures of welterweight boxing champion Kid Scanlan in Hollywood movies, as told by his manager, Johnny Green. "The book may be scoffed at by the more intellectual, but the wideness of its appeal is evident," commented the *New York Times* (July 25, 1920). *There's No Base Like Home* (Doubleday, Doran, 1920) consists of a series of letters from baseball star Ed Harmon to his friend Joe. Harmon brings his French wife, Jeanne, to New York, and she later goes into the movies, dragging her husband along with her. The *New York Times* (July 25, 1920) wrote, "In a certain way, Witwer's stories remind one of Keystone comedies, although, of course, they are not quite so far-fetched in their incongruous situations."

The central character in *Bill Grimm's Progress* (G.P. Putnam's Sons, 1926) is a New York taxi driver who becomes a prizefighter; his girlfriend helps him become a leading man in Hollywood films. *Yes Man's Land* (G.P. Putnam's Sons, 1929) bears some similarity to *Kid Scanlan* in that it is the story of a prizefighter, Gentleman Jack, who becomes a Hollywood star, and is narrated by the boxer's manager. "In this lightest of light fictions," wrote the *Saturday Review of Literature* (June 15, 1929), "Mr. Witwer gives us a good many canny observations on Hollywood. He makes flip but pertinent remarks on producers, actors, and hangers-on; even the infant talkies come in for their share of disrespect. Mr. Witwer is so conscientiously up-to-the-minute that his wisecracking book will need a glossary before many months have passed."

FLORENCE WOBBER. *Calico Orchids: Forthright Diary of "Little June East"* (Murray & Gee, 1942) documents its title heroine's work in radio in San Francisco and her later attempts to break into films. Purple prose at its worst.

P. (Pelham) G. (Grenville) WODEHOUSE (1881–1975) came to Hollywood in 1930, under contract to M-G-M. As he recalled in his 1957 autobiography *Over Seventy*, "I had a year's contract, and was required to do so little work in return for the money I received that I was able in the twelve months before I became a fugitive from the chain-gang to write a novel and nine short stories, besides brushing up my golf, getting an attractive sun-tan and perfecting my Australian crawl in the swimming pool." Wodehouse received two screen credits as a result of his sojourn at M-G-M: for the dialogue of *Those Three French Girls* (1930) and for additional dialogue on *The Man in Possession* (1931).

The first Wodehouse work to be adapted for the screen was his 1911 play *A Gentleman of Leisure*, filmed by the Jesse L. Lasky Feature Play Company in 1915. That same year, Essanay produced a two-reeler based on a Wodehouse work, *Rule 63*. Between 1918 and 1920, some seven pieces by Wodehouse were adapted for the screen: *Uneasy Money* (1918), *A Damsel in Distress* (1919), *Oh, Boy!* (1919), *The Prince and Betty* (1919), *Piccadilly Jim* (1920), *Oh, Lady, Lady* (1920), and *Their Mutual Child* (1920).

A Gentleman of Leisure was refilmed by Famous Players–Lasky in 1923.

Wodehouse's 1926 short story "The Small Bachelor" was the basis for the 1927 Universal feature of the same name. His 1926 musical *Oh, Kay!* was filmed by First National in 1928; his 1920 musical *Sally* by First National in 1929; his 1927 comedy *Her Cardboard Lover* by M-G-M as *The Passionate Plumber* in 1932; his 1929 English-language adaptation of *Kleine Komedie* by Universal as *By Candlelight* in 1933; his 1910 short story "The Watch Dog" by Liberty Pictures as *Dizzy Dames* in 1935. In 1936, Paramount filmed his 1934 musical *Anything Goes*, M-G-M filmed his 1917 novel *Piccadilly Jim*, and 20th Century–Fox filmed his 1934 novel *Thank You, Jeeves*. In 1937, 20th Century–Fox filmed *Step Lively, Jeeves!*, based on the writer's 1928 musical. In 1936, Wodehouse returned to Hollywood briefly, and adapted his 1919 novel *A Damsel in Distress* for RKO's release the following year.

In the United Kingdom, the first major television adaptation of a P.G. Wodehouse novel was "Code of the Woosters" by Central Television in 1991. Also in Britain, in 1962 the Wodehouse novel *The Girl on the Boat* was filmed by Knightsbridge as a vehicle for Norman Wisdom.

Hollywood Omnibus (Hutchinson, 1985) collects together the novel *Laughing Gas*, first published by Herbert Jenkins in 1936; five short stories from *Blandings Castle and Elsewhere*, first published by Herbert Jenkins in 1935; and one short story from *Plum Pie*, first published by Herbert Jenkins in 1966.

The story of ***Laughing Gas*** is recounted by Reggie Havershot, who has recently become the third Earl of Havershot, and he comes to Hollywood to extricate his cousin Egremont from an unfortunate liaison. It transpires that Egremont is besotted with Ann Bannister, for whom Reggie once had an affection, but en route to Los Angeles, Reggie is smitten by movie star April June. Once in Hollywood, Reggie develops a toothache, and at the dentist's office, he meets child star Joey Cooley, "the idol of American Motherhood." While the pair are under the influence of laughing gas, they exchange bodies. As Joey Cooley, Reggie discovers the true character of April June, who has the child star kidnapped as a publicity stunt. Escaping from his captors, Reggie is hit by a motorcycle driven by Joey in Reggie's body. The resulting accident permits the two to return to their rightful personae. Reggie decides to marry Ann, and Joey returns happily to Ohio, his career in ruins as a consequence of an unfortunate interview given by Reggie as Joey. (The effect of that interview is reminiscent of the aftermath to an interview Wodehouse gave the *Los Angeles Times* in 1931, in which he expressed his regret at being paid such a large sum by M-G-M without having done anything to earn it.)

The dialogue in *Laughing Gas* is strictly Wodehousian, with no acknowledgment of Americanese or Hollywood patter. Even the food consumed in Hollywood—steak and kidney pudding, sausages and pork pies—is British. The concept, which has been recycled by others, is a clever one, but the plot needed the pen of a contemporary writer such as Thorne Smith to move away from the banality and zero in on the sexual implications of the transmogrification, untouched by Wodehouse.

Blandings Castle and Elsewhere consists of short stories told in the bar-parlor of the Anglers' Rest. The star gorilla at the Perfecto-Zizzbaum Motion Picture Corporation of Hollywood is in reality a man in a monkey suit—"Balliol, you know ... an Oxford man"—in "Monkey Business." This knowledge helps a timid assistant director impress his extra girlfriend. "The Nodder" is a yes-man who gains influence with the studio management when he discovers that the company's child star is an elderly, hard-boiled midget. In "The Juice of an Orange," the Nodder from the previous story takes a pay cut and goes on an orange juice diet. "The Rise of Minna Nordstrom" chronicles the career of Vera Pebble from maid to movie star. "The Castaways" offers a caustic parody of the film industry's attitude toward screenwriters.

The bar-parlor of the Anglers' Rest is again the setting for the stories in *Plum Pie*. "George and Alfred" reminds the reader of the lot of the writer of additional dialogue in Hollywood — "he ranks, I believe, just above a script girl and just below the man who works the wind machine." George of the title is the writer, while his twin brother, Alfred, is a conjuror. The two are in Monte Carlo and inadvertently become involved in an attack on a Hollywood producer. After George saves the man's life, he is offered a new contract as "cousin by marriage," but insists that "brother-in-law" would be a more advantageous title.

Aside from the stories contained in *Hollywood Omnibus*, there are four more P.G. Wodehouse novels with film-related storylines. In *The Luck of the Bodkins* (Little, Brown, 1936), an English valet, Albert Peasemarch, is traveling on the train from New York to Hollywood and becomes involved in the problems of his fellow passengers, including producer Ivor Llewellyn and actress Lotus Blossom. When actress Carmen Flores dies in *The Old Reliable* (Doubleday, 1951), a former silent screen star acquires her estate, included in which is a diary that the silent star's butler and brother-in-law believe might have blackmail potential. After a year in Hollywood, Monty Bodkin returns to England in *The Plot That Thickens* (Simon & Schuster, 1971), and here he is hired by producer Ivor Llewellyn to write the history of the Superba-Llewellyn Studios. After various and typical Wodehousian adventures, Llewellyn is divorced and Monty engaged to his secretary. Ivor Llewellyn returns yet again in *Bachelors Anonymous* (Simon & Schuster, 1974), in which he is working at the British arm of his company, and trying to remain single with the help of a group called Bachelors Anonymous.

GARY WOLF. *Who Censored Roger Rabbit?* (St. Martin's Press, 1981) was the basis for the highly original 1988 feature film *Who Framed Roger Rabbit?*, a combination of live action and animation. The novel features tough Los Angeles private eye Eddie Valiant, who is hired by Roger Rabbit, a cartoon character or 'toon, who plays the straight man in the Baby Herman animation series. The 'toon wants Valiant to discover who is trying to buy his contract from the DeGreasy Brothers syndicate, and the investigation leads to murder and a steamy meeting with Roger's wife Jessica Rabbit, the lover of Rocco DeGreasy, in whose murder the 'toon is implicated. The author skillfully blends liberal doses of Raymond Chandler, Lewis Carroll, and the Warner brothers, and the end result is a book that some readers will agree with the publisher is "sheer delight," while others will dismiss it as nothing more than sheer silliness.

BERNARD WOLFE (1915–85) has used his early career as a writer of pornography and as a screenwriter at Universal-International Pictures/Tony Curtis Productions as the basis for a number of his novels. *Come On Out, Daddy*

(Charles Scribner's Sons, 1963) is a collection of short stories relating to a New York novelist, Gordon Rengs, "a serious writer of peripheral books," who is invited to come to Hollywood and write a script based on the life of Charlemagne for a Tony Curtis–type actor. While earning $2,000 a week for doing little, he gets involved with the sexual side of the film capital, including starlets, prostitutes, and homosexuals. Five of the chapters were previously published in *Playboy*. "It isn't a novel in the old-fashioned sense," wrote Budd Schulberg in *Book Week* (November 3, 1963). "It may not, suffering the defects of its abundant virtues, prove a permanent addition to Hollywood legend and literature in any sense. It is more like an ingenious, titillating, precocious, stimulating and comic monologue by a high-potency contemporary, a voice that deserves attention, but not quite so much as this gay, gifted garrulous book demands."

When writer Gordon Rengs returns to Hollywood from his Greek island in order to make money writing scripts in ***Logan's Gone*** (Nash Publishing, 1974), he gets involved with campus radicals, drugs, and extreme left-wing politics.

MARITTA WOLFF. *The Big Nickelodeon* (Random House, 1956) examines the sex lives of a group of Hollywood types, including a former screenwriter with whom a divorced woman falls in love, and a vagrant who falls in love with a homosexual but leaves him for a woman going through a sexual crisis. As here, Hollywood types do tend to lead desperate lives, and, after a while, it does make tedious reading. The opinion of the critic in the *New York Herald Tribune* (November 18, 1956) was that, "written with a high emotional beat, the book is interesting mainly for its portrayal of a strangely tangled group of people and the author's bitter criticism of the degenerating atmosphere of the world of celluloid."

PEGGY WOOD (1892–1978) was a major star of the American stage, married to poet and novelist John V.A. Weaver; her autobiography, *How Young You Look*, was published in 1941. Wood's novel ***Star-Wagon*** (Farrar & Rinehart, 1936) is the story of a New York actress and a reporter who come to Hollywood following their marriage; the novel recounts their experiences there. Beatrice Sherman in the *New York Times* (April 12, 1936) wrote, "The book is best when it is spoofing the temperamental stars, English actors and wire-pulling politics of the movie capital. But even when it goes romantic over lovers' quarrels or dramatic about an airplane smash it is very engaging, readable, light fiction."

LON RILEY WOODRUM (born 1901). ***If You Hear a Song*** (Zondervan Publishing, 1952) is the story of a decent yet tough man from Pittsburgh, who goes to Hollywood and finances a film promoting Eastern mysticism and starring a radio singer with whom he is having an affair. He is dragged deep into violence until converted to the Way of the Lord by a Sunday school teacher whom he marries and with whom he returns to Pittsburgh. The publisher specializes in religious books.

SARAH WOODS was the pseudonym of Sara Bowen-Judd. Prior to her death in 1985 Sarah Woods published 46 mystery novels featuring the insufferably boring and ultraconservative English barrister Anthony Maitland. In

The Case Is Altered (Harper & Row, 1967), Maitland is called upon by a young British film star, Jo Marston, to prove that her fiancé did not steal a collection of emeralds. Mrs. Maitland is, as usual, involved in the matter.

STUART WOODS (born 1938). *Santa Fe Rules* (HarperCollins, 1992) begins with film producer Wolf Willett learning that his directing partner, his wife, and an unidentified man believed to be Willett have been shot to death at his Santa Fe home. After completing final editing of his current film in secrecy, Willett returns to Santa Fe, where he is soon the chief suspect. Willett is not very happy that the obituaries on him and his partner named the latter as the creative force in the relationship, and the book concludes as Willett is about to begin work producing and directing his next film in partnership with a young female film editor who helped cut the previous work and with whom he has begun a sexual relationship. Despite attempts at being contemporary, *Santa Fe Rules* comes across as a plodding, at times almost tedious, mystery novel, and the conclusion, in which it is revealed that Willett's wife had a third sister unidentified until that point, is unfair to the reader.

The writing in ***L.A. Times*** (HarperCollins, 1993), which has nothing to do with the newspaper of that name, is uninspired. Vincente Michaele Callabrese is a good-looking New Yorker who works part-time as a muscle man for the Mafia. He is also a film buff and a student at NYU, and with a fellow student he produces a feature-length film, which he is able to sell at considerable profit to Leo Goldman, the head of Centurion Pictures. Goldman offers the young man a position as a production executive, and as Michael Vincent, Vincent Michaele Callabrese moves to Hollywood. He is talented and ruthless and a number of dead bodies line the path to his success, until he makes the mistake of taking on the Mob, which is supporting a Japanese takeover of Centurion. Crippled on orders of the Mafia bosses, Vincent is disgusted by the product Centurion is forced to produce by the Japanese. He decides to take revenge by killing both the Japanese and the Mafia representatives, but instead is gunned down. As he lies in a comatose state in the hospital, the widow of Leo Goldman, whom Michael had murdered, suffocates him.

"Slick but uninspired.... *Wait Until Dark* this isn't," writes *Kirkus* (November 15, 1993) of ***Dead Eyes*** (HarperCollins, 1994). The leading character is up-and-coming screen star Chris Callaway, who temporarily loses her eyesight in a fall. As might be expected, she has an ardent admirer who makes unwelcome advances, including tattooing her hand and sending her a dog's head. Eventually, the admirer is trapped in her newly built beachhouse by Chris, her gay hairdresser friend, and the cop with whom she is sleeping.

R. (Ralph) C. (Carter) WOODTHORPE (1886–19??). England's Dartmoor is the setting for ***Rope for a Convict*** (Crime Club/Doubleday, 1940), originally published in the United Kingdom as *Portraits of Characters*. The four principal characters are a screen star, her leading man, a director, and a 12-year-old boy. "Though the murder is incidental, there is detection, emotional concern, and narrative suspense," wrote Jacques Barzun in *A Catalogue of Crime* (Harper & Row, 1989).

WILLIAM WOOLFOLK (born 1917). *My Name Is Morgan* (Doubleday, 1963) is narrated by studio publicist Larry Whirter and is the story of producer Jack Morgan, who has reached the apex of his career with the production of the epic biblical drama *The Apostle*. Whirter is forced to promote Morgan as a great showman while secretly despising him.

The Beautiful Couple (World Publishing, 1968) are Jacquelyn Stuart and Brian O'Neal, who are separated and about to be divorced. Stuart has gone to Rio de Janeiro to work on her latest film, while O'Neal is in England, making side trips to his native Ireland, and working on a film version of *Oedipus Rex*, in which he stars and which he is also producing. As they deal with various problems on and off their respective sets, they recall many, many sexual encounters in their lives, including Stuart's two previous marriages. Her son is "kidnapped" by his father and her first husband, and in London O'Neal retrieves the boy for her. When Stuart has an accident, O'Neal flies to her side and attacks the wealthy industrialist who is her husband-to-be. In revenge, the industrialist pulls prospective funding for O'Neal's production. Stuart now flies to O'Neal's side and suggests that she should costar in the film as the mother, thus assuring the film's financing, and, as the reader knew from the start would happen, the pair is reunited. The novel is unintentionally patronizing toward the Irish and intentionally offensive to the homosexual community.

Maggie: A Love Story (Doubleday, 1971) is an unexciting rehash of the Marion Davies–William Randolph Hearst relationship. The principal character here is Maggie Dohaney, a showgirl in the Ziegfeld *Follies*, with whom newspaper tycoon Wallace Zachary Thorne becomes besotted. They begin a relationship that lasts for almost half a century. He decides to make her into a film star, but rejects her first film because she plays a comedic rather than a dramatic role. The film is remade and given its premiere at Grauman's Egyptian Theatre, even though the theatre had not yet opened. (Later, Maggie leaves her hand- and footprints at Grauman's Chinese Theatre three years before it opened.) Thorne builds a castle on the California coast called Sans Souci; Maggie lives there doing jigsaw puzzles and loans Thorne the money from the sale of her jewels in order to save his empire. The famous scandal in which Hearst shot producer Thomas H. Ince when he was supposedly making love to Davies is recreated, even down to having a gossip columnist (in real life Louella Parsons) there. And just as Parsons's daughter Harriet was lesbian, so is the gossip columnist's daughter here. A side plot involves a sister showgirl who marries a Rudolph Valentino–type leading man whose funeral is similar to that of the Italian-born star. The trouble with *Maggie* compared with the real-life saga of Hearst and Davies is that it has neither genuine romance nor legitimate fun.

ERIC WRIGHT (born 1929) has written a series of mystery novels featuring Toronto police Inspector Charlie Salter. In *Final Cut* (Charles Scribner's Sons, 1991), Wright notes the rise of filmmaking in Canada and that "Toronto had long since been discovered by Hollywood as an ideal location to imitate a medium-sized law-abiding American city, especially if the movie was set in the gentler past." Wright continues, "But if a story was actually set in Toronto, then someone was needed to keep the howlers out of the script." That need has provided employment for Salter's former boss, Staff Superintendent Orliff. He is working on a film at which a number of acts of sabotage have been directed, and when Orliff decides to go fishing, he arranges for Salter to pretend to take over his job while in reality investigating what is taking place on the set. After the screenwriter is murdered, the solution to the puzzle is found to lie in a minor incident that took place in Czechoslovakia.

Being a neophyte, Salter asks a lot of questions about film production, to which the producer provides answers. The making of a low-budget thriller in Toronto is covered in detail, but, as in previous Salter novels, what is more interesting is the inspector's home life and ongoing problems with his wife and sons (in this case, 16-year-old Seth's decision to become a ballet dancer). The initial plot outline might not seem particularly original, but Eric Wright's approach is always unique, as is the mystery's solution.

ROBERT WURLITZER (born 1938). *Slow Fade* (Alfred A. Knopf, 1984) is a short yet sprawling novel that centers on three main characters: Wesley Hardin, a veteran Hollywood director in the tradition of John Ford and Howard Hawks, who is fired from his latest film; his son Walker, who has just returned from India, about which he is writing a screenplay; and A.D. Ballou, a musician who loses an eye on Hardin's set and collaborates with Walker on the script. The book centers on Wesley Hardin's efforts to come to terms with his life at the age of 75, as he confronts a wife and assorted people who have worked with him in the film industry, and realizes that existence can only be better away from the movies. At the same time, his son uncovers the truth of his sister's death in India.

PHILIP WYLIE (1902–71) reintroduces Florida fishermen Crunch and Des (who first appeared in 1940 in *The Big Ones Get Away*) in *Salt Water Daffy* (Farrar & Rinehart, 1941). Here, the pair is offered a job in Hollywood to show how the big fish are caught. Unpretentious entertainment strictly for fishermen rather than film buffs.

RICHARD YATES (1926–92). *Disturbing the Peace* (Delacorte Press, 1975) documents the alcoholic decline of John Willer, a magazine advertising salesman, who is admitted to New York's Bellevue Hospital; the novel ends in a California mental institution. To get from New York to Los Angeles, he becomes involved with a woman he meets at an A.A. meeting, and agrees to work with her on a film titled *Bellevue*. "The novel is so cool and finely crafted that a truly harrowing experience seems occasionally only a disturbance of the peace," commented Barbara Nelson in *Library Journal* (December 15, 1975).

MICKEY ZIFFREN's first novel, *A Political Affair* (Delacorte Press, 1979), concerns a former movie star, Norah Jones Ashley, who is persuaded by the president to run as California candidate for the U.S. Senate against a conservative incumbent. The Ashley character is presumably based on Helen Gahagan Douglas, who lost the Senate race to Richard Nixon. There are dirty tricks galore as Norah's affair with a Mafia figure is exposed. She has also had an affair with her opponent, whose daughter is in love with Norah's Chicano organizer and whose son-in-law has a homosexual affair.

LEN ZINBERG. The central character in *What D'Ya Know for Sure* (Doubleday, 1947) is assistant director Pete Rand, who gives up his job in order to rehabilitate psychologically disturbed movie star Terry (Cherry) Evans. Cured, Evans marries Rand, and together they set out to make the type of film that Rand had always wanted to direct. A 20th Century–Fox Literary Fellowship novel.

BONNIE ZINDEL (born 1943). *Hollywood Dream Machine* (Viking Kestrel, 1984) is a novel with a Hollywood background for teenage readers.

PAUL ZINDEL (born 1936) is best known as the author of the 1971 play, and later film, *The Effect of Gamma Rays on Man-in-the-Moon Marigolds*. The central character in *When a Darkness Falls* (Bantam Books, 1984) is a successful Hollywood screenwriter whose personal life is in crisis as he struggles to pay the bills. He turns to cocaine and then to ritual murder as insanity takes over, with his ultimate aim the killing of his wife and children. *When a Darkness Falls* is a gripping suspense novel, its only fault being the early identification of the screenwriter as the serial killer.

WILLIAM K. (Knowlton) ZINSSER (born 1922) was film critic for the *New York Herald Tribune* (1955–58) and entertainment critic for the NBC *Sunday* show (1963–64). His film reviews were anthologized in *Seen Any Good Movies Lately?* (Doubleday, 1958). *The Paradise Bit* (Little, Brown, 1967) is a witty tale in which a Hollywood publicist promotes a new film titled *Desert Island for Two*, with a premiere on the unspoiled South Sea island of Tonji. The native inhabitants and local residents foil Hollywood's plans.

LEON ZOLOTKOFF (1866–19??). *From Vilna to Hollywood* (Bloch Publishing, 1932) is the story of a Russian émigré, Hershele Korbelnik, who changes his name to Harry Corbell and after World War I becomes the head of a studio. His career and life collapse when it is discovered that his marriage back in Vilna, Russia, was not dissolved as he had believed.

The Television Novel:
A Tentative Bibliography

This is the first attempt at compiling a bibliography of television-related novels. No claim is made that this listing is complete, but it does include all types of novels, including works intended for juvenile audiences.

Adams, Barbara. *Can This Telethon Be Saved?* Dell, 1987.
_____. *The Not-Quite-Ready-for-Prime-Time Bandits.* Dell, 1986.
_____. *Rock Video Strikes Again.* Dell, 1986.
Aiken, Joan. *Backing Round.* Doubleday, 1989.
Allen, Charlotte Vale. *Intimate Friends.* E.P. Dutton, 1983.
Allen, Steve. *The Murder Game.* Zebra Books, 1993.
_____. *Murder on the Glitter Box.* Zebra Books, 1989.
_____. *The Public Hating.* Dembner Books, 1990.
_____. *The Talk Show Murders.* Delacorte Press, 1982.
Amis, Kingsley. *I Want It Now.* Harcourt Brace Jovanovich, 1968.
Ansell, Jack. *Dynasty of Air.* Arbor House, 1974.
_____. *Giants.* Arbor House, 1975.
Aurthur, R. *Glorification of Al Toolum.* Rinehart, 1953.
Babbin, Jacqueline. *Bloody Soaps.* International Polygonics, 1989.
Bailey, Jill. *Polar Bear Rescue.* Steck-Vaughn Library, 1991.
Barden, Rosalind. *TV Monster.* Crown, 1988.
Barracca, Debra. *Maxi, the Star.* Dial Books for Young Readers, 1993.
Barris, Chuck. *You and Me, Babe.* Harper's Magazine Press, 1974.
Bauer, Laurel. *Vertical World.* St. Martin's Press, 1986.
Berenstain, Stan, and Jon Berenstain. *The Berenstain Bears and Too Much TV.* Random House, 1984.
Blackwell, Earl, and Eugenia Sheppard. *Skyrocket.* Doubleday, 1980.
Booth, Colleen E. *Going Live.* Charles Scribner's Sons, 1992.
Bora, Ben. *The Starcrossed.* Chilton Books, 1975.
Bradley, Rodrick. *TV Man.* Holt, Rinehart and Winston, 1981.
Brady, James. *Nielsen's Children.* G.P. Putnam's Sons, 1978.
Bragg, Melvyn. *Crystal Rooms.* Hodder & Stoughton, 1992.
_____. *Love and Glory.* Secker & Warburg, 1983.
Breen, Richard. *Made for TV.* Beaufort Books, 1982.
Brett, Simon. *Dead Giveaway.* Charles Scribner's Sons, 1985.
_____. *A Series of Murders.* Charles Scribner's Sons, 1989.
_____. *Situation Tragedy.* Charles Scribner's Sons, 1981.
Brown, Lizzie. *Broken Star.* St. Martin's Press, 1993.
Brown, Marc Tolon. *The Bionic Bunny Show.* Little, Brown, 1984.
Brown, Sandra. *The Silken Web.* Warner Books, 1992.
Buchwald, Art. *Irving's Delight: At Last! A Cat Story for the Whole Family!* David McKay, 1975.
Calhoun, Don. *Dando Shaft!* Stein and Day, 1965.

Calmer, Ned. *The Anchorman.* Doubleday, 1970.

————. *Late Show.* Doubleday, 1974.

Charters, Samuel. *Elvis Presley Calls His Mother After the Ed Sullivan Show.* Coffee House Press, 1992.

Clark, Mary Higgins. *I'll Be Seeing You.* Simon & Schuster, 1993.

Cohn, Nik. *King Death.* Harcourt Brace Jovanovich, 1975.

Compton, David Guy. *Windows.* Berkley Publishing, 1979.

Conford, Ellen. *Nibble, Nibble, Jenny Archer.* Little, Brown, 1993.

Cooper, Ilene. *Trouble in Paradise.* Puffin Books, 1993.

Corrigan, Mark. *Why Do Women?* Angus & Robertson, 1963.

Culligan, Matthew J. *The Seventy-Million Dollar Decimal.* Simon & Schuster, 1982.

DeAndrea, William L. *Killed in Paradise.* The Mysterious Press, 1988.

————. *Killed in the Act.* Doubleday, 1981.

————. *Killed in the Ratings.* Harcourt Brace Jovanovich, 1978.

————. *Killed on the Ice.* Doubleday, 1984.

————. *Killed on the Rocks.* The Mysterious Press, 1990.

————. *Killed with a Passion.* Doubleday, 1983.

Deaver, Jeffrey Wilds. *Hard News.* Crime Club/Doubleday, 1991.

DeLillo, Don. *Americana.* Houghton Mifflin, 1971.

Delligan, William. *Time Nor Tide.* E.P. Dutton, 1982.

DeMareo, Arlene. *Triangle.* New American Library, 1971.

De Vere White, Terence. *Chat Show.* Victor Gollancz, 1987.

Dewhurst, Eileen. *The House That Jack Built.* Doubleday, 1984.

Dick, Philip K. *Flow My Tears, the Policeman Said.* Vintage Books, 1993.

Dixon, Franklin W. *Danger on the Air.* Pocket Books, 1989.

Dudley, Dick. *When Jenny Grows Up.* Viking, 1990.

Evans, Carol. *Glad and Sorry Seasons.* Harper's Magazine Press, 1970.

Farrell, Gillian B. *Alibi for an Actress.* Pocket Books, 1992.

Ferguson, Alane. *Stardust.* Bardbury Press, 1993.

Fickling, G.G. *This Girl for Hire.* Pyramid Books, 1957.

Fisher, Carrie. *Surrender the Pink.* Simon & Schuster, 1991.

Fisher, Steve. *Giveaway.* Random House, 1954.

Flink, S. *But Will They Get It in Des Moines?* Simon & Schuster, 1959.

Fox, Peter, *Downtime.* Hodder & Stoughton, 1986.

Frankel, Valerie. *Prime Time for Murder.* Pocket Books, 1994.

Fraser, Antonia. *The Cavalier Case.* Bloomsbury, 1990.

————. *Cool Repentance.* W.W. Norton, 1983.

————. *Jemima Shore's First Case and Other Stories.* W.W. Norton, 1987.

————. *Oxford Blood.* W.W. Norton, 1985.

————. *Quiet as a Nun.* Viking Press, 1977.

————. *A Splash of Red.* W.W. Norton, 1982.

————. *The Wild Island.* W.W. Norton, 1978.

————. *Your Royal Hostage.* Atheneum, 1988.

Freeman, Benedict, and Nancy Freeman. *Lootville.* Henry Holt, 1957.

Friedman, Steve, and Rosemary Ford. *Station Break.* St. Martin's Press, 1993.

Gardner, Herb. *A Piece of the Action.* Simon & Schuster, 1958.

Gerson, Noel B. *Talk Show.* William Morrow, 1971.

Gilbert, Michael. *The Killing of Kate Steelstock.* Harper & Row, 1980.

Gilden, Mel. *The Return of Captain Conquer.* Houghton Mifflin, 1986.

Gill, B.M. *The Twelfth Juror.* Charles Scribner's Sons, 1984.

Gillette, Paul. *One of the Crowd.* Arbor House, 1980.

Gitlin, Todd. *The Murder of Albert Einstein.* Farrar, Straus & Giroux, 1992.

Goldsmith, Olivia. *Flavor of the Month.* Poseidon Press, 1993.

Gordon, Barbara. *Defects of the Heart.* Harper & Row, 1983.

Green, Gerald. *The Heartless Light.* Charles Scribner's Sons, 1961.
_____. *The Last Angry Man.* Charles Scribner's Sons, 1956.
Greenwood, John. *Mosley by Moonlight.* Walker, 1985.
Ham, R.G. *Peak in Darien.* John Murray, 1976.
Handy, Libby. *My Poppa Loves Old Movies.* Ashton Scholastic, 1989.
Hannibal, Edward. *Liberty Square Station.* G.P. Putnam's Sons, 1977.
Haran, Maeve. *Having It All.* Bantam Books, 1992.
Harris, Mark. *It Looked Like Forever.* McGraw-Hill, 1979.
Harris, Mark Jonathan. *Confessions of a Prime Time Kid.* Lothrop, Lee & Shepard, 1985.
Hayler, Sparkle. *What's a Girl Gotta Do?* Soho, 1994.
Haynes, Betsy. *Taffy Sinclair, Queen of the Soaps.* Bantam Books, 1985.
Heide, Florence Parry. *Banana Blitz.* Holiday House, 1983.
_____. *A Monster Is Coming! A Monster Is Coming!* Frederick Watts, 1980.
_____. *The Problem with Pulcifer.* J.B. Lippincott, 1982.
Heilbroner, Joan. *Tom the TV Cat.* Random House, 1984.
Helwig, David. *The King's Evil.* Beaufort Books, 1984.
Hicks, Clifford B. *Alvin Fernald, TV Anchorman.* Holt, Rinehart & Winston, 1980.
Hobson, Hank. *Death Makes a Claim.* Cassell, 1958.
Hochstein, Rolkine A. *Table 47.* Doubleday, 1983.
Hogan, William. *The Year of the Mongoose.* Atheneum, 1981.
Holt, Samuel. *One of Us Is Wrong.* T. Doherty Associates, 1986.
Hope, Laura Lee. *The Case of the Goofy Game Show.* Pocket Books, 1991.
Howar, Barbara. *Making Ends Meet.* Random House, 1976.
Howe, James. *Morgan's Zoo.* Atheneum, 1984.
Hubler, Richard. *Shattering of the Image.* Duell, Sloan & Pearce, 1959.
Hunter, Alan. *Gently Through the Woods.* Macmillan, 1975.
Irvine, R.R. *Freeze Frame.* Popular Library, 1976.
_____. *Ratings Are Murder.* Walker, 1985.
Irvine, Robert. *Barking Dogs.* St. Martin's Press, 1994.
Jackson, Alison. *My Brother the Star.* Pocket Books, 1990.
Jaffe, Rona. *An American Love Story.* Delacorte Press, 1990.
_____. *The Fame Game.* Random House, 1969.
Jenkins, Dan, and Edwin Shrake. *Limo.* Atheneum, 1976.
Jones, Rebecca C. *Germy Blew It.* E.P. Dutton, 1987.
Kamitses, Zoe. *Moondreamer.* Little, Brown, 1983.
Kanfer, Stefan. *The International Garage Sale.* W.W. Norton, 1985.
Kantor, Hal. *Snake in the Glass.* Delacorte Press, 1971.
Katz, John. *Sign Off.* Bantam Books, 1991.
Katz, Molly. *Nobody Believes Me.* Ballantine Books, 1994.
Kaye, Marvin. *Fantastique.* St. Martin's Press, 1992.
_____. *The Soap Opera Slaughters.* Crime Club/Doubleday, 1982.
Kelland, Clarence Buddington. *Key Man.* Harper, 1952.
_____. *Murder Makes an Entrance.* Harper, 1955.
King-Smith, Dick. *Ace, the Very Important Pig.* Bullseye Books/Alfred A. Knopf, 1992.
Kosinski, Jerzy N. *Being There.* Harcourt Brace Jovanovich, 1971.
Kotker, Zane. *Bodies in Motion.* Alfred A. Knopf, 1972.
Kovacs, Ernie. *Zoomar.* Doubleday, 1957.
Kunnas, Mauri. *Ricky, Rocky, and Ringo on TV.* Crown, 1986.
Lahr, John. *Hot to Trot.* Alfred A. Knopf, 1974.
Larson, Charles. *Someone's Death.* J.B. Lippincott, 1973.
Lasswell, Mary. *One on the House.* Houghton Mifflin, 1949.
Leonard, Lee. *I Miss You When You're Here.* Stein & Day, 1976.
Levy, David. *The Chameleons.* Dodd, Mead, 1964.
Lippincott, David. *The Voice of Armageddon.* G.P. Putnam's Sons, 1974.

Lively, Penelope. *Treasure of Time*. Doubleday, 1980.
Livingston, H. *The Detroiters*. Houghton Mifflin, 1958.
Locke-Elliott, Sumner. *The Man Who Got Away*. Harper & Row, 1972.
Lockridge, Frances, and Richard Lockridge. *The Long Skeleton*. J.B. Lippincott, 1958.
Lockridge, Richard. *Death on the Hour*. J.B. Lippincott, 1974.
Lupica, Mike. *Dead Air*. Villard Books, 1986.
Lynn, Jack. *The Turncoat*. Delacorte Press, 1976.
McCall, Dan. *Bluebird Canyon*. Congdon and Weed, 1983.
McCullough, Andrew. *Rough Cut*. William Morrow, 1976.
McCully, Emily Arnold. *Zaza's Big Break*. Harper & Row, 1989.
MacDonald, John D. *One More Sunday*. Alfred A. Knopf, 1984.
McInerny, Ralph M. *Quick as a Dodo*. Vanguard Press, 1978.
McKitterick, Molly. *Murder in a Mayonnaise Jar*. St. Martin's Press, 1993.
McNamara, John. *Revenge of the Nerd*. Delacorte Press, 1984.
McPhail, David M. *Fix-It*. E.P. Dutton, 1987.
MacVicar, August. *The Grey Shepherds*. John Long, 1964.
Madden, David. *On the Big Wind*. Holt, Rinehart & Winston, 1980.
Manes, Stephen. *The Boy Who Turned into a TV Set*. Avon Books, 1983.
_____. *It's New! It's Improved! It's Terrible!* Bantam Skylark, 1989.
_____. *The Oscar J. Noodleman Television Network*. E.P. Dutton, 1984.
Martin, John Bartlow. *Televising of Heller*. Doubleday, 1980.
Martin, William. *Nerve Endings*. Crown, 1984.
May, Derwent. *A Revenger's Comedy*. Chatto & Windus, 1979.
Mead, Shepherd. *The Big Ball of Wax*. Simon & Schuster, 1954.
Merrill, Robert, and Fred Janis. *The Divas*. Simon & Schuster, 1978.
Miles, Betty. *The Secret Life of the Underwear Champ*. Alfred A. Knopf, 1981.
Moore, Robin. *Pitchman*. Coward-McCann, 1956.
Morgan, Al. *Anchorwoman*. Stein and Day, 1974.
_____. *The Great Man*. E.P. Dutton, 1955.
Nessen, Ron. *The Hour*. William Morrow, 1984.
Oakes, Philip. *Miracles: Genuine Cases Contact Box 340*. John Day, 1971.
O'Connor, Jim, and Jane O'Connor. *Slime Time*. Random House, 1990.
O'Marie, Sister Carol Anne. *Murder in Ordinary Time*. Delacorte Press, 1991.
Orkeny, István. *The Flower Show and the Toth Family*. New Directions, 1982.
Palmer, Stuart. *Nipped in the Bud*. M.S. Mill/William Morrow, 1951.
Park, Barbara. *Almost Starring Skinnybones*. Alfred A. Knopf, 1988.
Parker, Chris. *Chaney's Choice*. Malvern, 1986.
Parker, Norman. *Don't Cry Little Girl*. Whitmore Publishing, 1970.
Parker, Robert B. *A Savage Place*. Delacorte Press, 1981.
_____. *Stardust*. G.P. Putnam's Sons, 1990.
Patterson, Richard North. *Private Screening*. Villard Books, 1985.
Paul, Barbara. *The Renewable Virgin*. Charles Scribner's Sons, 1985.
Pentecost, Hugh. *Past, Present and Murder*. Dodd, Mead, 1982.
Petersen, Paul. *The Series*. Dell, 1979.
Petievich, Gerald. *To Live and Die in L.A.* Arbor House, 1984.
Pinkwater, Daniel Manus. *The Magic Moscow*. Four Winds Press, 1980.
Polk, Cara Saylor. *Images*. St. Martin's Press, 1986.
Powers, Ron. *Face Value*. Delacorte Press, 1979.
Prior, Allan. *The Contract*. Cassell, 1970.
Quinlan, Sterling. *Merger*. Doubleday, 1958.
Rader, Paul. *Showdown at Mon Repos*. Dial Press, 1970.
Rae, Hugh C. *The Interview*. Coward-McCann, 1969.
Rebeta-Burditt, Joyce. *Triplets*. Delacorte Press, 1981.
Richler, Mordecai. *Joshua Then and Now*. Alfred A. Knopf, 1980.

Ritz, David. *Search for Happiness.* Simon & Schuster, 1980.

Robbins, Harold. *The Inheritors.* Trident Press, 1969.

————. *Spellbinder.* Simon & Schuster, 1982.

Roberts, Nora. *Private Scandals.* G.P. Putnam's Sons, 1993.

Robertson, Don. *Make a Wish.* G.P. Putnam's Sons, 1975.

Rogers, Edward A. *Face to Face.* William Morrow, 1962.

Ross, Walter. *Coast to Coast: A Novel About Corruption in High Places.* Simon & Schuster, 1962.

Rowe, Jennifer. *The Makeover Murder.* Doubleday, 1993.

Sargent, Sarah. *Jonas McFee, A.T.P.* Bradbury Press, 1989.

Scarborough, Chuck, and William Murray. *The Myrmidon Project.* Coward, McCann & Geohegan, 1981.

Schatell, Brian. *Sam's No Dummy, Farmer Goff.* J.B. Lippincott, 1984.

Schneck, Stephen. *Nocturnal Vaudeville.* E.P. Dutton, 1972.

Schneider, Howie. *Uncle Lester's Hat.* G.P. Putnam's Sons, 1993.

Schwartz, Jonathan. *Distant Stations.* Doubleday, 1979.

Shah, Diane K. *Dying Cheek to Cheek.* Crime Club/Doubleday, 1992.

Shannon, Jacqueline. *I Hate My Hero.* Simon & Schuster, 1992.

Shaw, Richard. *Lamprey's Legacy.* Beaufort Books, 1981.

Shyer, Marlene. *Adorable Sunday.* Charles Scribner's Sons, 1983.

Silverstein, Mickie. *Number One Sunset Blvd.* Zebra Books, 1982.

Slaughter, Frank Gill. *Gospel Fever: A Novel About America's Most Beloved TV Evangelist.* Doubleday, 1980.

Smith, Susan. *Terri the Great.* Pocket Books, 1989.

Snape, Juliet. *The Boy with Square Eyes.* Prentice-Hall, 1987.

Steel, Danielle. *Changes.* Delacorte Press, 1983.

————. *Heartbeat.* Delacorte Press, 1991.

————. *Secrets.* Delacorte Press, 1985.

Stern, Richard G. *Golk.* Criterion Books, 1960.

Stevens, Kathleen. *The Beast in the Bathtub.* Milwaukee: G. Stevens, 1985.

Stevens, Mark. *Summer in the City.* Random House, 1984.

Stimson, Tess. *Hard News.* Mandarin, 1993.

Stout, Rex. *Before Midnight.* Viking Press, 1955.

Streatfeild, Noel. *The Children on the Top Floor.* Dell, 1964.

————. *Gemma Alone.* Dell, 1969.

Sullivan, Eleanor, ed. *Scarlet Letters: Tales of Adultery from Ellery Queen's Mystery Magazine.* Carroll & Graf, 1991.

Susann, Jacqueline. *The Love Machine.* Simon & Schuster, 1973.

Symons, Julian. *The Pipe Dream.* Harper & Row, 1959.

Thomas, Michael M. *Hard Money.* Viking Press, 1985.

Tucker, John Bartholomew. *The Man Who Looked Like Howard Cosell.* St. Martin's Press, 1988.

Valin, Jonathan. *Natural Causes.* Congdon and Weed, 1983.

Vanderbilt, Gloria. *Never Say Good-Bye.* Alfred A. Knopf, 1989.

Vansittart, Peter. *Orders of Chivalry.* Abelard-Schuman, 1959.

Van Wormer, Laura. *Benedict Canyon.* Crown, 1992.

Vidal, Gore. *Messiah.* Little, Brown, 1954.

Wakefield, Dan. *Selling Out.* Little, Brown, 1985.

Warren, Cathy. *Roxanne Bookman Live at Five!* Bradbury Press, 1988.

Watson, Patrick. *Alter Ego.* Viking Press, 1978.

Westlake, Donald E. *I Gave at the Office.* Simon & Schuster, 1971.

Wildsmith, Brian. *Bear's Adventure.* Pantheon Books, 1981.

Willingham, Calder. *Providence Island.* Vanguard Press, 1969.

Wilson, Sloan. *Man in the Gray Flannel Suit II.* Arbor House, 1984.

Woiwode, Larry. *Poppa John*. Farrar, Straus & Giroux, 1981.
Woodruff, Una. *Catwitch*. Doubleday, 1983.
Ziefert, Harriet. *When the TV Broke*. Viking Kestrel, 1989.
Zimmerman, Ed. *Love in the Afternoon*. Bobbs-Merrill, 1971.

The Radio Novel:
A Tentative Bibliography

This is the first attempt at compiling a bibliography of radio-related novels. No claim is made that this listing is complete, but it does include all types of novels, including works intended for juvenile audiences.

Allen, Ted. *This Time a Better Earth.* William Morrow, 1939.
Andrews, Robert Hardy. *Legend of a Lady: The Story of Rita Martin.* Coward-McCann, 1949.
Ansell, Jack. *Dynasty of the Air.* Arbor House, 1974.
Armstrong, Charlotte. *Unsuspected.* Coward-McCann, 1946.
Baldwin, Faith. *Give Love the Air.* Rinehart, 1947.
———. *Men Are Such Fools!* Farrar & Rinehart, 1936.
Bayer, Olive Held. *Brutal Question.* Crime Club/Doubleday, 1947.
Beck, J. Warren. *Pause Under the Sky.* Swallow Press, 1947.
Bennett, Dorothy. *Murder Unleashed.* Crime Club/Doubleday, 1935.
Boyle, Thomas. *Only the Dead Know Brooklyn.* D.R. Godine, 1985.
Brown, Eugene. *The Locust Fire.* Doubleday, 1957.
Carpenter, Don. *Getting Off.* E.P. Dutton, 1971.
Carson, Robert. *Stranger in Our Midst.* G.P. Putnam's Sons, 1947.
Chaikin, Miriam. *Friends Forever.* Harper & Row, 1988.
———. *I Should Worry, I Should Care.* Harper & Row, 1979.
Christian, Kit. *Death and Bitters.* E.P. Dutton, 1943.
Coffee, Lenore. *Another Time, Another Place.* Crown, 1957.
Coffin, Carlyn. *Dogwatch.* Farrar & Rinehart, 1944.
Cohen, Roy Octavus. *A Bullet for My Love.* Macmillan, 1950.
———. *Danger in Paradise.* Macmillan, 1945.
Conford, Ellen. *Strictly for Laughs.* Pacer Books, 1985.
Coxe, George Harmon. *The Fifth Key.* Alfred A. Knopf, 1947.
Davis, Anne Pence. *The Customer Is Always Right.* Macmillan, 1940.
Davis, Frederick. *Thursday's Blade.* Crime Club/Doubleday, 1947.
Disch, Thomas M. *The Brave Little Toaster: A Bedtime Story for Small Appliances.* Doubleday, 1986.
Dorros, Arthur. *Radio Man: A Story in English and Spanish.* HarperCollins, 1993.
Echard, Margaret. *Stand-in for Death.* Crime Club/Doubleday, Doran, 1940.
Eichler, Alfred. *Death at the Mike.* Lantern Press, 1946.
———. *Election by Murder.* Lantern Press, 1947.
Elkin, Stanley. *The Dick Gibson Show.* Random House, 1971.
Freeman, Martin Joseph. *The Case of the Blind Mouse.* E.P. Dutton, 1935.
Fuller, Timothy. *This Is Murder, Mr. Jones.* Little, Brown, 1943.
Gary, Myra. *Little Jade Lady.* Arcadia House, 1948.
Goldman, Raymond Leslie. *Murder Behind the Mike.* Coward-McCann, 1942.
Gunther, John. *The Indian Sign.* Harper, 1970.

Hamilton, Virginia. *Willie Bea and the Time the Martians Landed.* Greenwillow Books, 1983.

Hargrove, Marion. *Something's Got to Give.* William Sloane, 1948.

Hearon, Shelby. *A Prince of a Fellow.* Doubleday, 1978.

Henderson, Donald. *A Voice Like Velvet.* Random House, 1946.

Hull, Helen R. *Through the House Door.* Coward-McCann, 1940.

Iams, Jack. *Into Thin Air.* William Morrow, 1952.

Jaynes, Clare. *Instruct My Sorrows.* Random House, 1942.

Jeffers, H. Paul. *Murder on the Mike.* St. Martin's Press, 1984.

Keene, Carolyn. *The Case of the Disappearing Deejay.* Pocket Books, 1989.

Kelland, Clarence Budington. *The Great Crooner.* Harper, 1933.

Korman, Gordon. *Radio Fifth Grade.* Scholastic, 1989.

Kovacs, Ernie. *Zoomar.* Doubleday, 1957.

Land, Charles. *Calling Earth.* Bourmar/Noble Publishers, 1978.

Lauferty, Lilian. *Baritone.* Doubleday, 1948.

Leonard, Lee. *I Miss You When You're Here.* Stein & Day, 1976.

Lipton, Lawrence. *In Secret Battle.* D. Appleton–Century Company, 1944.

Lockridge, Frances, and Richard Lockridge. *Killing the Goose.* J.B. Lippincott, 1943.

McDonald, Collin. *Nightwaves: Scary Stories for After Dark.* Cobblehill Books, 1990.

Matson, Norman Haghejm. *Doctor Fogg.* Macmillan, 1929.

Morris, Hilda. *The Tuckers Tune In.* G.P. Putnam's Sons, 1943.

Nadja. *Little Nina and the Radio.* Alfred A. Knopf, 1992.

O'Connor, Edwin. *The Oracle.* Reinhardt, 1952.

Oppenheim, E. Phillips. *The Dumb Gods Speak.* Little, Brown, 1937.

Panama, Norman. *The Glass Bed.* William Morrow, 1980.

Paul, Elliot Harold. *The Death of Lord Haw Haw.* Random House, 1940.

Pinkwater, Daniel Manus. *Fat Men from Space.* G.P. Putnam's Sons, 1977.

Powell, Dawn. *The Happy Island.* Farrar & Rinehart, 1938.

Powers, Ron. *Toot-Toot-Tootsie, Good-bye.* Delacorte Press, 1981.

Priestley, J.B. *Low Notes on a High Level.* Harper, 1954.

Rice, Craig. *The Corpse Steps Out.* Simon & Schuster, 1940.

Rinkoff, Barbara. *Elbert, the Mind Reader.* Lothrop, Lee & Shepard, 1967.

Rohmer, Sax. *Seven Sins.* R.M. McBride, 1943.

Runbec, Margaret Lee. *A Hungry Man Dreams.* Houghton Mifflin, 1952.

Sackville-West, Victoria. *Grand Canyon.* Doubleday, 1942.

St. Johns, Adela Rogers. *Field of Honor.* E.P. Dutton, 1938.

Sampson, Emma Speed. *Miss Minerva Broadcasts Billy.* Reilly & Lee, 1925.

Savage, Thomas. *Midnight Line.* Little, Brown, 1976.

Saxby, Charles. *Murder at the Mike.* E.P. Dutton, 1938.

Selinko, Annemarie. *Tomorrow Is Another Day.* Alliance Book Corporation, 1939.

Selman, Robert. *Once Upon a Crime.* William Morrow, 1947.

Shaw, Irwin. *Troubled Air.* Random House, 1951.

Sherman, Richard. *The Unready Heart.* Little, Brown, 1944.

Sherwood, John. *Death at the BBC.* Charles Scribner's Sons, 1983.

Shiel, M.P. *The Invisible Voices.* Vanguard, 1936.

Shirer, William L. *Stranger Come Home.* Little, Brown, 1954.

Smith, Chard Powers. *Turn of the Dial.* Charles Scribner's Sons, 1943.

Spinelli, Marcos. *Assignment Without Glory.* J.B. Lippincott, 1944.

Steegmuller, Francis. *A Matter of Accent.* Dodd, Mead, 1943.

Stewart, Alfred Walter. *The Counsellor.* Little, Brown, 1939.

Storm, Hans Otto. *Full Measure.* Macmillan, 1929.

Stout, Rex. *And Be a Villain.* Viking Press, 1948.

Toby, Mark. *The Courtship of Eddie's Father.* Bernard Geis Associates, 1961.

Treynor, Blair. *Silver Doll.* Henry Holt, 1951.

Twohill, Maggie. *Jeeter, Mason, and the Magic Headset.* Bradbury Press, 1985.
Uris, Leon. *Battle Cry.* Bantam Books, 1953.
Velter, Joseph Matthew. *Arctic S.O.S.* Harper, 1935.
Vickers, Roy. *The Whispering Death.* Jefferson House, 1947.
Wakeman, Frederic. *Hucksters.* Rinehart, 1946.
Widdemer, Margaret. *This Isn't the End.* Farrar & Rinehart, 1936.
Williamson, Maude. *Next Year Will Be Different.* Farrar & Rinehart, 1939.
Winchell, Prentice. *Where There's Smoke.* J.B. Lippincott, 1946.
Wing, Pat. *Take It Away, Sam!* Dodd, Mead, 1938.
Wouk, Herman. *Aurora Dawn.* Simon & Schuster, 1947.
Yates, George Worthing. *There Was a Crooked Man.* William Morrow, 1936.
Yudkoff, Alvin. *Circumstances Beyond Control.* Rinehart, 1955.

General Bibliography

Baird, Newton D., and Robert Greenwood. *An Annotated Bibliography of California Fiction, 1664–1970.* Georgetown, Calif.: Talisman Library Research, 1971.

Brooker-Bowers, Nancy. *The Hollywood Novel and Other Novels About Film, 1912–1982: An Annotated Bibliography.* New York: Garland, 1985.

Curtis-Fox, Terry. "The Hollywood Novel." *Film Comment* 21:2 (March/April 1985), 7–13.

Fine, David, ed. *Los Angeles in Fiction.* Albuquerque: University of New Mexico Press, 1984.

Franklin, Walter. "Hollywood in Fiction." *Pacific Spectator* 2:2 (spring 1948), 127–33.

Havig, Alan. "Hollywood and the American Heartland: Celebrities, Fans and the Myth of Success in the 1920s." *Journal of Popular Film and Television* 14:4 (1987), 167–75.

Johnson, Nora. "Novelists in the Dream Factory." *New York Times Book Review*, November 4, 1984, pp. 1, 38–39.

Leonard, John. "Hollywood Novels." *New York Times Book Review*, May 7, 1978, pp. 3, 36.

McMurtry, Larry. "The Hollywood Novel, the Hollywood Film." *American Film* 2:5 (March 1977), 6–7, 67.

Melcon, Alice Kesone. *California in Fiction.* Berkeley: California Library Association, 1961.

Moss, Gabriel. *The Nickel Was for the Movies: Film in the Novel from Pirandello to Puig.* Berkeley: University of California Press, 1994.

Schulberg, Budd Wilson. "The Hollywood Novel." *Films* 1:2 (spring 1940), 68–78.

See, Carolyn. "The Hollywood Novel: The American Dream Cheat." In *Tough Guy Writers of the Thirties*, edited by David Madden, 199–217. Carbondale: Southern Illinois University Press, 1968.

————. "The Hollywood Novel: An Historical and Critical Study." Ph.D. diss., University of California, Los Angeles, 1963.

Spatz, Thomas. *Hollywood in Fiction: Some Versions of the American Myth.* The Hague: Mouton, 1969.

Wells, Walter. *Tycoons and Locusts: A Regional Look at Hollywood Fiction of the 1930s.* Carbondale: Southern Illinois University Press, 1973.

Widmer, Kingsley. "The Hollywood Image." *Coastlines* 5:1 (1961), 17–27.

Wilson, Edmund. *The Boys in the Back Room: Notes on California Novelists.* San Francisco: Colt Press, 1941. Reprinted in *A Living Chronicle, 1920–1950*, Garden City, N.Y.: Doubleday, 1950.

Title Index

References are to page numbers.

Subject Index